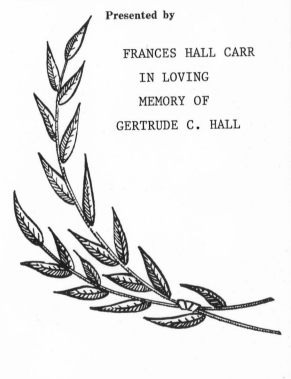

THE
MARX
BROTHERS

The Image of Anarchy—Groucho, Harpo, Chico, and Zeppo in a wrongfully discarded scene from *Horse Feathers* (1932). No still better captures the unique spirit of their comedy irreverence—the Marx Brothers complacently playing cards as the Apocalypse seems to rage around them, complete with what appears to be a burning cross. (Photograph courtesy of the Bob Cooper Collection.)

THE MARX BROTHERS
A Bio-Bibliography

Wes D. Gehring

Popular Culture Bio-Bibliographies

Greenwood Press
New York • Westport, Connecticut • London

791.43028
mart
p

Library of Congress Cataloging-in-Publication Data

Gehring, Wes D.
    The Marx brothers.

    (Popular culture bio-bibliographies, ISSN 0193-6891)
    Bibliography: p.
    Filmography: p.
    Discography: p.
    Includes index.
    1. Marx Brothers.   2. Marx Brothers—Bibliography.
3. Comèdians—United States—Bibliography.   I. Title.
II. Series.
PN2297.M3G44 1987   791.43'028'0922   86–31823
ISBN 0-313-24547-9 (lib. bdg. : alk. paper)

Library of Congress Catalog Card Number: 86-31823
ISBN: 0-313-24547-9
ISSN: 0193-6891

First published in 1987

Greenwood Press, Inc.
88 Post Road West, Westport, Connecticut 06881

Printed in the United States of America

⊗™

The paper used in this book complies with the
Permanent Paper Standard issued by the National
Information Standards Organization (Z39.48-1984).

10 9 8 7 6 5 4 3 2 1

Acknowledgments

All stills, except Figs. 10, 11, and the frontispiece, were provided by the Wisconsin Center
for Film and Theater Research. Fig. 10 came courtesy of the Museum of Modern Art/Film
Stills Archive. The Frank Dobias caricature (Fig. 11) originally appeared in the February
1936 *Photoplay* interview of Gummo, "THOSE MAD MARX HARES. . . ." It was photo-
graphed for reproduction in this volume by the University of Iowa Audiovisual Center. The
frontispiece came courtesy of the Bob Cooper Collection.

The author's poem, "GROUCHO & COMPANY or The Marx of Time" originally appeared
in The *Journal of Popular Film and Television* (1987). Reprinted with permission.

To Eileen, Sarah, and Emily; and Family

GROUCHO & COMPANY
or
The Marx of Time*

Groucho, Harpo, and Chico
Were the only Marxist party
America ever took to heart.

While Caesar divided Gaul into
Three parts, the three Marxes merely
Unleashed it . . . teaching Caesar to
    Beware the Ides of Marx.

The lecherous leader of
These men from Marx was
Groucho—their home-grown King Leer.

Groucho was also the only
Literary Brother—a regular
Book Marx in comic clothing.

Together their socialism of silliness
Seldom missed the Marx—a
Depression team treating various forms of
    depression ever since.

Truly, these are Marx of Time!

---

*The author appreciates being given this forum for his re-marx.

CONTENTS

ILLUSTRATIONS

PREFACE

The goal of this work is to present a combined biographical, critical, and biblio-graphical estimate of the Marx Brothers's significance in film comedy, the arts in general, and as popular culture icons. The book is divided into five chapters. Chapter 1 is a Marx Brothers biography, which explores the public and private sides of their lives. The focus is on Groucho, Harpo, and Chico—the dominant comedy team members and the only ones to develop clear and definable comedy personae. But where it is pertinent, the involvement of the less well-known Brothers, Zeppo, and Gummo, is, of course, examined.

Of the key three, Groucho decidedly evolves as the central player scrutinized in this group biography for three reasons. First, over time Groucho has unmis-takably been the Marx Brother most favored by the public (as well as the only one to launch a solo career after the group's demise), the available literature is overwhelmingly concentrated on him. For instance, easily the best group biog-raphy of the team is, ironically, one which purports to be only of the mustached one—Hector Arce's *Groucho*. Second, Groucho has added to this documentation by writing or co-writing eight books, versus a total of one by the rest of the team. Moreover, as the literary figures of old, Groucho left an additional body of writing in his copious correspondence, one volume of which was published be-fore his death. And third, Groucho outlived all his Brothers and was able to take a central role in the Marx Brothers revival of the 1960s and 1970s. Thus, he came to represent both the team and the final word on all things "Marxian."

Chapter 2 is a critique of the four ongoing broad influences of the Marxes—as unique icons of both comedy and the anti-establishment; as major contributors to new developments in American humor, from direct involvement in antiheroic humor during its beginnings to the idealized models they represent for more recent followers of black comedy; as pivotal early examples of what might best be called saturation comedy; and as a crucial bridge in American film comedy from the silents to sound.

Because no examination of artists would be complete without including some of their own observations, Chapter 3 is composed of three reprinted articles: Groucho's "My Poor Wife!" (1930) and "How to Be a Spy" (1946), and a comic interview with Gummo entitled "THOSE MAD MARX HARES: As Revealed by the Fifth Marx Brother to Edward R. Sammis" (1936). These particular pieces were chosen for three reasons. First, they richly showcase the Marxes's gift of humor, be it from the most famous Brother or the most obscure. Second, the Groucho essays are representative examples of his writing fluctuation between comical biographical reminiscences and less structured flights of comic monologue, more in the tradition of the team's films. However, in either case, Groucho frequently laces his prose with antiheroic characteristics. Third, the articles encompass a time span which almost exactly parallels the duration of the Brothers's screen career as a team.

Chapter 4 is a Marx Brothers bibliographical essay, which assesses key reference materials and locates research collections open to the student and/or scholar. The majority of the chapter is allocated to reference works and is divided into two sections. The first is devoted to book-length sources written about and/or by the Marxes. These materials are then subdivided into four categories: the Marx Brothers viewed by insiders, Marx on Marx, Marx critical studies, and Marx references. The second section of Chapter 4 is comprised of shorter works and includes articles, interviews, book chapters, and monographs. It is subdivided further into two parts: Marx Brothers critical and/or biographical pieces (categories often combined by authors writing on the Marxes), and Marx on Marx (including interviews). To facilitate the use of both sections as a reference guide, Chapter 5 is a bibliographical checklist of all sources recommended in Chapter 4. The checklist is meant to be a research guide, not an all-encompassing bibliography of the team (although it is more detailed than any other such listing currently on the market).

There is always a temptation to note every source of related interest, but this can open such a floodgate of material that pivotal works are shortchanged. Consequently, Chapters 4 and 5 maintain the most disciplined of configurations. The reader/researcher who must have additional related sources is invited to study the scores of notes which close the other chapters.

The pivotal research collections examined in Chapter 4 are found in the Library of Congress (particularly in the Manuscript Division; the Motion Picture, Broadcasting and Recorded Sound Division; and the Library Reading Room); the New York Public Library system, especially the Lincoln Center branch, which houses the Billy Rose Theatre Collection; the State Historical Society of Wisconsin (Madison); the Margaret Herrick Library at the Academy of Motion Picture Arts and Sciences (Los Angeles); the University of Iowa's (Iowa City) main library and its audiovisual center; American Film Institute (Los Angeles);

and the UCLA Theatre Arts Library within its University Research Library; and the film stills archives of the Museum of Modern Art (New York).

The appendixes contain a chronological biography, a filmography, and a selected discography. The chronological biography lists the names of the radio and television programs of Groucho and Chico, both in tandem and on a solo basis. The time line also notes some significant television guest appearances by the Brothers.

Few books are solely the result of one person, and special thank yous are in order for several individuals: Cooper C. Graham, film reference librarian, Motion Picture Division of the Library of Congress; Dorothy L. Swerdlove, curator, the Billy Rose Theatre Collection (New York City); John Gill, archivist, Academy of Motion Picture Arts and Sciences; three individuals from the State Historical Society of Wisconsin (Madison): Reference Archivist Harold L. Miller, Director of the Film Archive Maxine Fleckner Ducey, and Photo Archivist Timothy Hawkins; *The Freedonia Gazette* (a New Hope, Pennsylvania, journal devoted entirely to the Marx Brothers), Editor Paul G. Wesolowski; University of Wisconsin (Madison) Teaching Assistant Kevin Hagopian, who first brought the State Historical Society's Marx Brothers holdings to this writer's attention; film scholar Anthony Slide and film critic/author Leonard Maltin, each of whom shared an important reference source with the author; and Marx Brothers aficionado Bob Cooper, who granted permission to use the frontispiece still.

Closer to home, additional thank yous are in order for my department chairperson, John Kurtz, both for lightening my teaching load while this work was being finished and for his ongoing support of my writing projects; Janet Warrner, my typist and general troubleshooter; and Veva McCocky, interlibrary loan librarian at Ball State University's Bracken Library.

I also wish to acknowledge the encouragement and suggestions of friends, colleagues, and students—especially Thom Gulley (the recipient of Ball State University's first David Letterman scholarship), who volunteered to assist in the search for recent Marx Brothers literature.

Finally, I would like to thank both Dr. M. Thomas Inge and Greenwood Press, especially Acquisitions Editor Marilyn Brownstein, for making this project possible, and my family for their patience and understanding in seeing me through both the extensive research and the eventual writing. None of this would have been possible without their support.

1.

MARX BROTHERS
BIOGRAPHY

The only tradition in our family was our lack of tradition.[1]
— Harpo Marx on the childhood of the Marx Brothers

America's own peculiar brand of "Marxism" can be traced to 1887—the birth year of Leonard Marx, the oldest of the Marx Brothers.[2] Leonard, who later (and forevermore) would be re-christened "Chico" for vaudeville audiences, was followed in order by Adolph (1888, "Harpo"), Julius (1890, "Groucho"), Milton (1893, "Gummo"), and Herbert (1901, "Zeppo").[3] For the sake of familiarity and simplicity, the brothers will be referred to by their stage names throughout this work. It is also a tradition both Groucho and Harpo turned to when they became team biographers, as did other chroniclers from their family.

While all five were at some time part of the team (although never simultaneously), the best Marx Brothers "cast" listing is biographer Joe Adamson's tongue-in-cheek title: *Groucho, Harpo, Chico and Sometimes Zeppo.*[4] Gummo was part of the act only before entering the World War I armed forces. Zeppo replaced Gummo and was with the team through its first five commercially released films (all for Paramount). Thus, the key focus of this volume will be on Groucho, Harpo, and Chico, the group most commonly referred to as "the team" and the only members who devised clearly definable comedy characters.

The Brothers's parents were Simon ("Frenchie") and Minnie Marx, early 1880s Jewish immigrants who met and married (1884) in New York City. Frenchie (who shortened his name from Marrix to Marx in America) was from the French province of Alsace, which had been annexed by Germany after the Franco-Prussian War of 1871. Minnie's maiden name was Schoenberg; her family had immigrated from Dornum, Germany.

Frenchie and Minnie met at a dancing school he frequented because of his definite skirt-chasing tendencies, a characteristic his sons would share and in which they would later excel. (In fact, Frenchie's oldest son's nickname, Chico, was derived from the young man's girl—chick—chasing tendencies; therefore, Chico should be pronounced with the short i rather than the long e sound.) Minnie was nineteen when they married; Frenchie was four years her senior. The bride brought her parents Louis and Fanny along to the new household, and other Schoenbergs soon joined them. Hector Arce observed in his authorized biography of Groucho that while poor Frenchie had left his homeland to avoid "German subjugation," he had now "let down his guard and was irrevocably subjugated by . . . [another] German horde."[5]

Paying the rent was an ongoing challenge during the family's initial New York years. While there would be several flats (standing rent bills frequently drove the poor family into secretive, nomadic movements), their place on Ninety-third Street eventually would become their long-term New York home. Early Marx Brothers biographer Kyle Crichton termed the flat both a "last stand" and a "bus station," where "The door was never locked, there was a pot of coffee forever simmering on the stove, and the neighbors wandered in and out at random."[6] Such a state brings to mind the Marx Brothers's celebrated later stateroom scene in *A Night at the Opera* (1936). And it was in this Mad Hatter home base that their father also tried to operate a business.

Frenchie was a tailor, but it was a job description at best to be applied loosely. As son Groucho observed, "His record as the most inept tailor that Yorkville [New York City's Upper East Side, in Manhattan] ever produced has never been approached. This could even include parts of Brooklyn and the Bronx."[7] Unfortunately, Frenchie felt he was above the use of a tape measure. This resulted in very little repeat business, and Frenchie was forced to roam farther and farther outside the neighborhood as his reputation spread. Thus, family finances were meager, with "Misfit Sam's" (his nickname among customers) "income as a tailor hovering between eighteen dollars a week and nothing."[8]

Not surprisingly, Frenchie has often been seen simply as the buffoon, even within his own family.[9] But understanding Frenchie represents a key to understanding Harpo and his screen alter ego. In fact, in the space of ten pages in his autobiography, Harpo manages to describe his father and himself in nearly identical terms. Thus, while Frenchie worked hard, "He had no ambition beyond living and accepting life from day to day."[10] Of himself, Harpo wrote:

> I DON'T KNOW WHETHER my life has been a success or a failure. But not having any anxiety about becoming one instead of the other, and just taking things as they came along, I've had a lot of extra time to enjoy life.[11]

Harpo is also one of the few Marx Brothers biographers to address the most obvious question concerning Frenchie: Why would such an antiheroic tailor

1. Matriarch Minnie Marx as a young woman. (Photograph courtesy of the Wisconsin Center for Film and Theater Research.)

continue in what must have been a most frustrating profession? Harpo's answer was that his father was an "excellent judge of color and fabric" whose work was flawed by a "free-hand artist" philosophy which pooh-poohed frills like tape measures and fittings.[12]

Appropriately, when *Harpo Speaks!* was reissued in 1985, the comedian's composer son William drew another parallel between his father and Frenchie: Harpo "performed music the way his father ... performed tailoring: with an unerring feel for fabric and color [harmony] but very little for cutting and fitting [melody and tempo]."[13] Luckily for Harpo, while misfitted pants are obviously always misfitted pants, whatever flaws exist in Harpo's music are lost on his public.

Harpo lived for his music, regardless of its merits, and it is not unreasonable to assume that tailoring held a similarly mesmerizing quality for Frenchie. Moreover, this comedy team would later be celebrated for its flights of absurdity, and it does not seem inappropriate that the father of the Marx Brothers more than flirted with absurdity by remaining a tailor.

Frenchie's antiheroic profession had, however, another more direct tie with the future entertainment careers of his sons. Because Frenchie was hardly bringing home a tidy income—when he brought one home at all—the show business success of Minnie's brother Al Shean (changed from Schoenberg) seemed especially inviting. And Al's success was no little thing. At the beginning of the 1890s he had both organized and starred in the influential vaudeville comedy and musical act the Manhattan Comedy Four (which naturally sends one thinking of the later Four Marx Brothers, especially since Uncle Al's comedy writing for his nephews helped elevate them to big-time entertainment). Al is, however, best known as part of the vaudeville team of Gallagher and Shean ("Absolutely, Mr. Gallagher?" "Positively, Mr. Shean."), one of America's favorite comedy teams early in the twentieth century.

Minnie's family background, moreover, boasted other show-business roots. Her father had been a traveling ventriloquist and magician in Europe, with her mother playing the harp for the dancing that followed his act. This continued even after the birth of their three children. Thus, as critic and family friend Alexander Woollcott comically observed early on (1925), "The memory of those gypsy tours was hung with golden haze in the mind of Mrs. Marx [Minnie] in the after years when she was kept fairly busy carpeting the floor of her tenement flat with crawling Marxes."[14]

The old on-the-road days probably seemed all the more poignant after Minnie immigrated to America, because both her parents went into involuntary show-business retirement. Unfortunately, a new land does not always mean new opportunities, or as Groucho observed with tongue firmly in cheek: "For some curious reason there seemed to be practically no demand for a German ventriloquist and a woman harpist who yodeled in a foreign language."[15]

Still, since they were part of the Marx household, they represented a constant reminder of past glories. And as might be expected, Harpo's first harp was

2. Simon "Frenchie" Marx, the antiheroic tailor and father of the Marx Brothers. (Photograph courtesy of the Wisconsin Center for Film and Theater Research.)

actually his grandmother's. In Harpo's autobiography he also reminisces fondly about his grandfather's show-business tales and magic performances for a boy whose future trench coat pockets would produce magic all their own.[16]

Not surprisingly, with this kind of background, Minnie (who already was the dominant adult in the Marx household) became a stage mother. But in this story, the phrase "stage mother" knows only superlatives, from Woollcott's trend-setting, classic essay "A Mother of the Two-a-Day" (1925) to the Broadway musical comedy history of the family's early years, *Minnie's Boys* (1970). However, before examining those early lean years on the very fringe of the entertainment world, it is necessary to scrutinize further the beginning days of this immigrant family named Marx.

Minnie and Frenchie had lost their first baby, Manfred, to tuberculosis. Thus, the birth of Chico produced an even greater outpouring of affection than what might have been considered the norm for a childless household. This boy, whose dialect humor would later have most of the world thinking he was Italian, had the blond, blue-eyed, Germanic good looks of his mother.

Chico forever remained Minnie's favorite. And, as is often the case among favorites, his was the most unruly childhood of the five boys. As his daughter later observed, "Unfortunately, his 'street smarts' developed rapidly, and by the age of nine Chico had become a compulsive gambler."[17] He soon graduated to pool hustler and staying out all night with a gang; theirs was a tough neighborhood. Still, there was a foreshadowing of things to come—Chico had a talent for imitating accents. "In a tight spot he could pass himself off as Italian, Irish, German, or first-generation Jewish, whichever was most useful in the scrape he happened to be in."[18] Moreover, whether it was from that ongoing tidal wave of maternal affection, or merely additional maternal genes, Chico possessed his mother's warm, outgoing, persuasive personality. Chico's and Minnie's reservoirs of these traits would be invaluable to the future Marx Brothers team, from Minnie's long-term establishing push to Chico's later career coups as the group's unofficial manager. Fittingly, as critic Walter Kerr has observed, Chico's on-screen persona is also the only brother with whom audiences can feel "intimate" (one might like the others equally, but Harpo's "otherplanetary" nature and Groucho's "assault" style keep them somewhat distant.)[19]

These winsome traits notwithstanding, the young Chico's fascination with gambling (a lifelong addiction) would forever alienate the rest of the family. Frequently the loser, Chico had no qualms about pawning anything in, or out of, sight. Nothing was sacred, from his brother's harp to his father's latest tailoring job. Though frequently treated comically in later Marx Brothers chronicles (Groucho observed that the local pawnshop often had more Marx family items than their flat[20]), it was an ongoing trial that was never resolved.

For one thing, Frenchie was a reluctant disciplinarian who staged whisk-broom spankings outside the family's view (supposedly to save the others from unpleasant "spare the rod . . ." violence), and then merely pretended to spank the culprit. Moreover, the gambling habit behind Chico's pawning was merely a reflection of home life. While Frenchie had a near obsession for auction pinochle, Minnie was equally fascinated with poker. (Biographer Crichton even describes Minnie as feeling "guilty" that Chico had "inherited the failing from herself."[21]) Yet if reproachments were in order, Frenchie was the more likely candidate to receive one, because he even equated manhood with cards. One of the most poignant scenes in *Groucho and Me*, though the comedian softens it behind a layer of jokes (as was his custom), occurs when Frenchie tells Groucho he would "never be a real man" until he became a successful pinochle player.[22] No doubt added to the difficulty of stopping Chico's pawning beyond his status as Minnie's favorite and his masculinity in Frenchie's eyes, was the fact that often when he did come home it was only to sleep—sneaking in late and exiting early.

Harpo was the next oldest, and appropriately, noticing the parallels between Harpo and Frenchie, he was his father's favorite. As a child Harpo so resembled Chico that they often were mistaken for twins. In later years the physical resemblance often allowed Chico to "commit his adulteries in Harpo's name."[23] Even late in life Chico appeared on the television show *I've Got a Secret* as Harpo—his secret being that he really was Chico. One of the most repeated Marx family stories plays upon their look-alike status. Chico was the family piano player because there was lesson money only for one. But Harpo had managed to learn two numbers—"Waltz Me Around Again, Willie" and "Love Me and the World Is Mine"—not exactly an extensive musical repertoire. It was not long before Chico would land a piano-playing job in a silent film theatre, dazzling the management with his musical skills (maybe even revealing an early version of his classic "shoot the keys" technique). Yet very soon it would become apparent that this prodigy had suffered a musical regression. His collection of songs had all but disappeared, and very nearly the same sounds would emanate from the piano regardless of the action on the screen. Look-alike substitute Harpo would then be fired, and the Chico hand-me-down job system would be reactivated.

Other than a similarity of appearance, the Chico-Harpo relationship was largely of a teacher-student nature. Not surprisingly, the "education" focused on everything you wanted to know about gambling, from playing pool to avoiding dice games on a blanket. Harpo proved an excellent student. Groucho later observed in his *Memoirs of a Mangy Lover* that Chico and Harpo "were two of the best card players in the [United] States."[24] But Chico's gambling, or more precisely his gambling-related pawning, had a more interesting impact on Harpo. Chico's taking of everything not nailed down reaffirmed Harpo's "one day at a time" philosophy, especially in terms of not building up any stockpile of childhood treasures. Harpo's change went for readily disposable things from food to film tickets.

The threat of Chico's five-finger removal service could also inspire the surreal in Harpo, anticipating his comedy character by years. To safeguard a cherished pocket watch, Harpo removed its hands. No matter that it no longer told the time: it was now "Chico-proof."[25] Thus, unlike the nightmare symbolism of a handless clock in Ingmar Bergman's art house *Wild Strawberries* (1957), Harpo's action was an off-beat comic victory of life—perfectly in keeping with the reasons his later screen character became so celebrated.

Harpo's delightfully eccentric joys could also be a pathos-tinted window to childhood poverty. For example, though the Marx family had only one left-footed ice skate, Harpo managed to be entertained at length haphazardly making his way along the border of the frozen pond in Central Park. But even this takes on an air of luxury when juxtaposed with another of Harpo's unusual boyhood pleasures. A young fan of the baseball Giants when they still played in New York, Harpo never had the admission price to the Polo Grounds. But by standing on a high hill behind the park, he was able to see a narrow slice of left field—a slice which he nonetheless loyally watched. Appropriately, while other children collected baseball cards of yesterday's superstar Giants, Harpo's hero was the uncelebrated Sam Martes, the Giants' left fielder.[26] Had the pun-loving Chico and Groucho ever considered this baseball story, there might well have been the crack that Harpo was always coming out of "left field." Regardless, it is a bittersweet look at a difficult childhood. (Though baseball stories hardly constitute a sizable portion of the Marx Brothers's reminiscences, it is fitting that while the ethereal Harpo speaks of an average, obscure player, cynical Groucho's memories of youthful baseball attendance focus on the great but aggressive Ty Cobb.[27])

On other occasions the difficulties of Harpo's boyhood, and those of his brothers, surfaced much more baldly, from the tough cops to the ethnic street gangs that defined who you were and where you could go. It was a time when American literature was discovering naturalism, often with subject matter focused on the plight of this country's more recent immigrants. While the Marx family was not straight out of Upton Sinclair's *The Jungle*, times were not easy, and Harpo's autobiography sometimes has a matter-of-fact naturalism about it that can be shocking. For example, his description of what might be labeled the East River Breast Stroke—the "pushing away" motion of your hands—was "the only way you could keep the sewage and garbage out of your face" when swimming.[28]

While Chico was often self-centeredly absent, perhaps testing (as biographer Arce suggests[29]) the abundance of parental love with which he was showered, shy Harpo seems to have been unobtrusively present, soaking up the wealth of family and neighborhood eccentricities. Through a storefront window he studied the bizarre facial contortions (like crossed eyes painted on an overinflated balloon) of a cigar roller named Gookie as the man worked. Ingeniously, Harpo studied this accidental clown and practiced replicating his real mask in the reflection of the window. Once mastered and used for humor (initially to torment its rather humorless source comically), the now legendary "Gookie" represented a unique duality for Harpo—the beginning of Harpo as performer and the mask that would be his cornerstone visage throughout the life of his career and that of the Marx Brothers. In fact, the comic impact of Harpo's Gookie was such a guaranteed laugh that the stage Marx Brothers often used it

3. Groucho (left) and Harpo as children, with pet. (Photograph courtesy of the Wisconsin Center for Film and Theater Research.)

as a humor safety valve when their other material was not working. Woollcott, in a Harpo essay entitled *A Strong, Silent Man*, even comically credited the Gookie (which the critic likened to the mask of a "Neanderthal idiot") with strong staying power—"Strangers abruptly confronted with it are creditably reported to be heard for weeks thereafter screaming in their sleep."[30]

Groucho was the third oldest and middle son, though Zeppo was born late enough (1901) to constitute almost a second family for Frenchie and Minnie. Paradoxically, while Groucho's dominating cynical verbal patter would later make it appear he was the oldest of the three focus Marx Brothers, he was actually the youngest. Yet, first the sickly Gummo, whose poor health necessitated extra parental attention, and then Zeppo denied him the sometimes favored position of family baby. Indeed, the phrase "favored position" with respect to Groucho and his family seemingly never applied. Even as a child Groucho was aware of this—Minnie would eventually nickname him "the jealous one." Ironically, if an unequal distribution of parental love were ever justified, it was Groucho who should have been receiving the lion's share. As Chico observed, Groucho "was always trying to be the good son, while I was busy being the bad one—and yet Minnie always forgave me and loved me and was never that way with Grouch."[31] Biographer Arce opined that "Minnie's indifference was to adversely affect Groucho and shape his attitude toward women for the rest of his life."[32]

The frequently misogynist nature of Groucho's later humor, both on-screen and off, does, however, have other possible sources. For example, Groucho's comic attacks on the female might be the outgrowth of the womanizing nature of the older males in his young life—particularly Frenchie, Uncle Al, and Grandpa Louis.[33] It might also be the rather nonromantic fact that his introduction to sex came via a prostitute who also introduced him to gonorrhea. Indeed, when he later referred to the incident he often obsessively observed that it was a disease which never entirely left your body.[34] And Marx Brothers biographer William Wolf suggests Groucho's attitude evolved because he was never as successful with the girls as Chico.[35] Yet this latter possible cause might merely be an effect of his less-than-favorite-son status with Minnie. Regardless, "when it came to the ladies, he was tongue-tied and still mustering up courage to ask for a date long after Chico had tucked the lady in bed."[36]

This author would suggest one further hypothesis—the comic verbal cynicism of his mother. Groucho, like comedy contemporaries Charlie Chaplin and W. C. Fields, seems to have been profoundly influenced by his mother's sense of humor. Hannah Chaplin taught her boy mime and mimicry; Kate Dukenfield (Fields) was a model for her son's later caustic, under-his-breath asides. But Minnie's comic heritage was as master of the direct comic put-down.[37] And since Minnie ruled the family and husband Frenchie, his womanizing notwithstanding (and possibly because of it), it is possible that a young Groucho would assume the normal relationship between men and women to be one of verbal attack. But because Groucho was initially the family member most vulnerable to his mother's barbs, this theory too might move from cause to effect, since Groucho eventually assumed the mantle of verbal attacker out of self-defense.[38]

Regardless of the source of Groucho's comic misogyny (which was probably an uneven mixture of several if not all the possibilities suggested), one of his favorite stories nicely showcases how easily this characteristic was taking shape. As a teenager he had somehow managed to keep a nest egg of seventy cents from the sticky fingers of Chico. This would be just enough money for Groucho to take the reigning beauty of his apartment complex, one Annie Berger, to the theatre and still have carfare home. But Miss Berger quickly devastated Groucho's high finances by having the audacity to request a treat—some taffy. She then compounded the dilemma by not sharing. Groucho was now up against it, or at least someone was, because he had carfare home for only one. What to do? Groucho benevolently disregarded her selfishness and did the only fair thing, at least the only fair thing for a Groucho. He flipped her for the ride home. Miss Berger lost and was forced to walk home . . . in the snow . . . fifty-one blocks. Romance did not blossom.

Like Chaplin, whose later screen image of women is also anticipated in a famous reminiscence of a failed childhood romance (though unlike Groucho, Chaplin puts his heroine on a pedestal to worship), Groucho's anecdote is a fitting precedent for a screen character who would later spout such woman-baiting barbs as: "I can see you right now in the kitchen, bending over a hot stove, but I can't see the stove," or "Would you mind giving me a lock of your hair? . . . I'm letting you off easy. I was going to ask for the whole wig." (both from *Duck Soup*, 1933.)

In fairness to Groucho, raising the seventy cents for his less-than-romantic encounter had been an arduously sneaky task. No doubt taking a lesson from Chico, good boy Groucho had shortchanged his mother a penny on each of seventy trips to the store. Groucho's job was to buy the family bread, which cost a nickel for a fresh loaf. But the young businessman found he could purchase day-old bread for the more reasonable price of four cents a loaf, and thus was born a modest source of income.

It is also prophetic that this early tale of attempted romance is quite literally intertwined with pinching pennies. Because of his childhood poverty, Groucho (again like Chaplin and Fields) showed a much more loyal policy (tightness) toward his monetary affairs than to his marital ones. Appropriately, once major financial success came to the Marx Brothers, he was the one who still feared a return to poverty, and he economized accordingly. His son noted that even after Groucho became a major film star, not one movie production went by without his father noting the "real shock" he felt after meeting a former wealthy film performer working as an extra.[39] If his grouchy cynicism did not so perfectly match his nickname, one would be tempted to link his comic title with the "grouch" bags in which vaudeville performers sometimes carried their money (See Crichton's biography for more on the subject.[40]). It is tempting to describe both his comedy style and his coin purse with a punning aphorism such as: he

gave no quarter. But there were notable exceptions, such as the financial assistance he and his other brothers provided for the late years of gambler Chico.

Groucho was unlike his brothers in three additional, obvious ways. First,
while Chico and Harpo had decidedly Germanic looks with their light hair
and fair complexions, Groucho's prominent nose, dark coarse hair and dark
complexion favored their Jewish heritage. Significantly, Minnie (also Germanic
in appearance) thought of herself as more German than Jewish, and prolonged
her older boys' light hair with peroxide as it darkened with age.[41] These physical differences might also have contributed to Groucho's less-than-favored
position with his mother.

Second, Groucho was the resident bookworm of the family. Though he gave
different accounts as to why he left school in the seventh grade (boring institutional learning versus enticing show business versus the need for a job to help
support the family[42]), he had a lifetime commitment to reading, and eventually
discovered a talent for writing (see the bibliographical essay chapter). Thus,
Harpo noted that even the eight-year-old Groucho was too busy reading to play
cards with his older brothers.[43]

As children, however, Chico had displayed the greatest academic promise.
According to his teachers, he was gifted in math. But being Chico, he eventually
limited its application to gambling. Conversely, Harpo quite literally *dropped*
out of school during his second try at the second grade. That is, two bullies
enjoyed dropping him out of the window of their first-story classroom. After
several such exits, Harpo decided he would much prefer the more metaphorical
school of hard knocks *outside* the classroom. A popular legend (seemingly begun
by a young Harpo) had him held over in second grade for years because of an
infatuated teacher's resistance to losing him, though a 1933 article reverses the
situation, crediting his academic overtime to Harpo's own infatuation for a
beautiful blonde teacher.[44] Coincidentally this also matched the screen image
of his blonde-chasing Pan. But, the bullies aside, Harpo later notes in his autobiography that he found school impractical; it simply provided him with no
survival skills for a world he already knew to be less than easy.[45]

It was doubly ironic that when the Marx Brothers eventually found great
critical and commercial success on Broadway, it was the nearly illiterate Harpo
(as opposed to the bookish Groucho) to whom the literary intelligentsia was
attracted—both in their writing and in their socializing. This is best exemplified
in the life and writings of Alexander Woollcott, the patron saint of Marx Brothers
critics (for his early championing of their Broadway work) and later close friend
of Harpo.

Woollcott actually celebrates Harpo's minimal education in the aptly titled
comic essay, "I Might Just as Well Have Played Hooky." Joining Harpo as
the subject of this piece are Irving Berlin and Norman Bel Geddes—"three
[Woollcott] friends . . . whose total days at school if put end to end would
not even suffice to get one of them through the third reader and compound
fractions."[46] Yet, Woollcott wonders if schools "cramp" one's style, stating

the "lives of such men [the focus three] all remind us that it might well be a blessing . . . to be thrown out of school."[47]

Woollcott was not, however, above kidding about his friend's lack of education. His sneakily titled essay "My Friend Harpo" has a seemingly straightforward opening note: "BEING the brief history of an illiterate but golden-hearted clown, much admired by all who enjoy the inestimable boon of his acquaintance."[48] But the "golden-hearted clown" in question turns out to be Woollcott's dog, which had been named after the silent Marx Brother, though Woollcott's ambiguous descriptions of the canine have the reader long assuming it is the human Harpo.

The third manner in which Groucho differed from his brothers is that he was the only one who originally wanted to be in show business. Groucho's autobiography notes his early interest in show business; Harpo's autobiography traces the interests of the others. Chico would have preferred to become a professional gambler (something he very nearly qualified for anyway), Gummo an inventor, Zeppo a prize fighter, and Harpo a ferryboat piano player (a position some might have included in at least an entertainer's purgatory, but not Harpo).[49]

Appropriately, Groucho, the family outsider, described his entry-level position in show business (as a boy singer) thus: "I felt that for the first time in my life I wasn't a nonentity."[50] His performing aspirations were also assisted by the periodic flashy visits of his vaudeville star uncle Al Shean, an event not lessened by Al's custom of giving each of his poor nephews spending money, as well as scattering pennies among the neighborhood children. Groucho, "the jealous one," always strove for attention from his show-business-enamored mother, and this, too, might have been a factor in his choice of vocations. Like W. C. Fields, Groucho was also attracted to the idea of being able to sleep late. He comically comments on this horizontal "plus" for the entertainment profession in his first book, the 1930 *Beds*—"CONSIDERING that we spend a third of our time in bed—or, if you are an actor, two thirds."[51]

Groucho's 1905 beginning in show business, though an aborted one, was with the Leroy Trio. It was hardly a wow act, and the naive fifteen-year-old (who "knew as much about the world as the average retarded eight-year-old"[52]) soon found himself stranded in the wilds of Colorado. Not only had his partners disbanded the act without telling him, but they also had relieved him of his grouch bag funds as he slept.

As with the early careers of W. C. Fields and countless other pre–Actors Equity performers, this would not be the only time Groucho would find himself stranded. History would repeat itself in Dallas and again in Chicago. Though not yet tagged with the nickname Groucho, he was building an impressive portfolio of reasons for having it, especially when coupled with his "jealous one" background.

After these fiascos Groucho went home and briefly worked on the entertainment fringe as a delivery boy for a wig company in the New York City theatre district. But having been a performer, however minor league, Groucho would not take the comedown, and the job lasted only a few weeks. But the job was to be the catalyst for a major prank by Harpo, one that anticipates the later inspired comic lunacy of his screen character.

Groucho had brought home a box of wigs one evening for easier delivery the next morning. Naturally, he and Harpo could not resist breaking into the box and comically modeling a dozen different ladies' wigs before a mirror. Harpo was then stirred to dress as a hooker and play a gag on some nearby card-playing relatives, one of whom had an extreme fear of germs. Harpo's masquerade was a comic masterpiece, which nearly turned to bedlam when Harpo the hooker tried to kiss "Mr. Clean." The gag was comically compounded when several woman family members, including Minnie, tried to evict this harlot from the apartment. Eventually, Harpo de-wigged himself and the family hailed the prank a classic, though the women reportedly took several days to calm down. More important, however, the exploit tagged Harpo as the "family character," no small accomplishment in the Marx clan.[53]

Assumption of this particular character role, even as part of a prank, is of career importance for two reasons. First, it was a start for a young man who had shown neither much talent (other than his patented Gookie) nor much inclination for performing. Second, providing comedy from beneath a wig and costume anticipated the evolution of his comedy character as one of the Marx Brothers. Granted, they are different characters (though Harpo occasionally impersonated women later during his comedy career), but they both allow Harpo to perform from behind the protection of a disguise. Such protection was important for Harpo because as a young man he later wet his pants the first time he appeared on stage as part of a Marx Brothers act (but well before his wig-and-trench-coat days). As an old man he still appreciated the anonymity his costumeless private life allowed him. Thus, discovering the comedic freedom of a disguise would seem to be a very significant event. Indeed, Harpo himself related his later enthusiasm for the Patsy Brannigan character in *School Days* (his first stage appearance requiring a wig and a specific costume) to his comic masquerade as a harlot.[54]

While Harpo cornered the home entertainment market and Groucho was a periodic boy singer with an acting role to his credit (as the office boy in the 1906 production of *The Man of Her Choice*), Chico temporarily broke with the family and occupied himself with a number of life-on-the-edge sort of jobs, such as hustling pool and playing piano in a brothel. In 1907 he became a song-plugger for a Pittsburgh music house. But unlike writer/director Preston Sturges's famous later line from *Sullivan's Travels* (1941)—"If they [Pittsburgh residents] knew what they liked, they wouldn't live in Pittsburgh"—Chico had found himself and would soon team with a music house associate and enter vaudeville.

The initial merging of the Marx Brothers into a team occurred in 1907. Composed only of Groucho, Gummo, and a girl singer named Mabel O'Donnell, the

4. The Marx Brothers of 1908 (from left to right): Harpo, Groucho, and Gummo. (Photograph courtesy of the Wisconsin Center for Film and Theater Research.)

group was christened by Minnie "The Three Nightingales." Stage mother that she was, Minnie had decided it would be easier to find bookings for her two available sons (Harpo and Chico were working; Zeppo had just started school) if she made them a package. And traditionally, the more people in an act, the larger the salary. Despite later comically disparaging remarks by Groucho (such as Minnie must have never heard a real nightingale[55]), it was a successful act.

Mabel eventually was replaced (her voice always veered off key) by a young singer named Lou Levy. In a few months in mid-1908 Minnie Marx would make another change—with the addition of Harpo "The Three Nightingales" became a foursome. The most popular reason given for Harpo's addition is that the act was about ready to go on tour and Minnie was apprehensive about leaving this teenage son behind (one assumes she did not have the same anxiety about Zeppo because he was younger and still in school). This is the way Alexander Woollcott relates the story in his 1928 *New Yorker* piece, "Portrait of a Man with Red Hair" (Harpo), still another Marx Brother essay by the critic.[56]

Because Minnie almost kidnapped Harpo from his job (depending on the source, either as a bellhop or as a nickelodeon piano player) for his stage debut, there were probably additional factors. For example, Harpo credits the rush to both his mother's last-minute ability to obtain a good price on four instead of three new costumes for the act, and concern over competition from a quartet on the same bill. Groucho biographer Arce attributes Harpo's addition to manager Minnie (forever hungry to book her act) Marx's realization she had promised to provide a foursome instead of a trio.[57] Regardless of just how Harpo entered the act, this smorgasbord of possibilities is an excellent commentary on how pure happenstance often seemed to be the real guiding force behind the act.

The Four Nightingales began touring in small-time vaudeville as a juvenile act (despite its members being teenaged and older) late in the first decade of the twentieth century. Minnie capitalized on this by always obtaining half-price train fare, claiming each of the boys was thirteen. Eventually the act physically outgrew the ruse, though Minnie never surrendered. When a conductor eventually accosted her with "that kid of yours is in the dining car smoking a cigar and another one is in the washroom shaving," Minnie sadly shook her head and said, "They grow so fast."[58]

About 1910 Minnie made a much larger business decision concerning the group. She moved its home base from New York to Chicago because the latter city was more a booking haven for small-time vaudeville. Eventually a down payment was made on a three-story brownstone on South Chicago's Grand Boulevard, partly through the assistance of brother Al Shean. The mortgage was held by the banking concern of Greenbaum & Sons. Thereafter, whenever the boys would neglect their material on stage (such as the night they stopped their act to follow the slow progress of a beetle across the stage), Minnie would return them to a semblance of the performance by whispering from the wings: "Greenbaum!"

In Chicago The Four Nightingales became The Six Mascots—a short-lived singing and dancing act, beginning to add a modicum of humor to its material. The

5. The Marx Brothers after the 1912 addition of Chico (from left to right): Harpo, Gummo, Chico, and Groucho. (Photograph courtesy of the Wisconsin Center for Film and Theater Research.)

troupe was composed of Groucho, Gummo, Harpo, bass singer Freddie Hutchins, and two girl singers. However, when the girls left the group early, Minnie and her sister Hannah replaced them. The brief history of the Mascots generally focuses comically on its two maturely stout ingenues and the night they inadvertently sat on the same chair . . . until it collapsed beneath them. Some changes were deemed necessary.

Later in 1910 the brothers organized and began touring with a show called *Fun in Hi Skule*. The troupe would come to be called the "3 Marx Bros. & Co.," with a 4 replacing the 3 after the addition of Chico. This was a time in American vaudeville when the schoolroom routine, generally credited to Gus Edwards, was a popular comedy genre. *Fun in Hi Skule* had Groucho playing Mr. Green, the German Herr Teacher, complete with accent (dialect humor was still popular). Harpo was the country simpleton Patsy Brannigan, the kind of boy who drove teachers into early retirement. Gummo's Jewish boy was essentially a straight man.

Fun in Hi Skule was an important transition for several reasons. First, the emphasis of the act was now comedy. And this first use of Peasie Weasie material, a then-popular style of comic song (based upon word plays such as puns) in vaudeville and burlesque, would foreshadow the later nonstop verbal slapstick of the team's mature work. Second, Groucho's teacher was a mustached older man, anticipating the essentially dirty old man he would generally play in the future. Third, though Harpo's red-wigged bumpkin still spoke, his disruptive otherworldliness (both in appearance and in action) also anticipates his later comedy persona. Eventually, Harpo would also introduce his harp playing into this act. Fourth, *Fun in Hi Skule*'s cartoon-like satire of education is a primitive first cousin to what the Marx Brothers's later films do best—bringing anarchical comedy to frequently rigid institutional settings. Indeed, Groucho's attempt to teach a college biology class in *Horse Feathers* (1932; education is again the target of comedy) is in the spirit of the trials he suffered as Herr Teacher of *Fun in Hi Skule*. Fifth, Chico's joining the act the following year (1912) marked the first professional union of the three pivotal Marx Brothers—Groucho, Harpo, and Chico. Moreover, Chico came to the act already equipped with both his comic Italian accent and his delightful piano comedy. The latter includes his "shooting the keys" technique, where Chico's index finger extends out like a barrel from a fist gun (excepting a raised thumb as trigger), allowing him to tap-shoot pivotal keys individually with the *hand*gun's barrel. The technique would later become very popular with piano players.

The early on-the-road years were far from easy, though Groucho's frequent reminiscences are often peppered with enough humor to make them seem more like a comic odyssey. From the beautiful Muncie (Indiana) girl who invited him home and forgot to mention her husband, to the Orange (Texas) queen of uglies who had to be romanced so that the team could receive less inflammable food from the girl's mother, their Mexican boarding-house landlady, Groucho's misadventures seem forever funny—not to mention frequently sexual.[59]

6. Chico's patented "shooting the keys" piano-playing technique. (Photograph courtesy of the Wisconsin Center for Film and Theater Research.)

For a more realistic examination of the team's difficult early road years, it is again best to consult Harpo's autobiography. While not without his own comic reminiscences, Harpo describes these touring times as "unmitigated hell," making his tough, East Side New York streetwise childhood seem like an extended "recess."[60] With a small-time vaudeville focus on the Midwest and the deep South, the team had to contend with everything from the standard actor as low-life stereotype to prejudice against their Jewish heritage. (While Groucho is better known for his pronouncements on prejudice—his observation to a restricted club: since his son was only half Jewish, might not he be able to go into the water up to his knees?—Harpo is more thorough in documenting its ties in Marx Brothers family history.)

The ability of the Marx Brothers to survive, whether on the streets of New York or amid the rigors of small-time vaudeville, owes much to the strong force that was Minnie Marx. She did what was necessary for survival and eventual success, from maximizing her managerial efficiency with a family act to using Frenchie's one great skill—cooking—in order to bribe prospective vaudeville bookers by way of the culinary arts.

Minnie's wheeler-dealer skills were probably best showcased during the *Fun in Hi Skule* period. For example, because she had begun to manage and book additional acts, she rechristened herself Minnie Palmer, after a popular vaudeville star of the same name. She felt the name would give her expanded operation additional prestige, though it is unlikely she had not considered the possible windfalls through name confusion. This ploy was so effective that years later (1928) one of the first film articles on the Marx Brothers includes a lengthy notation on Mother Minnie but with actress Palmer's background.[61] In fact, when Jack Benny was interviewed for the 1973 *The Marx Bros. Scrapbook* (he had a close relationship with them in vaudeville), he still referred to their mother as Minnie Palmer.[62] For someone based in Chicago, as the Marx family then was, Minnie's choice of names also borrowed from the grandeur of the city's renowned Palmer House.[63]

When Chico joined the act (he is said to have unexpectedly turned up in the orchestra pit—at the piano—during a performance of *Fun in Hi Skule*, causing a comic battle royal in his reunion with his brothers), he gradually and unofficially assumed many of the group's managerial needs. In the years to come, as Chico's daughter Maxine Marx so insightfully observed in her biography of him, he was the "catalyst" behind the group's success.[64]

Chico as manager was important to the group for four reasons. First, while his personal gambling seldom fattened his bankbook, his gambler personality was ideal for the Marx Brothers. He was the member who challenged the more conservative Harpo and Groucho to higher goals, such as making the jump from vaudeville to Broadway. Second, he had a genuinely winsome personality, no small characteristic when negotiating. His phenomenal success with women showcased a more personal application of this trait. Third, Chico was Mr. Enthusiasm. He gave confidence to his managerial gambling, and in general, just lightened spirits around him. In contrast to the worrisome Groucho, upbeat Chico might just as appropriately have been nicknamed Happo. Fourth, Chico's life experience went beyond just being the oldest son and mother's favorite, though these were significant facts in a family operation run by the mother. Though his Marx Brothers seniority was slight, he had been the only brother to break with the family for a time and successfully go it alone. And while his pre-Marx Brothers team experience in vaudeville, as a trick piano player (doing audience requests blindfolded and with a sheet over the keys) and accompanist for such singing partners as cousin Lou Shean, had not set new records, he was accustomed to playing better quality houses—an expectation he brought to the team. All these things contributed to the great future success of the Marx Brothers.

Chico as performer was also very important to the group. Though his comedy character would eventually be eclipsed by that of Groucho's and Harpo's, he came to his entry level Marx Brothers show, *Fun in Hi Skule*, much closer to his later film persona than either of his brothers. That is, in a comedy act with a still verbal Harpo and a German-accented Groucho, Chico brought both his Italian dialect and his distinctive piano style. Moreover, his winning behind-the-scenes traits of personality and enthusiasm were even more important on stage:

> From the moment he sat down for his first piano speciality, *Fun in Hi Skule* had become his show. . . . Chico was not only the headliner, but he was the life of the troupe. No matter how flat the jokes fell or how sour the quartet sang, Chico was always there to jerk the audience aloft and get them roaring.[65]

In time *Fun in Hi Skule* had a second act called "Visiting the Old School Ten Years Later." This was a party given for Groucho's character (the teacher Mr. Green) where the *Hi Skule* participants of a decade prior are gathered. The party setting also happened to be a good excuse for the group's musical speciality numbers. By 1913 it had evolved that the schoolroom party reunion was now the opening, while the second act was the musical spotlight. The show was now called *Mr. Green's Reception*.

As variations on schoolroom material would occasionally surface in later Marx Brothers productions, especially *Horse Feathers*, the Marxes-at-a-party theme would be even more fruitful, occurring in much of their future stage work and films such as *Monkey Business* (1931) and *Duck Soup* (1933). Their "anything goes" humor is perfectly showcased in a party setting, where one expects the unusual and enjoys effronteries to elitists. Moreover, the Marxes bring "welcome insanity [to] the deadly affair that is supposed to be fun and never is."[66]

Though the gods of comedy had frequently avoided smiling upon their rough road through vaudeville, a change in the act took place in 1914. Ironically, the members were able to benefit from the temporary breakup of the Gallagher and Shean team. Uncle Al, now having the time, wrote and staged an act for them called *Home Again*. It is a show in two parts. It opens at the New York pier of the Cunard Line (where Groucho and family, including Gummo as his son, have returned from Europe); it concludes at a party at Groucho's villa on the Hudson. As before, the party becomes the perfect setting for both musical interludes and crazy comedy.

Groucho plays wealthy, elderly Henry Schneider, thus continuing his stage persona of an older German comedian. (Marx Brothers literature sometimes refers to this character as Mr. Green, since there had been some carryover in both Groucho's character and the show itself as it evolved from *Fun in Hi Skule* to *Mr. Green's Reception* to *Home Again*.) Gummo plays the handsome straight man, a limited part that Zeppo would inherit in a few years. Chico and Harpo, the team within the team (a phenomenon which had begun soon after Chico joined *Fun in Hi Skule*), are petty crooks who practice their trade by mingling with the dock crowds. They later make their entrance at Groucho's party with Harpo as a garbage man. This is a setup for the classic Groucho response to the announcement that the garbage man has arrived: "Tell him we don't want any." Though Groucho initially fights the girl-chasing anarchy of Harpo and Chico, he eventually joins their comic revelry.

Home Again was a major critical and commercial success. After a New York opening at the Royal Theatre (following several testing months on the road), *Variety* described it as "the best tab [loid] New York has ever seen . . . an act big time could depend upon for a future."[67] In two weeks *Home Again* opened to more praise at the celebrated Palace, the dream play date of every vaudeville act.[68]

Besides this rousing success, the show would display major change in the stage personae of Harpo and Groucho. One would occur immediately; the other would be necessitated by change in international politics. First, this is the production which begins Harpo's silent tradition. Uncle Al had inadvertently given him only three lines and when his nephew complained, the vaudeville veteran alibied that Harpo would be better off as a mime. Thus began a persona which made Calvin Coolidge seem like "an old chatterbox."[69] Second, the May 1915 German sinking of the *Lusitania* suddenly made anything to do with that nationality suspect, and Groucho's stage persona lost its Teutonic tendencies.

As if to give special significance to the 1914 birth of *Home Again*, as well as acknowledge their approaching celebrity, the Brothers would also receive their famous nicknames this year. The team was playing poker with monologist Art Fisher and discussing newspaper cartoon artist Charles Mager's phenomenally successful comic strip *Sherlocko, the Monk* (1910). The strip, which parodied Sir Arthur Conan Doyle's Sherlock Holmes, was populated with characters whose dominant idiosyncrasies were reflected in their names, which also ended with the letter "o." Sherlocko also interacted with characters from earlier, similar Mager strips.

Because of the strip's popularity, a number of vaudeville comedians adapted similarly inspired names. This is the backdrop into which Fisher dealt both cards and comic nicknames. Cynical Julius became Groucho; harp-playing Adolph became Harpo; girl (chick)-chasing Leonard became Chico (a typesetter later accidently dropped the "k" and the new spelling was retained), and the gumshoe-attired Milton became Gummo. (Herbert, not yet with the team, acquired the nickname Zeppo at a later date.[70])

That the Marx Brothers should have a comic strip connection, particularly with *Sherlocko, the Monk*, is appropriate for three reasons. First, the 1910s were a golden age for the comics, with strips like George Herriman's *Krazy Kat* (1913, universally considered the greatest strip) and George McManus's *Bringing Up Father* (1913) being in the vanguard of American humor. As this author suggested in the works *Charlie Chaplin: A Bio-Bibliography* (Westport, Conn.: Greenwood Press, 1983) and *W. C. Fields: A Bio-Bibliography* (Greenwood Press, 1984), one cannot fully understand the period's comedians without examining the era's cartoon strips. This is especially true of the Marx Brothers; their celebration of absurdity seems right at home among what were frequently antiheroic newspaper funnies. Thus, to find Marx Brothers's nicknames to be directly inspired from a strip is most fitting. Second, while there is no evidence that the Marx Brothers drew anything beyond their nicknames from the strip—though Groucho at least seems to have closely followed it for years—the basic comic premise of Sherlocko, to undercut an established authority figure, would soon be the comedy norm of the Marxes. This can be seen in their satire of specific figures (Napoleon and his advisers) in the stage production *I'll Say She Is!*, and in their more general putdown of government leaders in *Duck Soup*. Third, Mager's original Monk "o" strips (dating from 1904) had small apes in human clothing for characters. In time, they became somewhat humanized—yet more than a suggestion of their simian appearance remained. The Marx Brothers at their antisocial best, particularly in their Paramount films, always had an amoral spontaneity about them, which was more than a little animal-like. This is perhaps best typified by Harpo's close ties with animals, his girl chasing, and his deft placement of a leg (his) in the hand of unsuspecting strangers. It is therefore quite logical that all the team's Paramount films have animal-related titles: *The Cocoanuts* (1929), *Animal Crackers* (1930), *Monkey Business* (1931), *Horse Feathers* (1932), and *Duck Soup* (1933).

With their 1915 Palace success the Marx Brothers had reached the first of three career pinnacles—tops in vaudeville. In successive decades they would find comparable success on Broadway and then in film. (In the 1950s a solo Groucho would add still another triumph with his popular and critically acclaimed television show, *You Bet Your Life*.)

In an age before the national audiences of radio and television constantly necessitated new material, the Marx Brothers were able to tour for years in Uncle Al's *Home Again*. But while a degree of consistency was developing in their professional world (as much as possible for a team that enjoyed improvising), changes were coming to their private lives.

The ongoing war in Europe was the greatest usurper. Just as it had even managed to bring change to the bankable *Home Again*, it altered the Brothers's non-show-business activities. Most obviously, to play upon a war-related phrase, it changed what the Marxes would call their home front: in 1916 they moved from the Greenbaum house to a small farm near LaGrange, twenty miles outside Chicago. Since farming was supposed to be a draft-exempted occupation, Minnie most probably orchestrated the move to safeguard the act. Marx Brothers texts frequently note other, more positive, reasons, from patriotism (raising food for the war effort) to avoiding combat with Minnie's native country. Nevertheless, the change proved to be a total failure (other than possibly producing Herbert's nickname—Zeppo). Not only did the Brothers still receive the call to report for their service physicals, but any semblance of the rural life refused to rub off on them.

While becoming farmers had hardly been the original purpose for the move, the Brothers had initially attempted to get into the rural spirit, including rising early for chores. But, like the misplaced urban Tramp of Chaplin's rural *Sunnyside* (1919), the Marx Brothers had difficulty getting out of bed. Appropriately, the later *Beds*-penning Groucho was fond of describing how the first country morning they earnestly arose at five, but that each successive day the wake-up time was pushed back further . . . until it had eroded to noon. Even then they had an ulterior motive—to attend afternoon Chicago Cubs games at Wrigley Field.

Still, some agricultural tasks were attempted by these show business farmers. But, as was consistent with the ongoing irony of their lives, the most anarchic of public performers were frequently rather antiheroic private beings. With regard to the farm, this meant desired productivity, like egg-laying chickens, met with failure (though purchased eggs were sometimes planted in nests to impress city friends). Contrarily, bountifulness came from nonprofit areas, like the easy-to-raise guinea pig, which was supposed to be in great demand by the medical profession during the war period. Though the Marxes were soon overrun with guinea pigs, no market was in sight. They were forced to liberate their only bumper crop—a noble gesture, but hardly the stuff of big business.

Their call for physicals came in 1917, the year the United States entered World War I. But adding irony to irony, the supposedly sickly Gummo was the only one taken. Biographer Arce credits the exemptions to Groucho's poor eyesight, Harpo's albuminuria, and the recent marriage of Chico, who at thirty was also at the age ceiling.[71] But one more frequently reads that an arrangement was made. Gummo himself observed that his mother "realized that somebody in the family would have to go. . . . You couldn't expect the young one to go. Chico was married. Groucho and Harpo were important to the act. Mom said, 'We can do without you.'"[72]

Though the statement was nothing if not harsh, Gummo accepted it without rancor because he believed it and because he had always been an unhappy performer. In fact, even before his service obligation he had undertaken a "real world" sales position simultaneously with his stage work, in order to prepare for retirement as a performer. Drafted into the army, Gummo was in Illinois for the duration—being trained in Rockford and stationed in Chicago, where his commanding officers utilized his show business background to provide them with female companionship from the entertainment world.

After the war Gummo found success initially in the women's dress business and later as a show business agent. The man whose performing career seemed jinxed from his start as an undersized boy encased in Uncle Harry Shean's (Al's brother) ventriloquist dummy (an advantage which still could not save the act), was now comfortably and permanently off the stage. Zeppo followed him into the thankless straight man role.

Other pre-Broadway personal changes came via Chico's and Groucho's marriages. In 1916 Chico married a Pittsburgh nineteen-year-old named Betty Karp. She was a beautiful, straightforward Jewish girl, and Chico seems to have been especially taken with her ability to parry the sexual advances of the normally unstoppable Marx Brothers Don Juan. Still, because of that very sexual prowess, the union was something of a family surprise. Astonishment mixed with anger when the family found out about the ceremony only after the fact. (Groucho was so upset he did not invite Chico to his 1920 wedding.) Yet Chico's action was consistent with both his independent youth and his later family estrangement in early adulthood.

Since Chico continued his womanizing ways after marriage (in fact he was unfaithful on his honeymoon), one is tempted to define the union as another safeguard against being drafted. Yet, it might also have been an additional act of independence on Chico's part, inasmuch as his daughter later suggested Minnie encouraged her sons' womanizing in order to not "share her boys with another woman."[73] Moreover, the latter scenario is in keeping with the ongoing emergence of Chico as the leader of the team (save in money-holding situations).

In February 1920 Groucho married Ruth Johnson, a beautiful young gentile dancer featured with Zeppo in the *Home Again* troupe. (Betty Marx was also with the group as a chorus girl.) Despite being in Chicago, the couple had difficulty finding a clergyman who would marry a Jewish-gentile couple, especially one in the still less-than-respectable world of show business. Eventually an amusing solution presented itself—a Jewish ex-vaudevillian justice of the peace was discovered. Even then Groucho might have jinxed the find by his refusal to take the occasion seriously. For example, after the justice opened the ceremony with the traditional reference to holy matrimony, Groucho observed, "It may be holy to you, Judge, but we have other ideas."[74] Ironically, this spirit of anarchy, so central to Groucho's comedy persona, eventually would prove to be a severe liability in his personal relationships, especially with Ruth.

In 1930 Groucho comically touched upon the trials of living with him in a piece he authored for *Colliers*.[75] The wedding is described as very close to a Marx Brothers sketch, with all the performing brothers included. While this was logical for a period piece, accenting the Marx Brothers comedy team and avoiding anti-Semitism, the essay's title proved most appropriate for what would eventually be a failed marriage: "My Poor Wife!" However, with the birth of his son

Arthur the following year, Groucho would discover one of the joys of his life—the early years of parenting.

Professionally, the years between the Marx Brothers's 1915 Palace success and their 1924 arrival on Broadway were not entirely devoted to *Home Again*, though it was both the foundation for their later achievements and a periodic safety valve on which to fall back. Thus, in the fall of 1918 they had mounted a musical comedy that they hoped would carry them to Broadway. Called *The Street Cinderella*, it was unable to find an audience, largely because of the severe Spanish influenza epidemic then afflicting the country. Because of the disease, which would eventually kill tens of thousands, health officials restricted the Grand Rapids opening of *Cinderella* to an audience where both every other seat and every other row had to be empty. With many patrons also protecting themselves by handkerchief veils, the environment was not the most conducive for a musical comedy success. The tour never made it out of Michigan, and the Brothers returned to *Home Again* via the facsimile production *'N Everything*.

In 1920 they privately financed their movie debut in a silent short subject. Shot near the Fort Lee, New Jersey, theatre in which they were appearing, it was a film parody whose title also reflected what a Marx Brothers film then meant—*Humorisk*. It opened with love-interest Harpo wearing a top hat as he slid down a coal chute. He was juxtaposed by Groucho as the villian, whose film-closing fate was a ball and chain. *Humorisk*'s one sneak preview was not a success, and the film was subsequently lost or destroyed (sources vary). The Marx Brothers's film career would have to await the coming of sound, though Harpo would later play a supporting role in the silent *Too Many Kisses* (1925), and there would be 1926 negotiations between the team and First National.[76]

In February 1921 Marx Brothers friend and fan Benny Leonard, the popular reigning lightweight boxing champion, financed them in *On the Mezzanine Floor*. The act also featured the stagestruck boxer (including a comedy bout with the Brothers) as well as his girlfriend in a featured role. Written and staged by Herman Timberg, a Marx Brothers friend and performer from vaudeville, the production remained a hit even after Leonard went back to his real vocation. Thus, when the *Mezzanine* reached the Palace in mid-March, *Variety* described it as a comedy "riot . . . that's infallible . . . one of the very best acts that has hit the Palace this or any other season."[77] For someone with Broadway aspirations, especially the eternal optimist and unofficial Marx Brothers manager Chico, this review ended in a most provocatively positive manner: "It [the *Mezzanine*] should lift the Marx family right onto Broadway."[78] The act would assist in that transition, but in a manner neither the critic nor the Marx Brothers could ever have anticipated.

The *Mezzanine* is most important for introducing one of Harpo's signature scenes—the dropping of a seemingly endless supply of stolen silverware from his coat sleeve, topped by the appearance of a silver coffee pot.[79] That the avalanche of stolen silver was precipitated by the ongoing handshake of a hotel detective impressed with Harpo's honest face made it all the more comic.

Both Betty and Ruth permanently left the troupe during the *Mezzanine* run. Groucho and Ruth became parents for the first time in July 1921. While little has been recorded about the birth of Chico and Betty's only child (Maxine, born three years earlier), events surrounding the birth of Groucho and Ruth's Arthur are credited in Marx Brothers folklore as the cause of the comedian's greasepaint mustache. The proud father was said to have stretched one hospital visit too long and returned to the theatre with only time to apply the most cursory of stage mustaches. This greasepaint throwback to an earlier, more primitive make-up tradition (as opposed to the more realistic facsimile he had been applying with glue) was accepted by the audience, and Groucho forever switched to the less time-consuming process.

The Brothers were still doing a variation of the *Mezzaine* (*On the Balcony*) in the spring of 1922 when Chico decided they should take the act to England for the summer. Besides the added prestige a successful foreign tour could give the group, Chico would not have been blind to the added income it could also provide during the traditional off-season of American vaudeville—added income for which the gambling Chico was forever in need.

Prestige and money had been the twin reasons taking W. C. Fields, their comedy contemporary, to Europe for years. Moreover, it is likely that the triumphant return to England of Charlie Chaplin the previous September (1921) was also in their thinking. Besides the universal interest of what was then still a somewhat unique phenomenon—the idolatry accorded an international media star—Chaplin's well-publicized homecoming (see his own *My Trip Abroad*[80]) would have had added fascination to the Marxes because he was both their friend and the comedy idol of Groucho and Harpo (see especially "GROUCHO looks at CHARLIE"[81]). While they were, of course, an unknown quantity in Europe, it was assumed their low comedy tradition would be a hit.

The London reception of *On the Balcony* was not, however, up to Chaplin standards. In fact, it was not up to the more modest Marx standards. The audience threw pennies, the English version of giving the raspberry, provoking one of Groucho's most celebrated ad-libs: "We've come a long way to entertain you. The least you could do is throw silver." While it is still popular to credit the penny incident to the unhappy fans of an act the Marx Brothers had bumped from top billing (an explanation that originates in Groucho's letter in the August 11, 1922, *Variety*), British author Peter Dixon's detailed account of the tour makes it clear that it went much beyond a dissatisfied clique of fans.[82]

The problem was that British audiences had trouble following the zany comedy of the visiting Americans. Thus, the Marx Brothers soon returned to their more traditional, time-proven *Home Again*. Though this piece was better received, audiences still had difficulty understanding their humor. Moreover, the return home did not produce, to borrow from then President Harding, a return to "normalcy," Marx Brothers-style.

The English tour had upset the all-powerful E. F. Albee of the cadillac vaudeville circuit Keith-Albee, to whom the Marxes were under contract. Albee contended that the summer tour should not have been undertaken without his approval. When no understanding could be reached between all parties, the Brothers found themselves blacklisted.

Albee was powerful enough to make independent bookings difficult to find, and for a time the Marxes fought the system by joining the newly founded Shubert Brothers (Lee and J.J.) circuit. It was a demoralizing experience for the team, even before the circuit collapsed. The Shubert alternative was overextended, and the Marxes found themselves in playing conditions reminiscent of their apprenticeship days in grade Z vaudeville.

Being blacklisted is hardly the most conventional route to Broadway, but it proved to be the Marxes's catalyst . . . that, and Chico's ability to mix business with pleasure—or more precisely, business with gambling. Chico had met low-budget Broadway producer Joseph "Minimum" Gaites in a pinochle game. (The nickname, according to Harpo, stemmed from Gaites's totally pocketbook approach to auditioning performers—putting his back to the actor and asking, "So what's your minimum salary?"[83])

Gaites had a potential financial backer in James Beury, a wealthy Pennsylvania coal-mine owner. Beury had recently purchased Philadelphia's Walnut Street Theatre and was eager to back a show which would feature his girlfriend. Coincidentally, she happened to be a Marx Brothers chorus girl involved with Harpo. (In this case, Chico's mixture of business and pleasure was quite possibly assisted by a few dealings of Harpo.)

Add to this "Minimum" Gaites's recent producing of two short-lived shows—*Love for Sale* and *Gimmie a Thrill*—shows with lots of sets and salvageable script material. The sum total, though obviously threadbare around the corners, would be enough to put on the proverbial show, save for someone to headline. Chico made sure that headliner was the Marx Brothers. The result was the musical comedy revue *I'll Say She Is!*, with writers Will B. Johnstone (book and lyrics) and Tom Johnstone (music) performing the script operation which combined old and new. True to Gaites's nickname, Beury was providing only a modest budget, and the Philadelphia opening would be during the normally taboo June heat. But the revue was a hit.

As with earlier Marx Brothers productions, the plot line was thin—a beautiful, rich girl looking for thrills from a love match, a logical situation for a story born of productions entitled *Love for Sale* and *Gimmie a Thrill*. The new title, *I'll Say She Is!*, was simply a then-popular slang affirmative to anyone's acknowledgment of a pretty girl. This thrill-seeking rich girl was presented with various adventures from a courting doctor, lawyer, merchant, chief, rich man, poor man, beggar man, and thief. Eventually she is allowed to imagine herself as Napoleon's wife Josephine.

The second-half Napoleon scene was the revue's key sketch, and it was cowritten by Groucho. It revolved around Napoleon's (Groucho) frequent returns from the front to thwart the sexual advances of his advisors Gaston (Harpo), François (Chico), and Alphonse (Zeppo) upon Josephine. In this case, however, Josephine was more than happy to meet the advisors halfway. Thus, a suspicious, tracking Groucho observes, "They say a man's home is his castle. Mine must be the Pennsylvania Station. Come out, come out, wherever you are."[84] The sketch also featured such celebrated and later recycled Marx Brothers lines as "Beyond the Alps lies more Alps, and the Lord 'Alps those that 'Alps themselves" and the exchange "'Why, that's bigamy.' 'Yes, and it's bigamy, too.'" Appropriately, and probably not accidently for a group that so thrived upon puns, the Marxes's leading lady Josephine had a stage name—Lotta Miles—based upon her then well-known modeling and association with the Springfield Tire Company.

There was irony in the sketch's attempted cuckolding of a brother, because Betty Marx's early married days with the troupe had found Harpo, Groucho, and Gummo all making nonstop passes.[85] And Chico was even less concerned than the comically watchful Groucho of the Napoleon scene. Chico later told his brothers to quit, but he was not angered by their actions, growing as they did from their previous on-the-road sharing of girls. One is reminded of a much earlier incident from their childhood, when their father was caught in bed with one of Minnie's perennially visiting relatives. Though the other woman had been a young cousin, with Frenchie the instigator, the girl was the one driven from the house. As biographer Arce suggests, the Marx Brother boys were given a message: it was fine to play around, and if problems followed, the female was to blame.[86] When related to Betty Marx's experiences, one might add the double corollary that all-in-the-family affairs were acceptable, and if scenes arose, the immediate family—the Marx Brothers—took precedence. As if to document this cinematically, the close of their later motion picture *Horse Feathers* (1932) was a wedding ceremony where Thelma Todd became the shared bride of grooms Groucho, Harpo, and Chico—all of whom began to wrestle romantically with her as the credits come up. Appropriately, the Marx Brother first involved romantically with Todd (Zeppo) is not included in the wedding finale.

After its unique summer 1923 success in Philadelphia, *I'll Say She Is!* was taken on the road. Though the troupe was initially concerned about mediocre business in Boston, the box office returned in Chicago, and the Brothers worked their way to a Broadway opening. Not only would they have a thoroughly audience-tested vehicle (a stage tradition they would try to maintain even during later MGM film productions), but they were drawing upon years of vaudeville experience. While not exactly the "Marxes's greatest hits" (though familiar material abounded, from Harpo's sleeve-dropping silverware to the aforementioned Napoleon lines), *I'll Say She Is!* showcased a veteran team doing what they did best—making people laugh.

I'll Say She Is! opened at Broadway's Casino Theatre on May 19, 1924, and the Brothers Groucho, Harpo, Chico, and Zeppo immediately had a phenomenal hit, critically and commercially. Through the years several stories have adhered to this legendary night. The two most honored highlight Minnie and critic Woollcott on the subject of attendance. Minnie was not to be denied witnessing the crowning achievement of her managerial mother career, despite the need to be carried into the theatre because of a broken leg (which occurred during a dress fitting for the auspicious occasion). Conversely, Woollcott seems to have been inexplicably unaware of just who or what the Marx Brothers were and less than enamored about finding out. However, it was as if Minnie had provided her boys with the ultimate rendering of the theatre's traditional good luck phrase—to "break a leg." The influential Woollcott not only attended the production, but he led the ensuing critical hosannas. The title of his *New York World* review, however, nicely capsulized his Marx Brothers favorite: "Harpo Marx and Some Brothers."[87] (Arce has questioned the now time-honored story of Woollcott's reluctance to attend the production and quotes an excerpt from Woollcott's review to substantiate his revisionism.[88] However, a closer reading of Woollcott's entire review would seem to negate such a position.)

The group that had inadvertently been pushed upward by a vaudeville boycott had now reached a second career pinnacle. The Marx Brothers would follow *I'll Say She Is!* with two other very successful Broadway shows—*The Cocoanuts* and *Animal Crackers*. Though they were soon celebrated New York eccentrics, their basic interests (solidified after years of touring) did not so much change as become more fully experienced. This is best exemplified by Chico's gambling habit.

During the last on-the-road production of the 1925 post-Broadway tour of *I'll Say She Is!*, Chico turned up missing. His whereabouts remained unknown for days. When he did surface, it became apparent Chico had gone on the lam in order to avoid physical reprisals, or worse, from gamblers/gangsters to whom he owed money. His daughter Maxine's affectionate biography of her father revealed both that she felt as a child "it wouldn't be beneath Daddy to put me up for security . . . to cover a gambling debt" and that his gambling fascination focused upon "pitting himself against the odds, the longer the better: the final result mattered very little."[89]

One could liken Chico to the title character in Dostoevsky's *The Gambler*, who is obsessed by his habit: "a strange sensation built up in me, a kind of challenge to fate, a kind of desire to . . . stick out my tongue at it . . . a terrible craving for risk took possession of me."[90] While there can be no easy answers for such self-destructive tendencies, Dostoevsky scholar Edward Wasiolek's thoughts on the subject bear examining:

> The daring to risk the last gulden on the irrational turn of the wheel gives him [Dostoevsky's gambler] what the fixities of position, money, and love do not: the feeling of being open to the irrationalities of the turning wheel . . . the irrationalities of human life. Dostoevskii [also a chronic gambler who once pawned his second wife's wedding gown] knew and said many times that the deepest urge in human beings is the revolt against definition and the fixities of life.[91]

Possibly for Chico, with his chaotic, immigrant child-of-the-streets beginnings, the ongoing life-on-the-edge risk of gambling provided the only norm with which he was comfortable. (Interestingly, he was the only brother to maintain his

7. An early, darkly comic photo documentation by Chico of his gambling obsession. (Photograph courtesy of the Wisconsin Center for Film and Theater Research.)

immigrant persona throughout his performing career.) Regardless, the inherent anarchy which was the Marx Brothers was deeply rooted in Chico. The Broadway successes of the 1920s merely allowed him to take bigger gambling risks.

While Chico's personal world eschewed reason, Groucho, the group's most verbal on-stage attacker of the phenomenon, strived for it in private life, from attention to his Wall Street investment portfolio to his lifelong fascination with books. Of more importance than these, however, was his interest in children. Arthur Marx has said of the 1920s Groucho: "No son ever had a more doting father than I had. Or a more conscientious one. Or a more entertaining one. Or a father who was more of a buddy."[92] The man who enjoyed having his baby son on tour (even though it meant Groucho's late-night reading would be sentenced to diaper-ridden hotel bathrooms) had more daytime hours for the family once the act reached Broadway. A house was eventually purchased in Great Neck, Long Island, and six-year-old Arthur was joined by sister Miriam.

Unlike W. C. Fields (Groucho's later rival for king of screen comedy cynics), Groucho genuinely enjoyed the company of children. (Fields's observation that he preferred children well-done was seemingly not limited to his film persona.) Groucho's niece Maxine offers an even broader endorsement of Groucho's attitude toward children: "I loved him almost as much as Daddy because his love was offered unconditionally, coming as spontaneously as it comes from a child."[93] Maxine also provides the student of Groucho with what must have been one of the comedian's favorite lines to children. She remembers a Groucho tendency to ask her young friends (when they visited the theatre) whether they were married or not.[94] Over thirty years later the same question was delightfully preserved on film when a very young Melinda Marx (Groucho's daughter by his second wife, Kay Gorcey) appeared on Groucho's televised *You Bet Your Life.* Undoubtedly, Groucho's interest in children was a reflection of his own childhood's less-than-favored-son status.

Unfortunately, Groucho's childlike love was largely limited to children. With adults he often seemed distrustful and in need of preserving his cynically wise-cracking persona. Thus, he was not always easy to be around, especially for Ruth and the wives to follow. Paradoxically, Groucho's domestic free time and child-doting nature added pressure to his first marriage because of his tendency to supervise. While greater male involvement in the household is now considered essential to a marriage, Groucho tended to dominate; this created friction for two reasons. First, he frequently exercised total control, from hiring a live-in housekeeping couple who spoke only German (which Groucho knew because of his family background, but Ruth did not) to sending "her away from the table to eat dinner by herself in the kitchen" on those occasions when they argued about the family budget.[95] Second, Groucho's frequent domestic usurpations violated what was to have been her domain after she was forced from the act. (True to Marx Brothers form, when Ruth had earlier given Groucho an "either/or" choice about who stayed in the act after performing differences with Zeppo had arisen, Groucho opted for his brother.)

There were also other, more fundamental differences between Groucho and Ruth. Groucho, consistent with his bookish, loner nature, was not a party type; Ruth, the dancer, was. Late in the 1920s Groucho had observed privately to long-time Chicago friend Dr. Samuel Salinger (originally the family doctor for Minnie's clan):

> You know me well enough by this time to know that I dislike nightlife and clubs, and only go when there is no out . . . try and remember I might be a good companion . . . any[where] outdoors where I could be away from the hooey and hoopla that the night club thrives on.[96]

A partial Groucho compromise might have involved active membership in the ongoing partying of the literary Algonquin Round Table group (they called themselves the "Vicious Circle") where Harpo had become Woollcott's social protégé. (The group's fluctuating cast included Woollcott, Robert Benchley, George Kaufman, Dorothy Parker, Franklin P. Adams, Ring Lardner, Heywood Broun, Donald Ogden Stewart, and Edna Ferber.) And though Groucho did involve himself somewhat, his lack of formal education often made him feel uncomfortable. In fact, his son observed that in such situations Groucho often used his talent for verbal slapstick to distract from the weighty subject at hand, from punning deep-dish vocabulary to concurrent requests by other guests. One such widely applauded foray into what was really a comic cover-up was the following: "You want some ice water? I'll give you an onion. That'll make your eyes water."[97] His feeling of educational inferiority probably helps explain how he came to be an early 1930s subject in one of friend Will Rogers's syndicated weekly articles. While the down-home populist Rogers and the cynical Groucho would hardly seem to be both a party duo and friends (which they were), the Oklahoma humorist writes affectionately of their disruptively loud singing of old songs at both a small dinner party and a large formal gathering—singing not unlike the Marx Brothers's comically enthusiastic rendition of "Sweet Adeline" at the beginning of *Monkey Business* (1931). Rogers also provides a rare comic review of the Brothers's music:

> Now here is a funny thing about those Markses [*sic*], Groucho can play as good on the guitar as Harpo can on the Harp, or Chico on the piano. But, he never does. So he is really what I call an ideal musician, he can play, but don't.[98]

It should be added that in the 1932 presidential campaign the Four Marx Brothers comically touted Rogers for the top spot and themselves as an ensemble vice president. Somehow Franklin Delano Roosevelt survived this challenge, though Groucho did achieve a cinematic presidency twice during this time period (of Huxley College in *Horse Feathers*, 1932, and of Freedonia in *Duck Soup*, 1933).

Another basic difference between Groucho and Ruth was his egalitarian nature (the misanthropic image notwithstanding) when it came to not playing upon his fame (another tie with Will Rogers?), something Ruth would have preferred. For example, Groucho would not use his name when making reservations: "I don't like restaurants where you have to be a celebrity in order to get in."[99] This "declare yourself" conflict could also continue while waiting for a table at the restaurant, for Groucho without makeup enjoyed complete anonymity until late in his career, when he essentially appeared as himself on *You Bet Your Life.*

An additional egalitarian difference with his wife was Groucho's ongoing desire to include the children in every activity, from dinner party seating arrangements to travel plans (vacations and performing tours alike). Such inclusion naturally made him a further hit with his children, as well as the envy of niece Maxine, who was frequently left behind by Chico and Betty. His son also highly approved of Groucho's unorthodox stance on certain foods no real child would include on the menu. Thus, Groucho disliked eggplant, artichoke, and cauliflower au gratin, calling them "trick vegetables."[100]

One might comically close the subject of Groucho and egalitarianism by noting some previously unpublished 1931 tongue-in-cheek observations on the dangers of plastic surgery (which he preferred to call "plastered surgery"). Writing to his friend Dr. Salinger, a plastic surgeon who had recently authored a book on the subject, Groucho questions alterations to the "extraordinary proboscis" of prominent Americans (Fannie Brice's then well-known "beak" operation being his example). But then Groucho makes more general his comic warning:

> you and your medical brethern [sic] should be very careful with your knives, lest in time you erase all individuality from this country, and make us a race of straight faced citizens with all the personality of so many smoked white fish. . . . Employ your scalpel economically and only in times of great emergency, and by so doing you will help to retard the standardization that is rapidly smothering what was once supposed to be a free nation.[101]

His main purpose here is still humor. In fact, he closes his letter with "Gentlemen; I thank you," as if he were finishing one of his own movie monologues of false sincerity. But in the context of both the complete letter and Groucho's general egalitarianism, the comedian was most definitely mixing a message with merriment.

Groucho's economizing created another conflict with his wife—a phenomenon travel seemed to accent. While the other Marxes journeyed in style, the Groucho clan generally went the bargain-basement route. Moreover, if Groucho had a philosophy, it was to live a life of extreme moderation, from watching his diet to getting plenty of rest (though he eventually suffered from insomnia).[102] While exercising both economy and moderation undoubtedly has ties to his near-poverty childhood, it is also most fitting for a screen persona forever skewering the excesses of the idle rich.

A final, though crucial, problem between Groucho and Ruth was his sense of humor, and just when he would choose to use it.[103] Again, like his screen character, the private Groucho enjoyed lobbing humor into serious settings, from his own first wedding (see earlier example, note 74) to disembarkation through customs. The latter really occurred, though it sounds suspiciously like the cinema difficulties the Brothers experience disembarking in *Monkey Business* (where they each individually attempt to get through customs by imitating Maurice Chevalier). And it is probably the most comically memorable private incident in which Groucho's sense of humor ever embroiled him. After an ocean voyage to Europe, Groucho wrote "smuggler" under occupation on a customs form. Officials were not amused, and the family was detained several hours while their baggage was thoroughly searched. Initially inconvenient, now funny, it seems a small price to pay for sharing the world of Groucho. But the story continues. After their lengthy delay, something moved Groucho to ask Ruth, in the healthiest of whispers, where she had hidden their opium. This time the family members were subjected to a strip search. Living with an inspired comic anarchist exacted a high price.

Incidents like this "opium smuggling" affair were probably not, however, entirely a product of his anti-establishment sense of humor. Groucho also had an almost masochistic tendency to push a gag too far, as if to make some egalitarian statement, such as everyone can and should act like his stage persona. Unfortunately, this stance seldom works for the common man, which is what the private Groucho was generally assumed to be. Traveling as Julius Marx, without his comic greasepaint, frock coat, and patented dirty-old-man crouch, he was not accorded Groucho privileges, nor did he seem to want them. As with his restaurant habits, he was loath to have his adopted name come to the rescue. Maybe it was his own ongoing joke about world hypocrisy—where the anarchist comedian's message is applauded in the public arena, but its application is forever damned in the private one. Or, possibly he just enjoyed the real shock value anonymity gave his comic audacity. Indeed, in cult figure old age, after any semblance of anonymity was gone, he frequently complained he could no longer insult people; they expected and actually savored such behavior. Ironically, for Groucho *not* to insult eventually became more of an insult.

Ruth's differences with Groucho, as well as the general pressures of being married to a celebrity, led to their parting in 1942 and also no doubt contributed to her alcoholism. But the early years of their marriage, particularly when both children were young, were fairly amiable, despite the conflicts. In fact, family friend and author Norman Krasna (who also teamed with Groucho to write both the screenplay for *The King and the Chorus Girl*, 1937, and the play *Time for Elizabeth*, 1941) was inspired enough by their family to use it as a pattern for a comedy play. Called *Dear Ruth* (1944, though the title's Ruth is actually a daughter in the production), Groucho is represented by the witty Judge Hairy Wilkins, whose title probably reflects Groucho's real-life decision-making nature. Ruth surfaced as the pleasantly vacuous wife Edith. While the judge sounds very much like Groucho (at one point even being compared to him[104]), Edith has a rather Gracie Allen eccentricity about her, with material either going over her head or being unconsciously funny. For example, after meeting a soldier who is about to be shipped into an unknown war zone (the play was initially performed during World War II), Edith says of the government's policy: "I think that's very inconsiderate of them, not telling you."[105] As another character observes, "I think you've hit on the best definition of war I've ever heard. Just one inconsideration after another."[106] Furthermore, the Wilkins family (which also had two children, though both girls—Ruth and Miriam) acted much the way one assumes a Groucho Marx household would. An example is Edith's explanation of a family tradition based upon a pun:

> Any word that sounds like thanks, we say "You're welcome." . . . It's a joke we used to have with the children. What is it that looks like a truck, and has a caterpillar tread, and can climb trenches? . . . You're supposed to say "Tanks" [addressed to a family guest, the judge provides the correct answer] "You're welcome."[107]

While *Dear Ruth* was obviously not without entertainment embellishments (Arce describes the play family as "impossibly wholesome"), the Groucho clan was still the model, with the plot-turning Miriam closely patterned after real daughter Miriam.[108]

In the play a teenaged Miriam creates a homefront comedy dilemma by writing love letters to numerous servicemen using her older sister's name and photograph (thus the title, *Dear Ruth*). The play was a major critical and commercial success on Broadway, where it opened in late 1944. It became a popular hit movie in 1947 and was followed by two sequels: *Dear Wife* (1949) and *Dear Brat* (1951).

If the Marx Brothers's ascendency as New York (and later Hollywood) celebrities gave Groucho more opportunity to focus on parenting (plus reading) and Chico on gambling (plus more gambling), Harpo gifted himself with a childhood, "everything I'd missed out on when I was a kid."[109] Always an ardent disciple of fun over success, Harpo found the Algonquin group to be composed of similar spirits. In fact, Harpo's fun-filled, day-to-day philosophy was probably most comically articulated by the Algonquin's inimitable Robert Benchley in his essay, "A Little Sermon on Success":

> I take Life as it comes, and although I grouse a great deal and sometimes lie on the floor and kick and scream and refuse to eat my supper, I find that taking Life as it comes is the only way to meet it.[110]

Appropriately, Benchley's humor here and throughout his work frequently assumes a childlike nature. And the free-spirited Harpo described the Algonquin or "Woollcott gang" as the decade's most "famous delinquents."[111] Though the 1920s was the decade in which the American public found leisure-time activities in a big way (largely made possible by a shorter work week and technology such as the automobile and radio), "Woollcott's gang" was leisure leagues ahead of them. Games abounded in the group, ranging from parcheesi to badminton. But nothing seems to have come close to their collective fascination with croquet, an obsession that resulted in obtaining a special permit to play in Central Park and an attempt to convert a New York City rooftop into a court. Harpo even reserved one room of his apartment just for his English croquet mallets, maintaining a lower temperature to safeguard the wood.

Again, the writing of Benchley—see "How to Break 90 in Croquet"—chronicles best and most comically the "gang's" fascination for the game. For example, he suggests gripping the croquet mallet "with both hands something in the manner of a flute-player, only more virile, you bend over the ball, with the feet about two feet apart and both pointing in the same direction."[112] Benchley's essay also provides satirical in-joke humor at the expense of leader Woollcott. The latter, who was especially corpulent (looking "like something that had gotten loose from Macy's Thanksgiving Day Parade"[113]) and prone to play croquet in loud-colored clothing, is the model for Benchley's advice on costume—wear "a loose-fitting, rather vulgar, blazer of some awning material."[114] If there was ever any doubt (Woollcott's name is never mentioned), the Gluyas Williams caricature that follows this passage is obviously of the critic.

Harpo fit into Woollcott's game-playing literary group for three reasons in addition to the enthusiastic sponsorship of the critic. First, while Harpo mirrored the group's fun-loving philosophy, he brought something fairly rare to the gang: he did more listening than talking. One can never overestimate the importance of a listener to a creative group in search of an audience. Unlike Groucho, he did not feel a need to compete on an equal intellectual level.

Second, while Harpo often played student to these Algonquin "professors" (Oscar Levant later noted Harpo's "fascination for savants and celebrities"[115]), the Marx mime was no novice in the ongoing game playing of the group. He both enjoyed and excelled at their physical activities, from cards to croquet. Bookish Groucho, seemingly the most logical Marx Brother for Algonquin inclusion, was not so "athletically" inclined.

Third, though Harpo could not match the verbal wit of such Algonquin colleagues as Woollcott or George S. Kaufman, his mime and comically anarchistic tendencies complemented and sometimes completely dwarfed the comedy actions of the others. For example, when tourists invaded the beach of Woollcott's Neshobe Island (Lake Bomoseen, Vermont), private playground for the "gang," it was Harpo who cured the snoopers by comically attacking in the nude, save for his red wig, the ever-present Gookie, and a trusty ax. The tourists left . . . quickly.

Harpo, however, was not limited to playing a surrealist savage. He could also compete in the "gang's" word games. Acclaimed Woollcott biographer Howard Teichmann has recorded that Harpo won a Benchley-inspired contest for the best capsule review of *Abie's Irish Rose*, a play then enjoying a phenomenal commercial success, yet despised by Benchley and most New York critics. Harpo's mini-review: "No worse than a bad cold."[116] His prize was never having to see the play again.

Harpo's close friendship with Woollcott, born of those Algonquin years, later found its way to Broadway in *The Man Who Came to Dinner* (1939), a play inspired by the entertainingly volatile world of Woollcott. Written by friends Moss Hart and Kaufman, Woollcott (Sheridan Whiteside in the play) described the work to Harpo: "What the boys have done is bring out the worst and the best in me."[117] The character patterned after Harpo was Banjo, a girl-chasing zany who first appears with a nontraditional Christmas gift for Sheridan: "This brassiere was once worn by Hedy Lamarr."[118] Yet, behind Banjo's eccentricities is one of the play's most sensitive characters and the friend who most helps Sheridan save a young romantic couple (a task which was also frequently asked of Harpo in his MGM films of the period). The play was a great critical and commercial success and was adapted to the screen in 1941.

Despite the added attention the 1920s Marxes could now give their old pleasures and/or aspirations (a childhood for Harpo, parenting and reading for Groucho, and more gambling for Chico), they were still very busy on stage. The team played in *I'll Say She Is!* from 1923 to 1925, and then followed it with another major hit—*The Cocoanuts* in 1925-1928 (both sets of dates include tours). After the Model-T economy measures of *I'll Say She Is!*, *The Cocoanuts* was a Cadillac, thanks to the now proven Broadway success of the Marxes. Moreover, Kaufman, then America's greatest comedy playwright, wrote the show, and the acclaimed Irving Berlin provided the music (though for once a hit song was not forthcoming).

The Cocoanuts satirized the current Florida land boom. Though a musical play, as opposed to the Marxes's usual collection of sketches, the army of *Cocoanuts* customers was not coming because of a strong plot. For example, in 1927 Groucho wrote that the plot was missing and a prize would be offered to anyone who could reveal its whereabouts. He closed his plea with: "Remember, it is not necessary to see the show to win the prize. In fact, it is better if you don't see the show."[119] Though records do not reveal whether Groucho's "Whatever Has Become of Our Plot Contest" ever produced a winner, *The Cocoanuts* definitely proved to be one.

The records do, however, show several memorable firsts for the production. *The Cocoanuts* introduced Margaret Dumont into the Marxes's world. She would appear in their next Broadway show, *Animal Crackers*, and seven future Marx films. For many she came to represent "the fifth Marx Brother." She generally played a stuffy mountain of a dowager who was the perennial high-society target of the Brothers, off whom they bounced roughhouse comedy and assorted fruit (*Duck Soup* conclusion) whenever she was towed into range. She most frequently played straight woman to the comic slander of Groucho, who, though forever courting her bank account, could never resist unloading a barrage of comic insults. The barbs were all the funnier because at no time did they ever seem to register with her. Groucho always claimed Dumont's comic mystification to lines like, "I'm prepared to fight for your honor, which is more than you ever did" was no act. Author and former Marx Brothers film publicist Teet Carle strongly endorsed that assessment, adding that Groucho's attacks did not alienate audiences because they "liked to believe she [Dumont] was never hurt by insults—simply because they seemed to go over her head."[120]

The Cocoanuts was also the first professional teaming the Marxes had with Kaufman, who would co-write (with Morrie Ryskind) both the stage version of *Animal Crackers* and the screenplay for *A Night at the Opera* (1935). Kaufman and *Cocoanuts* are also centerstage when Groucho's ad-libbing is discussed. It was during this play that one of the most celebrated Marx Brothers anecdotes was born. A backstage Kaufman interrupted a friend (who varies according to the source) to move closer to the action. Upon returning to a now disgruntled individual, who questioned the interruption, the playwright said, "I thought I heard one of the original lines of the show."

The Marx Brothers, particularly Groucho, had been ad-libbing for years. It began on an early vaudeville stop in the South when they had lost their audience to a runaway mule outside the theatre. When the customers eventually wandered back inside, the angry brothers abandoned their normal material and started using both the audience and the region as comic targets. But what started as a satirical approach to primal therapy had another bonus: the audience loved it.

The ad-lib thus became a norm in Marx Brothers work. In fact, one reason they were such hits on Broadway was the repeat business they received from fans who were curious to see what comic evolutions had occurred. The repeat attraction of the Brothers, as well as the extreme to which they would go for an ad-lib, are best brought out in an article by a fan and friend who also happened to be a major entertainment critic—Heywood Broun (also of the Algonquin Round Table). Writing in his *New York Telegraph* newspaper column, "It Seems to Me," he confessed to having seen *The Cocoanuts* twenty-one times and the still-playing *Animal Crackers* a dozen times, but "I hope to catch up, as the season is still young."[121]

Broun also inspired the most personalized of ad-libs (directed at an audience of one—Broun) during, of all times, the opening night of *Animal Crackers*:

> When Groucho examined the stolen painting, he said, "It looks like an early Broun." It earned a loud, proud laugh from [me], but the rest of the audience sat stony wondering what "an early Broun" might be. I believe the line was dropped after that and that it is restored only on such nights as I stand in the wings.[122]

This kind of ad-lib activity, from the obscure verbal reference to the unexplained appearance of a nonplayer on stage, seems to have been a Marx Brothers norm. It is testament to both a loyal audience and the Brothers's own self-confident comic audacity.

Though Groucho was the champion of the traditional ad-lib, he frequently received plenty of slapstick inspiration from wordless Harpo, who had to develop most of his visual gags. For example, *Cocoanuts* was the first time Harpo introduced another of his signature routines—chasing a pretty blonde while honking his horn. After the initial unannounced honking intrusion, an already onstage Groucho observed, "First time I ever saw a taxi hail a passenger." Harpo then attempted to catch Groucho without an ad-lib by chasing the girl back across the stage almost immediately. But Groucho once again had a winning response: "The nine-twenty's right on time. You can always set your clocks by the Lehigh Valley."

The ad-lib aura was also strengthened by two additional factors. First, Groucho possessed the ability to make even his scripted lines sound as though they were ad-libbed. And, since the best comedy is spontaneous, or delivered to seem that way, Groucho's ad-libbing reputation was enhanced all the more. His later award-winning tenure on *You Bet Your Life* came about because of a now-celebrated bit of ad-libbing he did with Bob Hope on a 1947 all-star radio broadcast. And, naturally, the great solo success he had with the quiz show, where he spent more time needling guests than playing the game, further enhanced his ad-libbing reputation (although ironically, his television show was not without scripting).

Second, the scripted "ad-lib" was not unknown to their Broadway material, either. In the text for the stage production of *Animal Crackers*, a supporting character makes scripted "mistakes" to comically feed Groucho's Captain Spaulding:

Chandler: Tell me, Capt. Chandler —er —er —Spaulding. (Business)

Spaulding: Yes, Spaulding. You're Chandler. You're Chandler and I'm Spaulding. It's the switching from the light to the heavy underwear. . . .

Chandler: Tell me, Captain—er—er—

Spaulding: Spaulding. You're Chandler and I'm Spaulding.

(To Audience) Could I look at a program a minute? It might be intermission for all he knows.[123]

The same suggested sense of spontaneity can be found in the film adaptation, where the scene is essentially repeated, though there are some dialogue changes.

Following the *Cocoanuts* road show tour, the Marx Brothers closed the production for a summer 1928 rest. Though it has sometimes been stated that the team then did their relaxing in Europe, only Harpo made the trip. Accompanying Alexander Woollcott, Harpo was introduced to European high life, from the Riviera and Monte Carlo to southern Italy. He also met numerous artists and developed friendships with, among others, George Bernard Shaw and Noel Coward. Morrie Ryskind described Harpo as becoming a "vogue" in 1928 Europe.[124]

The most immediate impact Harpo's trip had on his Brothers was to delay rehearsals for their third Broadway show, *Animal Crackers*, until late summer. Groucho writes briefly about both the delay and the cause in another Salinger letter. But the letter better exemplifies the frequent earthiness of Groucho's subject matter in the Salinger correspondence. For example, Groucho observes, "Harpo is arriving home to day . . . and I am sure that one of the things he won't declare at the Customs Offices will be a slight dose of Mussolini Gonorrhea."[125] (Like all Marx Brothers, or should one say most males in their extended family, Harpo was very active sexually. To his credit, Harpo was still single, being the last unmarried Brother.)

Harpo's trip did, however, have a plus side for the team. His European "vogue" seems to have added to the special-event aura that graced the Broadway run of *Animal Crackers*. For example, Ryskind remembers the last-minute chaos of trying to get Somerset Maugham (another of Harpo's new European friends) into the sold-out *Animal Crackers* opening. And, as Ryskind comically understated, "When Somerset Maugham was fighting to get into your show you knew something was right!"[126]

Animal Crackers occupied their talents into 1930. Kaufman and Morrie Ryskind co-authored the play, with music by the team of Bert Kalmar and Harry Ruby. Again, the plot was sketchy; again, it did not matter. The story loosely revolved around the high-society reception being given by Mrs. Rittenhouse (Margaret Dumont) for the famous African explorer Captain Spaulding. As noted previously, a party was the perfect setting for the Marxes's comedy, and this was no exception. *Animal Crackers*, which opened on October 23, 1928, would be their greatest Broadway hit. Kalmar and Ruby even gave Groucho the one thing *The Cocoanuts* had lacked—a popular song. The now celebrated number, "Hooray for Captain Spaulding," eventually would become Groucho's theme song. (The song's first line, "Hello, I must be going," not only is a nice comic capsulation of Marx Brothers absurdity, but it also served as the title of Charlotte Chandler's 1978 Groucho biography.)

Though the Marxes still did not always respect the printed page (scripted comedy mistakes notwithstanding), Kaufman and Ryskind had outdone themselves on the comic dialogue, providing a gold mine for later would-be impressionists. The most recycled bit was probably African explorer Groucho's reminiscence: "One morning I shot an elephant in my pajamas. How he got in my pajamas I'll never know."

While the Marx Brothers were already well-established figures of comic absurdity, the stage production of *Animal Crackers* seemed to find them even more eccentrically inspired. Because modern science has yet to invent a meter for measuring the causes of comic nonsense, no exact explanation is available. But their increased zaniness, on stage and off, is not without possible hypotheses. For example, by this time their popularity had reached very heady levels—for fans and critics alike they seemed incapable of doing wrong. What more carte blanche invitation to be outrageous could there be, especially for a team that never needed an invitation to be outrageous? Thus, they quite possibly realized that stagewise there would be no topping their latest ludicrousness. (Appropriately, this would be their last Broadway play.)

One might also hazard the suggestion that the increased craziness of the Marxes during *Animal Crackers* was due to the comic silliness born of sheer exhaustion. Not only was this their third successive Broadway hit without a substantial break, but for six weeks of *Animal Crackers*'s Broadway run the Marxes worked an entertainment double shift. During the day they resurrected *The Cocoanuts* for Paramount (two weeks of rehearsals and four weeks before the cameras) at the company's Astoria studio on Long Island. During the evening they returned to the Broadway stage for *Animal Crackers*. Privately, in a letter that began by mentioning how tired he was recently, Groucho candidly noted not looking forward:

> to the agonies and drudgery of rehearsal, with an occasional slapping of a chorines [*sic*, chorus girl's] fanny as she glides by, as the only break in the monotony. After that, we hope to go into actually doing the cursed thing, which I imagine will be even worse than rehearsing. This thing of learning the part of the Cocoanuts over again is sickening, it has all the thrill of a warmedover potroast, and giving in to a dame that you were through with many years ago, but its [*sic*] all for the money, and what the hell are you going to do about it.[127]

There was, however, no denying the film production, owing to the public's phenomenal fascination with these two "new" commodities—sound movies and the Marx Brothers.

What of these *Animal Crackers* eccentricities? Whereas no Marx Brother activity lacks such stories, something that increases the historian's pleasure while at the same time increasing his workload, *Animal Crackers* is especially rich and varied in its examples. For instance, one can footnote the doting father Groucho. Arthur Marx writes warmly of Groucho's occasional impromptu inclusions of his son and daughter in the production.[128] Not infrequently, Arthur was invited to ride onstage with Groucho in his African sedan chair (carried aloft by four strong natives of Captain Spaulding's jungle entourage). Though Groucho would disembark at Margaret Dumont's reception and comically contest the cost of a sedan chair ride from Africa to New York, no explanation would ever be made of the wide-eyed little boy in short pants who remained in the chair. Along the same lines, Groucho once shortened a Harpo performance on the harp to allow a very young Miriam to sing "Show Me the Way to Go Home."

In contrast to parental pride, *Animal Crackers* could also showcase that the accidently erotic Harpo's entrance to the reception already had comic surprise. After surrendering his coat to the butler, he was revealed to be wearing only swim trunks . . . usually. One night, however, he cut his always dominating game-playing activities too close to the opening curtain. And, in his haste to get in costume, he neglected to pull on his trunks over the most modest of briefs. Thus, when he disrobed that night, the audience became especially attentive. And Harpo's hurried exit from the scene needed no pretty girl incentives, nor did Groucho's ad-lib, which encouraged customers to buy tickets early for tomorrow's show, when Harpo would be wearing even less.

There are many other *Animal Crackers* stories, from management-banned critic Walter Winchell being smuggled into the theatre and made up to look like a Harpo stand-in so he could watch the show from backstage, to the surrealistic shock of Margaret Dumont (whose gullibility made her a popular target) the night she opened a chest on stage and was confronted with a nonstop parade of exiting Grouchos. Groucho biographer Arce states the bottom of the chest and the floor below it had been removed for this gag, enabling orchestra members and available crew—all made up as Groucho—to perform comic magic.[129] An examination of the play's script, however, suggests some sort of passageway might already have been in existence for the chest Captain Spaulding described as "a match box for an elephant."[130] That is, the "match box" was largely a special prop for the surprise appearance, from it, of the Professor (Harpo), near the close of Act I.[131] Though the script at this point is almost shorthand in its brief description of several Harpo routines centered around the chest, it seems that a passageway would have been necessary for the things Harpo was both taking from and placing into the chest.

This is not, however, to distract from the comic beauty of Dumont's shock at the parade of Grouchos that poured forth from the trunk one night—which was decidedly *not* in the script. It merely demonstrates the existence of a passageway, an "open" invitation for such pranks to take place. For example, on another night it would be Groucho who would be surprised by an unscripted trunk appearance of an associate who demanded an overdue birthday gift. Though the joke was lost on the audience, other than registering as more absurdity from the world of the Brothers Marx, Groucho was so comically surprised that for once he could produce no ad-lib. Possibly he was thinking of an earlier performance when this surprise trunk guest had made another unbilled appearance—dragged on stage by the Marxes. Regardless, it was no wonder the production received prodigious repeat business; there was always something new.

Though a further inundation of *Animal Crackers* stories hardly seems necessary, their prolific numbers and the comic joy with which they are brought forth is reminiscent of film critic Andrew Sarris's later comments on the nightclub performances of Dean Martin and Jerry Lewis—that the comic anarchy of their live shows was never adequately captured on screen.[132] Though this is not to equate Martin & Lewis on a comedy plane with the Marx Brothers, it does showcase a real difficulty in transferring any heavily spontaneous performance from stage to screen. For the Marx Brothers, there would be the added liability of starting their team film career (disregarding *Humorisk* and Harpo's solo performance in *Too Many Kisses*) at the beginning of the sound era.

Because of primitive sound technology, the movements of both performers and cameras were severely limited in most film productions. Actors were forced to hover around the all-important hidden microphone, and cameras were encased in glass-fronted boxes to keep their running noise from being recorded. *Cocoanuts* screen adaptor Morrie Ryskind remembers the production being inundated with technical horror stories, from a cameraman "who would frequently stagger out of the [soundproof] box for air!" to such comically maddening problems as

"If a fly buzzed on the set, it sounded like an airplane."[133] Robert Florey, the film's co-director (with Joseph Santley), added: "Because the camera was in a box it couldn't pan [move horizontally from a fixed position]. If the camera was turned you'd end up with a photograph of the inside of the box."[134] Thus, as Groucho observed, "If this movie is more static . . . it's because our movements were hampered [by camera and microphone restrictions].[135]

The Marxes's most trying encounter with sound during the *Cocoanuts* production threatened what is now the film's most famous scene—Groucho's attempt to explain the blueprints of a land development project to Chico. During this pun-ridden dialogue Groucho makes the mistake of innocently noting a viaduct, and Chico unloads the team's most famous pun: "Why a duck?" The viaduct dilemma is then discussed at comic length, necessitating more attention to the blueprints. Unfortunately, the noise from handling the stiff blueprint paper was ruining the sound recording. Innumerable takes were done before an answer surfaced—the papers were soaked in water.

The film opened in May 1929 and was an immediate critical and commercial success. Seeing the film today, one frequently wonders what all the excitement was about. However, its static, canned theatre nature makes it an excellent choice for a film classroom studying the transition to sound. While it is a model of many early sound limitations, it is made palatable by the still lively humor of the Marxes. It also represents an invaluable time capsule for the theatre historian, who is provided with a close facsimile of a 1920s Broadway play. And, while the theatre historian is aware of the period's entertainment expectations, today's viewer is disappointed by *The Cocoanuts*'s time commitment to the singing love interest of Broadway stars Mary Eaton and Oscar Shaw. Besides lacking any screen chemistry (singularly, or as a couple), their musical rendezvous always derail the Marxes's comedy momentum. Though not all 1920s film critics were enamored of the couple either, the period's views on comedy dictated a frag-mented presentation. Thus, Ryskind observed: "You have to have a [comedy] break and a change of pace. So the two lovers [enter] . . . . You didn't have ice cream [i.e., comedy] all the way through, you know!"[136] Appropriately, what is now considered the Marxes's greatest film, *Duck Soup*, is also the one most religiously molded to nonstop comedy (without even musical solos by Chico and Harpo).

The Cocoanuts is most interesting for what it reveals about the Marxes's comedy arsenal—it came to the movies nearly full-blown. To one familiar with their years in vaudeville and Broadway, this should hardly seem a surprise, and this study has noted pivotal characteristics as they have evolved. Still, old scripts and articles do not capture every comic quirk of their performances, especially the delightful but generally unscripted visual peculiarities of Harpo. Moreover, to see such polished comedy personae at the birth of their commercial film career is still mesmerizing, even when one is seemingly prepared for the encounter.

A greatest hits potpourri of the Marxes comedy bits from *Cocoanuts* would represent an unwieldy list, but some would bear noting. Groucho and Chico engage in one of their typical verbal duels, with Groucho attempting to be the semi-rational one. But being rational can never stand up to the comically possessed language tunnel-vision of Chico, such as the steamroller obsession of his "Why a duck?" And when Chico moves on to "Why-a-no-chicken?", even Groucho begins to see the futility of his ways: "I don't know why-a-no-chicken. I'm a stranger here myself." Thus, they are complete comedy anarchists, dismantling the language as well as the world around them.

Cocoanuts also features a prime example of Groucho's comic misogyny masquerading—as is the norm—as romantic patter. Again, the target (and very much the target) of this unlikely romance is Margaret Dumont, who repeats her stuffy socialite from the stage production. Thus, when Groucho comically undercuts her, he efficiently scores humor points against women, romance, and cultural elitism simultaneously.

The *Cocoanuts* film antics of Chico and Harpo, the most frequent team-within-the-team, also include several comedy standards which would appear often in future films. For example, on three occasions they indulge in their own special brand of fisticuffs, where no punches are ever landed. Yet, Harpo always emerges ahead because of his distractingly comic haymaker windup, which allows him to surprise Chico periodically with a kick to the rump. Another of their familiar routines highlighted in *Cocoanuts* might be labeled "wrapped up in each other." Beginning with being seated next to each other, they first cross their legs over each other, then intertwine their arms, and finally lean their heads together. Like the elaborate handshakes of some lodge brothers, this comically bizarre, linking reflex ritual somehow seems appropriate for the two Marxes most often together.

Individually, familiar patterns are also present, from the solo musical performances of Chico and Harpo (in addition, Harpo does a clarinet number) to Groucho's machine gun-like verbal ability. Director Florey also added to Harpo's otherworldliness by having him eat part of a telephone (in actuality made of chocolate) and drink from an ink well (filled with Coca-Cola).[137]

The key difference between *Cocoanuts* and the Marxes's later films (besides their becoming more cinematic) was a matter of comic intensity. Their trademark enthusiasm is somewhat lacking. Marx biographer Adamson suggests it is a product of their first time playing without an audience.[138] It might also have been boredom with recreating, once again, a property they had played for several years. Or perhaps, it was simply fatigue from having just left their beds, because they continued to perform nightly during the film production. Regardless, for the sound-and-music-mesmerized public, it was an entertainment gift.

Through the years *Cocoanuts* co-director Florey has sometimes been blamed for flaws in the film (the other credited director, Santley, seems to have been more of an assistant). For example, Groucho frequently later claimed Florey, who had come to the United States from France in the early 1920s, did not fully understand English. It has also sometimes been claimed he did not understand the Marx Brothers and/or was without a sense of humor, which is probably redundant. These accusations can hardly be true, however, since other production participants—including Harpo—remember Florey's only problem as being an extension of his sense of humor. That is, whenever the Brothers ad-libbed, Florey would laugh so hard he would drown out what was being recorded on the sound track, necessitating a retake. Eventually, Florey's uncontrollable laughter sentenced him to a soundproof booth with the cameraman, directing via hand gestures.[139] Naturally, this is strange behavior for someone with an English and/ or humor problem.

Any misunderstandings that might have existed beyond the film's number one anxiety producer (beginning their film careers during the difficult early sound era) centered around the sheer challenge of directing something involving the Marx Brothers. In the 1970s Florey observed, "You couldn't direct the Marx Bros. any more than you could a Chaplin [Florey was associate director of Chaplin's 1947 *Monsieur Verdoux*] or a clown who had been doing the same number for many years."[140] Other than *Duck Soup*'s Leo McCarey, none of the Marxes's subsequent directors would manage an auteur stamp either. Moreover, as Florey observed privately in correspondence with film scholar and archivist Tony Slide, Paramount "had decided to 'experiment' with the Brothers without spending too much."[141] Thus, even if the Marxes had been more directable, Florey was creatively locked into a production which would use such economical canned theatre givens as painted backdrops which, in a drafty soundstage, sometimes swayed slightly in the finished film. Still, at the beginning of the sound era, the film was a great success.

To borrow a Dumont phrase from the later *Duck Soup*, 1929 was turning into a "gala day" for the Marxes. (Groucho's in-film rejoinder was agreement, because he could only handle "a gal a day.") Between a hit film and a hit Broadway musical comedy, the Brothers had sandwiched an April return to the Palace, where they commanded the highest group price tag ever for vaudeville's premier theatre—$7,000 a week.[142] Groucho also added a solo triumph—the publishing of his first book, *Beds* (copyrighted 1930, but serialized earlier in *College Humor*). For bookworm Groucho, "It was the thrill of my life, a fellow with little education and a tall, blonde stenographer joining . . . Shakespeare, Tolstoy and Longfellow. I could well imagine afterlife . . . discussing with them such subjects as tall, blonde stenographers."[143]

Though this quote, from the introduction for the 1976 reissue of the book, kids the significance of the publication, one still senses Groucho's pride at becoming a member of that group he most admired—writers. But Groucho did not put on any smoking-jacket literary airs in turning author because, when one of the girl-chasing Marx Brothers wrote a book entitled *Beds*, it was an obvious sexual tease for an era when censorship minimized what an author could say about it, comically or otherwise. Still, it was timely, inasmuch as in the 1920s America had just discovered Freud and the complexities of sex. Quite possibly, its comic timeliness was brought to his attention by the 1929 publication of the James Thurber and E. B. White volume *Is Sex Necessary?*, a book he recommended. The volume by Thurber and White, two authors he greatly enjoyed, is, however, more a direct parody on the era's obsession with the clinical mumbo-jumbo of sexuality, whereas Groucho might have described his own work as pretty much *skirting* the issue. Thus, *Beds* assumes a more comic furniture perspective than frolocking fun, even though a fictitious editor's note informs the reader that Groucho neglected to write anything on "The Advantages of Sleeping Alone," and the author later describes being mistaken as Freud.[144] Regardless, Groucho's stockpile of successes for 1929 made it easy for him to declare: "everything's coming up grosses."[145]

There is no record, however, as to whether Groucho, the practical cynic who seems to have been born old, sensed approaching tragedy after these accomplishments. But come it did. On September 13, 1929 (a Friday), Minnie Marx died of a cerebral hemorrhage. But as Woollcott's *New Yorker* obituary gently suggested, it was more the death of the reluctantly retired—where one's all-consuming goal had been accomplished.[146] The proverbial "parade gone by," in this case the Marx Brothers, had, however reluctantly, passed her by.

In death as in life, conflicting stories surround the exact circumstances of her passing. The most logical scenario has her and Frenchie eating a large evening meal at Zeppo's, followed by ping pong and a drive home, when she suffered a stroke. Frenchie brought her back to Zeppo's, where, after her sons hurriedly gathered, she died in the early morning hours. The most common conflicting story has the whole family gathered for one last time, with the animated Minnie of old reminiscing about their lively collective past. This idealized memory was a tribute that granted Minnie family leadership one last time, as when she saw future stardom in a motley, underaged crew named the Marx Brothers.

Groucho, in an unpublished letter written shortly after Minnie's death, observed:

> The swiftness of the entire happening makes it a little terrifying.
>
> In the afternoon she was at the theatre watching a rehearsal joking and laughing. Four hours later she was gone. The only grain of comfort, if there can be one, was the fact that it was merciful. . . . It's a thing we all have to face, but to each one it's a harrowing experience.[147]

The brothers had taken turns sitting with Minnie before she died, and almost appropriately, Harpo the mime was with her at death—appropriate, because after her stroke she was unable to speak or move. Yet, at the end, she was desperately trying to communicate. Harpo instinctively understood her request. The mother who at one time had put peroxide in the bath water of young Chico and Harpo in order to prolong their blondness wanted her own blonde wig straightened. The deed accomplished, Minnie managed a smile and slipped away.

While Minnie's death was a common loss for the Brothers, the second shock of 1929 hit Groucho and Harpo the hardest. The infamous stock-market crash wiped them out financially. (All texts that address the subject agree on this, but an unpublished, undated Groucho letter from the period states he was "teetering on the edge of a pauper's grave" but did not go under.[148]) Like those of many other crash victims, their stock holdings had been bought on the margin. This practice of paying outright only a varying fraction of the stock's worth allowed an amazing number of Americans to both play the market and ultimately be devastated by its collapse. When the market started to plummet in late October, it was initially hoped that by covering those margins a total loss could be averted. Thus, Groucho and Harpo were financially bled further by daily phone calls from desperate brokers asking for additional funds to cover margins. Harpo ultimately went into debt.

Each lost personal fortunes of $250,000, though Harpo's setback was more on paper (inflated stock values), whereas Groucho's involved a greater loss of hard currency.[149] Both because of actual loss and temperament, Groucho took the crash the harder. Thus, while Harpo, like his screen character, was able almost immediately to shake off the loss, the crash is frequently cited as the real beginning of Groucho's insomnia. Once more, an irrational modern world had caused Groucho to suffer. Just as he had been a model son who received *less* parental attention, so he had been financially frugal since childhood, a trait strongly continued in the management of his adult home. None of his performing brothers, including the fun-loving and still-single Harpo, had ever been so disciplined. The added irony was the knowledge that Chico's gambling and general spendthrift ways had turned out to be the better "investment," a bit of illogic that immensely pleased Chico, who did not miss the opportunity to kid Groucho about it. In fact, this is reminiscent of so many Groucho-Chico film confrontations, where absurdity generally wins, for example, Chico's selling of an endless supply of supplemental betting books to Groucho in the later *A Day at the Races* (1937), or their discussion of the missing painting in *Animal Crackers* (1930) and Chico's suggestion to question the people in the house next door. When Groucho asks, "Suppose there isn't any house next door?", Chico calmly replies, "Well, then, of course we got to build one."

For many these were the beginnings of desperate times; some even refused to go on. At the time Groucho observed privately that "window space was being rented in high office buildings."[150] In later, more cynical times he publicly punched up the observation: "The roof over my room was so crowded with people jumping that they had to take numbers."[151]

Luckily for the Marx Brothers they were a very popular act at the beginning of a lucrative feature-film career. Luckier still for the team, though not yet apparent, the Great Depression would encourage the 1930s film comedy popularity of harder, older, and more cynical comedians—comedians like the Marx Brothers (particularly Groucho), W. C. Fields, and Mae West. This worldly slant was in direct contrast to the previous decade and its favored film comedians. Both the Jazz Age and its clowns were generally optimistic and youthful. Consequently, the depression made the Marx Brothers's style of humor more "contemporary."

When the market collapsed, the team was on tour with *Animal Crackers*. The work was both therapeutic and financially necessary. Their next major project would be adapting *Crackers* to the screen. During the shooting, Groucho was privately

> more skeptical about the success of this one [film adaptation] every day. I have seen so much of Animal Crackers as a play and as a movie, that it doesn't seem possible that there is any place in the wide world an audience so stupid that they would laugh at the bilge in Animal Crackers.[152]

Years later, with the hindsight of the adaptation's great success, Harpo noted they "stuffed audiences" with the production for three years.[153]

Animal Crackers was the second of five films made under contract for Paramount. Like *The Cocoanuts*, it was shot at that company's Astoria, Long Island studio. Groucho described the experience as "leading the life of a dock walloper. Up in the dewy morn at seven and six thirty, at the studio at nine, and at nine thirty ready to shoot."[154] While *Animal Crackers* also suffers from a canned theatre nature, the technical limitations are not as severe as in *The Cocoanuts*. Moreover, it is made more palatable than *Cocoanuts* by the increased screen time of the Marxes (including Zeppo), thankfully at the expense of the romantic subplot and non-Marx musical numbers (director Victor Heerman having lobbied for a greater Marx Brothers focus). However, even when the new technology was cooperating, and the Marxes were not ad-libbing themselves into problems such as a laughing director, unexpected troubles could occur. Lillian Roth, the young heroine of *Animal Crackers*, observed:

> Groucho and I had a scene that had to be shot over at least ten times. . . .
> My line, when we stumbled on a fake painting, was, "Oh, if we could only find the real painting!" Groucho's line was, "I know who the thief is. Here's his signature." "Who is it?" I asked. "Rembrandt," he said. "Don't be silly, he's dead," I retorted. Groucho snarled, "Then it's murder." I burst into giggles every time he said that, ruining the take. The line itself wasn't so hilarious, but I knew Groucho was going to say it with the big cigar jutting from his clenched teeth, his eyebrows palpitating, and that he would be off afterwards in that runaway crouch of his; and the thought of what was coming was too much for me.[155]

The Marxes's performances are more assured than they were in *The Cocoanuts*. And as if to reflect that film assuredness, Zeppo is even allowed some comic audacity at Groucho's expense. As Groucho's secretary, Zeppo eliminates the whole body of a dictated letter because he found it unimportant. However, Groucho still eventually wins, getting even additional laughs by further dictating to Zeppo, "Alright, send it that way and tell them the body will follow." (The scene had also been in the Broadway production, but Zeppo material had never been as sacred as the material of the others. For example, most of his role had been cut from the film adaptation of *The Cocoanuts*.)

While all Marx Brothers films are about the illusion of things not being what they seem—from language to life-styles—*Animal Crackers* seems especially rich with examples. They range from Harpo's surreal opening scene (after Harpo takes real potshots at a statue of two figures, they come to life and return the gunfire) to celebrated art patron Roscoe W. Chandler (Louis Sorin) turning out to be a Czechoslovakian fish peddler named Abe Cabiddle. (While the latter name is semantically funny to begin with, it is undoubtedly a comic reference to the very popular period newspaper cartoon character Abe Kabibble, from Harry Hershfield's strip *Abie the Agent*, begun in 1914. Hershfield's Abe was a business-man who tried everything to move his product. Thus, Chico's revelation about Chandler is both funny and comically informative.) What plot there is also nicely reflects the state of illusion, with two art copies frequently being substituted for a famous painting. Of course, one might merely begin and end with the comic outrageousness of Groucho being cast as a great African explorer.

Animal Crackers is also the Marx movie in which high society receives its most literal beating. Though the phenomenon most quickly brings to mind Groucho's abusive tongue, *Animal Crackers* also showcases Harpo, running off Margaret Dumont's wealthy guests with gunfire and landing punches to the society matron's stomach—punches that comically raise her into the air. As film critic Allen Eyles observed, it is "a visual metaphor [of] society becoming a punchbag for the Marx Brothers."[156] As dark comedy it anticipates W. C. Fields's booting of Baby LeRoy in *The Old-Fashioned Way* (1934) and possibly directly influenced the bit in Mel Brooks's *Blazing Saddles* (1974) in which an elderly pioneer lady takes several punches to the tum-tum and then, in direct address to the audience, observes, "Have you ever seen such cruelty?" Interestingly enough, the Dumont-as-punching-bag scene does not occur in the script for the stage version.

Another variation, though a more familiar one, between the stage script and the film adaptation, was the incorporation of Harpo's silverware-dropping routine into the latter. In fact, it had become such a signature routine even then that Groucho observes at this point in the film: "I can't understand what's delaying the coffee pot." The pot promptly falls out. (Later in the 1930s Harpo would characterize his occupation as dropping silverware.)

As with the film *Cocoanuts*, the screen adaptation of *Animal Crackers* was a critical and commercial success—*Variety* called it a "dough [moneymaker] film."[157] Thus, even technical limitations could not derail the popularity of the Marx Brothers's humor or its growing timeliness for the age. One is reminded of Benchley's *Life* (the humor magazine, not the later pictorial) review of the Marxes's poverty-stricken *I'll Say She Is!* While not blind to its technical flaws, he still celebrated the Brothers's sheer comedy greatness by observing, in his own delightfully comic way: "Not since sin laid its heavy hand on our spirit have we laughed so loud and so offensively . . . [picking] ourself out of the aisle follow-ing each convulsion."[158] Paramount's comedy "experiment" had become a unique success. Their next cinema stop would be Hollywood.

Before their 1931 migration to California, however, there were some lucrative stage dates to fill and a minor brush with politics. Marx friend and critic Heywood Broun—or if one notes his idolatry of the team, friendly critic Broun—ran for Congress in 1930. Trying to represent a New York City district, he understandably attracted major support from the entertainment profession, including the Marxes. Appropriately, Broun even had free headquarters in the Algonquin Hotel. Thus, on the night of October 14, 1930, Groucho found himself introducing Broun over the New York radio station WABC (of the Columbia Broadcasting System). What follows is a short excerpt from Groucho's comically rambling political (?) speech, a speech that also nicely anticipates the absurdity of his later *Duck Soup* cinema politician Rufus T. Firefly:

Man and boy I have known Heywood Broun for thirty years. He has known me for thirty years. This makes a total of sixty years and brings us down to the fiscal year of 1861, when conditions were much as they are now. My father was out of [a] job at the time, the farmers were complaining about the prices and the prices [Prices] who lived next door were complaining about my father. . . .

And so, pupils of the Pratt Street Grammar School, we have come together today to observe Arbor Day and plant a tree in honor of the Polish explorer, Heywood Broun. Let us hope that one day the frozen Yoken [*sic*] wastes will give him up. Let us hope that something will give him up. Perhaps he will give himself up. I gave him up long ago.[159]

Unfortunately, Socialist candidate Broun finished third in a three-horse race. Groucho biographer Arce suggests that Broun's Algonquin-led big-name support had been more dilettantes than real campaigners.[160] As an example he tells of a huge celebrity rally, with master of ceremonies Woollcott orchestrating the lengthy hosannas for Broun. Just as this late 1920s beautiful people gathering was about to close, Groucho asked the crowd how many were from Broun's district. Fewer than a handful were.

Groucho's involvement in the campaign is important for three reasons, besides the Arce implication that dilettantism was another item that separated the mustached one from the Algonquin group. First, Groucho's radio involvement and his consideration of district residency showcase his practical nature. A commitment equals meaningful involvement. The Marx Brothers literally fought their way out of childhood poverty and the lowest entertainment ranks. The world they frequented during much of their career in vaudeville even necessitated their carrying blackjacks (a flexible loaded club) for protection. They persevered both on and off stage and eventually made the most of their talents. Second, supporting a Socialist was not a fad liberalism for Groucho. The comedian was generally to the political left throughout his life. For example, as late as the Watergate 1970s, Groucho found himself temporarily in hot water for suggesting it would be best for the country if someone would just shoot then-President Richard Nixon. Though this was a bit extreme, even for this anarchist comedian, it is valid to state, as did Groucho biographer Charlotte Chandler, that he "tended to be quite democratic, with a small *d* as well as a capital *D*."[161] Third, Groucho was forever the cynic, whether it was the comic deprecation of Broun in the radio introduction or the timing of his residency statement at what had been an upbeat rally. His direct-to-the-heart approach, without necessarily showing any heart, was a frequent source of conflict for Groucho in his personal relationships, not unlike his sometimes masochistic sense of humor—as in his on-going disembarkation gag about smuggling opium. To incorporate the diplomacy Groucho so often neglected, one might simply say he was, frequently, a wet blanket.

While this late-1930 involvement in politics was not a winner, Groucho and his brothers were much more successful in their chosen field. They signed for a very lucrative short-term vaudeville tour on the Radio-Keith-Orpheum (RKO) Circuit and would soon follow this with another London engagement.

At the beginning of their RKO tour, Groucho was hospitalized for an emergency appendectomy, but somehow a Groucho appeared on stage. How was this possible? Zeppo went on as his cynical brother, and the audience thought it was Groucho. Eventually, the truth came out because there was still a brother missing. (This might be seen as another compliment to Zeppo—noticing he was gone—since critics generally saw him as expendable.) Groucho later said that Zeppo "got such huge laughs that, out of self-protection, I got out of the hospital as fast as I could."[162]

This apparent Zeppo metamorphosis was really no metamorphosis at all. The seemingly invisible Zeppo was really an underrated talent, frequently considered the funniest of the Brothers in real life—a view that Groucho endorsed.[163] In fact, Jack Benny, who roomed with Zeppo on a vaudeville tour, observed: "Zeppo off stage was like Groucho on stage."[164] And Groucho later said of Zeppo's early-1930s exit from the group: "His roles were thankless, and much of the time all he was required to do was show up. It's not that he didn't have the talent; he simply had three older brothers ahead of him."[165]

Interestingly, Harpo and Chico had once exchanged roles on Broadway with no one being the wiser. And without a missing brother, as was the case in Zeppo's role switch, friends and associates later refused to believe it had happened. Obviously, this too demonstrated great comic diversity. But besides being look-alikes, they were already recognized comedy talents. Zeppo's switch was more unique because it was in the stereotyped understudy-makes-good category. It even improves upon this convention, inasmuch as the standard understudy was merely an unknown, and Zeppo was often considered a known no-talent. What seems generally neglected, however, is Zeppo's comment that he "understudied" all their parts, and had once "got away with" substituting for Harpo.[166] Thus, Zeppo was not only the team's straight man, but he was also a built-in family understudy—a situation that merits more attention.

Despite Zeppo's surprising success, RKO was not happy about paying full price for a less-than-full complement of Marx Brothers. Zeppo continued to appear as Groucho during the first week's run in Chicago, but the tour was then postponed until Groucho could return.

Groucho was on stage in a week, but because he could do only two instead of the four daily shows agreed upon, RKO subtracted $800 from the team's $9,000 weekly salary.[167] The conflict over the number of stage appearances seems to have dogged them throughout the tour, because as Groucho related privately at the time (December 6, 1930), the team's last stop (Detroit) was iffy until the week before it was to open: "It has now been definitely settled and the sturdy settlers of Michigan will have to endure the slings and arrows of the outrageous Marxs [sic] four times a day, with the customary additional performances when the business warrants it."[168] Groucho then goes on to add a more earthy commentary on recovery rituals for appendectomy victims:

> I get plenty of time here to woo the festive muse, and also to feel any unlucky ladies who happen to be on the bill. It [i]s the only kind of exercise you can possibly get, and unquestionably the best kind anyway. You can gather from these remarks on sex, that the wounds of Strauss and the scars of nature are rapidly healing up, and that I will soon be back on the happy humping grounds, doing my best to appease the unsatisfied habits and longings of what was once known as the gentler sex.[169]

Groucho disapproved of Chico's lack of discretion in his nearly nonstop affairs, but Groucho was not without his own fixation as these and many other similar passages revealed in other letters. In his later book, *Memoirs of a Mangy Lover*, he comically called himself a "man whom destiny had marked as a potential sex maniac."[170] Though tongue-in-cheek, his comic diagnosis hardly seems very wide of the mark.

The Marx Brothers set sail for London shortly before Christmas in 1930. They were to appear at the Palace Theatre in Charles B. Cochran's 1931 *Varieties*. As in their recently finished tour stop in Detroit, negotiations had continued to the eleventh hour. The phenomenal popularity of the team had put them in the most superior of bargaining positions. In December Groucho had written:

> the only thing that is holding it [their London Palace appearance] up, is the fact that we have made such absurd demands in the way of financial concessions that no manager with a spark of manhood in him could possibly comply with our insane requests. We are doing this purposely, as we do not care to go, but if we have to we will sell ourselves as dearly as possible.[171]

Evidently, there was not "a spark of manhood" in the booking manager, because they were soon traveling to England. It was truely a time of heady success; due to the box office of *The Cocoanuts* and *Animal Crackers*, Paramount renegotiated their contract on board ship before they left.

The Marx Brothers's original contract had given them $75,000 per picture. Their third Paramount film would pay them $200,000. They would also receive

50 percent of the net profits! There was so much pie in the sky that even tight-fisted Groucho loosened up and booked deluxe sailing accommodations.

The Marx Brothers children remembered the trip in radically different ways. Chico's daughter Maxine was crushed because she had to stay behind; Groucho's Arthur and Miriam were appropriately ecstatic at being included, as was their father's habit, in the travel plans. Unfortunately, especially for the easily seasick Groucho, it was a particularly rough passage. For example, Arthur remembers that one evening in the dining salon "after a particularly violent lurch of the ship, my Aunt Betty [Chico's wife], dressed to the teeth in a beaded Chanel creation, fell over backwards in her chair and slid across the dance floor on her back."[172]

As is not uncommon for people suffering from seasickness, Groucho rarely turned green while on deck in the fresh air. Below deck was another matter, and this created tensions with the evening social calendar of wife Ruth, especially since Groucho would seem so healthy topside during the day. Appropriately, this situation favored Groucho's normal daytime activities with the children.

Of more concern to Ruth was his stubborn independence and anti-elitism. A major row was precipitated because Groucho did not want to enjoy the honor of eating with the captain:

> Why do I have to eat dinner with a total stranger, just because he happens to be a Captain of a leaky scow? I'd rather eat with the kids. Besides, the Captain'll expect me to be funny. I don't want to have to be funny if I don't feel like it.[173]

Such situations were an ongoing commentary on the challenge of being married to "democratic" (as well as stingy) Groucho and often were terribly funny—his original rejection of the messenger bringing the invitation was, "Tell the Captain he's a lousy driver. He has no right to leave the bridge just to have dinner." Later to Ruth he intoned, "Do I ask him [the Captain] to come down here for free and tell me what he knows about seamanship?"[174] This particular example of anti-establishment irreverence is also especially significant career-wise, because the Marx Brothers's next picture, *Monkey Business*, was largely set on an ocean liner with the team (especially Groucho), frequently at odds with the captain. In fact, as stowaways, they were constantly trying to avoid the captain. And one cinematic confrontation with the captain has specific echoes of Groucho's earlier real-life dialogue. He tells the film captain, "I don't care for the way you're running this boat. Why don't you get in the back seat for a while and let your wife drive?"

Groucho also received an unexpected holiday frustration on the crossing. It did not occur to him until they were actually celebrating Christmas that for once he would not be able to pursue his favorite holiday tradition: exchanging gifts given to him.

While the crossing was "rough" in just about every imaginable way for Groucho, the Marx Brothers were a major critical and commercial success at the London Palace. Groucho observed privately at the time: "We opened here last night [January 5, 1931] and were, surprisingly enough, a big hit. The pictures, both Animal Crackers, and Coconuts [*sic*] were both smashes here, and through them, the Londoners became sufficiently acquainted with our styles, to get a fair idea of what we are doing."[175]

Their forty-minute performance, part of a variety bill, culled the best material from *Cocoanuts* and *Animal Crackers.* Appropriately, that additional "Marx Brother" was performing with them—Margaret Dumont. After their successful opening, Groucho could not resist reminding the audience of the Brothers's less-than-pleasant opening during their last London appearance.

Ironically, the anarchistic Marxes were much sought after by members of the royal court. Besides being comic celebrities, their easygoing directness was no doubt part of their appeal. For example, when Maxine later asked her father what one says to a duke, assuming some sort of court protocol was required, Chico replied in basic New Yorkese: "Hi ya, Dook."[176] Harpo and Chico spent a great deal of time playing cards, with the latter finding a bridge friend in the duke of Manchester. Groucho, the frustrated author, seemed to divide his time between meeting favorite writers and giving his children a historical tour of London. Of course, it was history according to Groucho. His explanation for Henry the Eighth's penchant for beheading wives was, "Because it was cheaper than paying alimony."[177]

Beheadings notwithstanding, Groucho was most impressed by the civilized nature of the British. But if one item might have produced agreement among the Brothers about the host nation, it would have been cold living conditions. Groucho observed at the time in correspondence that in "the frigidity of their rooms, heavy underwear ... [was] absolutely essential."[178] Groucho would later observe, "If you are familiar with the discomforts of a cold-water flat in Soho it may help you understand why the British Empire has steadily declined over the years."[179] The latter observation is in an essay fittingly entitled "A Hot Time in the Cold Town Tonight," which comically describes a successful but frigid all-night London gambling session with Chico and Harpo.

Cold temperatures and heavy underwear notwithstanding, it was a very heady trip for the Marxes, both professionally and socially. Not surprisingly, however, Groucho did manage to end the trip on a sour note when he tried his ongoing disembarkation smuggling joke in clearing customs. Later, though, he might have alibied the incident as work-related, for one of the most inspired scenes in their next film would be a comic broadside against the event called customs.

After the climatic cold of Britain, the planned 1931 move to California no doubt sounded all the more promising. Paramount would have liked the Brothers to come earlier, but the Broadway success of *Animal Crackers* had delayed the move, as well as necessitating their one-time work schedule of two-shift days, combining stage and screen. While their new Paramount contract sent them to sunny California, the lucrative terms had been the prime but not the sole motivation. There were other factors. First, the Brothers wanted to work less—to get away from the daily grind of a Broadway show. The three focus Marxes were all over forty now, with each having already individually logged a minimum of twenty entertainment years.

Second, the depression and sound movies (which took both audiences and stellar performers from the stage) made Broadway successes increasingly more difficult. In fact, *Variety*'s review of the Marxes's current picture, *Animal Crackers*, had even dispensed with its standard critical remarks to examine the stage versus sound film conflict: "why 'Animal Crackers' on the stage at $5.50, when even the ruralities know they will see it later on the screen at 50 or 75c?" Later the same essay states, "in this Paramount picture they [the Marx Brothers] are just the same [as on stage]."[180] Moreover, at approximately the same time the Marxes set sail for Britain, fellow comedy cynic W. C. Fields was opening on Broadway in *Ballyhoo*. Though it showcased some of Fields's best material, the production would have a short, commercially troubled run.[181] Thus, 1931 would also find W. C. Fields heading west to Hollywood.

Third, even before their mother's death the Brothers had wanted to relocate their parents to a warmer climate. When they moved to California, their father came along. Frenchie died there May 11, 1933, at age seventy-two. Paralleling his own marriage, when Minnie brought her immigrant parents along, Frenchie spent most of his life in this new world of California at the home of Zeppo and his wife (actress Marion Benda, whom he had married in 1928). Frenchie appeared as an extra in two scenes in his sons' first California film, *Monkey Business*. Appropriately, at least for a member of the Marx family, he was inadvertently included as an extra in one too many scenes. Thus, as the ship on which the Marx Brothers are stowaways docks in the film, Frenchie turns up as part of the crowd both on decks and on the pier. How fitting for the father of the Marx Brothers, in his first and last film, to be both coming and going at the same time! It is a surrealism befitting his sons, especially his favorite, Harpo, the most surreal of the clan.

The Marxes's first Hollywood film is also their first cinematic one, as opposed to the two previous "canned theatre" productions. Between the greater technical expertise to be found in the industry's home base, and the general added knowledge another year (since the Brothers's last film) meant in the transition from silent to sound films era, the team was cinematically static no more. As if to accent this greater mobility, *Monkey Business* could be defined as an ongoing chase film, especially on board ship.

Monkey Business, also their first film written directly for the screen, is distinct from their earlier stage adaptations in two key ways. First, as Allen Eyles suggests, the comedy is more unrelentingly biting.[182] But Eyles somewhat exaggerates the point. For example, what could be more comically aggressive than Harpo's literal comedy punches to Dumont's tummy in *Animal Crackers*? Moreover, in contrast to their later, more homogenized MGM (Metro-Goldwyn-Mayer) films, one could call all their Paramount films more comically aggressive. Still, there is an increased comedy hardness in *Monkey Business*. As comedy anarchists the Marxes never soften or let up, from the actual slapstick of Harpo's other-worldly Punch and Judy show to Groucho's cool verbal machine-gunning of gangster Alky Briggs (Harry Woods). But this author is especially reminded of Groucho's matter-of-fact cynicism when, after pretending to be a doctor and diagnosing a still-horizontal fainting victim, he addresses the gathering crowd: "Will you all get close so he won't recover? Here, right this way [Groucho directs where they are to stand]. Step right around here."

Eyles seems hesitant to suggest that the less sympathetic nature of the *Monkey Business* Marxes is a product of the first appearance of S. J. Perelman as a Marx Brothers writer. Yet, for the student of American humor, Perelman's presence seems an unmistakable key to the film. Perelman, to whom Robert Benchley later in the 1930s would bequeath comic leadership in "the dementia praecox field," has now long been celebrated as one of America's great darkly comic writers, a master of the most complex verbal slapstick. Thus, it seems, however, only natural to link him to both the film's hard comedic edge and the very verbal "highly literate script" which Marx Brother authors Paul D. Zimmerman and Burt Goldblatt credit to Perelman.[183]

The second distinctive way in which *Monkey Business* can be separated from the earlier Marx stage adaptations, as well as much that followed, also has possible Perelman roots. *Monkey Business* spends much of its time parodying the gangster film (as opposed to the Marxes's more typical ongoing potshots at high society, and their later comedy attacks on establishment institutions, such as college life in *Horse Feathers* or governments in *Duck Soup*). *Monkey Business* does, however, in a broader context, satirize an era in which wealthy gangsters were buying themselves into high society.

The gangster film was in its original heyday at the time. Gangsters were front-page news during the Prohibition years, and filmmakers capitalized on this timeliness and the appropriateness of the phenomenon for early sound films, when the public was easily fascinated by the noisy violence of the genre. In fact, at the time of *Monkey Business*'s original release (September 19, 1931), two of the genre's most pivotal films had already appeared—*Little Caesar* (1930), and *Public Enemy* (1931). And the early 1930s popularity of these tough-guy films was a major factor in the later implementation of an enforceable film censorship code in 1934. Thus, while Groucho's nonsensical verbal mishandling of gangster Briggs remains hilarious today, in 1931 it must have been even more comic:

[Tough new gang leader Briggs points a gun at Groucho from the classic extended gangster's pocket.]

Briggs: Do you see this gat?

[Groucho looks in the pocket.]

Groucho: Cute, isn't it? Santa bring it for Christmas? I got a fire engine.

[Later in the same conversation.]

Briggs: Is there anything you've got to say before I drill ya?

Groucho: Yes, I'd like to ask you one question.

Briggs: Go ahead.

Groucho: Do you think that girls think less of a boy if he lets himself be kissed? I mean, don't you think that although girls go out with boys like me—they always marry the other kind?

The same year that the Marx Brothers parodied gangster films, Laurel & Hardy were doing *Pardon Us*, a takeoff on another early 1930s crime genre—the prison film, especially *The Big House* (1930).

When examining parody, Perelman again comes to mind, as his comedy essays frequently parody the film industry and its various genres. In fact, Perelman reveals in a later article that his first impression of a Hollywood studio (after he and Will B. Johnstone, who had written the Marxes's *I'll Say She Is!*, were signed for *Monkey Business*) was that of an assortment of genres (beginning with the "gangster epics") for which he had little respect.[184] Indeed, regardless of who receives credit, an argument could be advanced for *Monkey Business* as an on-going parody of several Hollywood genres, besides its gangster focus. For example, when underworld kingpin Joe Helton (Rockliffe Fellowes) expresses admiration for Groucho, even though "you're a funny kind of a duck," the comedian drawls:

Sheriff, I ain't much on flowery sentiments, but there's somethin' I jes' got to tell yuh. . . . Shucks, man, I'd be nuthin' but a pizenous varmint and not fitten to touch the hem of yo' pants if I didn't tell you you've treated me squar, mighty squar, and I ain't forgettin' it.

Groucho then strolls away bowlegged, takes a ten-gallon hat from a passing cow-boy (Groucho is at a party where many guests are in costume—a perfect setting for genre parody), returns to Helton, and says, "Sheriff, I ain't forgettin!" Groucho again strolls away bowlegged and exits the film frame. This is followed by comically creative use of off-screen space—western parody style. A horse neighs and Groucho shouts: "Whoa theah, Bessie, whoa theah," and one hears hoofbeats. Just prior to this scene, Groucho had a comic run-in with a guest costumed as an Indian, creating additional parody of the western genre. (Since the silents, the western films had only known great success. *Cimarron* even won the Academy of Motion Picture Arts and Sciences Best Picture Oscar for 1930-1931, the only western ever accorded that honor. Consequently, western parody was also very timely in 1931.)

Film critic William Wolf briefly describes the film as "spoofing sex appeal," noting the replacement of Margaret Dumont by the inviting blonde Thelma Todd.[185] Even without the added sexual comedy tension the sexy Todd provides, there are numerous takeoffs on the romantic film, from the integration of the love interest into the team (Zeppo plays the romantic male lead) to Groucho caught in mid-conversation at the party, surrounded by admiring girls, one of whom is stroking his chest: "No, you're wrong, girls. You're wrong. In the first place, Gary Cooper is much taller than I am."

One of Groucho's love scenes with Todd reveals a further genre parody delineation. When they meet on the terrace and she asks why he is there, a very dramatic Groucho says, in part: "Come, Kapellmeister, let the violas throb; my regiment leaves at dawn." Perelman has revealed this was the beginning of a long parody of a similar scene in Eric von Stroheim's 1925 melodrama *The Merry Widow*.[186] But in this case, Groucho kept the parody to the quoted line, stating the maxim he often used when he felt comedy material was too esoteric: "The trouble is that the barber in Peru [Indiana] won't get it." As in money management, Groucho's approach to comedy leaned toward the tried and true.

For a surprise of surprises, the Groucho-Todd romantic encounter in her ship stateroom can even be seen as a parody of Groucho as lover. Unlike Margaret Dumont, who is neither physically attractive nor frequently mentally attuned to Groucho's sexual suggestions, Todd is both inviting and *inviting*. Indeed, as if to underline her similar sexuality wavelength she quotes from an earlier, delightful bit of Groucho dialogue, a comic anthem to sexuality: "I want excitement. I want to ha-cha-cha-cha." She then breaks into dance, as Groucho did after uttering these lines. That Groucho does not take her up on the "Ha-cha-cha-cha," period restrictions on screen sexuality notwithstanding, is an interesting calling of the Groucho sexual bluff.

Further examination of the later love scene brings one back full circle to more parody of the gangster genre. For example, shortly after Groucho has given his abbreviated von Stroheim speech Todd denies him a kiss, saying: "My husband might be inside, and if he finds me out here he'll wallop me." Groucho replies, "Always thinking of your husband. Couldn't I wallop you just as well?" Besides "wallop" being a funny-sounding word, it also comically focuses on another aspect of why the early 1930s cinema gangster was so popular—his rough treatment of women. Be it Clark Gable's general manhandling of Norma Shearer in *A Free Soul* (1931) or Cagney's celebrated grapefruit to Mae Clarke's kisser in *Public Enemy*, it was part of 1930s cinema gangster's machismo, and added to his sexual charisma. Thus, Groucho's offer to be a substitute gangster walloper is comically akin to his mild protest of resembling the then young and sexy Gary Cooper.

Despite these *Monkey Business* differences, most views undoubtedly saw it as more inspired fun from the Marxes. That it was, however, not always fun behind the scenes had been nicely chronicled by Perelman, who records a fascinating look at the Marx Brothers entourage shortly after their return from Europe. (See the Perelman material examined in the bibliographical chapter overview, especially his *Show* essay.) Perelman (then a cartoonist and essayist whose work had regularly appeared in the humor journals *Judge* and *College Humor*) and Johnstone had impressed the Marxes with a script idea for them to be ocean liner stowaways. Although it was originally conceived as a radio program idea, Groucho pushed it as a premise for their next movie. Thus, while the Marxes were in England, Perelman and Johnstone labored in Hollywood over their script under the loose-ship guidance of their Paramount supervisor Herman Mankiewicz (now best known as the later co-author, with Orson Welles, of the screenplay for *Citizen Kane*).

The anxiety once produced by the refrain "The British are coming" had nothing on the emotions of Perelman and Johnstone when informed by Mankiewicz that the Marxes are coming. That the Brothers were sailing from Britain should have been seen as an omen . . . a bad omen (though the team was not coming from a bad British reception, as Perelman invariably states). Mankiewicz might have added to his—the Marxes are coming—refrain some additional "and coming and coming." The group that finally assembled before the writers for a script reading numbered nearly thirty, and the entourage arrived like any invading army, in reverse order of importance. Frenchie Marx and a pinochle-playing companion (cards now being Papa Marx's main pastime) arrived first. Zeppo and his wife were the next family members to arrive, and they had brought along several Afghan hounds purchased in Britain. Initially, the dogs were no problem because they were still digesting the upholstery of a Packard they had dined upon earlier. Harpo then appeared with a blonde on each arm. The Marxes's unofficial team captain, Chico, soon followed, with his wife and a wirehaired dog, which promptly declared war on Zeppo's Afghans. As if waiting for the first available chaotic moment, Groucho and his wife then arrived. Other visitors included recent gagmen acquisitions by Groucho, Harpo, and Chico (plus the mini-entourages of the gagmen) and Paramount representatives such as Mankiewicz, who was accompanied by his then screenwriter brother Joseph. The final tally, if you "counted noses and paws," was twenty-seven people and five dogs.[187]

The "honor" of reading the lengthy script fell to Perelman because he had *lost* the coin flip to Johnstone. Great writers are frequently mediocre readers, especially when they are intimidated by their audiences. All the above applied to Perelman, along with the added weight of including every technical film production notation in his oration. The effect was less than socko, more like snoozo.

When Perelman was finally, mercifully done, a less-than-happy Chico asked Groucho for his opinion. Groucho, no doubt savoring his position of power, took his time replying, pausing to light a cigar. Finally, he unloaded a simple but devastating two-word salvo: "It stinks." Entourages being what they are, there was quick agreement, and the Marx army filed out. Perelman's and Johnstone's Hollywood career threatened to end before it started.

By the following day, however, the Marxes saw some good in the screenplay. So, Perelman and Johnstone worked on the script for several more months with the assistance of an assortment of gagmen, cartoonists, and writers, though only Arthur Sheekman would share eventual writing screen credit, for "Additional dialogue," with Perelman and Johnstone.

Though there are several differences between the final script (dated April 21, 1931) and the finished film, the most interesting is the scaled-down conclusion. Instead of the Zeppo-Briggs barn fisticuffs, with comic ringside commentary by Groucho, the script had originally called for an elaborate finale at a warehouse brewery. While there is still a Zeppo-Briggs fight (Briggs ends up being socked into a vat of beer), the written ending more thoroughly plays upon stereotypical icons of the gangster genre—"bootleggers' equipment; cases of liquor, bottles, demijohns, barrels, kegs of beer . . . a rum sloop . . . lashed to the dock, . . . a 'bubbling' vat of beer."[188] Indeed, nearer the close is a delightfully written scene that even tops W. C. Fields's classic anti-social liquor activities in *International House* (1933), most pointedly, the ongoing stream of beer bottles which fall from Fields's autogyro (part plane and part helicopter), a wonderful sight gag itself, as he attempts to fly to Kansas City but ends up in China.

The *Monkey Business* topper scene finds Harpo enjoying a swim in another vat of beer: "Harpo's head comes up with a smile. He spurts a little beer out of his mouth—[one hears] the honk of a horn—he disappears out of sight in the beer again."[189] The scripted finale was probably scrapped for cost and technical reasons. In addition to the more ambitious bootlegger setting, the warehouse had a steam hoist whose moving long arm and attached pincher figured prominently in the final comedy battle. Also lost was an artistically symmetrical fade out with Groucho, Harpo, and Chico once again singing in barrels, as they had in the film's beginning, on another ship (Joe Farina's private yacht, while Zeppo and Farina's daughter kissed nearby). In the tradition of this increased gangster focus, the final script additionally has a more comically menacing Groucho: "How would you like to be shot, sideways, or in a group?" or "Listen, Big Mans [sic], there's a certain somebody out to shoot you in your fat little tummy and that certain someone is me."[190] Despite the changes, the September 1931 release of *Monkey Business* gave the team still another major hit.

Coupled with their new film was a new home, California, but the Brothers remained consistent to their basic personality traits. The Groucho Marxes rented a series of modest homes, while the rest of the team went in for more luxurious settings. (Perelman would later state Groucho's "passionate avocation" was "the collecting and cross-fertilization of various kinds of money."[191]) Appropriately, however, before later buying a home, Groucho would rent a bungalow in the more impressive Garden of Allah, which at that time housed such transplanted Eastern writers (Groucho's kind of people) as Robert Benchley and Dorothy Parker. (Harpo and Frenchie initially had had separate bungalows at the Garden, too.) Socially, Chico and Harpo moved more in the fast lane than Groucho. Thus, Chico spent a great deal of time in Aguascalientes, Mexico, where the racetrack and gambling casino attracted a number of Hollywood high rollers; Harpo hob-nobbed with California's elite after he was nearly "adopted" by the William Randolph Hearst-Marion Davies circle.[192] Zeppo was already showing an interest in becoming an agent, his later occupation after breaking with the team.

Groucho's description of a Palm Springs party attended during the production of *Monkey Business* nicely demonstrates his ongoing scorn for the pompous and the petty. Observed Groucho:

> Von Sternberg [the elitist director/cinematographer who added the "von" himself and is best known for a 1930s series of pictorially striking films starring Marlene Dietrich] with baggy wide pants and a cane trying awfully hard to forget that he was born in Brooklyn and not Vienna. The place was afire with repartee, wiseys, who was the best director, what their [*sic*] next part was going to be, who was humping who, why this supervisor was fired, why Carl Laemme Jr. [*sic*, Laemmle, Universal's head of production] was going to displace Thalberg [MGM production head and later the Marxes's patron at the studio] as the little Napoleon of the silver screen, and all the claptrap that goes to make a Hollywood conversation one of the dullest on earth.[193]

Maxine Marx remembers a "glorious" first California summer at a Malibu beach house Chico and Betty had rented.[194] Film star neighbors like Joan and Connie Bennett made it a schoolgirl's dream, though Maxine was happiest at being able to see more of the father she idolized. When the Marx Brothers families had initially moved west in early 1931, Maxine had stayed behind with a cousin in order to continue at Woodmere Academy, where she would return in the fall.

That Uncle Groucho and his family came for an extended visit while Maxine's parents went on a short trip is also an early example of Groucho's California economizing. Groucho had asked specifically about coming out to enjoy Chico's beach, a variation of his lifelong appreciation of swimming pools—other people's swimming pools. He avoided renting or buying homes with pools, though, in all fairness to Groucho, his reasoning was not entirely tightness. The absence of a pool also cut down on unwanted guests! Groucho's resolve on guests was probably strengthened by Harpo's nearly open-door policy, which frequently had his residence taking on the nature of a free hotel. (See especially Oscar Levant's "Memoirs of a Mute," which includes a comic chronicle of Levant's feud with the silent Marx Brothers as the now celebrated hypochondriac musician continued to stay at Harpo's home.[195]) In addition, Harpo ranked second only to Chaplin as the 1930s Hollywood personality visiting celebrities most wanted to see.

Business and old ties still frequently brought the Marxes east, however. Groucho, Chico, and Harpo appeared for two performances (August 20 and 21, 1931) in Heywood Broun's Broadway *Shoot the Works!*, a cooperative revue for needy actors. After the smash opening (September 1931) of *Monkey Business*, there was also another lucrative vaudeville tour in the East. These non-Hollywood ties were enough to make the Brothers consider shooting their next film, what became *Horse Feathers*, back at Paramount's Astoria (New York) studio. In addition, it seemed inevitable that the Four Marx Brothers would eventually become Three, especially if Zeppo's interest in the business end of film were coupled both with his absence from *Shoot the Works!* and with Groucho's "sly curtain speech in which he expressed gratification that the three brothers could get along without the fourth."[196] But Zeppo was again with the team for *Horse Feathers*, which was eventually shot in Hollywood.

The August 1932 release of *Horse Feathers* provided the Marxes with still another critical and commercial film success. It also gave them the unique honor of making the cover of *Time* magazine (August 15, 1932), though the recognition was as much a hosanna for their nonstop body of film successes. The short two-page article was largely taken up with a plot synopsis and a family history. But in its brief summation of each brother's screen persona, two frequent past press tendencies continued: Harpo merits the most attention, while Zeppo is nonchalantly slammed. Both tendencies are best exemplified through comic quotes: Harpo "pursues women with the abandon of a satyr and the stamina of Paavo Nurmi [a period runner]" and Zeppo acts "poorly enough not to detract from the antics of his confreres."[197]

At the time Groucho was modestly self-deflating about the *Time* cover, a *Horse Feathers* scene which found all four Brothers in a chariot-like ash can. He privately described it as "their natural habitat."[198] (But at the same time he is critical of another period piece which offered suggested changes for the film. See notes 60 and 61 in Chapter 4.) The added attention a *Time* cover generates was no doubt especially rewarding because of the lengthy *Horse Feathers* production delay necessitated by the injuries Chico sustained in a serious automobile accident (April 9, 1932). In an April 1932 letter, Groucho observed:

> I have been so busy running to the hospital to see Chico that I have'nt [*sic*] had time to do anything. . . . He had a Dr. Speirs, who all the quacks out here assured was a capable surgeon, so we are hopeful he will mend without any kind of a future limp [Chico had one knee shattered]. The whole thing is a mess; it sets us back [the production of *Horse Feathers*] six to eight weeks . . . and all in all is a general nuisance, but then so is Chico, and I guess we should be thankful that it was'not [*sic*] any worse.[199]

The production delay had been especially frustrating because the shooting was nearly completed and it was within a few weeks of a preview. Ironically, the main scene left to shoot was also the most physical—the football finale. An extended waiting period for the audience's response to any popular art production can be painful for the participants, but it was especially so for the perennial pessimist with the matching name—Groucho.

In the finished film Chico's lack of mobility in the football scene is not overly disconcerting, especially since his comic quarterback's rendition of signal calling still makes him part of the action. The only bothersome moment occurs when an obvious extra substitutes for Chico in a shot where it is necessary to include him among running players. Conversely, one possible *Horse Feathers* in-joke related to Chico's knee injury was his sideline request of two passing stretcher bearers to drop him off at the forty-yard line.

Chico's limited mobility notwithstanding, the film continues the more cinematic tradition in Marx films ushered in by *Monkey Business*. Thus, *Horse Feathers* showcases everything from a football game (shades of Harold Lloyd's football finale in *The Freshman*, 1925) to Chico and Harpo sawing themselves through the floor—possibly the inspiration for Terry Gilliam's darker rendition of a similar surprise entrance in his black comedy *Brazil* (1985), which pays direct homage to the Marxes by including an anti-establishment figure watching *The Cocoanuts*.

While it is only natural that the Marxes's first Hollywood film should parody industry staples like the gangster picture and other genres, *Horse Feathers* has a much broader and more universal base of comedy attack—higher education and America's ongoing fascination with college football and winning at any cost. Thus, while all Marx Brothers films find some then-contemporary values to satirize (such as the Florida land boom of *The Cocoanuts*) and/or entertainment media to parody (see especially Dennis P. deLoof's provocative analysis of *Animal Crackers* as a parody of Eugene O'Neill's *Strange Interlude*[200]), *Horse Feathers* is unique because its dual attack on collegiate education and football is still of mainstream satirical interest. This is not to forget that such perennial Marx Brothers targets as romance and elitism are forever relevant in their earlier films, but *Horse Feathers* more fully maximizes their satire skills for the general audience.

Interestingly enough, as was the case with the conclusion of *Monkey Business*, an elaborate scripted finale of *Horse Feathers* was essentially dropped.[201] After their football victory there was to have been a bonfire celebration. However, Harpo makes a mistake. Instead of starting the campus bonfire, he ignites a campus building.[202] Thus, rather than the brief comic wedding that unites the trio of Groucho, Harpo, and Chico to college widow Thelma Todd at the film's close, *Horse Feathers* was tentatively scripted to end with the burning of the college.

Unlike the aborted ending of *Monkey Business*, the deleted conclusion of *Horse Feathers* represents a greater potential loss. As the scene from this book's frontispiece demonstrates (a fiery close was shot but not used), what could be a more appropriate image of the antisocial Marxes than card playing complacently while a chaos they created rages around them? In fact, with the cross-like burning of two beams in the still's background, there is more than a suggestion that the raging chaos around the Brothers could be of apocalyptic dimensions, which makes their complacence all the more darkly comic.

The frontispiece scene had not yet been written in the tentative script of February 11, 1932, but there was already a nihilistic quality to what was transpiring on the burning campus. For example, Groucho enters a burning building seemingly to save Jennings, the leader of the rival college. Instead, he exits with a diploma.[203] Is this more nonsense or a black comedy reward for sending the villain to his just desserts? Appropriately, at least in this irrational world, he hands the diploma to Zeppo.

Of the images that make the actual film, three of the most memorable belong to Harpo, though one provides not comedy delight but a nihilistic chill: the silent one, with mad delight, shovels a pile of books into a raging fire. One can, of course, make viable comedy excuses for Harpo, or merely recycle Chico's explanation from their next film, *Duck Soup*, when Harpo rips up a telegram after closely examining it: "He gets mad because he can't read." But seen today against the 1930s backdrop of book-burning Nazi Germany, the scene is more than a little disconcerting.

Classically happier Harpo images occur, however, elsewhere in *Horse Feathers*. Especially wonderful is the scene where a tramp asks him for coffee money and Harpo produces instead a steaming cup of the liquid from the magic pocket of his trench coat. More comic sorcery on high is provided in answer to Groucho's admonition, "Young man, you'll find as you grow older you can't burn the candle at both ends." Harpo produces a candle doing just that. These are two of the most delightful if not *the* most delightful examples of the pocket wizardry that is Harpo's ongoing "wardrobe."

Curiously, sometimes rather analogous to the candle incident represents the whimsical comic highlight at the close of Norman Krasna's aforementioned Groucho family-focused *Dear Ruth*. The Groucho daughter figure, both based upon and named after real daughter Miriam, drunkenly quotes from the Edna St. Vincent Millay poem, "A Few Figs from Thistles," where the candle that burns at both ends is acknowledged not to last long but still is celebrated for its "lovely light."[204] (As Groucho biographer Arce sadly observed, in the case of the real Miriam, "Within a few years, life would tragically be imitating art."[205]) If Arce had noted the *Horse Feathers* connection, he might have added that the real magic of Harpo's candle, or any favored cinema moment, is the timelessness of it, as opposed to one's ever-changing life. To borrow a title from author/director Peter Bogdanovich, film truly represents *Pieces of Time*.

With the success of *Horse Feathers*, the team was more popular than ever. In fact, as Chico's daughter later observed, the Marxes had wanted to take a year off for lucrative stage appearances but financially troubled Paramount insisted they begin work on a new film.[206] Groucho and Chico did manage to have a short-lived radio program, *Flywheel, Shyster, and Flywheel*, which began November 28, 1932. Reviews were mixed, but it was initially picked up for an additional thirteen weeks. As the title implies (doubly), Groucho was an opportunistic lawyer (with Chico as the office process server). But the program also recycled past Marx Brothers movie material and in at least one case, provided new content for future films. That is, as George Oppenheimer, a writer for both the radio program and the Marxes's later *A Day at the Races* (1937) remembers, his all-time favorite pun (which would resurface in *Duck Soup*) had Chico in a court of law:

"All-a right," said Chico. . . . "I ask-a you a question. What is it has four legs, a trunk and is naked?"

Whereupon the prosecuting attorney shouted, "That's irrelevant."

"At'sa right," said Chico.[207]

Because Oppenheimer credits the pun to Groucho and his writer/friend Arthur Sheekman, it is also a good additional example of Groucho's ongoing contributions to the Marxes's material, something frequently noted but seldom exemplified.

The year 1932 had been so good for the Marx Brothers that the financial Jack Benny of the team bought a California home. Said Groucho, "I fought this off as long as I could, but . . . here I am, just another yokel. From now on you can expect nothing in my letters but climate."[208] The following year was more in keeping with the general pessimism of Groucho.

On March 9, 1933, the team temporarily broke with Paramount. The *New York Times* had the Marxes "serving notice on the studio executives that they considered their contract breached because of assorted non-payment of certain [substantial] sums of money, as well as the transfer of their contract from one [Paramount] corporation to another."[209] The depression had come to Hollywood, and Paramount was in financial trouble.

On April 3 the Marxes received their incorporation permit (as The Marx Brothers, Inc.) and continued plans to produce their next film. On April 15 the California State Corporation Department granted the team permission to incorporate. Their announced positions inside Marx Brothers, Inc., were a comic commentary on their individual images, public and private. Thus, tightwad Groucho was made treasurer, voiceless Harpo president, girl-chasing Chico the secretary, and the forever slandered as do-nothing Zeppo had the classic do-nothing position—vice president. Their first picture was to be an adaptation of Kaufman and Ryskind's Pulitzer Prize-winning *Of Thee I Sing*. Adequate funding was not forthcoming, however, and after their differences were settled with Paramount in May, the team returned to that studio for *Duck Soup* (released in November 1933).

Unfortunately, for the first time in the Marxes's film career, they did not have a hit. While *Duck Soup* was not quite the failure more recent critics have sometimes suggested, for many 1933 patrons the film followed the *New York Sun*'s analysis: "Below Their [the Marxes] Standard."[210] Ironically, today's student of comedy frequently sees this nihilistic satire on the absurdity of government as the team's best picture. Why was this unrecognized at the time? Sociological film historian (and now screenwriter/playwright) Andrew Bergman convincingly points at timing: "After a year of Roosevelt's energy and activism, government, no matter what else it might be, was no absurdity."[211]

Appropriately for a film now considered so significant, *Duck Soup* was the only one for which the team had a real auteur, Leo McCarey, as director. Mc-

Carey, who had teamed and molded Laurel & Hardy in the silent era and who would later win Oscars for *The Awful Truth* (1937, Best Director) and *Going My Way* (1944, Best Director and Best Original Story), did the seemingly impossible—he left a discernable comedy stamp on a Marx Brothers film. The uniqueness of this becomes more apparent when one juxtaposes McCarey's "Do it visually" motto with the tendency of Groucho's blitzkrieg verbal patter to dominate Marx Brothers films.[212] (*Duck Soup* would seem to showcase Harpo more than any other Marx Brothers film except *Love Happy*, 1949, which is essentially a Harpo-Chico vehicle.) That McCarey would be able to showcase so much purely visual material, to the point of even using Groucho in the celebrated silent mirror sequence (where Harpo, dressed like Groucho, comically becomes Groucho's "reflection"), is a tribute to McCarey's comedy talents. This should not, of course, obscure the fact that there was still a wealth of verbal material, with screenplay credit being given to Bert Kalmar and Harry Ruby, with additional dialogue by Arthur Sheekman and Nat Perrin.

In the American Film Institute's unpublished "Leo McCarey Oral History" (conducted by Peter Bogdanovich), McCarey observed; "My experience in silent films influenced me very much, and so usually I preferred Harpo."[213] The Oral History also includes the seemingly obligatory note by Marx Brothers directors that the Marxes were both a challenge to work with and difficult to keep together. Still, McCarey generally managed. In fact, he was successful enough that the most rare of anecdotes has been passed down from *Duck Soup*: the director played a gag on the Marxes. The Brothers's contract specified that they were not to begin shooting a scene after six in the evening. This created a natural conflict with the often improvisational McCarey, who later prided himself on always having had crews who would both let him wait for an idea and then not interrupt the creative process, regardless of what time it got to be. After having heard the Marxes's six o'clock exit line once too often, McCarey decided to turn the tables. Late in the day he had his assistant distract the team while he supposedly went to the telephone. Instead, McCarey went home. The Marxes were kept busy right up until the magic hour (with, one assumes, more contract references), when the assistant informed them that McCarey was home in bed but should be recovered by the first thing in the morning. As Marx Brothers author Adamson observed:

> McCarey was the only man on earth who could teach the Marx Brothers a lesson and come out of it with his life. But you'll notice he planned the gag so he'd be miles away from them when the punchline came.[214]

McCarey's touch is more obvious in the ongoing meetings between Harpo and the excellent comedian/character actor Edgar Kennedy (who had worked under McCarey during the Laurel & Hardy years). Kennedy runs a lemonade stand while Harpo is an assistant of sorts at Chico's peanut and hot dog stand. The first conflict has Harpo and Chico reducing Kennedy to distraction by a hat routine which keeps their bonnets moving from head to head in a combination "noodle" version of musical chairs and the old shell game. Though hat routines obviously predate McCarey, they have always been an integral part of his comedy, even before the celebrated hat exchanges of Laurel & Hardy. (For example, see the McCarey-directed Charley Chase short subject *His Wooden Wedding*, 1925.)

In the context of a Marx film, the rotating hats are a delightful variation on changing identities—things not being what they seem. Thus, by the end of the routine Kennedy is so disoriented that he begins taking on characteristics of the Marx Brothers. For McCarey, a pioneer in the evolution of the comic antihero in American film comedy, the scene demonstrates the inherent frustrations (focus on Kennedy) to be found in what should be the most innocent of encounters (Chico explaining his problems with Harpo).

In the second conflict between Harpo and Kennedy, McCarey uses the "tit-for-tat" gag he first introduced with Laurel & Hardy, what film historian John McCabe more descriptively describes as "reciprocal destruction."[215] A comedy conflict arises, and the participants take turns destroying each other's properties. Thus, what begins with Kennedy "paying" for a bag of peanuts by painting Harpo's outstretched hand with hot-dog mustard eventually escalates to Kennedy's overturning of the Marxes stand and Harpo's use of his rival's lemonade tank to wash his own feet. Such wading expeditions are seldom good for lemonade sales, and Kennedy is frustrated once again. This is a typical example of how McCarey enjoys presenting the comic chaos of the world in the everyday situation—a misunderstanding. And as a central comedy focus of the film suggests, similar misunderstandings can lead to war. Herein lies part of the layered richness of *Duck Soup*—the reiteration of a common theme in seemingly different contexts.

The third Harpo-Kennedy meeting is the briefest and most bizarre. Harpo has taken time out from a Paul Revere-like ride (warning of the approaching enemy) to visit the shapely wife of Kennedy. The husband's arrival home necessitates that Harpo hide. Unlike the stereotypical closet that Groucho's comic audacity allows him to use in *Monkey Business*, under somewhat similar circumstances, Harpo's choice is pure surrealism. He chooses the bottom of a drawn bathtub of water, from which he comically surfaces after poor Kennedy settles in for what was to be a relaxing soak. Besides representing main*stream* Harpo comedy of the absurd (heightened by the fact that the viewer does not know ahead of time where Harpo has hidden), the scene is typical McCarey in terms of comedy victim. One laughs at, yet comically sympathizes with, this poor schmuck who cannot even escape Marxian madness in what should be the security of a hot tub. There are few comedy heavies in McCarey's world (note also the unbelievable patience of Louis Calhern's Ambassador Trentino during his spy conference with Harpo and Chico), and *Duck Soup* is immeasurably richer for it.

The initial failure of *Duck Soup*, now recognized as a great film, to receive the recognition it deserves fit the kind of Marx year 1933 was becoming. Their contractual arrangement with Paramount was now completed, and *Duck Soup* was hardly a strong bargaining tool, especially with a studio of which the Marxes were less than enamored. There would be no more Paramount films. The Marxes suffered more than a regression in the entertainment business; brother Gummo's clothing business went bankrupt in 1933. Ironically, this would bring him back into the entertainment world as a successful agent. An October 1933 *Los Angeles Times* article also had him considering writing a biography of his brothers and such tales as how Groucho "stuck a hatpin in the bellows of the church organ and promptly resigned his [paid choir singer] post, under pressure."[216] But like a lot of Marx projects in 1933, nothing came of the book.

The year's best news for the family was Harpo's trip as cultural ambassador to the Soviet Union. Again the name of Alexander Woollcott surfaces, for Harpo's close friend was largely responsible for initiating the trip. Franklin Roosevelt had entered the White House, and the diplomatic recognition of the Soviet Union was at hand. It was Woollcott's idea that Harpo be the first American performer to entertain in Moscow after this recognition took place. But this was no pipe dream. Woollcott was both an ardent New Dealer and a close friend of the president's wife. Harpo was, however, reluctant. He had grown very fond of the California sun and did not even have an inclination to go to Canada, let alone the Soviet Union.[217] Eventually, Harpo's mind was changed, and he left for the Soviet Union in November 1933.

Harpo was an unknown commodity in Russia. Traveling with an assorted number of props, from bottles marked poison to a massive number of table knives for his silverware-from-the-sleeve routine, he even had some trouble entering the country. There were further delays once in Moscow when he was subjected to some audition-like interviews. Eventually, differences were worked out, and he was a great success in Russia. His repertoire of material, showcased at different points in a revue, features two harp bits, his clarinet-bubbles routine, and a pantomime scene from the opening of *The Cocoanuts*, with additional material from *I'll Say She Is!*[218] The pantomime sketch included essentially his running amuck at a hotel desk, tearing up mail and drinking ink, and using the proverbial Gookie. And herein lay Harpo's only need for a special adaptation of his work. Without changing his hotel zaniness, the bits were included in a story format, which his Russian theatre advisors felt necessary. It seems that Soviet audiences, at least in 1933, needed some foundation to their comic insanity.

To those who would ask if Harpo attempted to play upon his surname, the answer is yes. In Leningrad "He told the Soviet press through his interpreter that he was Karl's distant cousin, and they greeted him warmly."[219] But Harpo's playfulness was not unreciprocated. After one performance he was congratulated by Foreign Minister Maxim Litvinov, then the number two man in the Soviet Union. When they shook hands a shower of table knives fell from one sleeve . . . Litvinov's. Harpo was a hit.

At a press conference upon his arrival back in the United States (January 9, 1934), he was asked if he had converted to communism. He replied he had been too busy being converted to vodka and caviar.[220] It was a funny line, which the

New York Times even used in part as the title of its article noting Harpo's return (see previous note). Two not-so-funny things that had considerably dampened Harpo's traveling had not, however, made the *Times*'s coverage. First, Harpo had traveled by train through Germany. And though Hitler had only recently come to power, Harpo was sickened by the steps already being taken by the dictator against his own Jewish citizens. Second, upon leaving Moscow Harpo was given a more personalized worry—the United States ambassador (William C. Bullitt) asked the comedian to smuggle some letters back to New York. In complete secret agent style the epistles were strapped to one of Harpo's legs and covered by his sock. Today the thought of a 007 Harpo, or possibly just 00 Harpo, seems like additional comic surrealism. But at the time Harpo was more than a little concerned. (Real government agents relieved him of the documents just before the ship docked in New York, but unfortunately history has never recorded just what the silent one was carrying.)

Work had already begun on a Marx Brothers musical comedy return to Broadway in fall 1934. Though this did not materialize (because of a second chance in film), a January article in the *New York Herald Tribune* tied the prestige of Harpo's trip to the already more serious goals of the team: "a unified plot with humor in its situations rather than in its wise-cracks, a wish that has undoubtedly been considerably bolstered by Harpo Marx's recent appearance in Russia."[221]

The 1934 lull in the Marxes's momentum was the final catalyst for Zeppo's retirement from the team. On March 30 Groucho made public the letter he had received from Zeppo:

> I'm sick and tired of being a stooge. You know that anybody else would have done as well as I in the act. When the chance came for me to get into the business world I jumped at it.
>
> I have only stayed in the act until now because I knew that you, Chico and Harpo wanted me to. But I'm sure you understand why I have joined Frank Orsatti in his theatrical agency and that you forgive my action. Wish me luck.
>
> Love, Zeppo.[222]

The break had been a long time in the making. For example, Zeppo had been surprisingly candid in a January 1929 interview: "I'm not suited to the musical comedy stage; [I] should have been in straight comedy, and not with my brothers. They make me feel so self-conscious that I suffer. It's developed an inferiority complex in me."[223]

Interestingly enough, fifty years later in his last interview, Zeppo revealed one very positive benefit of joining the team—it kept him out of jail, or worse. At the time his mother demanded he join the group because of Brother Gummo's defection to the military: "I was a real bad boy. I was a kid, but I carried a gun and I stole automobiles."[224] Working as a Chicago mechanic during the day, Zeppo palled around evenings with another young tough. And the very same night he opened with the team, this friend was involved in a shooting death, which put him in prison for twenty years. Zeppo originally had had plans to be along that evening. The man eventually ended up in organized crime and met a violent death. As Zeppo observed, "that story shows how close my life would have been completely like his. I don't know what would have happened to me if my mother hadn't called me."[225] Thus, it is quite possible Minnie was playing the role of mother instead of agent the day she forced Zeppo into show business.

The same month as Zeppo's defection (March), Groucho and Chico returned to radio with the pun-entitled *Marx of Time* program, in which they comically discussed the day's news.[226] The program actually predated the then-in-development monthly screen-magazine series *The March of Time*, which was launched in 1935. Besides representing their inability to resist a pun, their new comedy look-at-the-news format was possibly also influenced by the sometimes adult comedy, at least for the more public 1930s radio airways, of their standard movie material. *Variety's* lengthy review of their earlier radio program voiced concern over a skit where lawyer Beagle (Groucho) comically turned out to be the mysterious other man in his client's divorce case:

> That's fine stuff for children! Chances are that if the Marxes proceed with their law office continuity along lines like this they will never be able to hold a kid listener. . . . Because parents don't want their children to hear about bad wives and divorces.[227]

Their new approach was, however, even less successful than the first, and they were canceled after eight weeks.

In Zeppo's 1929 interview he had mentioned straight comedy, but in 1934 it was Groucho who momentarily entered the field. He starred briefly in a summer theatre production (Lakewood, Maine) of Ben Hecht and Charles MacArthur's *Twentieth Century*. As the volatile Broadway producer Oscar Jaffe, Groucho could not have picked a better role for which to take off his mustache, and he was well received.

His original purpose for being in the area was a country vacation. But his description of the holiday in a letter, besides being very funny correspondence, gives the distinct impression of someone who would be ready for a local role—any role—to keep moss from forming on his north side:

> As you know I am up in the Maine woods, and it is lovely. Theres [sic] a thrilling piece of news, and one that will probably set your heart to palpitating wildly. I am up in the woods. Hundreds of thousands of people are at this very moment up in the woods and writing to their friends that they are up in the woods. This is as insipid a line as anyone could write. If it is written to anyone who is in the city, it could only make them angry or envious, and if it is written to someone in the woods, it could only be received with apathy and boredom. At any rate I am up in the woods.[228]

Metaphorically speaking, the Marx Brothers team was also "up in the woods." There was talk of other studios picking them up, but no strong offers were forthcoming. Eventually, as had happened in the past, Chico's card playing got things going again. Irving Thalberg, MGM head of production, was a bridge-playing friend of Chico's. Thalberg "decided" he wanted the Marx Brothers, although "Mr. Persuasion" (Chico) probably had something to do with it. Regardless, support from the "Boy Genius" of Hollywood—later the model for the title character of F. Scott Fitzgerald's unfinished *The Last Tycoon*—was no little accomplishment. But there would be a price. Thalberg had specific thoughts on reshaping both the team and their relationship to the story, however thin the story might be. In fact, a stronger, more plausible story was something Thalberg wanted, as well as better pacing of comic lines—to eliminate responsive audiences drowning out other comic lines. Thalberg said *Duck Soup* "was a very funny picture, but you don't need that many laughs in a movie."[229] He went on to suggest he could do twice the gross with half the jokes, if he could incorporate a more believable story. He also wanted to add a romance to interest women. (The antisocial cynicism and sometimes womanizing, sometimes misogynous nature of Depression clowns like W. C. Fields and the Marx Brothers hardly endeared them to most women.) To broaden their audience still further, Thalberg wanted the Marxes's characters made more sympathetic, something that was most specifically directed at the antisocial personae of Harpo and Groucho. Moreover, eccentric comic behavior should be more directly tied to the plot, as in the assistance of the film's romantic couple.

Though these ideas obviously received a mixed reaction from the Marxes, one Thalberg suggestion met with great enthusiasm—that they road test much of the material for their first MGM film. The Marxes's first two movies had been based on well-established stage hits that had also known extensive tours. This, of course, had not been the case with their three subsequent films. Moreover, their last film, *Duck Soup*, which had received the poorest initial reception of their work, had no doubt seemed their most tentative in production. Director McCarey's normal working habits, a product of his silent film comedy past, had involved bringing in ideas on scraps of paper and shooting material in an improvisational or nearly improvisational manner daily. Though the Marxes's *Duck Soup* entourage of writers and gagmen had somewhat blunted this approach for McCarey, he still clearly left his signature on the film. Therefore, when *Duck Soup* then did not do the business expected of it, it would seem logical this would represent more evidence for using road-tested material. Though the Marxes had handpicked McCarey, any production doubts they might have had would not be unique to them. In 1937, because of McCarey's unorthodox working style, the stars of the director's classic *The Awful Truth*, Cary Grant and Irene Dunne, attempted (unsuccessfully) to buy out of their contracts during production. But unlike *Duck Soup*, the greatness of *The Awful Truth* was recognized immediately.

In September 1934 the Marxes signed a potentially lucrative three-film contract with MGM. They would receive 15 percent of the gross profits, as opposed to the more traditional net profit deals. As the Marxes well knew after their court battle with Paramount, where net profit obligations were in question, studios could be very good at *creative* bookkeeping when it came to their figures on even the most commercially successful films. Over a year later the *New York Times* would claim MGM and the Marxes had "a peculiar type of contract" where "there would be no picture" if their material did not tour successfully.[230] But by then the Marxes's summer 1935 tour of material for *A Night at the Opera* (which the article also addressed) had been such a great success that any such stipulation, written or otherwise, was a moot point. The November 1935 release of the film underlined the point, by returning the Marxes to the world of critical and commercial film success.

A Night at the Opera is a very funny film. It contains two of the Marxes's most famous sketches—the stateroom scene, where the Brothers and everyone this side of the moon are squeezed into a munchkin-sized sleeping compartment, and the Groucho-Chico examination of a contract, something that should be part of the curricula of every law school. The film also gave new impetus to a motion picture career which, while certainly not over, had been unduly slowed. Still, the overall movie is flawed by the changes brought to the Marxes.

Some Marx Brothers texts denigrate such reservations as the qualms of cinéastes, but one has only to like the team to sense the misdirection. Or, in some cases, one has only to listen to the audience during *A Night at the Opera* screening—the stony silence that greets the early beating of Harpo (to build viewer sympathy), or the less-than-polite noises that "welcome" each Kitty Carlisle-Allan Jones love song.

In all fairness, not all these "developments" were new to the Marxes. For instance, love story subplots had burdened their films before, especially *The Cocoanuts*. (*Cocoanuts* screen adaptor Morrie Ryskind, who also co-scripted *A Night at the Opera*, defended the mixing of comedy and a love interest. See note 136.) And in *Animal Crackers* Chico and Harpo had modestly assisted the romantic couple. But the key point is that in their later, more comically stream-lined Paramount films they had either moved beyond such plot devices or drastically sublimated them. In fact, *Duck Soup* had been so stripped down that there had been neither a love interest (beyond Groucho's return to the romantic baiting of Dumont) nor the musical solos of Chico and Harpo. The toned-down love focus of *Monkey Business* and *Horse Feathers* had been made palatable by keeping it in the Marx family, with the romantic lead going to Zeppo in the former, and being shared by the Brothers in the latter.

A Night at the Opera is more disturbing, however, for putting a rational cause above their normal allegiance to pure comic anarchy. For instance, while the film is a delight when it both physically and philosophically undercuts the pomposity of high art (opera), there is a jarring inconsistency, a comic hypocrisy, about the Marxes suddenly allowing the traditional opera production to con-tinue after the right players have been substituted. One longs, instead, for the irreverent consistency of *Duck Soup*'s close where, despite the victory of their side, Freedonia, the Marxes cannot keep from bombarding Groucho patron Margaret Dumont with fruit when she begins her pompously high art rendition of their national anthem. (Originally, there had also been an opera scene scripted for *Duck Soup*.[231]) The team's nothing-sacred pelting of Dumont is unadulterated Marx Brothers. Anything less negates their comic anarchy. One can only wish they had aimed some fruit at Carlisle and Jones during *A Night at the Opera*'s conclusion.

The film is also disturbing when it attempts to give Harpo and Groucho pathos, be it the beating of Harpo by the singing villain Lassparri (Walter King) or Groucho being booted down three flights of stairs by a minor character. Such actions are not consistent with their aggressively comic personae. An excellent period demonstration of this occurs in Walt Disney's nearly parallel release of *Mickey's Polo Team* (January 4, 1936, to *A Night at the Opera*'s November 15, 1935, opening). Disney's polo cartoon has Mickey, Donald, Goofy, and the Big Bad Wolf competing against Harpo, Chaplin, and Laurel & Hardy. Harpo is easily the roughest comedy player, no small accomplishment when your competition includes the Big Bad Wolf. The cartoon Harpo's ensemble of tricks, perfectly in keeping with the live-action Paramount Harpo, includes everything from a boxing glove that springs from his hat to the coat-hidden appearance of a blowtorch (produced just as magically by the real Harpo in *Duck Soup*). The fact that the cartoon Harpo steals the show and that Disney is not exactly a poor surveyor of popular culture tastes suggest that a comically unsympathetic Harpo had not yet overstayed his welcome. Moreover, an argument could be made that *A Night at the Opera*'s success with mid-1930s audiences was not so much because of Thalberg-engineered changes but rather due to Thalberg's financial generosity. Most importantly, this meant a willingness to pay the $100,000 it would take to get George Kaufman involved in the production. For the Marxes and much of the country, Kaufman (who co-scripted with Ryskind, plus additional material by Al Boasberg) was at or near the top of America's stockpile of comedy writers. Also important was the tour, which generated both some quality material (such as the stateroom scene) as well as publicity. In fact, it seemed so successful at the time that some thought it represented the wave of the future in testing film material.[232]

Regardless of how you define its success, *A Night at the Opera* put the Marxes back on top. And as if to symbolize this rise in fortunes, a week after the film's opening Harpo, in the form of a huge balloon, appeared in the grand finale of Macy's annual Thanksgiving Day parade. Because Harpo often dominates the artistic hosannas given the group, it was also appropriate that Harpo the balloon would be held down during the parade by three Grouchos and three Chicos. Harpo the human was also involved in the parade, and from another lofty position. He provided laughter from the Macy marquee as the crowd awaited the parade. One newspaper account "predicted that Harpo, in person, will throw a comical fit when he meets himself."[233]

Thalberg's orchestration of the Brothers's next film, *A Day at the Races* (released June 1937) was also a great success, and even outgrossed *A Night at the Opera*. However, Thalberg's untimely death during the production not only saddened the Marxes, but it also left them without a sympathetic patron at MGM. Things were also less than happy on two of the three Marx Brothers home fronts. The marriage of Chico and Betty was now especially chilly. While both his nonstop affairs and his gambling were ongoing problems, the former vice was at least something that was generally limited to short-term sexual contacts as opposed to emotional relationships. For example, one Chico-Betty story which nicely demonstrates this situation finds the couple out on the town. While Chico is at the theatre, a pretty girl smiles at him and he acknowledges her with a nod but later asks Betty who it was. Betty is said to have responded along the lines of—oh, she's the one who nearly broke up our marriage last week.

While this is not exactly a story of marital bliss, it does showcase through humor a certain reluctant acceptance of Chico's infidelities. And despite his flaws, he was a very warm and funny man to be around—generous to a fault with both his companionship and his money. Though this in no way justifies his womanizing or gambling, it is not impossible to imagine a scenario where Betty, who still inexplicably loved him, could reach some reluctant acceptance of Chico's "habits." Such acceptance, however, was to change after his relationship with Ann Roth, the younger sister of Lillian Roth, the love interest of *Animal Crackers* who had found it so hard to keep a straight face while shooting with Groucho (see note 155).

Biographer Arce suggests the Chico–Ann relationship began during this film, in which the girl had a small part, but Chico's daughter claims it was a "girlish crush" (Ann was then just fourteen) that later became serious.[234] Regardless, by 1934 something serious had developed between Chico and Ann. Things came to a head after Chico had spent an inordinate amount of time in New York, allegedly on radio negotiations but primarily to visit Ann. She demanded Chico make a choice. He decided in her favor but was unable to execute the change. Chico, the team's gregarious, gambling negotiator, was not good at this kind of confrontation.

Betty fought the idea of a divorce, using everything from business (endangering the impending MGM contract—Thalberg and his actress wife Norma Shearer were fond of both Chico and Betty) to family (the needs of daughter Maxine).[235] His brothers were equally adamant. They were surprisingly loyal to Betty, considering their own womanizing ways. However, Betty's ongoing perseverance in a difficult marriage had impressed them, and no doubt reminded the brothers of the history of headaches (primarily gambling-related) Chico had caused them. Besides mentioning this checkered past, they too brought up the issue of alienating Thalberg. The key factor, though, seems to have been Betty's use of Maxine, who quite literally begged Chico not to go. Thus, his relationship with Ann was over. The strong-willed Betty, whom Harpo affectionately called "Napoleon," had won, right down to having Chico formally end the romance by phone while she listened on another line.[236] But after this it was a marriage in name only. As the alienation grew between her parents, the daughter blamed her mother.

Maxine's own estrangement from Betty was fed by her mother's tendency to take out her marital frustrations on the child.

As the second half of the 1930s progressed, Groucho's children, Arthur and Miriam, were also privy to some intense scenes between their parents. Essentially the conflict here was Ruth's increased drinking, a reflection of her difficulties in coping with marriage to Groucho. After their fights Groucho frequently told the children they were the only reason he was continuing the marriage. Ironically, both children came to *wish* strongly that their parents would divorce, though, like Maxine, they sided with their father.[237]

All was not totally dark on the domestic front. Harpo married for the first and only time September 28, 1936. The bride was actress Susan Fleming. Theirs would easily be the happiest and most successful of Marx Brothers marriages. Appropriately, one of Susan's previous starring films was the classically zany *Million Dollar Legs* (1932), which comically chronicles the politics of the land of Klopstokia, where Fleming is the daughter of the president—W. C. Fields. The film anticipates the world of *Duck Soup*'s Freedonia, though it was much more successful at the box office. Having W. C. Fields as a "father" seems to have been a good training ground for marrying a Marx Brother. Harpo and Susan would eventually adopt four children (Billy, Alex, Jimmy, and Minnie). In tribute to close friend Alexander Woollcott, Harpo gave his first son (William) the middle name Woollcott, while his second son was christened Alexander. Daughter Minnie's name honored, of course, the comedian's mother. Harpo and Susan created a strong family unit. This included authoring their own domestic Bill of Rights, which was long on comedy and gave the freedom to be unorthodox. It was just the sort of document you would expect from a raincoat-garbed Pan figure who frequently honked a horn.[238]

In the late 1930s and early 1940s the tennis skills of Arthur Marx also created much joy in the Groucho household. Arthur would evolve into one of the country's top-ranked amateur players. As early as 1937 Zeppo claimed Groucho's favorite recreation was "Bragging about Arthur's tennis."[239] A bittersweet reflection on that status is also the title of Arthur's later combination autobiography/Groucho biography—*Son of Groucho*, which would frequently be the headline wording for sports page accounts of his tennis.

The late 1930s was also the source of what was initially seen as a happy solution to Chico's gambling problem. Groucho and Harpo, who wanted both a solvent old age for Chico and a guarantee that they would not have to support him, arranged an agreement (when they re-signed with MGM in 1938) that a large portion of their older brother's income be banked. Their leverage on Chico was the double fact that Groucho and Harpo neither needed the additional funds, nor were they now as enamored of filmmaking, especially after the death of Thalberg. Conversely, the gambling, spendthrift Chico always needed the money; thus, he agreed reluctantly. Initially the plan worked and a considerable nest egg was banked, but the naturally self-destructive Chico eventually found a way around it. He ran up huge gambling bills with people who were capable of anything if they were not paid. With Chico's life literally on the edge, Groucho and Harpo relented. Chico soon had his money . . . momentarily. This was heralded as the proverbial last straw by his brothers, but, as in most close families, future aid to Chico would be forthcoming. Not surprisingly, however, in later years Chico's prodigal son nature became the number one topic of conversation between Groucho and Harpo.

Chico's amoral philosophy of life had been producing largely private family tension since before Harpo's childhood "Chico-proofing" defense of a watch by removing its hands (see note 25). But in 1937 Chico and Groucho were subjected very publicly to another ethical question. On November 1 the Brothers were convicted of copyright infringement, using gag material in a radio broadcast from a previously rejected script. Their defense was that their script had been prepared by their late friend and writer Al Boasberg, and they were unaware of any similarities with previously submitted material.

The case was closely followed in the entertainment community, something that is underlined by the large number of period articles on the trial in the Marx Brothers files at the library of the Academy of Motion Picture Arts and Sciences (Beverly Hills, California).[240] Biographer Arce claims it was the first time a Hollywood entertainer had been convicted on a charge of criminal plagiarism.[241] Academy files suggest the Brothers initially did not take the trial very seriously, treating it almost as if it were one of their movie courtroom scenes. But the seriousness of the situation was soon brought home to them, just as it was further accented by their eventual conviction. A front-page *Los Angeles Examiner* headline the following day provided a sobering, concluding overview: "Marx Bros. Fined, Escape Jail Term."[242]

Both Brothers had to pay the maximum fine of $1,000, but they also could have been given a year in jail. A serious Chico observed in the same *Examiner* article: "That's a relief. We'll be glad, Groucho and me, to shell out a thousand each. But jail—. Say, that's a terrible thought." The Los Angeles paper described an even more somber Groucho, who "smiled wryly. For once he tried to be funny and failed when he said, 'Well, I was expecting the worst, so I'm well satisfied.'"

Groucho and Chico issued a statement in which they reiterated their innocence of any intentional wrongdoing and appealed the ruling. Their conviction was upheld in April 1938, almost a year to the day after their initial indictment. By then, however, Groucho was able to put things back in a comedy perspective: "We might take it [the case] to the United States Supreme Court but it's pretty hot in Washington during the summer and they've got a rotten ball club [Washington Senators] there."[243]

The years 1936 and 1937 had thus been a roller-coaster ride for the Marxes, with such conflicting emotional events as the death of Thalberg, the marriage of Harpo, the copyright conviction, and a hit movie. Other Marx Brothers events of interest during this time include an unusual closing night, Groucho as screenwriter, and another lucrative film contract. The closing in question was the

August 18, 1936, end of their *A Day at the Races* road show (the stage testing of film material which had begun with *A Night at the Opera* having been continued). Three things made this appearance especially memorable. First, Harpo broke a long stage silence and made a curtain speech at the production's close. Second, the anarchical Marxes practiced what they preached "by destroying all their scenery and stage props before the amazed spectators."[244] And third, the mad final show seemed a fitting metaphor for a mad period of testing material. This is best summarized by merely noting the title of a *Variety* article on the closing: "Marx Bros. Use 11 Different Acts in 11 Shows in Windup Vaude Wk."[245] It was also appropriate that the tour should have such a resounding finale, because road tests would not be fully supported after Thalberg's death. Without their mentor, the team found that MGM would claim road tours were too expensive. Thus, the Marxes were made to help subsidize tours for both *Go West* and *At the Circus* (their last road testing of movie material). Whether as a rationalization for the change in policy or merely as added support, Chico had observed there was a problem in having new material stolen when showcased in public long before it was committed to film.[246]

In 1937 Groucho co-scripted an innocuous film comedy with close family friend and writer Norman Krasna, who later would author *Dear Ruth*. Entitled *The King and the Chorus Girl*, it was a quasi-screwball comedy at a time when that genre was at the height of its popularity. Of more interest, however, were superficial story parallels with the then-recent abdication of King Edward VIII of England for the love of a commoner, Wallis Simpson. But Groucho and Krasna's work, which originally had been titled *Grand Passion*, had been written before what was then called "the story of the century." *The King and the Chorus Girl* was produced by Warner Brothers, with Mervyn LeRoy directing and featured Joan Blondell, Fernand Gravet, Edward Everett Horton, and Jane Wyman in the principal parts. Besides the appropriateness of a solo Marx Brother being attracted to the screwball genre, there were few discernible Groucho touches, other than a well-placed pun or two.

That same year Marx Brother agent Zeppo negotiated a very profitable contract with RKO for his Brothers to star in the film adaptation of the hit Broadway play *Room Service*. (The team had fulfilled their initial MGM contract.) The deal generated a lot of attention because the $225,000 RKO had paid for *Room Service* was at that time the highest purchasing price ever for film rights to a play. Zeppo, who had already become a very successful agent on his own, regularly used a comically self-disparaging remark in bargaining for his Brothers—when negotiations stalled he threatened to return to the team. The line was reminiscent of the Zeppo jokes that used to circulate every time his retirement from performing seemed imminent. One such example would have Groucho telling their current producer he had bad news . . . Zeppo was quitting. But when the really pleased producer would comfort Groucho with a restrained "that is not so bad" answer, the comedian would lower the zinger: their asking price would now, of course, go up. That Zeppo could use a variation of this gag in his new career is probably the best indication of the confidence he was now feeling.

There were to have been three RKO films, but *Room Service* (1938) did not work as a Marx Brothers picture. As Chico observed late the next year in a *New York Sun* interview, "It was the first time we had tried doing a play we hadn't created ourselves. And we were no good. We can't do that. We've got to originate the characters and the situations ourselves."[247] In another 1939 article the team called *Room Service* their "worst" film "because it was too sane [a traditional, straight comedy], and we had always to be thinking of the plot!"[248] *Room Service* would be their only RKO picture.

The Brothers would return to MGM for three more films before their first retirement from movies. The films were *At the Circus* (1939), *Go West* (1940), and *The Big Store* (1941). Though often entertaining, and an improvement upon *Room Service*, the films were not on a par with their earlier movies. The Thalberg formula, without Thalberg present at least to guarantee the maximum in quality (such as paying the $100,000 necessary to bring Kaufman briefly west for *A Night at the Opera*), resulted in merely average comedies. Marx Brothers scholar Thomas H. Jordan observed that Groucho's rallying cry to his brothers in *Go West*, "Come on, miracle men," as they go off to grant the heroine's requested miracle, is "perhaps the most depressing line ever delivered in a Marx film." That is, "For anyone hoping for a comic miracle in *Go West* that line spells disaster. With it they explicitly cancel their free spirits and irreverent characters and align themselves in a good guys-bad guys confrontation."[249] Jordan is remiss only in not stating that this kind of situation is a frequent problem in all the Marxes's MGM films. However, it is most pronounced in the last three that they made for the company. In fact, disappointment over *At the Circus* provoked long-time Groucho friend and correspondent Dr. Samuel Salinger to write the comedian about the Marxes "being chained to the same routine" and "The trouble with all of your pictures is that when you boys aren't doing your stuff the supporting cast, story and action fall to unprecedented depths."[250]

Writing could have made the difference. There are rare moments in these last films that rival their best work, such as the opening of *Go West*, where Groucho attempts to swindle Chico and Harpo for the extra money he needs for a train ticket west. By a convenient comedy coincidence, Harpo also needs additional funds for his ticket. As is the team's comedy norm, wheeler-dealer Groucho runs amuck when he interacts with his wise fool Brothers. But the film then goes nowhere until its inspired racing train finale, when Harpo's trusty ax and the disposable wooden railroad cars keep them in fuel. The ending undoubtedly was inspired in part by Buster Keaton's epic train classic *The General*. Moreover, as Marx film critic Allen Eyles has observed, despite the funny close, "it would be just about as amusing if it features Abbott and Costello or Martin and Lewis."[251] But at this point in the Brothers's film career, anything funny seemed to outweigh the distinctly "Marxian" approach.

Not surprisingly, in October 1939, just prior to the production of *Go West*, Groucho wrote to friend and author Arthur Sheekman and his wife: "The boys at the studio have lined up another turkey for us. . . . I saw the present one [*At the Circus*] the other day and . . . on leaving the theater, vowed that I'd never see it again."[252] Such feelings hardly make for enthusiastic filmmaking. While some strong comedy writing probably would have changed that, it was also true that team members were all at or near fifty years of age and feeling it. Thus, earlier in 1939 Groucho had written Sheekman:

> I'm getting too old for rushes [the daily screening of the just completed unedited film footage]—the projection rooms, or at least the ones they give us, are either a long climb, or in an air-conditioned cellar, and I've decided to wait until the picture plays the Marquis before seeing it. At least if I don't like it, I might win the [raffled] Chevrolet.[253]

Groucho was not, however, at a loss for things to do. In another 1939 letter, this time to Dr. Salinger, he apologized for not having written earlier: "I've been shooting all day [*At the Circus*] and pounding out radio scripts in off hours."[254] Despite the copyright conviction, Groucho and Chico were still in demand on radio.

During the first half of 1939 Groucho and Chico were regulars on a big-budget, one-hour radio program called *The Circle* (also known as *The Kellogg Show*, for the production's sponsor). As the title, *The Circle*, suggests in part, the program was a celebrity round table, where entertainment stars discussed an assortment of subjects, from the arts to death and taxes. The Brothers were a popular part of *The Circle*, with probably the most commented-upon contribution being the Sunday night they improvised their normally six-minute spot into nearly twice its length. Though Groucho and Chico regularly mixed scripted material with ad-libs, this was ambitious even for them.

This comedy "success," a term contested by some of *The Circle*'s preempted guests, seems to follow a formula that *New York Post* writer Aaron Stein had prescribed for them in 1937. In a rave review of Groucho and Chico's guest appearance on the *Lanny Ross-Charles Butterworth Show*, Stein suggests:

> The ideal arrangement would be to have them guest star on some show at least once a week. Turn them loose on an established series and they tear it apart . . . they are at their very funny best when they are given some form of orderly procedure to disrupt.[255]

Appropriately, Stein has articulated the reason for the Marxes's success in any medium. He might only have added that their comedy works best when the "orderly procedure" has grown pompously self-important, which would seem to have been the case with *The Circle* program. Stein's hypothesis on why they had not yet succeeded as radio regulars was their need to self-destruct somebody else's world. Inadvertently, however, he also offered another possible reason. His lengthy opening bemoans the fact that Harpo is hardly appropriate for radio and looks forward to the day when television will be in every home and "the air will be full of Harpo Marx . . . just the thing we need to clear the air."[256] Certainly the sense of an incomplete set of Marx Brothers did not aid the Brothers's radio onslaughts, with regard to their own program. Consistent with this is the fact that the only sustained success Marx radio programs had were Groucho's 1940s accomplishments as a solo.

By 1940 Groucho had decided radio was his future. In another letter to Arthur Sheekman, Groucho observed:

> I'm shaping my ambitions in other directions [from film] and discussing a radio show that I might do with Irving Brecker. It's kind of Aldrich Family except that we hope to make it a little funnier. By that I don't mean joke, joke, joke but a kind of human interest story with a slightly wacky father, who, of course, would be me.[257]

Brecher later described the program as "a family comedy . . . the first comedy on radio where the father was amusing."[258] Sponsors were not forthcoming, but the program later became very popular under the title of *The Life of Riley*, with William Bendix playing the put-upon father. While Brecher possibly overestimated the first-time nature of this type of radio father, it was still a fairly fresh radio concept which also, in part, reflected the view Groucho had of himself at home. His son Arthur observed that the domestic Groucho of this period "enjoyed" very much "playing the [comic] martyr."[259] For example, when Arthur's sister Miriam once remarked how funny the Ritz Brothers were, Groucho comically feigned indignation and told his traitorous daughter that maybe the Ritz Brothers could buy her that new bike she wanted.[260]

This comic antihero development needs to be focused upon, because it is an apt description of the increased comedy writing (for print) Groucho would do in the early 1940s. There would be another comedy book (*Many Happy Returns: An Unofficial Guide to Your Income-Tax Problems*, 1942) and the publication of numerous freelance works, especially in *This Week*, the Sunday supplement of the *New York Herald Tribune*. (See Chapter 3 of this volume for reprint examples of this work.) Thus, in August 1941 Groucho wrote to fellow cynic Samuel Salinger: "Despite your sneers at my literary efforts, I'm constantly implored by most of the important national weeklies to contribute to their pages."[261] The same letter also mentioned writing a play with Norman Krasna, what would later become *Time for Elizabeth*.

While the worldly-wise movie wise guy Groucho does not divorce himself from these writings, except for the much subdued father in *Time for Elizabeth*, Groucho the author addresses more the everyday frustrations of the average person, in turn revealing the comedian's similar victimization. He comically denies this in the opening of *Many Happy Returns*: "This book . . . was not written for the average man. It was written only for the fellow who can scrape up a dollar."[262] And one can even see the recycling of a Groucho wise guy movie scene. That is, early in *Many Happy Returns* he builds a comedy diatribe against the possible nature of the prospective reader (which escalates from "Dear Reader" to "swine"), just as he had done in *Duck Soup*, when he becomes more and more comically angry about a possible insult from Ambassador Trentino (Louis Calhern).[263] But his selection of subject matter, both in this book (and in such later works as the *Memoirs of a Mangy Lover*, 1963) as well as his early 1940s freelance material, which addresses everything from faulty body parts ("Groucho Marx Turns Himself in for Scrap") to thoughtless guests ("Do You Know Enough to Go Home?") points at the frustrations of the antihero.[264] Thus, the aggression of this comedy is more often directed at the insanity of a given situation, such as the tax program, as opposed to an individual comedy victim.

This antihero focus might best be capsulized by a literary-related request in another Groucho letter to Salinger. Groucho's son Arthur was to be visiting the Chicago surgeon shortly, and the comedian requested his friend take the young man to Clarence Day's *Life with Father*.[265] Day was one of the pioneer anti-heroic writers. *The* American humor historian Walter Blair includes him in *The New Yorker* pantheon (with Robert Benchley, James Thurber, and S. J. Perelman) that was most responsible for helping usher in this comedy phenomenon.[266] Day's *Life with Father* is also something of a look at antiheroic roots, revealing the beginnings of this comedy even in one of those seemingly more capable Yankee fathers of the past—just the sort of antihero insight an interested party (like Groucho) might want his son to see. The Marx Brothers also played an important, though often unappreciated, role in the evolution of the comic antihero in American humor (see Chapter 2, "The Marx of Time"). But the most traditional image of the antiheroic (frustration) when related to the Marxes invariably focuses on Groucho, either in his comic film problems at the hands of his Brothers, or in his solo writing for print.

The term antiheroic might also be used to describe Groucho's widely quoted reason for the first breakup of the team. Announced during the film production of *The Big Store* (1941, but then sometimes entitled *Bargain Basement*), Groucho observed in the April 10, 1941 *Los Angeles Herald*:

> When I say we're sick of the movies, I mean the people are about to get sick of us. By getting out now, we're just anticipating public demand, and by a very short margin. Our stuff simply is growing stale. So are we.[267]

Marx spokesperson Groucho, who was speaking between takes on *The Big Store* set with Brothers Chico and Harpo in attendance, went on to add:

> What happened to us was that we were defeated by our own speciality. The fake mustache, the dumb harp player and the little guy who chased the ladies, all were funny at first. [He seems to have inadvertently referred to Harpo's character twice. If "harp" is changed to "piano," Chico will be represented.] But it became successively harder with each picture to top the one before. We couldn't get out of the groove, without getting out of the movies. So we decided to get all the way out.
>   It means splitting up a team . . . a team of brothers . . . and that means a

certain amount of sadness. But everything passes, sadness included. Anyhow, I prefer never to work again than to make another Marx Brothers picture.[268]

Groucho's strong close to this quote indirectly reveals what only time could demonstrate about his comments—that he was the one Brother most bothered by being typed as the "fake mustache" sort. He would be the only one to reject actively continuing the delightful cartoon-like physical characteristics and actions of his character in the future. For example, in an August 11, 1942, letter he explained to Samuel Salinger why he rejected a Broadway show that had been expressly written for him: "The play wasn't bad but it didn't fill what I wanted. I wanted to play a legitimate character and they wrote a musical-comedy Groucho, so I asked them to let me out."[269] Moreover, both when his later popular radio program *You Bet Your Life* debuted, and then when it moved to television, Groucho had to fight the demands of others that he resurface in his frock coat and his greasepaint mustache and eyebrows. When the program's head writer Bernie Smith (though credited as a director so as to not distract from what was to be an ad-lib image) initially made such a demand in 1947 for the radio program, Groucho responded: "The hell I will. That character's dead. I'll never go into that again."[270] When the program moved to television (in 1950, though continuing concurrently for a time on radio), the same demands were made by others. Though not without a point—home viewers would now, after all, be able to see Groucho—the comedian would not be swayed. *You Bet Your Life* director Robert Dwan later said of the new Groucho:

Playing himself and not a clown was a major change in his whole [comedy] approach. Now he established a whole new Groucho character. It was partly based on Dr. Hackenbush [Groucho's character in *A Day at the Races*] and the others [the various movie variations of the until then standard Groucho persona] but this was not the same guy at all, and it allowed him to do things and to react in other ways.[271]

This new Groucho was not unrelated to his comically more subdued, sometimes antiheroic, author and his image of himself as frustrated father. Groucho is not without an occasional regression to the past persona, such as the return of the Marxes in *A Night in Casablanca* (1946), but this was much less the case after the beginning of *You Bet Your Life*.

Conversely, Harpo and Chico essentially maintained their Marx Brothers personae for the rest of their careers. In fact, probably the most famous non-team appearance made by either Harpo or Chico involved recycled movie material. A May 1955 television appearance on *I Love Lucy* had Lucy and Harpo recreating the mirror scene from *Duck Soup*, the key variation merely being that the common costume was now Harpo's, as opposed to the look-alike Grouchos of the film. Harpo also did a harp rendition of "Take Me Out to the Ball Game" (a song which figured prominently in the Marxes's *A Night at the Opera*), and

Fred (William Frawley) and Ricky (Desi Arnaz) appeared in the television finale dressed as Chico and Groucho, respectively.

Ironically, at the time of the announced breakup (1941), Harpo also seemed directed toward straight entertainment. The two most frequently mentioned Harpo projects at that time were joining Alexander Woollcott in a limited stage revival of *The Yellow Jacket* (for British war relief) and in *The Man Who Came to Dinner*, with the friends playing characters based upon themselves. But Harpo's regression to type during two productions of *The Yellow Jacket* nicely foreshadowed his future loyalty to his characters, because, if Harpo could return to "Marxism" during a Chinese ritual drama, where he played "The Property Man" in Chinese costume and make-up, then it was not likely that any future role would ever sufficiently divorce him from his preferred character.[272]

Chico's post-movie team career was touring with "his" band, though as a rave March 1942 *Cleveland Press* review observed, after noting his comedy at the piano produces "applause in a volume rarely accorded these days," Chico was essentially a comedy front for the orchestra.[273] Chico's daughter Maxine later described his contribution as opening with some jokes, introducing the show, pretending to conduct, calmly eating a banana near center stage, and eventually doing his piano solo.[274] There was no denying Chico's drawing power, however; Groucho was even moved to observe in a November 1942 letter that his brother's "success is extremely gratifying to us [the Marx Brothers]."[275] As with Harpo, Chico drew upon his Marx Brothers movie identity past. He wore the same comedy costume, featured his patented piano solo, and even titled his act "Chico Marx and his Ravellies," Revelli having been his name in both *Animal Crackers* and *The Big Store* (at the time the most recently and purportedly last of the team's films).

Chico was on the road for three reasons. First and foremost was the need to earn an income. Unlike his two performing Brothers, whose savings allowed them more leisure in any future career moves, Chico's gambling necessitated an ongoing salary. Second, touring enabled him to leave what had become an untenable situation at home. His relationship with wife Betty had not survived the Ann Roth affair. Third, after a lifetime of touring, Chico purported to enjoy the road, though in an interview just prior to the debut of "Chico Marx and his Ravellies" at Brooklyn's Flatbush Theatre there was a treadmill sadness in his observation: "I like to work, so I decided on the band and I'm just where I started thirty years ago, pounding the piano keys."[276] The boy who had started his piano "tricks" (such as the trademark "shooting the keys") in order to break the boredom of practice, stating, "Even good music will get stale if hammered out continuously," had returned to being a solo.[277]

Chico's vagabond existence was in marked contrast to the world of Harpo and Groucho. Harpo and wife Susan would adopt three of their four children (Alexander, James, and Minnie) in the early 1940s. And while Groucho and Ruth separated in late 1941 and divorced the following year, Groucho was given custody of Arthur and Miriam. After Arthur entered the service, Miriam would be official hostess of the house and an occasional Groucho "date" at special events.

In conjunction with the economic freedom of Chico's Brothers, both Groucho and Harpo spent a great deal of time entertaining troops stateside during World War II. In a letter from June 1943, Groucho describes this activity:

> We are knee-deep in service camps and, although the work is arduous and tiring, the audiences are an inspiration and I feel that I am making a minute contribution to the war effort. I would go to the Blood Bank but I doubt whether they would accept anything that runs through my veins.[278]

Groucho showcased more of his war effort by attaching to the letter an anti-heroic article he had authored on the trials and tribulations of tending his Victory Garden (an activity then encouraged among all citizens). Unfortunately, Groucho's garden just was not growing:

> I have scattered cow dung, Hitler's speeches and most of Du Pont's more expensive chemicals over their stunted growths, but so far all I have to show for my trouble is a small bed of wild marihuana, a sprig of mint and a dislocation of the trunk muscles that has an excellent chance of developing into a full-blown rupture.[279]

Groucho was also busy in radio. He was a regular guest on the *Rudy Vallee-Joan Davis Sealtest Show* during 1941 and 1942. In addition, he was guesting on the radio programs of such other stars as Bob Hope and Bing Crosby. But he was eager to have his own program. Besides wanting to succeed in this medium as he had in every other, he felt radio was a "very soft racket." According to Arthur, his father was especially taken with radio because one did not have to memorize lines or apply makeup and wear costumes, and there were minimal rehearsals.[280]

He finally received his own program in 1943—*The Pabst Show*, a half-hour variety program sponsored by Pabst Blue Ribbon Beer. A November 1943 letter described how he was able to combine radio and entertaining the troops: "We play a camp every other week . . . [and] we not only do a radio show [from location] but afterward we put on a vaudeville show."[281] The same letter noted how he was also regularly involved with a number of overseas shows like *Mail Call*, which were shortwaved to servicemen.

Unfortunately, Groucho was only with *The Pabst Show* for a year, being replaced by Danny Kaye in 1944. Groucho sometimes insinuated that he was replaced because of what he had managed to do to the nervous main speaker at the one-hundredth anniversary celebration of Pabst in February 1944. Groucho had gotten the elderly son of the founder, Edward Pabst, mildly drunk . . . on Miller's Beer.

With this development Groucho's focus again became service camps. And the popularity of his appearances seems to have played a large part in the film reteaming of Groucho, Chico, and Harpo for 1946's *A Night in Casablanca*. This is significant because Marx Brothers literature invariably credits the reteaming as an act of charity for the (as always) financially troubled Chico. While helping Chico was no doubt a factor, Groucho stated in a 1945 letter:

> The first thing I'm asked when I play service camps is, "When are you fellows going to make another picture?" As a matter of fact, this was one of the reasons for my return to the screen. . . . I don't care for movie acting and I'm not particularly eager about any other kind (other than radio and service camps) so I am doing this partly for my bank roll and partly for the boys—and when I say "the boys," I'm not referring to Harpo, Chico and Gummo.[282]

A Night in Casablanca was an independent production distributed by United Artists, with the Brothers receiving a percentage of the profits. While this comic tale of hidden Nazi loot was not the Marx Brothers at their best, the general critical consensus was that it was just good to have them back. The now celebrated critic James Agee summed it up best in his review in *The Nation*: "the worst they might ever make would be better worth seeing than most other things I can think of."[283]

The film probably has become most famous for the series of letters Groucho purportedly wrote to the Warner Brothers legal department concerning the studio's supposed contesting of the title use of Casablanca. The issue was whether Warners, because of its earlier classic film *Casablanca* (1942), had exclusive rights to titular use of the city. The question generated a great deal of comic interest in both 1945 (when the film was in preproduction) and 1967, the year when some of Groucho's correspondence was published in book form, with the comedian's responses to the Warners opening the volume.[284]

Groucho's Warner letters are indeed humorous, fluctuating from comic outrage to outrageous comedy. For example, he asserts that if Warner Brothers has exclusive rights to Casablanca, then the Marxes have a similar claim to Brothers, because "Professionally, we were brothers long before you were."[285] But in an obviously unpublished 1945 letter to longtime correspondent Samuel Salinger, Groucho revealed:

> We spread the story that Warners objected to this title purely for publicity reasons. They may eventually actually object to it, although I don't think so. . . . At any rate, the publicity has been wonderful on it and it was a happy idea. I wish they would sue, but, as it is, we've had reams in the papers.[286]

Groucho nearly received his wish. Warners eventually lodged a formal complaint, but it was ironed out quickly in arbitration.[287]

While the Warner Brothers controversy had been manufactured (at least initially) in secret, Groucho was also involved in a much more public event in 1945; he married for the second time. The bride, Kay Marie Dittig Gorcey, was the former wife of "Dead End Kid" Leo Gorcey, and Groucho's daughter Miriam had inadvertently played matchmaker. Kay, who was not much older than Miriam, was trapped in an abusive relationship with Gorcey. Miriam played social worker and offered her friend sanctuary. Unfortunately for Miriam, when a relationship developed between her father and Kay, followed by marriage and then by the 1946 birth of a daughter (Melinda), Miriam felt very much displaced. For a possessive daughter who had been acting as hostess of the Groucho domain it was a difficult series of events to handle. It no doubt contributed to her growing dependence upon alcohol, something she later chillingly credited to fulfilling her father's low opinion of women.

In 1947 Chico suffered a heart attack while performing in Las Vegas, though it has been claimed the "attack" was really a hoax to get himself out of town before he lost more money gambling. The flaw in the false attack story is that Chico never knew when to stop. Regardless of exactly what happened, Chico's gambling-need to work-gambling treadmill had led to heart problems in 1947. He would go into temporary retirement under the care of his then companion and later wife, Mary DeVithas.

At a time (1947) when one Marx Brother was officially retired and another was generally acting the part (Harpo), Groucho's career as a solo was just now about to begin. It was merely on a radio quiz show, and many felt it a great comedown for the former president of Freedonia and other lofty comedy titles. Groucho himself observed privately, "It's not too distinguished a set up, but you know me, I have no shame."[288]

The show was, of course, *You Bet Your Life.* And while Groucho's stake was not exactly his life, it was certainly taking a career risk. *Newsweek* later observed: "Marx fans mourned that it was like selling Citation to the glue factory."[289] But the quiz show format proved a perfect entertainment setting for an older, more subdued Groucho for comically conversing with and kidding noncelebrity guests, the actual quiz itself being of decidedly secondary importance. First broadcast October 27, 1947, the program started slowly but by recording it long and then editing it down for pace (which would be continued later when it moved to television), it caught on in popularity.[290] *Newsweek*, which, like many other publications, had initially panned the program, eventually featured the *You Bet Your Life* Groucho on its cover (May 15, 1950), stating, "the program has turned Marx back up an amazing comeback road. And he, in turn, has given radio a real transfusion."[291] Their cover page caption said it with more comically metaphorical wit, however: "Groucho Marx: A Sharp Knife in Stale Cake."

At one point in ninety-second place among commercial radio ratings, it was at the time of the *Newsweek* cover article number six.[292] In fact, as was befitting a Marx Brother, *You Bet Your Life*'s commercial popularity even had a touch of the bizarre. Groucho lost his first sponsor (Elgin-American) because he was *too* popular. Insofar as Elgin-American could not keep up with the product demand created by the program's popularity, the company figured, why keep advertising? With a "problem" like that Groucho and company had no trouble attracting the

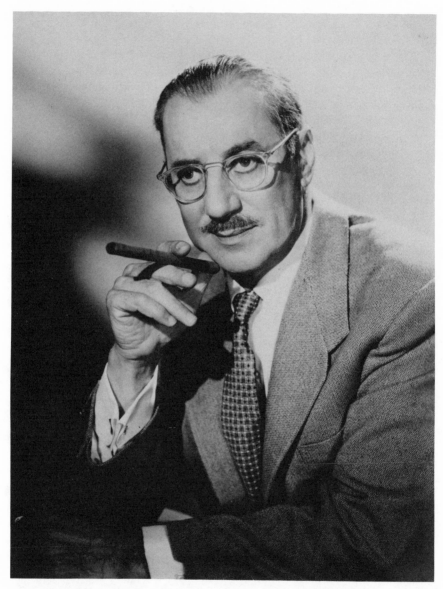

8. Groucho during the long run of *You Bet Your Life*. (Photograph courtesy of the Wisconsin Center for Film and Theater Research.)

sponsor De Soto-Plymouth. Critically, the success was equally impressive. In 1949 Groucho received radio's greatest tribute—a Peabody Award as best entertainer. In 1951 he received television's highest honor—an Emmy for most outstanding personality.

Besides *Newsweek*'s 1950 cover story, the year was especially memorable for several other reasons. Probably most significant, especially for a little boy who had always saved his pennies, was the amazingly lucrative contract Groucho signed to jump networks, from CBS to NBC (his original program had debuted on ABC). NBC guaranteed Groucho "$760,000 annually over a ten-year period, and in addition . . . when the program is on the air, $4,800 weekly for 39 weeks a year . . . [plus] 38 per cent of its profit on the *You Bet Your Life* package."[293]

This year also marked the first appearance of a book-length biography of the team (Crichton's *The Marx Brothers*), the American release of their last film (*Love Happy*), and *You Bet Your Life*'s achieving the dual status of both radio *and* television show. All these may or may not have been factors, but Groucho's Emmy was for this most visible (1950) year.

On the serious side, this was also the year he went through his second divorce. Citing mental cruelty, Groucho received the divorce decree May 12. Interestingly enough, among his charges was: "It was necessary for me to run the house. I did everything, ordered the meals, kept the servants in line, did the marketing and things like that."[294] These were items his first wife Ruth often had difficulty doing because of Groucho's interest in the home. Other complaints included his wife's not going out with him, seldom attending his weekly radio show, and avoiding his visitors to their home. Groucho's corroborating witness was his brother and personal business manager Gummo, who would later in the year help orchestrate the lucrative NBC contract.

Without turning this into a catalogue of Groucho cover stories, it is especially important to note that the following year (December 31, 1951) he graced the front of *Time* magazine. This event might be accorded credit as the topping accolade on his road to solo success. Nearly twenty years before (August 15, 1932) he was one of four brothers showcased on *Time*'s cover; he alone was now front and center. And just as significantly, it was not as a character in costume but rather as he appeared in real life.

The 1951 cover article did not mention the earlier *Time* honor, but its opening remarks brought it readily to mind. Whereas the 1932 article had most highlighted Harpo, this piece noted:

> Professionally, the other Marx Brothers haven't worn nearly so well. Harpo, once the rage of several continents, has just finished a series of television commercials for a milk company; Chico does his hoary piano routine and Eyetalian dialect around nightclubs; Gummo, who quit the act for good to become a World War I doughboy, is his brother's agent; Zeppo, now out of show business altogether, manufactures airplane parts.[295]

You Bet Your Life had truly accorded Groucho an entertainment rebirth.

While the program is still popular in syndication today (the original *You Bet Your Life* ran until 1961), two long-term controversies continue to surface: the nature of his comedy target guests and the show's publicized ad-lib nature.

The premise of the first complaint was essentially that the movie Groucho used insult humor against appropriate, deserving subjects, from stuffy society matrons to crooked big business financiers. Essentially, anyone who took himself too seriously was a valid target. In contrast, the argument continues, Groucho's television show unleashed these insults upon the average everyday person, who became an undeserving victim instead of a comic target.

Obviously, the show's ongoing popularity puts proponents of this position in the minority. But it still merits a brief rebuttal, keying upon a foundation already established in this chapter—that the television Groucho was not quite the same as the movie fellow. First, he is obviously an older, more subdued individual, both in appearance and actions. Sitting atop a long-legged stool, without either the showstopping greasepaint or the patented loping walk, his comic cynicism does not register as unduly aggressive. Groucho himself observed: "That small box [a television set] is no place for frenetic comedy. Casual shows like ours are the ones that last."[296] At the risk of sounding blasphemous, his soft voice and high perch sometimes even make him seem positively fragile.

Second, the movie Groucho at his best buries his comedy target under an avalanche of words. On television he lets the comedy victims be their own worst enemies—they are the ones who talk. As Groucho noted: "I don't prod. When some contestant puts his foot in his mouth, I just push it in a little further."[297]

Third, on those occasions when the television Groucho seems more like his movie version, the targets are also generally similar. That is, the *You Bet Your Life* guest is usually Mr. Average. But there are occasional minor celebrities. On those occasions Groucho admitted:

> Sure, I'll go after a visiting fireman, say a big-shot politician or something. The audience loves that . . . it's their alter ego at work. How often do you get a chance to insult a big-shot stuffed shirt—and before 30,000,000 people.[298]

Fourth, unlike the movie Groucho, who could never go too far with an insult, the *You Bet Your Life* star is more sensitive to decorum. For example, his program conversation with a retired admiral, whom he had been needling, revealed that the man had been a naval hero. Groucho promptly responded, mildly penitent: "Well, that's about as big a thrill as anybody could have. I didn't know you were quite that much of a war hero. I wouldn't have cracked all those bum jokes about you."[299] Groucho later explained, "I wasn't taking any chances in case any listener might have been offended."[300]

Fifth, while the movie Groucho is most often self-serving, the television Groucho seems, through the vehicle of the show, to try to be genuinely helpful. Thus, as quiz shows go, the *You Bet Your Life* questions are not that difficult. The guest couple could also discuss the question between them. And, if they still failed, there was always a consolation prize dependent upon merely answering a gag question, such as "Who is buried in Grant's Tomb?" or "Who is the President?" That this is, indeed, a softer Groucho is best echoed by what he invariably says on these occasions: "Nobody leaves here broke." Moreover, the show even has a benevolent stuffed duck that occasionally drops from nowhere with a one hundred dollar bill if a guest happens to say that night's secret word. ("It's a common word, something you see every day.")

Sixth, a final corollary to this issue of Groucho's personae must note that by the 1950s, if not earlier, the comedian had become so synonymous with the comic insult that people were more apt to be upset if they were *not* insulted, at least mildly.[301] This public affection helps explain the ongoing popularity of both the show and Groucho himself. By seeming to reveal the man behind the greasepaint mask, *You Bet Your Life* gave Groucho greater popularity than he had ever known. Thus, instead of Thalberg's flawed attempt to soften the comically harder movie Groucho, one now had a *new*, more benevolent figure who did not seem an effrontery to what had gone before. The always insightful Marx Brothers critic Allen Eyles was even so moved as to state, "Groucho decisively abandoned the old screen image to become a friendly, avuncular figure, if with a roguish eye for the prettier guests."[302]

The second *You Bet Your Life* controversy focuses on the show's ad-lib nature. Though Groucho had always had talent along these lines, and his ability to ad-lib with Bob Hope during a 1947 radio special had originally attracted producer John Guedel (the man behind *You Bet Your Life*) to the comedian, the show was hardly the pure ad-lib vehicle it originally was purported to be. Guests were coached on what to say to Groucho, and the comedian (without meeting contestants beforehand) was prepared for these comedy feeds with appropriate jokes based upon the background of the guests. An off-screen blackboard with cues further helped Groucho with his "ad-libs." The show was not, however, without real Groucho ad-libs. Moreover, because an hour of footage was shot (on film) each week, there was the comic freedom to pick from a large assortment of material, scripted and otherwise. (This editing process also acted as an unofficial program censor, inasmuch as Groucho's real ad-libs would be blue, at least by 1950s standards.)

The interesting thing about the ad-lib controversy is that it persists. As early as a 1954 *TV Guide* cover article, entitled "The Truth About Groucho's Ad Libs," the situation has been public knowledge.[303] This brief essay assumed a positive, upbeat position on the issue, praising (defending?) the show for bringing the audience the professionally best entertainment possible. The uncredited author of the article could not resist, however, recycling an in-the-know gag about the program's ad-lib nature: "That show has all the spontaneity of a Swiss watch."[304] But besides being both funny and to the point, the Swiss watch metaphor also reinforces the article's praise of the program's professional quality. In addition, when the *TV Guide* author still states "that the show seemingly has more genuine spontaneity than any other major show on the air," he has also unintentionally provided a key clue for the ongoing ad-lib controversy. That is, for comedy to be effective it needs to be spontaneous *or* at least seem that way. And though Groucho was a great ad-libber, he was equally adept at making scripted material seem like it was off-the-cuff, something which also has been examined earlier in his stage work. Thus, a logical hypothesis as to why one continues to run into articles revealing "The Truth About Groucho's Ad Libs" is that viewers no doubt continue to be surprised that so much of *You Bet Your Life* was preplanned.

One interesting outgrowth of this issue of planned "spontaneity" is an additional point for the defense that the television Groucho is not too hard on his guests. Because the contestants are part of a largely prepackaged program (and not randomly selected from the audience that evening, as home viewers once thought), they are hardly, as comedian/author Steve Allen observed, "Unwilling" victims made "to cower before the rapier wit of the cruel master."[305] But regardless as to one's feelings on these issues, *You Bet Your Life* was one of the most popular programs of the 1950s. And as Groucho had said in a letter back in that pivotal 1950, "to come up with a spectacular success after all these years I find enormously satisfying."[306]

Though all but forgotten now, in Groucho's first season on television (1950–1951), he was not the only Marx Brother appearing regularly on the small screen. Chico had a live, half-hour musical comedy on ABC entitled *The College Bowl*, in which he was cast as the owner of a campus soda shop. Having come out of retirement the previous year because he needed the money, Chico and *The College Bowl* produced no long-term support; the show was canceled after a single season. The campus setting justified the large, young supporting cast, which included a teenaged Andy Williams. Chico retained the piano and his Italian accent, but it was a low-budget show that did not showcase him to his best advantage.

Periodically, Chico and Harpo played some nightclub dates together. The act was largely bits and pieces from their movies with, of course, their musical solos. Though Harpo did not need the money, his teaming with Chico was not merely obliging a hungry brother. He genuinely needed to perform periodically, something also revealed by his ongoing involvement in benefit shows. His son Billy later revealed another reason behind one of the most ambitious Chico-Harpo teamings, their three-month 1949 tour of the British vaudeville circuit, topped off with a month's stand at the London Palladium.[307]

It seems Billy was fascinated by the comic vaudeville tales that Groucho, Chico, and Harpo forever reminisced about whenever they got together. Vaudeville became some sort of magic land for Billy. Thus, when the boy was twelve (the year poets sometimes mark as the end of childhood, though Harpo was an ongoing argument against this fancy), Harpo decided Billy should see what vaudeville was like firsthand. Billy and his mother Susan accompanied Harpo and Chico on tour, with the boy even being given a small part in the act. Dressed as an angel, he would roll out his father's harp when it was time for the solo. As he exited the stage, he was also given his own laugh, because the backside of this angel had the sign "EAT AT REVELLI'S CAFÉ."[308]

While one of the Marx Brothers's sons was learning about the trade firsthand, another would soon be chronicling it—Arthur wrote the well-received biography *Life with Groucho* in 1954. No doubt inspired by his father's great respect for writers, the former tennis star and World War II veteran was just now beginning to come into his own as a writer. Though it was an entertaining, warmly written look at his father, a more complete picture would not appear until the 1972 appearance of the darker *Son of Groucho*. (Though both works have been drawn upon for this chapter, see also Chapter 4, "A Marx Brothers Bibliographical Essay," for a more pointed comparison.)

The same year *Life with Groucho* appeared, the comedian married for the third time. The bride was Eden Hartford, whom he had met on the 1951 set of his film *A Girl in Every Port* (1952). Eden's fashion model/actress sister Dee Hartford (and later wife of film director Howard Hawks) had a role in the movie. Once again there would be a threesome in the home, paralleling the earlier combination of Groucho, daughter Miriam, and second wife Kay. This time the grouping was Groucho, second daughter Melinda (by Kay), and Eden. Though custody of Melinda had originally gone to her mother in the 1950 divorce, it returned to Groucho in 1952 after Kay had developed a drinking problem, unfortunately following in the paths of Ruth and Miriam Marx.

Eden hardly represented the displacement figure to Melinda that Kay had symbolized to Miriam. While the mid-twenties Eden was almost forty years younger than Groucho, Melinda was hardly of school age. Still, the youngest Marx had become something of the house mistress in the two years her father had had custody. A later and ongoing example of stress for Melinda were her appearances on her father's television shows. Though initially merely fun, they later would be difficult for her. Not surprisingly, Groucho was exhibiting the stage parent tendencies of his own mother.

Previous to the July 16, 1954, Groucho-Eden marriage there had been much speculation in the press as to whether they had wed earlier in the summer. This was a result of Eden having accompanied Groucho and Miriam when he made a much publicized trip to Europe, where he filmed some commercials for De Soto (his television sponsor) and showed his daughter their ancestral home.

The stay-at-home Groucho became more socially active with his marriage to Eden. And though they, too, would eventually divorce in 1969, theirs was, at least for Groucho, a fairly amiable marriage. Moreover, even after a divorce in which she received almost a million dollar settlement, the two frequently appeared together socially. When once asked about this, Groucho gave a much quoted reply: "I want to be near my money."

For a few years, beginning in 1957, Groucho and Eden spent part of each summer in summer stock productions of the comedian's (and Norman Krasna's) *Time for Elizabeth*.[309] She also appeared in the 1964 television production of the play. One of their first joint acting ventures, *The Story of Mankind* (1957), was also the last film in which Groucho, Chico, and Harpo appeared. It was not a reteaming, however, as they had no screen time together. In a production full of celebrities playing in historical episodes, Groucho appeared as Peter Minuit (Eden was the Indian girl he charmed); Harpo was a harp-playing Sir Isaac Newton; and Chico, in what had to be a major industry in-joke, was cast as a monk who advised Columbus. The film, which was not a success, had attempted to follow the then-recent and very popular all-star cameo-packed production *Around the World in Eighty Days* (1956).[310]

There would, however, be one last time the Brothers would appear together, though for Groucho it was still a cameo. In March 1959 Chico and Harpo starred in the *G.E. Theater* television production *The Incredible Jewel Robbery*. Groucho and his *You Bet Your Life* wooden duck made an unbilled appearance (due to his contract with a rival network) at the teleplay's close. Interestingly enough, other than the surprising close with Groucho, probably the production's best scene was Harpo in disguise resurrecting the old movie Groucho. *The Incredible Jewel Robbery* was done entirely in pantomime, except for Groucho's closing after being fingered in a police lineup: "We won't talk until we see our lawyer." Comically fitting, sly Groucho had just been bested one final time by his brothers. Harpo had not just playfully imitated Groucho; he had used the mustached one's identity while robbing a store. Some things, thankfully, just never change.

Interestingly enough, there might have been another television teaming. In 1959 the Brothers had almost completed a television pilot for comedy writer Phil Rapp entitled *Deputy Seraph*, "as in sheriff, or seraphim."[311] The project died in mid-pilot when Chico, because of hardening of the arteries, could not be insured for a weekly television series. Chico and Harpo were to be bumbling angels who righted wrongs on earth, with occasional assistance from Deputy Seraph Groucho, who would star in every third episode. (As with *Love Happy*, funding for creative projects for the Marxes generally necessitated all three be involved, even if Groucho's part was somewhat tangential.) This Marx Brothers *Highway to Heaven* concept made allowances for the advanced ages of the three by having them do their *heavenly* work only from above, with certain earth-bound characters being taken over, at appropriate times, by the *spirits* of the Brothers. On paper, anyway, the comedy possibilities were intriguing, from, as invisioned by Phil Rapp, an "elegant dowager" suddenly grabbing a cigar and "walking with a lope," to a "stuffy concert pianist suddenly start shooting the keys."[312] But it was not to be. And until the 1980s, it was basically forgotten. Yet it seems more than fitting that this late, almost public teaming should have Marx Brother justice continuing from on high.

Chico died of heart disease in 1961. Harpo, following in seniority and with similar physical problems, died after heart surgery in 1964, though thankfully not before writing (with Rowland Barber) the autobiography *Harpo Speaks!* (1961). Groucho lived much longer, dying of pneumonia in 1977. He was able to witness the rebirth of intense Marx Brothers popularity in the anti-establishment 1960s. While his autobiography *Groucho and Me* had appeared in 1959, there would also be several other books (generally with collaborators—see Chapter 4). In addition, he frequently appeared on television during the 1960s, he hosted two short-lived series on the order of *You Bet Your Life* (one in Britain, *Groucho*, and one in the United States, *Tell It to Groucho*), and eventually even saw the mid-1970s revival of interest in *You Bet Your Life*. In 1970 he witnessed the brief run of the play *Minnie's Boys* on Broadway, while in 1972 he returned to the stage himself with his one-man show, appearing at Carnegie Hall. Also in 1972, just after his Carnegie Hall show, the French government made him a *Commander dans l'Orde des Arts et des Lettres*. (The awarding of the prestigious decoration took place at Cannes, with Groucho afterwards attending that city's internationally known film festival.)

In 1974 Groucho received a special Oscar from the Academy of Motion Picture Arts and Sciences for the "brilliant creativity and unequaled achievement of the Marx Brothers in the art of motion picture comedy." In accepting the award, he wished that Harpo, Chico, and Margaret Dumont might have been there. In addition, he thanked his mother and Erin Fleming, his then companion/caretaker, who would later be involved in two Groucho controversies. First there would be an ugly 1977 Groucho conservator fight between Erin and the comedian's son, Arthur. After Groucho's death the executor of his estate, the Bank of America, instituted an ongoing court battle against Fleming for funds she had received through her association with the comedian, plus punitive damages.[313]

It is a sad day when a comedian of such acid wit, probably *the* comedian of acid wit, reaches the point where a conservator fight breaks out. But sadness touches all people, including the clowns. The earlier closing acts of Chico and Harpo were, in other ways, no less difficult. In a way, time was cruelest to Chico and Harpo. But this was not because their solo careers never evolved past the team, as did younger Brother Groucho's. To achieve the true status of the clichéd "legend in your own time" should certainly be heady enough stuff for anyone, without wishing for the double whammy success of Groucho the teammate *and* solo star. Though unfortunate, the sadness of Chico and Harpo is not even that they died before the phenomenal 1960s revival of interest in the team, of the 1970s Academy recognition, and all the fanfare attached to the re-release of *Animal Crackers*. After all, the Marxes had never really been out of style, especially with the accessibility to old films that 1950s television had magically provided.

No, time was cruelest to Chico and Harpo because they aged, and their comedy personae were of the nonaging sort. Groucho had been playing old men since his schoolmaster days in their classroom act. And what was his funny lope but a comic variation of age's stooped walk? Ironically, aging, if anything, merely enhanced his comedy, whether as the greasepaint Groucho or the more subdued *You Bet Your Life* figure. That the man of so much sexual comedy innuendo should actually reach the age of his comic dirty old man merely enriched the humor. He even officially became crowned King *Leer*.

PCP-24140

9. All five Marxes—Gummo (bottom) joins his brothers (from the top down) Groucho, Zeppo, Harpo, and Chico on the set of their greatest film, *Duck Soup* (1933). (Photograph courtesy of the Wisconsin Center for Film and Theater Research.)

Conversely, the comedy personae of Chico and Harpo were synonymous with youth. They were Puck and Pan, figures of mystery and magic. Harpo especially seemed a god of comedy slumming on earth, from his otherworldly nature (be it his silence or his Gookie) to his sorcerer's pockets and his special affinity with children and animals. How could such figures—at their best defying everyone and everything—age? It deadened their comedy, allowing pity to slip in. That age should constitute a problem for their comedy personae was, however, evident even before the team broke up. It is distracting, especially concerning Harpo, as early as the 1946 *A Night in Casablanca*. Thus, while there were other late-life bits of sadness, be it Chico's 1959 need to tour in *The Fifth Season* despite being in poor health or Harpo's decision to remain active at the end, regardless of a poor heart, that age should line their masks of comedy seems the cruelest trick of all.

But enough along these lines. This book is a Marx Brothers celebration. And their forever younger, iconoclastic figures permanently live on in their films . . . films that continue to defy time, just as they continue to make us laugh. Minnie would have been proud.

NOTES

1. Harpo Marx (with Rowland Barber), *Harpo Speaks!* (1961; rpt. New York: Freeway Press, 1974), p. 24.

2. Numerous listings can be found for the date of Chico's birth, but August 1887 seems the most likely.

3. The exact birth dates of the other Marx Brothers are not so vague, but some differences do exist. For full details, see this volume's Chronological Biography.

4. Joe Adamson, *Groucho, Harpo, Chico and Sometimes Zeppo* (New York: Simon and Schuster, 1973).

5. Hector Arce, *Groucho* (New York: G. P. Putnam's Sons, 1979), p. 26.

6. Kyle Crichton, *The Marx Brothers* (Garden City, N.Y.: Doubleday & Company, 1950), pp. 2, 4.

7. Groucho Marx, *Groucho and Me* (1959; rpt. New York: Manor Books, 1974), p. 15.

8. Ibid., pp. 15, 23.

9. See especially Arce's *Groucho*, p. 39.

10. Harpo Marx, *Harpo Speaks!*, p. 21.

11. Ibid., p. 11.

12. Ibid., p. 21.

13. William Marx, "Afterwords, II," in *Harpo Speaks!* (1961; rpt. New York: Limelight Editions, 1985), p. 480.

14. Alexander Woollcott, "A Mother of the Two-A-Day," in *Going to Pieces* (New York: G. P. Putnam's Sons, 1928), p. 38. This article originally appeared in the *Saturday Evening Post*, June 20, 1925, pp. 42ff.

15. Groucho Marx, *Groucho and Me*, p. 29.

16. Harpo Marx, *Harpo Speaks!*, p. 29.

17. Maxine Marx, *Growing Up with Chico* (Englewood Cliffs, N.J.: Prentice-Hall, 1980), p. 3.

18. Harpo Marx, *Harpo Speaks!*, p. 31.

19. Walter Kerr, "Chico, the Utterly Indispensable Marx," *Los Angeles Herald-Examiner*, February 24, 2981, p. 86.

20. Groucho Marx, *Groucho and Me*, p. 22.

21. Crichton, *The Marx Brothers*, p. 10.

22. Groucho Marx, *Groucho and Me*, p. 24.

23. Maxine Marx, *Growing Up with Chico*, p. 56.

24. Groucho Marx, *Memoirs of a Mangy Lover* (New York: Bernard Geis Associates, 1963), p. 132.

25. Harpo Marx, *Harpo Speaks!*, p. 58.

26. Ibid., p. 40.

27. Groucho Marx and Richard J. Anobile, *The Marx Bros. Scrapbook* (New York: Grosset & Dunlap, 1974), pp. 13, 40. Groucho includes a later picture of himself with Ty Cobb in the comedian's *The Groucho Phile* (1976; rpt. New York: Pocket Books, 1977), p. 482.

28. Harpo Marx, *Harpo Speaks!*, p. 38.

29. Arce, *Groucho*, p. 29.

30. Alexander Woollcott, "A Strong, Silent Man," *Cosmopolitan*, January 1934, p. 108.

31. Maxine Marx, *Growing Up with Chico*, p. 172.

32. Arce, *Groucho*, pp. 33, 62.

33. See Arce, *Groucho*, p. 75; Arthur Marx, *Son of Groucho* (New York: David McKay Company, 1972), p. 15.

34. See Groucho Marx and Richard J. Anobile, *The Marx Bros. Scrapbook*, p. 12; Arce, *Groucho*, pp. 61–62.

35. William Wolf, *The Marx Brothers* (New York: Pyramid Publications, 1975), p. 23.

36. Hector Arce, "Introduction," in *The Groucho Phile*, p. xv.

37. Arce, *Groucho*, p. 39.

38. Ibid.

39. Arthur Marx, *Son of Groucho*, p. 11.

40. Crichton, *The Marx Brothers*, p. 167.

41. Arce, *Groucho*, p. 32.

42. Groucho Marx, *Groucho and Me*, p. 54; Groucho Marx, *The Groucho Phile*, p. 11.

43. Harpo Marx, *Harpo Speaks!*, p. 32. (Again, one is reminded of Chaplin and Fields, recipients of even less formal education, who like Groucho became self-educated adults through a great personal drive to learn.)

44. Clara Beranger, "The Woman Who Taught Her Children to Be Fools," *Liberty*, Winter 1972, p. 55. This article originally appeared in *Liberty*, June 3, 1933. It also reappeared in the Summer 1976 issue of *Liberty*.

45. Harpo Marx, *Harpo Speaks!*, p. 28.

46. Alexander Woollcott, "I Might Just as Well Have Played Hooky," in *Long, Long Ago* (New York: World Book Company, 1943), p. 179.

47. Ibid., p. 182.

48. Alexander Woollcott, "My Friend Harpo," in *While Rome Burns* (New York: Grosset & Dunlap, 1934), p. 37.

49. Harpo Marx, *Harpo Speaks!*, pp. 23–24.

50. Groucho Marx, *Groucho and Me*, p. 57.

51. Groucho Marx, *Beds* (1930; rpt. Indianapolis: Bobbs-Merrill Company, 1976), p. 17. Arce claims the book was ghostwritten by Arthur Sheekman. See Arce, *Groucho*, pp. 168–169; and this volume's Bibliographical Essay.

52. Groucho Marx, *Groucho and Me*, p. 55.

53. Harpo Marx, *Harpo Speaks!*, p. 65.

54. Ibid., p. 108.

55. Groucho Marx, *Groucho and Me*, p. 80.

56. Alexander Woollcott, "Portrait of a Man with Red Hair," *The New Yorker*, December 1, 1928, p. 34.

57. Harpo Marx, *Harpo Speaks!*, pp. 94–95; Arce, *Groucho*, pp. 67–68.

58. Groucho Marx, *The Groucho Phile*, p. 18.

59. Groucho Marx, *Groucho and Me*, pp. 125–129; Groucho Marx, *Memoirs of a Mangy Lover*, pp. 156–164.

60. Harpo Marx, *Harpo Speaks!*, p. 98.

61. B. F. Wilson, "The Mad Marxes Make for the Movies," *Motion Picture Classic*, February 1928, p. 48.

62. Groucho Marx and Richard J. Anobile, *The Marx Bros. Scrapbook*, p. 44.

63. Arce, *Groucho*, p. 77.

64. Maxine Marx, *Growing Up with Chico*, pp. 14, 60. See also critic Walter Kerr's excellent combination review of the book and general analysis of Chico's importance to the team—"Chico, the Utterly Indispensable Marx," pp. 81, 86.

65. Crichton, *The Marx Brothers*, p. 130.

66. Adamson, *Groucho, Harpo, Chico and Sometimes Zeppo*, p. 153.

67. *Home Again* review (Royal theatre), *Variety*, February 12, 1915, p. 16.

68. See *Home Again* review (Palace), *Variety*, February 27, 1915, p. 19.

69. Woollcott, "A Strong, Silent Man," p. 108.

70. Groucho credits the nickname Zeppo to the then-contemporary Zeppelins over World War I London. Harpo claims the athletic Herbert received his nickname from an act that featured a Mr. Zippo. But the most logical explanation comes from Chico and Gummo: Zeppo is a variation of the rural nickname Zeb, which Herbert later acquired while working on the family's next common home—an Illinois farm. Crichton, *The Marx Brothers*, pp. 167–168.

71. Arce, *Groucho*, p. 101.

72. Groucho Marx and Richard J. Anobile, *The Marx Bros. Scrapbook*, p. 21.

73. Maxine Marx, *Growing Up with Chico*, p. 22.

74. Arthur Marx, *Son of Groucho*, p. 22.

75. Groucho Marx, "My Poor Wife!" *Colliers*, December 20, 1930, pp. 15, 59.

76. "Marx Bros. Picture," *Variety*, March 24, 1926, p. 26.

77. "The Mezzanine Floor" review (Palace), *Variety*, March 18, 1921, p. 17.

78. Ibid.

79. Harpo Marx, *Harpo Speaks!*, p. 142.

80. Charlie Chaplin, *My Trip Abroad* (New York: Harper & Brothers, 1922).

81. Grace Simpson, "GROUCHO looks at CHARLIE," *Motion Picture*, May 1936, pp. 39, 82.

82. Peter Dixon, "First Appearance in Europe!" *The Freedonia Gazette*, Winter 1981, p. 9; Julius H. Marx (Groucho), "Marx Bros.' Explanation [letter]," *Variety*, August 11, 1922, p. 2.

100   The Marx Brothers

83. Harpo Marx, *Harpo Speaks!*, p. 163.

84. Groucho Marx, *The Groucho Phile*, p. 45.

85. Maxine Marx, *Growing Up with Chico*, p. 21.

86. Arce, *Groucho*, p. 45.

87. Groucho Marx and Richard J. Anobile, *The Marx Bros. Scrapbook*, p. 61.

88. Arce, *Groucho*, pp. 125–126.

89. Maxine Marx, *Growing Up with Chico*, pp. 77, 100.

90. Fyodor Dostoevsky, *The Gambler, With Polina Suslova's Diary*, ed. Edward Wasiolek and trans. Victor Terras (1866; rpt. Chicago: University of Chicago Press, 1972), pp. 31, 158.

91. Edward Wasiolek, Introduction to *The Gambler, With Polina Suslova's Diary*, by Fyodor Dostoevsky, p. xxxvii.

92. Arthur Marx, *Son of Groucho*, p. 44.

93. Maxine Marx, *Growing Up with Chico*, p. 36.

94. Ibid.

95. Arthur Marx, *Son of Groucho*, p. 68.

96. The Groucho Marx letter mistakenly later dated "1930?" in "The Groucho Marx Papers," Box 1, Folder 1 (Correspondence with Dr. Samuel Salinger, 1928-1938), State Historical Society of Wisconsin Archives, Madison, Wisconsin.

97. Arthur Marx, *Son of Groucho*, p. 63.

98. Will Rogers, "The Singing Don't Hurt" (December 24, 1933, syndicated weekly newspaper article), in *Will Rogers' Weekly Articles*, vol. 6, *The Roosevelt Years, 1933-1935*, ed. Steven K. Gragert (Stillwater: Oklahoma State University Press, 1982), p. 84.

99. Arthur Marx, *Life with Groucho* (New York: Simon and Schuster, 1954), p. 55.

100. Arthur Marx, *Son of Groucho*, p. 64.

101. The Groucho Marx letter labeled "1931," in "The Groucho Marx Papers," Box 1, Folder 1.

102. Arthur Marx, *Son of Groucho*, pp. 160, 187; Arthur Marx, *Life with Groucho*, p. 214.

103. Arthur Marx, *Life with Groucho*, p. 53.

104. Norman Krasna, *Dear Ruth* (New York: Dramatists Play Service, 1944), p. 7. See also Arce, *Groucho*, p. 225.

105. Krasna, *Dear Ruth*, p. 104.

106. Ibid.

107. Ibid., p. 58.

108. Arce, *Groucho*, pp. 225, 265.

109. Harpo Marx, *Harpo Speaks!*, p. 178.

110. Robert Benchley, "A Little Sermon on Success," in *No Poems Or Around the World Backwards and Sideways* (New York: Harper & Brothers, 1932), p. 230.

111. Harpo Marx, *Harpo Speaks!*, p. 178.

112. Robert Benchley, "How to Break 90 in Croquet," in *From Bed to Worse Or Comforting Thoughts About the Bison* (New York: Harper & Brothers, 1934), p. 27.

113. Harpo Marx, *Harpo Speaks!*, p. 169.

114. Benchley, "How to Break 90 in Croquet," p. 29.

115. Oscar Levant, "Memoirs of a Mute," in *A Smattering of Ignorance* (Garden City, N.Y.: Garden City Publishing Co., 1942), p. 54.

116. Howard Teichmann, *Smart Aleck: The Wit, World, and Life of Alexander Woollcott* (New York: William Morrow and Company, 1976), p. 133.

117. Ibid., p. 261.

118. George S. Kaufman and Moss Hart, *Three Plays by Kaufman and Hart: Once in a Lifetime, You Can't Take It With You, The Man Who Came to Dinner* (New York: Grove, 1980), p. 291.

119. Groucho Marx, *The Groucho Phile*, p. 61.

120. Tete Carle, "'Fun' Working with the Marx Brothers? Horsefeathers!" *Los Angeles Magazine*, October 1978, p. 145.

121. Heywood Broun, "It Seems to Me," *New York Telegraph*, 1928, n.p., in "The Groucho Marx Papers," Box 1, Folder 1 (included in Correspondence with Dr. Samuel Salinger, 1928-1938), State Historical Society of Wisconsin Archives, Madison, Wisconsin.

122. Ibid.

123. "Animal Crackers" script, in "The Groucho Marx Papers," pp. 1-37, Box 1, State Historical Society of Wisconsin Archives, Madison, Wisconsin. (At the time of this author's visit the script was mistakenly thought to be that of the film adaptation.)

124. Groucho Marx and Richard J. Anobile, *The Marx Bros. Scrapbook*, p. 80.

125. The Groucho Marx letter later dated "1928" in "The Groucho Marx Papers," Box 1, Folder 1.

126. Groucho Marx and Richard J. Anobile, *The Marx Bros. Scrapbook*, p. 80.

127. The Groucho Marx letter mistakenly later dated "1930?" in "The Groucho Marx Papers," Box 1, Folder 1.

128. Arthur Marx, *Life with Groucho*, pp. 109-110.

129. Arce, *Groucho*, p. 150.

130. "Animal Crackers" script, in "The Groucho Marx Papers," p. 58 of Act 1, Box 1.

131. Ibid., p. 60 of Act 1.

132. Andrew Sarris, "Make Way for the Clowns," in *The American Cinema: Directors and Directions, 1929-1968* (New York: E. P. Dutton and Company, 1968), p. 243.

133. Groucho Marx and Richard J. Anobile, *The Marx Bros. Scrapbook*, p. 80.

134. Ibid., p. 117.

135. Groucho Marx, *The Groucho Phile*, p. 75.

136. Groucho Marx and Richard J. Anobile, *The Marx Bros. Scrapbook*, p. 80.

137. Ibid., p. 116.

138. Adamson, *Groucho, Harpo, Chico and Sometimes Zeppo*, p. 92.

139. Harpo Marx, *Harpo Speaks!*, p. 271.

140. Groucho Marx and Richard J. Anobile, *The Marx Bros. Scrapbook*, p. 116.

141. Robert Florey letter dated May 31, 1975, to Tony Slide, from the private collection of historian and archivist Slide.

142. Arce, *Groucho*, p. 159.

143. Groucho Marx, *Beds*, p. 7.

144. Ibid., pp. 15, 29.

145. Ibid., p. 5.

146. Alexander Woollcott, "Obituary [of Minnie Marx]"—subject of his "Shouts and Murmurs" column, *The New Yorker*, September 28, 1929, p. 54.

147. The Groucho Marx letter labeled "Death of his Mother," in "The Groucho Marx Papers," Box 1, Folder 1.

148. The Groucho Marx Carlton Hotel (Washington) letter later dated "1929, 1930," in "The Groucho Marx Papers," Box 1, Folder 1.

149. The figure for Groucho's loss occurs frequently in Marx Brothers literature; Harpo's comes from his autobiography, p. 277. The latter is described as an on-paper loss; the Groucho references imply a greater loss of real currency.

150. The Groucho Carlton Hotel letter.

151. Groucho Marx, *Beds* (the updated introduction), p. 8.

152. The Groucho Marx letter of May 9, 1930, in "The Groucho Marx Papers," Box 1, Folder 1.

153. Harpo Marx, *Harpo Speaks!*, p. 283.

154. The Groucho Marx letter of May 9, 1930.

155. Lillian Roth (with Mike Connolly and Gerold Frank), *I'll Cry Tomorrow* (New York: Frederick Fell, 1954), p. 85.

156. Allen Eyles, *The Marx Brothers: Their World of Comedy* (New York: A. S. Barnes & Co., 1969; rpt. New York: Paperback Library, 1971), p. 55.

157. *Animal Crackers* film review, *Variety*, September 3, 1930, p. 19.

158. Robert Benchley, "The Marx Brothers" (June 5, 1924, *Life*—the humor magazine), in *Benchley at the Theatre: Dramatic Criticism, 1920-1940*, ed. Charles Getchell (Ipswich, Mass.: Ipswich Press, 1985), p. 35.

159. Groucho Marx's October 14, 1930 radio introduction for Heywood Broun, in "The Groucho Marx Papers," Box 1, Folder 1.

160. Arce, *Groucho*, p. 176.

161. Charlotte Chandler, *Hello, I Must Be Going: Groucho & His Friends* (Garden City, N.Y.: Doubleday & Company, 1978), p. 303.

162. Groucho Marx, *The Groucho Phile*, [p. 107].

163. Charlotte Chandler, *Hello, I Must Be Going: Groucho & His Friends*, p. 187.

164. Groucho Marx and Richard J. Anobile, *The Marx Bros. Scrapbook*, p. 45.

165. Groucho Marx, *The Groucho Phile*, [p. 113].

166. Groucho Marx and Richard J. Anobile, *The Marx Bros. Scrapbook*, p. 174.

167. Arce, *Groucho*, pp. 176-177.

168. The Groucho Marx letter dated "Dec 6 30," in "The Groucho Marx Papers," Box 1, Folder 1.

169. Ibid.

170. Groucho Marx, *Memoirs of a Mangy Lover*, p. 7.

171. The Groucho Marx letter dated "Dec 6 30."

172. Arthur Marx, *Son of Groucho*, p. 88-89.

173. Arthur Marx, *Life with Groucho*, p. 147.

174. Ibid., pp. 147, 148.

175. The Groucho Marx letter dated "Jan 6 31," in "The Groucho Marx Papers," Box 1, Folder 1.

176. Maxine Marx, *Growing Up with Chico*, p. 61.

177. Arthur Marx, *Life with Groucho*, p. 153.

178. The Groucho Marx letter dated "Jan 6 31."

179. Groucho Marx, *Memoirs of a Mangy Lover*, p. 133.

180. *Animal Crackers* film review, *Variety*, September 3, 1930, p. 19.

181. See the author's *W. C. Fields: A Bio-Bibliography* (Westport, Conn.: Greenwood Press, 1984).

182. Eyles, *The Marx Brothers: Their World of Comedy*, pp. 76–77.

183. Paul D. Zimmerman and Burt Goldblatt, *The Marx Brothers at the Movies* (1968; rpt. New York: Berkley Publishing Corporation, 1975), p. 47.

184. S. J. Perelman, "The Winsome Foursome," *Show*, November 1961, p. 37.

185. Wolf, *The Marx Brothers*, p. 56.

186. Mel Calman, "Perelman in Cloudsville," *Sight and Sound*, Autumn 1978, p. 248.

187. Perelman, "The Winsome Foursome," p. 38.

188. *Monkey Business*, Final Script (April 21, 1931), Box 1, Folder 6, State Historical Society of Wisconsin Archives, Madison, Wisconsin, p. M-11.

189. Ibid., p. M-18.

190. Ibid., pp. E-11, E-12.

191. S. J. Perelman, "Week End with Groucho Marx," *Holiday*, April 1952, pp. 132–133. (Later this would appear as "I'll Always Call You Schnorrer, My African Explorer"—see Chapter 4 of this text.)

192. Arce, *Groucho*, p. 198.

193. The Groucho Marx letter later dated "1931, April?" in "The Groucho Marx Papers," Box 1, Folder 1.

194. Maxine Marx, *Growing Up with Chico*, pp. 63–68. (Maxine mistakenly labels it summer 1930, whereas it was 1931.)

195. Levant, "Memoirs of a Mute," p. 59–60.

196. "Marx Brothers in Revue," *New York Times*, August 21, 1931, p. 20.

197. "Horse Feathers" (cover article), *Time*, August 15, 1932, p. 25.

198. The Groucho Marx letter later dated "1932?" in "The Groucho Marx Papers," Box 1, Folder 1.

199. The Groucho Marx letter dated "1932, April," in "The Groucho Marx Papers," Box 1, Folder 1.

200. Dennis P. deLoof, "A Constructive Analysis of Three Early Marx Brothers Films," in "TFG's First Special Issue" of *The Freedonia Gazette*, Spring 1984 (complete issue devoted to the essay).

201. The dropped conclusion for *Monkey Business* was in the Final Script (April 21, 1931), while with *Horse Feathers* it was shot but not used. See the Tentative Script (February 11, 1932), in Special Collections, Margaret Herrick Library, Academy of Motion Picture Arts and Sciences, Beverly Hills, California.

202. *Horse Feathers*, Tentative Script (February 11, 1932), p. L9.

203. Ibid.

204. Krasna, *Dear Ruth*, p. 140.

205. Arce, *Groucho*, p. 295.

206. Maxine Marx, *Growing Up with Chico*, p. 71.

207. George Oppenheimer, *The View from the Sixties: Memories of a Spent Life* (New York: David McKay Company, 1966), p. 100. See also Gerald Weales, "Duck Soup," in *Canned Goods as Caviar: American Film Comedy of the 1930s* (Chicago: University of Chicago Press, 1985), p. 82.

208. The Groucho Marx letter later dated "1932?"

209. "Marx Break Reported," *New York Times*, March 10, 1933 (of a March 9 event), p. 18. For this and related coverage of the Marxes's walkout, see: "Marx Brothers Files," Billy Rose Theatre Collection, New York Public Library at Lincoln Center.

210. "Marx Brothers Files," Billy Rose Theatre Collection.

211. Andrew Bergman, "Some Anarcho-Nihilist Laff Riots," in *We're in the Money: Depression America and Its Films* (1971; rpt. New York: Harper and Row, 1972), p. 37.

212. Pete Martin, "Going His Way," *Saturday Evening Post*, November 30, 1946, p. 65. See also the author's: *Leo McCarey and the Comic Anti-Hero in American Film* (New York: Arno Press, 1980), and "The Director as Keeper of the Screwball Sanatorium," in *Screwball Comedy: A Genre of Madcap Romance* (Westport, Conn.: Greenwood Press, 1986), pp. 73–111.

213. Peter Bogdanovich, "Leo McCarey Oral History" (Los Angeles: American Film Institute, 1972), p. 66.

214. Adamson, *Groucho, Harpo, Chico and Sometimes Zeppo*, p. 221.

215. John McCabe, *The Comedy World of Stan Laurel* (Garden City, N.Y.: Doubleday and Company, 1974), p. 64.

216. "Marx Brothers Files," Billy Rose Theatre Collection.

217. Harpo Marx, *Harpo Speaks!*, p. 297.

218. Ibid., p. 316.

219. Kipp Wessel, "Comrade Harpo," *The Freedonia Gazette*, November 1980, p. 8.

220. "Harpo Marx Back, A Caviar Convert," *New York Times*, January 10, 1934, p. 24.

221. "Marx Brothers Files," Billy Rose Theatre Collection.

222. Ibid.

223. Sylvia B. Golden, "Confessions of the Marx Brothers," *Theatre Magazine*, January 1929, p. 48.

224. Barry Norman, "Zeppo's Last Interview" (Part 1), *The Freedonia Gazette*, November 1981, p. 5. (The interview was drawn from a 1979 transcript originally done for an episode of the BBC-Television show *The Hollywood Greats* that focused on Groucho.)

225. Ibid., p. 6.

226. "Marx Brothers Files," Billy Rose Theatre Collection.

227. "Refineries 'Five-Star Theatre' For Every Type of Radio Listener," *Variety*, December 6, 1932, p. 34.

228. The Groucho Marx letter later dated "1934, July," in "The Groucho Marx Papers," Box 1, Folder 1.

229. Groucho Marx, *Groucho and Me*, pp. 234–235.

230. Douglas W. Churchill, "News and Gossip from Hollywood: The Marxes as Guinea Pigs for a State-Screen Experiment," *New York Times*, October 20, 1935, Section 10, p. 5.

231. *Duck Soup*, First Buff Script (June 22, 1933), pp. G1-12, in Special Collections, Margaret Herrick Library, Academy of Motion Picture Arts and Sciences, Beverly Hills, California. See also in Special Collections the F. D. Langton synopsis of the Final Script for *Cracked Ice/Grasshoppers* (early titles for what became *Duck Soup*), n.d., and Mirian Valentine's synopsis of the Final Script for *Duck Soup*, n.d.

232. Churchill, "News and Gossip from Hollywood. . . ."

233. "Marx Brother Files," Billy Rose Theatre Collection.

234. Arce, *Groucho*, p. 175; Maxine Marx, *Growing Up with Chico*, p. 107.

235. Maxine Marx, *Growing Up with Chico*, pp. 109-110.

236. Ibid., p. 111.

237. Arthur Marx, *Son of Groucho*, p. 168.

238. For a more exacting look at these family rules, see Harpo Marx, *Harpo Speaks!*, p. 434.

239. Kirtley Baskette, "Hoodlums at Home," *Photoplay*, July 1937, p. 113.

240. "Marx Brothers Files," Special Collections, Margaret Herrick Library.

241. Arce, *Groucho*, p. 258.

242. "2 Marx Bros. Fined, Escape Jail Term," *Los Angeles Examiner*, November 2, 1937, pp. 1, 4.

243. *Los Angeles Examiner* article from April 1938, in the "Marx Brothers Files," Special Collections, Margeret Herrick Library, Academy of Motion Picture Arts and Sciences, Beverly Hills, California.

244. "Marx Bros. Use 11 Different Acts in 11 Shows in Windup Vaude Wk.," *Variety*, August 26, 1936, p. 89.

245. Ibid.

246. "Marx Brothers Files," Billy Rose Theatre Collection.

247. Eileen Creelman, "Picture Plays and Players: Chico, the Piano-Playing Marx, Talks of 'Marx Bros. at the Circus,'" *New York Sun*, November 14, 1939, p. 16, in the "Marx Brothers Files," Billy Rose Theatre Collection.

248. Marie Seton, "S. Dali & 3 Marxes =   ," *Theatre Arts*, October 1939, pp. 734-735.

249. Thomas H. Jordan, "The Marx Brothers," in *The Anatomy of Cinematic Humor* (New York: Revisionist Press, 1975), p. 96.

250. A Dr. Samuel Salinger letter to Groucho dated "January 29, 1940," in "The Groucho Marx Papers," Box 1, Folder 2.

251. Eyles, *The Marx Brothers: Their World of Comedy*, p. 156.

252. Groucho Marx, A Groucho letter dated "October 27, 1939," in *The Groucho Letters: Letters from and to Groucho Marx* (New York: Simon and Schuster, 1967), p. 21.

253. Groucho Marx, A Groucho letter dated "June 24, 1939," in *The Groucho Letters*, p. 20.

254. The Groucho Marx letter dated "May 26, 1939," in "The Groucho Marx Papers," Box 1, Folder 2.

255. Aaron Stein, "Mad Marxes Guest Star on Radio," *New York Post*, September 15, 1937, n.p., in "Marx Brothers Files," Billy Rose Theatre Collection.

256. Ibid.

257. Groucho Marx, A Groucho letter dated "October 10, 1940," in *The Groucho Letters*, p. 26.

258. Groucho Marx (with Hector Arce), *The Secret Word is GROUCHO* (1976; rpt. New York: Berkley Publishing Corporation, 1977), p. 3.

259. Arthur Marx, *Life with Groucho*, p. 215.

260. Ibid., p. 216.

261. The Groucho Marx letter dated "August 14, 1941," in "The Groucho Marx Papers," Box 1, Folder 2.

262. Groucho Marx, *Many Happy Returns: An Unofficial Guide to Your Income-Tax Problems* (New York: Simon and Schuster, 1942), p. 15.

263. Ibid., p. 10.

264. Groucho Marx, "Groucho Marx Turns Himself in for Scrap," *This Week, New York Herald Tribune* Sunday Supplement, November 8, 1942, p. 6; Groucho Marx, "Do You Know Enough to Go Home?" *This Week, New York Herald Tribune* Sunday Supplement, March 23, 1941, pp. 6, 29.

265. The Groucho Marx letter dated "June 6, 1940," in "The Groucho Marx Papers," Box 1, Folder 2.

266. Walter Blair, *Native American Humor* (1937; rpt. San Francisco: Chandler Publishing Company, 1960), p. 169.

267. Frederick C. Othman, "Marx Brothers, Sick of Movies, to Quit," *Los Angeles Herald*, April 10, 1941, p. 2.

268. Ibid., p. 13.

269. The Groucho Marx letter dated "August 11, 1942," in "The Groucho Marx Papers," Box 1, Folder 2.

270. Groucho Marx, *The Secret Word is GROUCHO*, pp. 17, 21.

271. Ibid.

272. See *Harpo Speaks!* (pp. 410–413) for the comedian's account of his involvement in *The Yellow Jacket*.

273. "Views and Reviews at the Palace: Chico Marx and His Piano Head Stage Show; Western on Screen," *Cleveland Press*, March 28, 1942, n.p., in "Marx Brothers Files," Billy Rose Theatre Collection.

274. Maxine Marx, *Growing Up with Chico*, p. 148.

275. The Groucho letter dated "November 17, 1942," in "The Groucho Marx Papers," Box 1, Folder 2.

276. "Chico Marx in Vaudeville" (otherwise unlabeled article), in "Marx Brothers Files," Billy Rose Theatre Collection.

277. Background on Chico's piano tricks is from the *Go West Pressbook*, part of which was reproduced in Winter 1984 issue of *The Freedonia Gazette*, p. 11.

278. The Groucho letter dated "June 29, 1943," in "The Groucho Marx Papers," Box 1, Folder 2.

279. Groucho Marx, "Groucho Beats Brow and Plow," an otherwise unidentified Los Angeles newspaper article, attached to a Groucho letter dated "June 29, 1943," in "The Groucho Marx Papers," Box 1, Folder 2.

280. Arthur Marx, *Life with Groucho*, p. 247.

281. The Groucho letter dated "November 24, 1943," in "The Groucho Marx Papers," Box 1, Folder 2.

282. The Groucho letter dated "May 31, 1945," in "The Groucho Marx Papers," Box 1, Folder 3.

283. James Agee, *A Night in Casablanca* (review), *The Nation*, May 25, 1946,

p. 636; rpt. James Agee, *A Night in Casablanca* (review), in *Agee on Film*, vol. 1 (New York: Grosset and Dunlap, 1969), p. 201.

284. Groucho Marx, *The Groucho Letters*, pp. 13–18.

285. Ibid., p. 14.

286. The Groucho letter dated "May 31, 1945."

287. Paul G. Wesolowski, "Brother Against Brother," *The Freedonia Gazette*, Winter 1983, p. 4.

288. The Groucho letter dated "October 3, 1947," in "The Groucho Marx Papers," Box 1, Folder 3.

289. "Master Marx," *Newsweek*, May 2, 1949, p. 53.

290. *You Bet Your Life* (review), *Newsweek*, November 24, 1947, p. 57 (brief negative review); "Groucho Rides Again" (cover article), *Newsweek*, May 15, 1950, p. 57.

291. "Groucho Rides Again," p. 56.

292. Ibid., p. 57.

293. Groucho Marx, *The Secret Word is GROUCHO*, p. 46.

294. "Groucho Marx Sheds Wife as He Plays Court Scene in Real Life," *Los Angeles Times*, May 13, 1950, n.p. cited, in "The Marx Brothers Files," Special Collection, Margaret Herrick Library.

295. "Groucho Marx" (cover article), *Time*, December 31, 1951, p. 29.

296. "The Stupider the Better," *Newsweek*, September 2, 1957, p. 52.

297. Ibid.

298. Bob Salmaggi, "Candid Quipster," *New York Herald Tribune* magazine supplement, July 27, 1958, p. 6, in "Marx Brothers Files," Billy Rose Theatre Collection.

299. "Groucho Rides Again," p. 57.

300. Val Adams, "Groucho in Mufti," *New York Times*, April 23, 1950, Section 2, p. 9.

301. For a 1950s example of this, see p. 6 of Salmaggi's article.

302. Eyles, *The Marx Brothers*, p. 189.

303. "The Truth About Groucho's Ad Libs," *TV Guide*, week of March 19–25, 1954, pp. 5–7. (On p. 6 the article claims to be the first time these things have been revealed in print.)

304. Ibid., p. 5.

305. Steve Allen, "Groucho Marx," in his *The Funny Men* (New York: Simon and Schuster, 1956), p. 239.

306. The Groucho letter dated "December 11, 1950," in "The Groucho Marx Papers," Box 1, Folder 3.

307. William Marx, "Afterwards, II," in *Harpo Speaks!*, pp. 478–479.

308. Ibid., p. 479.

309. "Eden Marx," *The Freedonia Gazette*, Summer 1984, p. 11.

310. Arce, *Groucho*, p. 374.

311. Ted Newson, "Marx Bros.' Forgotten TV Pilot," *Los Angeles Times Calendar* section, July 19, 1981, p. 6.

312. Ibid.

313. See both the "Marx Brothers Files," Special Collections, Margaret Herrick Library, and "Erin Fleming, Who Made His Life Worth Living," *The Freedonia Gazette* (issue-long essay), Summer 1983.

2.

THE MARX OF TIME

I write by ear. I tried writing with the typewriter but I found it too
unwieldy.[1]
                                                     —Groucho in a letter to author E. B. White

How does one measure the influence of the Marx Brothers? Their impact upon
American humor and upon American popular culture in general has been immense. Moreover, their comedy has made a distinct imprint upon Western civili-
zation itself—lofty stuff for a comedy team that struggled for years in the lower
depths of vaudeville. This cultural Marx Brothers metamorphosis is also ironic,
since the most distinctive characteristic of their comedy has always been its
iconoclastic nature. Thus, while in *Horse Feathers* (1932) the Brothers comically
dismantle university life, today's university dissects *Horse Feathers* for educational purposes. But before examining the more philosophical ramifications of
their work, permit this author to relate a personal story that nicely showcases
the ongoing impact of the Marx Brothers upon our culture.

In doing research on a book of this nature, it is, of course, necessary to visit
archives scattered across the country. Away from family and after long hours in
some special collections library, one naturally searches for diversion. For the student of film, as for many others, this often means going to a movie. Thus, on
one research trip for this volume the author managed to take in two then-current
commercial theatre releases: Woody Allen's *Hannah and Her Sisters* (1986) and
Terry Gilliam's *Brazil* (1985). Though both are comedies in the broadest sense of
the word, they are radically different. The former film, like so much of Allen's
work, fluctuates between humor based upon the problems of a strongly defined
personality comedian (Allen) and a romantic comedy that frequently parodies
love itself. But unlike the guarded optimism which frequently closes Allen films,

Hannah and Her Sisters ends upon a decidedly upbeat note. The film even manages to include the two most archetypal elements of comedy's classic formula for a happy ending—the new beginnings symbolized by both a marriage and a child's birth. In contrast, *Brazil* is the blackest of comedies. Gilliam, best known as the only American member of the British comedy troupe Monty Python, has fashioned a film without hope—a nightmare comedy of the future. Like a slapstick *1984, Brazil* offers the standard black comedy message: not only is the individual insignificant, but he is forever fated to contribute to his own demise.

Both of these very different films, however, used the Marx Brothers as cultural symbols of equally different things. In *Brazil* the anti-establishment heroine watches *The Cocoanuts* (1929) on television. In this case the Marxes represent two things—an iconoclastic ideal for a radical, and comic prophets who recognized early the inherent pointlessness of the modern world. In *Hannah and Her Sisters* a suicidal Allen wanders into a screening of *Duck Soup* (1933). Prior to this he had been asking himself: If the world is without reason, why go on living? But slowly the comedy magic of the Marxes envelops him. Here the Marxes symbolize pure comedy, those random moments of joy which make life worth living. Allen leaves the theatre completely revitalized, once again a believer in hope and in the modest milestones (marriages, births . . .) of the modern man.

Here, then, was a Marx Brothers researcher who tried and failed, on two successive nights, to find a simple, momentary escape from his focus of study. That failure would seem to say a lot about the ongoing significance of the Marxes, especially since *Hannah and Her Sisters* and *Brazil* have known great critical acclaim.

Allen's recognition of the importance of the Marxes is doubly important because he has evolved into one of America's greatest creative artists. His accomplishments range from an Oscar for best motion picture to the O. Henry Award for best short story. And in 1986 the nominating theatre critics for the Pulitzer Prize in drama even recommended that his screenplays be made eligible for the competition. This is especially relevant here, for besides calling Allen "America's Ingmar Bergman," the critics' action had been precipitated by the fact that the only narrative script they had agreed upon in their 1986 nominating capacity was the Marx Brothers-influenced *Hannah and Her Sisters.*[2]

One might even say the spirit of the Marxes brings out the best in Allen. His most pointed previous highlighting of them, or more specifically Groucho, had come at the opening of his most acclaimed film—the Academy Award-winning *Annie Hall* (1977). At that time he had quoted Groucho's famous real-life put-down: "I would never want to belong to any club that would have someone like me for a member." But not before *Hannah and Her Sisters* had Allen so baldly showcased the importance of the Marxes's comedy art. Morever, he offered no verbal or printed lead-in (such as even a "now showing" movie poster) as to whom or what the *Hannah* viewer was about to see in this movie-within-a-movie. The *Duck Soup* excerpt, from "The Country's Going to War" number (where the Marxes brilliantly satirize the unthinking jingoism that welcomes war), is simply presented without fanfare as the comic masterpiece that it is. And remember, Allen's narrative goal in the scene is to present a symbol of comedy at its greatest—again, high praise for these former low-level vaudevillians.

Addressing broader lines this chapter's opening question—How does one measure the influence of the Marx Brothers?—four subjects come to mind: their significance as cultural icons, their richly ambitious influence upon schools of comedy, their impact upon modern entertainment, and their easing of the transition from silent to sound comedy.

First, with the world's ever-increasing marketing, their importance as cultural icons is neither to be denied nor to be avoided. Caricatures of them appear on nearly anything that can be purchased. Their much-hawked images rank with Chaplin's tramp figure (Charlie) and the con man caricature of W. C. Fields as probably the most universally recognized of American film icons. But their significance as images goes beyond mere sales.

As with Chaplin and Fields, caricatures of Groucho, Chico, and Harpo have become an enduringly popular logo for Americans, even for those who have not seen a complete Marx Brothers film. This is possible because it has become a common cultural heritage to know what they represent. Most specifically, the Marx Brothers as icons symbolize two things: pure comedy and anti-establishment spirit. Expanding briefly upon the former, the Marxes are not only funny, they look funny, whether you are watching them in a film or studying a caricature. Most memorable are Groucho's greasepaint mustache and eyebrows, the latter so comically powerful that the comedian refused to raise them when doing road tours of movie material, because they would win a laugh for any line. Add a cigar and a bent-over lope and you have Groucho. For Harpo's image one sees the curly blond hair, a battered top hat, a magic trench coat, an old autmobile horn, and a face crazily contorted into his comic Gookie, with perhaps a harp in the background. Chico's visual signature is largely limited to a vacuous face and a somewhat dunce-cap-like hat, both of which comically compliment his wise fool immigrant persona. If a piano is stationed nearby, one hand will be in the toy-gun-like pose necessary to "shoot the keys." Thus, as is true of the most traditional of clowns, one would be prone to laugh at them visually without prior knowledge of who, or what, they were.

Their significance as comedy symbols is doubly underlined by the frequent stage shows that include impersonations of one or more Marx Brothers. An excellent overview of this phenomenon can be found in back issues of another example of Marx Brothers fascination—*The Freedonia Gazette*, which bills itself as "*The* Magazine Devoted To The Marx Brothers" (see Chapter 4, "A Marx Brothers Bibliographical Essay").[3] Along these same lines one should note the ongoing stage revival productions of two Marx Brothers celebrations that originally played on Broadway: *Minnie's Boys* and *A Day in Hollywood/A Night in the Ukraine* (two independent one-act shows, with the second showcasing the Marxes). Appropriately, *Minnie's Boys* is a musical comedy biography of sorts, while *A Night in the Ukraine* embraces more the spirit of the Marxes, being, as it is, loosely drawn from "The Bear"—a short story by Chekhov! To flesh out completely the full complement of possible contemporary Marx Brothers stage experiences, one of the team's own Broadway productions, *Animal Crackers*, is also currently seeing revivals.

Besides being symbols of pure comedy, the Marx Brothers also represent the ultimate in anti-establishment icons. As Martin A. Gardner has so thoroughly revealed in his 1970 doctoral dissertation, their talent for satirizing society can be grouped into three broad categories. They comically undercut history, politics, and the economy; manners and customs; and literature and popular entertainment, though this final category is best defined as parody.[4] While one most frequently associates them with the comic usurpation of high society (manners and customs, especially as personified by Margaret Dumont), their satire and parody seems to touch nearly every aspect of American culture. Thus, *Duck Soup* is a satirical send-up of politics that makes comic inroads into governmental policy on everything from the economy to diplomacy, managing effectively to scramble American history along the way, from Harpo's rendition of Paul Revere's ride to the then-current state of world depression. *Horse Feathers*'s dismantling of university life comically managers to skew a range of literature and popular entertainment from Theodore Dreiser's *An American Tragedy* to college football. In fact, the ongoing *Horse Feathers* lampooning of the significance placed upon college football (even in 1932) makes a nice metaphor on the universality of their satire upon all that is American; as more and more commentators on the American scene have noted, football represents an excellent microcosm of American society.[5] Certainly the aggressive, anything-for-a-victory attitude often seen in American football and American life is perfectly burlesqued in the Marx Brothers's rendition of the game. This is especially true at the contest's conclusion, when an instrument of war (another metaphor for football and American competition) is used to win—Harpo's chariot-like trash cart.

The Marx Brothers–football analogy can also be expanded more broadly. That is, part of the modern fascination with football is its multifaceted execution, which reflects the complexities of today's world, as opposed to the simpler one-thing-at-a-time progression of the more nineteenth-century sport of baseball. The Marx Brothers represent that same principle of entertainment diversity in comedy, both in terms of the humor types exhibited in their team, as well as their tendency to be entirely unpredictable in what they do for a laugh. This broadness of type and target also brings one full circle back to their importance as satirical anti-establishment icons. This is because their work seldom kayos one subject at a time. It is a complex, multilayered use of satire and parody that invariably draws one in, even if not every comedy jab connects. The viewer is simply mesmerized by both the amount and the diversity of the comedy.

The second broad influence of the Marxes, after their significance as comedy/ anti-establishment icons, is in their impact upon schools of comedy. Most specifically, this means their involvement in the center stage blossoming of the comic antihero in American humor, best typified by *The New Yorker* writing of authors like Robert Benchley and James Thurber.[6] But unlike so many of their contemporary screen comedians, such as Leo McCarey's Laurel & Hardy and W. C. Fields, they did not essay the figure of frustration in the comic antiheroic, modern absurd world. Instead, the Marxes donned the mantle of comic absurdity as a defense and beat the world gone mad at its own game. In fact, they were cocky enough to "take what order there is in life and impose chaos on it."[7] The latter daydream victories of Thurber's Walter Mitty were business as usual for the Marxes.[8] Groucho is, however, often victimized by his Brothers, and in these encounters Groucho becomes the more traditional antiheroic male. Moreover, Groucho's solo writing for print more fully embraced the antihero's frustrations.

The Marxes acknowledge this tie to what they call "lunatic" comedy in a 1939 article in *Theatre Arts* magazine, observing they were "followers" of such lunatic antiheroic writers as Stephen Leacock, Donald Ogden Stewart, and Robert Benchley.[9] The label "lunatic" is merely a characteristic of a comedy movement that generally focuses upon the comic frustrations of an antiheroic male, or what American humor historian Norris W. Yates frequently refers to as the "little man."[10] The authors noted by the Marxes all belong to this school of comedy, though today a more representative grouping, as noted in the previous chapter, would be: Benchley, Thurber, Clarence Day, and S. J. Perelman.[11] Even the nonsense literary example that film comedy historian and critic Gerald Weales notes as being most similar to the world of the Marxes, from Donald Ogden Stewart's *Mr. and Mrs. Heddock Abroad* (1924), finds the zany Groucholike verbal patter belonging to a supporting character who, to a great extent, is victimizing an antiheroic or "little man"—Mr. Heddock.[12]

. Since the Marxes, however, fully accented the "lunatic" characteristic, and some period literature used that label, it is natural they should recycle it. (Moreover, much of the humor point in antiheroic comedy is the absurd nature of the modern world.) In fact, speaking of recycling, the full *Theatre Arts* quote linking the three Marxes to this type of comedy is taken basically verbatim from critic Alva Johnston's detailed analysis of the team in a 1936 article.[13]

Regardless of how one interprets the resurfacing of the "lunatic" comedy statement, its repeating would seem to underline a period awareness of the connection by both the team and its most astute critics. And though the Marxes label themselves "followers," their initial Broadway triumph in *I'll Say She Is!* (1924), which was essentially a zany anthology of their "Greatest Hits" from years of vaudeville, places them in the vanguard of the movement. Their 1920s centerstage ascension as Broadway's resident crazies, on and off stage, makes them natural participants in this comedy evolution. As Gerald Weales has suggested in his justification for crediting the Marx Brothers's involvement: "it is more useful to think in terms of a shared intellectual and social climate [in 1920s New York, the center for the ultimate literary articulation of the movement] in which lunacy, verbal and physical, could flourish."[14]

For purists still distracted by the presence of Marx Brothers playwrights and screenwriters, it should be kept in mind that while the Brothers did not control their film productions in the unquestioned total auteur manner of a Chaplin, they were, like W. C. Fields, largely undirectable. Moreover, Groucho was often involved, though uncredited, with the writing, and later emerged as an author himself. Harpo, though not as concerned with the overall scope of the play or film as was Groucho, was generally the key "author" for his own visual material. In addition, much of the team's classic material for both stage and screen was first tinkered with daily as the Brothers either toured or tested it on the back roads of America. And finally, even the Marxes's involvement with a pivotal antiheroic "lunatic" writer like S. J. Perelman (on *Monkey Business*, 1931, and *Horse Feathers*, 1932), can be qualified with the team having exerted the influence, as opposed to the more traditional credit going to Perelman.[15]

Weales credits William Troy's negative review of *Duck Soup* as making an important connection between the Marxes and this comedy movement.[16] Troy had observed: "Like the whole 'crazy-fool' humor of the post-war epoch, it [Marxian humor] consists in a dissociation of the faculties rather than a concentrated direction of them towards any particular object in the body social or politic."[17] Troy might have exemplified his "dissociation of the faculties" analysis with the following *Duck Soup* conversation between the president of Freedonia (Groucho) and a peanut vendor (Chico):

Groucho: Now listen here. I've got a swell job for you, but first I'll have to ask you a couple of . . . important questions. Now, what is it that has four pair of pants, lives in Philadelphia, and it never rains but it pours?

Chico: 'At'sa good one. I give you three guesses.

Groucho: Now, lemme see. Has four pair of pants, lives in Philadelphia. Is it male or female?

Chico: No, I no think so.

Groucho: Is he dead?

Chico: Who?

Groucho: I don't know. I give up.

Chico: I give up, too. . . . [Chico insults Groucho]

Groucho: Just for that you don't get the job I was going to give you.

Chico: What job?

Groucho: Secretary of War.

Chico: All right, I take it.

Groucho: Sold!

The Groucho–Chico conversation nicely showcases their ability to personify the absurdity of the antiheroic modern world without also playing its comic victim, though Chico mildly gets the better of the argument. More often than most of their humor contemporaries, the Marxes comically vaccinated themselves against a zany world by assuming part of that zaniness themselves. Interestingly enough, this crazy comedy antidote is generally more apt to appear in the women who populate the comic antiheroic world, from the Looney Tunes Gracie Allen of (George) Burns & Allen, to the Thurber grandmother who thought electricity would leak from sockets without light bulbs.[18] But as eccentric as these women were, they made decisions (Thurber's grandmother was always screwing in bulbs) and then got on with living. Meanwhile, the comic antihero male generally attempts to make sense of it all (women and the world) and goes near crazy trying. Moreover, he cannot proceed with understanding and, since there is no understanding. . . .[19] (In the film genre of screwball comedy this same type of antihero male-eccentric female dicotomy exists. It merely represents a more sophisticated feature-length variation which was able to broaden the audience for the antiheroic misfit.)

Thurber later more fully articulates this antiheroic male-female difference in the story "Destructive Forces in Life," concluding:

> the undisciplined mind [that of the woman] runs far less chance of having its purpose thwarted, its plans distorted, its whole scheme and system wrenched out of line. The undisciplined mind, in short, is far better adapted to the confused world in which we live today than the streamlined mind [the disciplined mind of the man]. That is, I am afraid, no place for the streamlined mind.[20]

While the Marxes were much more likely to assume the "undisciplined" mind normally attributed to the female in this comedy movement, it should again be noted that interactions within the team often had Groucho playing the more traditional antihero male. This is best exemplified by the close of the long comedy dialogue between Groucho and Chico in the 1930 *Animal Crackers*. (This conversation includes Chico's classic irrational crime-solving suggestion to build a house next door in order to question the people who would then live there.) Thus, the "undisciplined mind" of Chico has both so fractured reason and the language that Groucho's "disciplined mind" is eventually reduced to incoherency in trying to make sense of Chico. The mustached one stumbles out of the scene mumbling "Ahh, ahh. . . ." Though this in-family victimization of Groucho to antihero status is not nearly so frequent as Groucho's own comedy attacks on an absurd world, they do regularly occur. Examples would include the standing gag in *Duck Soup* that Harpo and his motorcycle sidecar will always leave Groucho behind, the tootsie fruitsie ice cream scene in *A Day at the Races* (1937) where Chico sells Groucho a library of unnecessary betting books, and Chico's almost sadistic prevention of letting Groucho board the train in *At the Circus* (1939). Moreover, what Marx author Allen Eyles calls "Harpo's *tour de force* in outsmarting Groucho," the *Duck Soup* "mirror" scene imitation of Groucho, is argumentatively the greatest of all Marx Brothers scenes.[21]

10. Groucho, Harpo, and Chico "cutting up" for a publicity still. Groucho's precarious position is a fitting commentary on his frequent screen status, with regard to his Brothers. Note also that Harpo is showcasing his famous Gookie and Groucho is clenching one of his trademarks—a cigar. (Photograph courtesy of The Museum of Modern Art/Film Stills Archive.)

Added detail has been given to this examination of the Marxes's second broad influence, their involvement in the evolution of antiheroic comedy in American humor, for three reasons. First, unlike their high visibility as icons of comedy and the anti-establishment, their links to the world of the comic antihero are not always immediately apparent. Moreover, it is made more complex by Groucho's dual status—as comic aggressor outside the family (the stance which most readily comes to mind), and as the sometimes antiheroic male within the team. It is not that unlike the duality managed by his 1930s contemporary W. C. Fields, who fluctuated between his comic antihero male and that of carnival huckster—as well as sometimes joining them in the same role, as Groucho did his duality.[22] Second, understanding the Marxes's ties to antiheroic comedy makes Groucho's much more pronounced use of comic frustration in his solo writing considerably less jarring. Students of the Marxes frequently have expressed surprise over this apparent disparity, but the seeds of the antihero male were always in the Groucho persona, and comic interaction with his Brothers even made them surface, on occasion, in the team films. Third, joining the Marxes's often aggressive use of absurdity to the world of antiheroic comedy makes all the more understandable the ongoing pervasive influence of their comedy today. The same qualities which attracted surrealist Salvador Dali in the 1930s moved French Theatre of the Absurd pioneer Eugene Ionesco to declare the three biggest influences on his (Ionesco) work were actually Groucho, Chico, and Harpo Marx.[23] Theatre of the Absurd historian Martin Esslin agrees on the significance of the team to a movement that has also been called black comedy.

Like most things, black comedy is not inherently new, but its increased pervasiveness is. Thus, in a modern world that appears more and more unhinged, the Marxes seem even more contemporary. Moreover, their humor was often black to begin with. This is especially true in *Duck Soup*, where the foolishness of war is so effectively undercut, from the jingoistic joy given the approaching war (which is further universalized by the frequent military uniform changes in the scenes to come), to Groucho's accidental machine-gunning of his own men. Indeed, the very cause of war in *Duck Soup*, Groucho's comic paranoia about the intentions of Ambassador Trentino (which satirizes the paranoia often connected with the decisions of American government[24]), has direct ties with the even darker comic paranoia of *Dr. Strangelove*'s Sterling Hayden. Playing General Jack Ripper, he believes fluoridated water is a Soviet plot to assist in the takeover of America. Thus, one frequently thinks of the Marxes when communicating about the ironic absurdity of the modern world. This would include award-winning, dark comedy film director Billy Wilder's early 1960s plan to use the Marxes in a *Dr. Strangelove*-type satire; the more recent view of celebrated satirical playwright Dario Fo's darkly comic *Accidental Death of an Anarchist* as a "Left-Wing *Duck Soup*," and the Marx ties to *Brazil* with which this chapter opened.[25] More visible popular culture footnotes to the Marxes's influence on today's dark comedy are countless. They range in diversity from the obvious debt Alan Alda owes Groucho for the anti-establisment, womanizing Hawkeye

Pierce of *M*A*S*H* to the frequent tendency among political cartoonists to comment on the escalating absurdity of today by including the Marxes in their drawings. For example, *The Freedonia Gazette*, which regularly includes these cartoons in its pages, has a devastatingly comic one in its November 1980 issue. A reprint of a *Washington Star* syndicated Marx Brothers caricature, this one has the team as Pentagon heads preparing for a second mission after their involvement in the infamous failed hostage rescue under the Carter administration. Its black comedy detail might best be summed up by the fact that Chico is reading a booklet on "Helicopter Maintenance" (a helicopter breakdown having doomed the first mission).[26] Thus, the Marxes's inherent black comedy tendencies were the deciding factor in the author's choice of the *Horse Feathers* still used as this volume's frontispiece—a showcase of comic casualness at the apocalypse which seems chillingly contemporary.

The Marxes's third broad influence on Western culture has been their impact upon the complex, multifaceted phenomenon that is modern entertainment. For starters, the team might be called a cross section of American humor, from the fast-talking Groucho and the dialect comedy of Chico to the mime of Harpo, which was forever supplemented by cartoon-world sound effects. One might even count Zeppo as an example of the romantic light comedian for which sound comedy increased the need. Regardless of Zeppo, when the Marxes's comic diversity was married to their propensity for a scatter-gun range of satire topics, the entertainment possibilities were almost overpowering. In fact, Irving Thalberg's MGM homogenizing of the Marxes, coupled with his addition of more traditional story elements (see Chapter 1), was, in part, an attempt to make them more palatable to a general audience by making them less irrational. After the disappointing reception given *Duck Soup*, their last Paramount film and typical of their work for that studio, Thalberg thought the diversity of their comedy was too much for the 1930s audiences. Not surprisingly, today's more demanding viewer prefers the comically complex actions of the Marxes's Paramount films, especially *Duck Soup*, to their later work. Marx author Thomas H. Jordan quite logically observes:

> They were without question the most prominent forerunners of the rapidly-paced saturation comedy reintroduced to modern audiences through such television programs as *Laugh-In*, *The Ernie Kovacs Show*, *That Was the Week That Was*, and in Britain, *The Goon Show* and *Monty Python's Flying Circus*. Few modern film comedies have been able to re-create the headlong rush of humor which characterizes the Marxes.[27]

Related to this, Jordan goes on to note what has always been a popular refrain about the team—a key reason for their ongoing popularity—"their films can be seen many times without losing their appeal, for there are so many gags and jokes that no one can possibly remember more than a small number."[28] However, it should be underlined that the Marxes are still able to maintain their distinctive comedy character significance in this world of comedy chaos. Unlike other comedy team participants in similarly complex humor onslaughts, be it Olson & Johnson in *Hellzapoppin* (1941, which had also been an earlier success on Broadway), or Rowan & Martin in *Laugh-In*, the Marxes maintain center stage both by their talent and the simple fact that they monopolize the comedy roles. Unlike *Laugh-In*, which most people have forgotten was actually entitled *Rowan & Martin's Laugh-In*, there has never been a danger of forgetting the title characters in a Marx Brothers film.

Surprisingly, the influence of one Marx Brother has also been credited with setting just the opposite model (from saturation comedy) for television. Groucho Marx's casual conversations while sitting on a stool for the noncreatively visual *You Bet Your Life* was, according to television historian Max Wilk, instrumental in the similarly casual nature of many television programs that followed, especially the variety show.[29]

The Marxes's fourth broad influence was their early demonstration of the comic artistry *potential* of sound films, despite the often canned-theatre nature of their first two movies. To the student of film comedy, their cross section of American humor team made the transition from silents to sound more palatable—especially with the mime of Harpo acting as a salve on the painful loss and/or decline of so many silent comedy stars. In fact, as early as 1937 perceptive cultural critic Gilbert Seldes observed, "The arrival of the Marx Brothers and the reappearance of W. C. Fields saved screen comedy."[30] While Seldes goes on to credit Disney with being the ultimate sound replacement for the silent slapstick short, the live action team diversity of the Marxes (especially at a time when sound was decentralizing the formerly single comedy character focus of the silent films), demonstrated that film comedy's future could still be bright. Moreover, the Marx Brothers's early film success was so great that they paved the *movie* way for a whole series of other zany period comedy teams, such as the Ritz Brothers and Olsen & Johnson. Indeed, MGM's failed early-1930s attempt to team Buster Keaton and Jimmy Durante does not seem so unlikely if seen as a variation upon a Harpo-Groucho duo.

These, then, have been the four ongoing broad influences of the Marxes—as unique icons of both comedy and the anti-establishment; as major contributors to new developments in American humor, from direct involvement in antiheroic humor during its beginnings to the idealized models they represent for more recent followers of black comedy; as pivotal early examples of what might best be called saturation comedy; and as a pioneer measuring stick for the great potential of sound film comedy. One must never, however, lose sight of their greatest and continuing impact—they make people laugh. There are no greater gifts.

NOTES

1. Groucho Marx, *The Groucho Letters: Letters from and to Groucho Marx* (New York: Simon and Schuster, 1967), p. 133. The title of this chapter was also the name of a short-lived Groucho and Chico 1930s radio program.

2. Jeannie Williams, "Woody's film sparks Pulitzer tiff," *USA Today*, Weekend edition, April 18–20, 1986, p. 1A.

3. Paul G. Wesolowski, *"TFG* Reviews *Groucho,"* *The Freedonia Gazette*, Winter 1985, pp. 7–8. This review lists Wesolowski's top five Marx Brothers impersonation stage shows.

4. Martin A. Gardner, "The Marx Brothers: An Investigation of Their Films As Satirical Social Criticism," Ph.D. dissertation, New York University, 1970.

5. See especially Michael R. Real, "The Super Bowl: Mythic Spectacle," in *Television: The Critical View*, 3d ed., ed. Horace Newcomb (1976; rpt. New York: Oxford University Press, 1982), pp. 206–239.

6. See especially Wes D. Gehring, *Leo McCarey and the Comic Anti-Hero in American Film* (New York: Arno Press, 1980).

7. Joe Adamson, *Groucho, Harpo, Chico and Sometimes Zeppo* (New York: Simon and Schuster, 1973), p. 156.

8. James Thurber, "The Secret Life of Walter Mitty," in *My World and Welcome to It* (New York: Harcourt, Brace and Company, 1942), pp. 72–81.

9. Marie Seton, "S. Dali + 3 Marxes =   ," *Theatre Arts*, October 1939, p. 734.

10. Norris W. Yates, *The American Humorist: Conscience of the Twentieth Century* (1964; rpt. Ames, Iowa: Iowa State University Press, 1967).

11. See Walter Blair, *Native American Humor* (1937; rpt. San Francisco: Chandler Publishing Company, 1960), p. 169.

12. Gerald Weales, "Duck Soup," in *Canned Goods as Caviar: American Film Comedy of the 1930s* (Chicago: University of Chicago Press, 1985), p. 58; Donald Ogden Stewart, *Mr. and Mrs. Haddock* (New York: George H. Doran Company, 1924), pp. 123–137.

13. Alva Johnston, "The Scientific Side of Lunacy," *Woman's Home Companion*, September 1936, p. 12.

14. Weales, "Duck Soup," p. 58.

15. J. A. Ward, "The Hollywood Metaphor: The Marx Brothers, S. J. Perelman, and Nathanael West," *The Southern Review*, Summer 1976, p. 660.

16. Weales, "Duck Soup," p. 57.

17. William Troy, *Duck Soup* review, *The Nation*, December 13, 1933, p. 688.

18. James Thurber, "The Car We Had to Push," in *My Life and Hard Times* (1933; rpt. New York: Bantam Books, 1947), p. 41.

19. See Wes D. Gehring, *Screwball Comedy: A Genre of Madcap Romance* (Westport, Conn.: Greenwood Press, 1986).

20. James Thurber, "Destructive Forces in Life," in *Let Your Mind Alone! and Other More or Less Inspirational Pieces* (1937; rpt. New York: Universal Library, 1973), p. 18.

21. Allen Eyles, *The Marx Brothers: Their World of Comedy* (1966; rpt. New York: Paperback Library, 1971), p. 106.

22. See Wes D. Gehring, *W. C. Fields: A Bio-Bibliography* (Westport, Conn.: Greenwood Press, 1984).

23. Ionesco's *The Shepherd's Chameleon* review, *Time*, December 12, 1960, p. 63; Gardner, "The Marx Brothers," pp. 2–3; Martin Esslin, *The Theatre of the Absurd* (Garden City, N.Y.: Doubleday & Company, 1961), pp. 263–237.

24. For more on this, see Gardner's "The Marx Brothers," p. 94.

25. Lance Morrow, *Accidental Death of an Anarchist* review, *Time*, March 12, 1984, p. 70.

26. *The Freedonia Gazette*, November 1980, p. 17.

27. Thomas H. Jordan, "The Marx Brothers," in *The Anatomy of Cinematic Humor* (New York: Revisionist Press, 1975), p. 90.

28. Ibid., pp. 91–92.

29. Max Wilk, *The Golden Age of Television* (1976; rpt. New York: Delacorte Press, 1977), p. 92.

30. Gilbert Seldes, chapter 5, in *The Movies Come from America* (New York: Charles Scribner's Sons, 1937), p. 41.

3.

MARX ON MARX:
AN ARTICLE,
AN INTERVIEW,
AND A COMEDY ESSAY

Since no in-depth examination of a family of artists would be complete without including some of their own observations, this chapter includes the reprinting of the Groucho article "My Poor Wife!" (*Colliers*, December 20, 1930); an interview with Gummo, "Those Mad Marx Hares: As Revealed by the Fifth Marx Brother to Edward R. Sammis" (*Photoplay*, February 1936); and a Groucho comedy essay, "How to Be a Spy" (*This Week* magazine, *New York Herald Tribune*, February 16, 1946).

While Groucho might have revealed several other self-critical reasons for calling Ruth "My Poor Wife!" (see Chapter 1), this is still an entertainingly warm look at what might be called the "make 'em laugh syndrome" of comedians. That is, their need to be funny and the recycled material this subjects their spouses to as old material is repeated for new guests. Near the essay's close he also indirectly acknowledges a comedy habit that sometimes got him into trouble—making outlandish "Groucho" statements (without benefit of costume and greasepaint) to strangers and not revealing who he was.

"Those Mad Marx Hares" is a delightfully funny look at Gummo, the most obscure of the Marxes. Besides demonstrating that all the Brothers had comedy skills, it provides some interesting family background (such as Gummo's long-term pre-*A Night at the Opera* belief that Harpo's screen persona should be made more sympathetic), as well as obscuring a few things (see the bracketed notes within the text). The interview is also graced with Frank Dobias's amusing group caricature, which has also been reproduced for this chapter.

Groucho's "How to Be a Spy" is one of many comedy essays he wrote during his lifetime. This piece from the 1940s, probably his most prolific journal-writing period, recommends itself for several reasons. First, besides being funny, it manages to showcase both the archetype screen Groucho and the comic antihero so often present in his writing (or his film encounters with his Brothers).

Second, while its comic espionage focus is an obvious plug for the Marxes's *A Night in Casablanca* (which by itself makes for an interesting tie between his fiction and film), the then topical nature of espionage is just the sort of subject on which Groucho preferred to write. For example, during World War II he comically examined such topics as "Groucho Marx Turns Himself in for Scrap" and "How to Build a Secret Weapon" (see Chapters 1 and 4). Moreover, his frequent "How to . . ." stance is another parallel that his comedy writing shares with Robert Benchley, whose essays he greatly admired (see Chapter 2). For both men, the "How to . . ." theme was a perfect comic premise from which to get comically derailed during a lecture-like "talk" (essay, though both authors used variations of this in their films).

Third, the essay is replete with the verbal slapstick for which Groucho is famous. In fact, this author's only hesitation about using this piece was that it seemed overstocked, closer to his film character than his writing persona. Possibly, this was again a conscious plug for the Marxes's then-forthcoming film. Ultimately, such a full showcasing seemed to outweigh the reservations. Indeed, there might even be a renewed negative insight, that his writing—or any writing— would be more comically effective if one could see a filmed Groucho performing it. Groucho himself had underlined this point during the MGM material testing tours. The complaint was made that Groucho was not "selling" the material with such patented gestures as the raised greasepaint eyebrows. His response was that when thus helped along, he could get a laugh with any line. Underselling was just his way of finding what was intrinsically funny.

Fourth, the final section of the essay, when applying spy business to archetypal boring, visiting neighbors, "Mr. and Mrs. Pratt," effectively demonstrates Groucho's ability to bring even espionage back to the underlying theme of so much of his 1940s writing. In fact, earlier in the decade he had written "Do You Know Enough to Go Home?", an essay fully devoted to getting unwanted guests out of the home (see Chapter 4). This Pratt segment is, however, extra fun, because Groucho's suggestions go to the comic extreme, not unlike the dark humor of an S. J. Perelman.

All in all, the article, interview, and comedy essay that follow present the most famous and the most obscure Marx Brother in a variety of print selections. Fittingly, for a comedy team, the material is amusing, as well as informally insightful. And the informal setting is often the most revealing.

"MY POOR WIFE!"

By Groucho Marx

Although Mr. Marx doesn't say so, this article is really a warning to any young woman who thinks she would like to marry a comedian—any comedian.

The lady—a new acquaintance—tittered as she was leaving our house. Turning to my wife, she said:

"If laughing makes people fat, how do you manage to keep your figure: Why, you must spend most of the time in hysterics, having a comedian for a husband."

My wife smiled, or rather tried to smile, and I felt ashamed. I knew how many times Ruth had heard the jests, wisecracks and puns that I had uttered during the evening, and I wondered how long her beautiful patience could last.

How often (I couldn't help thinking), how often she must have wished she had married a plumber or an undertaker, who, although he might talk shop at home, would hesitate to work at it after hours! I had seen my wife wince when I told the story (again) about the Scotchman who painted red stripes on his son's thumb so the child would think he had a peppermint stick. She had heard the story five (possibly six) times before, even though it was, I still hope, new to our guests. She had even laughed a little during the second and third recitals of the anecdote. And the second time she had actually directed the conversation to small talk about thrift.

But there are limits to human endurance. . . . Oh, I know that a theater usher has to hear the same joke as often as two or three hundred times a year (when the show's a hit); but then that's the usher's *job*. And I doubt that my wife could have been happy as an usher.

Then why, you ask (and it's about time you were taking an interest in what I'm saying), why do I tell and re-tell all these trifling japes and nifties? Why don't I become a quiet, unclownish husband like Mr. Smith, the grocer, or Mr. Jones, who delivers our coal?

Dear, dear reader, you are now going to hear about the curse of my profession. When a man is in the comedy business, people expect him to be comical at all times. A violinist can leave his fiddle at home; a pianist can forget to bring his music; but a comedian has no excuse. If he isn't conspicuously funny, he's regarded as a rather dull and disappointing fellow.

Let a stage clown go to a party and completely forget his profession, and people will say: "Oh, he's all right behind the footlights, but isn't he uninteresting when you meet him: I suppose he just isn't a *natural* comedian." Thereupon the

Reprinted from *Colliers*, December 20, 1930, pp. 15, 59.

poor man develops a first-class inferiority complex and begins slinking down alleys for fear that a mad critic will bite him.

There are, of course, a few men—men braver than I—who are in the business of being funny and yet will not hesitate to indulge in a quipless evening, no matter how many eager auditors are around them, hopefully waiting for something to laugh at.

Ring Lardner, for example, is one of the wittiest men in America; certainly he is the most humorous. But when away from his typewriter, Ring is content to be as solemn and unfunny as a New England preacher dedicating a new funeral chapel. I have spent evenings with Lardner when he didn't say one funny thing. I have spent evenings with him when he didn't say anything at all.

George Kaufman is another of America's First Wits; and he, too, is considered a grave gent by people who meet him for the first time. "Great playwright," they say of George, "and a funny writer, but he didn't say one amusing thing all evening."

And I ought to cite Ed Wynn, too, among the heroic gentlemen in the comedy business who can (when away from the theater) puff at their pipes and ask whether Radio is likely to go up a few points during the next day and how do you think the Giants will hit the old apple around next season?

Courageous men, Lardner, Kaufman and Wynn. How my wife must envy their wives!

Not, of course, that she wasn't sufficiently warned before our marriage. Ruth was a dancer (I might add, a *good* dancer; in fact, I'd *better* add a good dancer) in our vaudeville act when we met; and, although I tried to keep her from hearing me repeat my off-stage comedy in our courtship days, I wasn't altogether successful. And I was weak. I couldn't always resist making fresh use of a good anecdote, or what I considered a snappy bit of repartee, whenever there was a new listener to hear it.

The wedding itself might have changed Ruth's mind, but it didn't. It was the only comical wedding I have ever attended.

We were married in Ruth's home in Chicago; and of course my brothers (also in the comedian business) were present. Harpo was in a particularly mirthful mood.

Just as the clergyman—he was a most dignified old gentleman—began to say the words that were to make Ruth my wife and permanent audience, he coughed and made a funny noise with his throat.

Unfortunately, it was just such a sound as that which served as a signal for a comedy bit in our show. On the stage, when the straight man did an "er-r-r," Harpo would pretend to become frightened and would quickly fling himself under the carpet.

Yes, it happened at the wedding. The clergyman had no sooner cleared his throat than Harpo was under the carpet; the wedding became giddier than any skit I have ever seen in the revues. Everybody but the clergyman laughed.

Matrimonial Monkeyshines

As Harpo left his hiding place under the rug, Chico began wishing me luck in Italian dialect [Chico was actually not in attendance], and Zeppo asked the preacher if it would be bad taste for him to sing a little ditty about his yearnings for Alabammy.

I, of course, had no part in these monkeyshines. It was my wedding, a solemn day in my life. A day of dignity. And it's only because Ruth's memory isn't as good as mine that she says I answered the preacher in Moran-and-Mack fashion. Oh, I might have walked up to the altar doing a modified fox trot (I was rather proud of my dancing in those days), but I did not—I most certainly did not—talk like Moran and Mack.

For my part, I can only wish that my comedy during our married years had been easier for Ruth to bear. To be sure, she has never once complained. More often than not, in fact, she has encouraged me.

I can remember (with no pride at all) remarking that I could tell the age of a chicken by the teeth. "But a chicken *has* no teeth," Sam Harris—I think it was Sam Harris—said, and I replied: "No, but *I* have." There was a round of laughter in the room.

Personally, I thought this a pretty terrible crack, but the Marxes believe that the customer is always right.

The next time we had chicken for dinner, and a few friends at the house, I found myself saying once more that I could tell the age of a chicken by the teeth. And it was Ruth—Ruth herself—who said, "but a chicken *has* no teeth."

But to be perfectly honest with you, I must confess that I brought up the subject of a chicken's age three or four days later. . . . And it was four months before my wife served chicken again. She said she had grown tired of poultry, but down in my heart I knew.

It is with honest humility that I am citing my worst offenses in after-working-hours comedy, because I want you to know the extent of my wife's grievances. I can remember when Reigh Count—or was it Man o' War?—won the Kentucky Derby in the rain, and the papers referred to him as a good mudder. And I said, "And does the mudder eat his fodder?"

Well, George White, who was present at the time, had won a few nickels on the horse. Consequently he was in good humor at the time. He laughed. And you can't guess how laughter can spoil a comedian.

The next night, when Reigh Count was mentioned again, Ruth said—very slyly, I thought—"he's an awfully good mudder, isn't he?" Dear, dear Ruth! That, I knew, was my cue. So quick as lightning—as though the thought had just struck me—I went into my little joke.

Four days later, when Eddie Cantor mentioned the Kentucky Derby, Ruth neatly changed the subject. Nothing was said about mudders and fodder.

Then there was the time when we went fishing in Long Island Sound and the man who rented the boat and fishing equipment said the bait would cost us eleven dollars. I said it would be cheaper to cut up the children for bait; and Ruth became annoyed. She said it wasn't a nice thing to say; the man might take me seriously; and . . . anyway, I knew she was right. But my objection to the remark was that it had fallen pretty flat. The boatman merely stared at me and held out his hand for the eleven dollars.

I am not, to be sure, *always* weak. Only a month ago when the grocer talked about the "pesky kids" who swiped cherries from the stand in front of his store, I restrained myself from asking if a *pesky* was a skeleton key in Russia. And never—may I never hear another laugh if I'm lying to you now—have I said that the best way to tell a bad egg is to break it gently.

Because I wear a painted mustache and a comical costume on the stage and in the movies, I seldom am recognized by strangers. Which is quite a handicap (or maybe a blessing) for some of my off-stage comedy.

You see, people are always a little quicker to laugh at a professional funny man than they are at a person in another profession or business. When we moved to Great Neck, I went to one of the village confectioners and asked for some candy for the children.

What Makes a Joke a Joke

"Just a few dainties to make the kiddies sick," I told the clerk and he gave me a frigid stare—and the candy.

A month later, after the confectionery man had learned that I was a comedian, I happened to drop in for more candy.

"The kiddies want to get sick again," I said, and the clerk shook the counter with his laughter. Surely this wasn't any more amusing than when I had said a similar thing before. But the fact that I was a comedian made a difference.

Now this confectioner chuckles when I merely walk into his store. He has, I think, a frustrated yearning to be some comedian's "straight man," or foil.

Ruth as no such wish.

For ten years she has been listening to my oft-repeated flippancies; she has heard me say the same things again and again—serious things as well as skittish.

Even all this—all that I have been telling you here in Collier's—Ruth has heard before.

I'm sorry for my wife.

"THOSE MAD MARX HARES"

As Revealed by the Fifth Marx Brother to Edward R. Sammis

Discovered, Gummo Marx! Daffier than the others!
He tells—with gestures—just how crazy they all are!

[Original *Photoplay*] Editor's Note: With everyone going around saying, "Did you hear that one the Marx Brothers pulled in 'A Night at the Opera'?", we felt we just had to have a story on the Mad Marx Hares. Knowing from bitter experience that it was practically impossible to get any of them to remain in one place long enough to talk for publication, we sent out a reporter to ferret out the fifth Marx Brother, Gummo Marx, who used to be in the act years ago, and is now associated with Brother Zeppo in his talent agency. Gummo's intimate revelations of the private life of the Marx Brothers follow.

"Why is it," I demanded, coming straight to the bush instead of beating around the point, "that you Marx Brothers are nearly always together lately, except when you're apart?"

It was Gummo Marx to whom I put the question. Probably you have never heard of Gummo. You have never seen him on the screen and you never will unless he loses his reason. (Gummo has forgotten what his reason was, but he sticks to it just the same.)

Gummo is known far and wide, or at least wide, as the sane Marx Brother. In fact, Gummo is so sane that he quit the act fourteen years ago and went into the clothing business.

I had been told that Gummo was one Marx Brother to whom you could put an uncivil question and expect a civil answer. So here I stood in his Broadway office. The only catch was that Gummo didn't seem to be listening.

"Why is it!" I began again. But he checked me with a gesture.

Gummo remained silent while the cigar he was slowly swallowing traveled from just under the lobe of his right ear to just under the lobe of his left ear and back again.

Then he faced me without flinching, and answered fearlessly:

"Yes and no."

A moment later he was pacing the floor.

"Do you want to know why the Marx Brothers are always together?" he said. "I'll tell you why. Suspicion—intrigue—collusion! That's why. What has the career of the Marx Brothers become: An elimination contest.

"It's this way: I left the act and business immediately began to pick up.

"Zeppo left, and the next picture 'A Night at the Opera' is terrific. Now the suspense is terrific. Who will be next?

Reprinted from *Photoplay*, February 1936, pp. 26–27, 89.

11. Frank Dobias's caricature of the Marx Brothers in transition. (From the original 1936 article "THOSE MAD MARX HARES . . .") The drawing highlights the three main Marxes, while flanking them with fragmented images of the two Brothers who quit the act—Gummo (the leg) in front and Zeppo (the head and tie) at the end.

"That's what the boys started asking each other right after the preview. In fact, they all drew lots. Chico claimed his lots were under water, so he called the deal off. What Groucho called it is nobody's business.

"But someone's got to go. That's progress. Why, I can foresee the day when their pictures will be billed, 'Absolutely no Marx Brothers Whatever Positively!' And then won't they pack them in!"

"And what," I asked, "are these brothers of yours really like?"

"So you want to know about father," said Gummo reflectively.

I did not say I wanted to know anything about father so Gummo began:

"It seems that one day he was sitting up in the balcony watching the boys down on the stage when two men in front of him got to arguing about whether Harpo was really dumb or whether he could talk.

"The old man reached over and tapped one of them on the shoulder and said, " 'He can talk all right.'

"The man turned around incensed.

" 'All right,' he said to the old man, 'I'll bet you ten dollars he can't.'

"My father looked at him with a gleam in his eye and said,

" 'What odds will you give me?' "

Gummo flicked six inches of ash from his cigar and continued:

"You see how it was. We never had a chance to make an honest living. So there was nothing left for us to do but go on the stage. We started out as acrobats, building a human pyramid, but somehow we got off on the wrong foot, and our house of cards (we never could decide who was the greatest card) came tumbling down."

"Very interesting," I said, "but what are these brothers of yours really—"

"So you want to know how Groucho got his moustache," chuckled Gummo. "Well, that's quite a story. It seems that Groucho used to make up a moustache of crepe hair for every show. Then one day, Harpo found a bald spot in his wig, just before curtain time. And he stole all of Groucho's crepe hair to patch it up. So Groucho had to go on with a moustache of burnt cork. But he made a tremendous discovery. Burnt cork didn't tickle like crepe hair. It changed Groucho's whole nature. He used to be gruff, glum and surly. Now he's impossible." [Many Marx Brothers stories, like legend, have variations. This is one of them. The standard explanation, however, is that Groucho arrived too late at the theatre—after visiting his newborn son in the hospital—to glue on his crepe mustache properly. Thus, he applied the quickest available substitute.]

"True, no doubt true," I interrupted, "but what are these brothers of yours—"

"I knew you'd ask that one," laughed Gummo. "Everyone does. Well, the way we got our names was this. When we were in vaudeville, there was a cartoonist, Art Fisher, playing on the same bill with us, who gave us those names.

"Where he got them, heaven knows. Of course, Harpo was playing the harp, but I'm sure that had nothing to do with it. Chico was a cheeky sort of guy—so what? Zeppo was playing a rube named Zep—pure coincidence. I, Gummo, was always gum-shoeing around—a happenstance. And then there was Groucho. He couldn.t have been named for his disposition. Groucho isn't really like that. He's worse." [Gummo was possibly protecting Chico by not noting the real Chico pronunciation—chico- "girl"-chasing—because Chico had recently had a serious affair for which his Brothers had pressured him not to get divorced, in part to protect the making of *A Night at the Opera*. And Zep, for a time, really was "playing a rube" on the Marx family farm in Illinois. See Chapter 1.]

"Authentic, undoubtedly authentic," I nodded. "But tell me, what are these—"

"Why did I quit the act?" Gummo resumed. "I'll tell you why I quit the act. I went to war to get a little peace. When I returned I went into the clothing business.

"The boys tried to even up old scores by getting me back into the act. I retaliated by trying to get them into the clothing business. But there wasn't a chance. They didn't like my taste.

"When we were all playing together they used to steal each other's clothes. They wouldn't even steal mine."

"Quite," I said, "but tell me what are—"

"So I stayed in the business, thinking that was where you got money without working. They became comedians. And they expected *me* to laugh at *them*!

"All this time we kept in very close touch. I'd touch them before they got a chance to touch me.

"When they went to the Coast, I wrote them long letters every week.

"As soon as they got them they'd tear them up without reading them.

"Then they'd write letters to me. At least I think they did.

"I don't know, because I always tore their letters up, too.

"It's a wonderful system.

"Nobody knows what the other is thinking. Besides, it saves filing.

"Then, one day I got a wire from them telling me to sell my business and join them on the Coast.

"I sold my business that same day and took a plane for Hollywood. [Gummo actually had gone bankrupt.]

"When I got there I found they'd flown to New York.

"The only word they'd left for me was a note saying 'April Fool.' But I didn't get the point because it was in July.

"So I took another plane to New York, and bought my business back for twice what I sold it for. [There is more than one tale about aerial Marx Brothers gags, or what they might have labeled a "plane" practical joke.]

"A few weeks later the boys walked into my office and tried to get me to go to Hollywood with them. But I was smart this time. It took them six months to persuade me they weren't kidding.

"So I joined Zeppo in the agency business. You know Zeppo has become one of the most successful agents in Hollywood. He has a sure-fire formula. He goes to a producer and offers one of his actors for a picture. If the producer turns him down, Zeppo threatens to go back on the screen.

"Then the producer says, 'I can't use your actor, but I'll pay him anyway, rather than see that happen.'

"As soon as we all got together, we got as far apart as possible. I came back to New York.

"Now I'm the eastern end of Zeppo. Or Zeppo is the western end of me, depending on how you look at it.

"Harpo shuttles back and forth between. We tried pacing him with a mechanical rabbit like they do whippets. But we couldn't keep the rabbits. Harpo could scare even a mechanical rabbit.

"Now we pace him with a blonde and we have no trouble. The blonde has it."

"An aborbing narrative," I observed, "but tell me what are your brothers really like? Take Groucho—"

"You take Groucho. Goodness knows I've tried to take him often enough. But he always takes me—for plenty."

"Speaking of Harpo—" I prompted.

"Who's speaking of Harpo?" he retorted. "Nobody's said a word about him. But since you've brought up an unpleasant subject, have you noticed that Harpo is more wistful, more appealing in the new picture?"

I said I hadn't noticed it.

"Well, they can't blame me for that," he said, "I thought of it years ago. I must have written them a hundred letters urging them to play up that boyish quality of his. But I know they never read my letters. So they needn't go around blaming me for it.

"Let them blame Thalberg. It's probably his idea. [Irving Thalberg, head of production at MGM—the parent company for *A Night at the Opera*—had worked closely with the team, and was responsible for the softening of their characters.]

"Say," said Gummo suddenly, "there's one thing you haven't asked me. You haven't asked me what the boys are really like. Well, since you haven't displayed any interest whatever, I'll tell you.

"Look at Groucho, if you can stand it. I can't. Groucho is the family man. Likes to sit around home and smoke my cigars or play with his kids.

"Harpo is a family man, too. Any family that's handy. You'd better keep yours under lock and key.

"Chico, now, is a crack bridge player. He's so good he's almost half as good as he says he is. I'm telling you that for nothing although I'd hate to tell you how much it cost me to find it out.

"And Harpo: Who mentioned Harpo? Well, Harpo's hobby is collecting old harps, only he hasn't started yet.

"Outside of that he plays croquet. He won't be happy until he beats [drama critic and close friend Alexander] Woollcott, and I doubt if he'll be happy then.

"You have to be careful what you say to Harpo. I told him once he'd go a long ways before he found an audience which would appreciate him. So he went to Russia. [In late 1933, largely because of Woollcott, Harpo became the first American performer to entertain in Moscow after the United States recognized the Soviet Union.]

"Now he's always talking about going to Budapest.

"In the picture, where his lips are moving and you can't hear a word he's saying, he's talking about going to Budapest.

"I didn't see the picture, but I understand it was so funny even the audience laughed. I stayed home instead and wrote a six page criticism of it.

"It proved a great help to the boys. They tore it up without reading it.

"Right now we're all trying to find a story for their next picture.

"Hundreds of people are working on stories for them.

"The only trouble is the stories all have plots. They'll go right into production as soon as they can find a story without a plot.

"I'm working on one myself. Only I'm having trouble getting the story long enough to make it worth their while to tear up."

"I can see," I observed, "that it must be quite a responsibility being the only sane Marx Brother."

"I'll say it is!" he snorted. "In fact, it's driving me nuts!"

"HOW TO BE A SPY"

By Groucho Marx

You, too, can learn to swallow secret documents.
You, too, can master the art of facing a firing squad.
Here are some straight facts from a warped mind

The public may be surprised that I am able to write on the subject of espionage. As a matter of fact, the public may be surprised that I am able to write. But the truth is that my latest picture, "A Night in Casablanca," is so fraught with international intrigue that I have become an expert in that field. Thus, I decided I must write this vital article which every man, woman and child in the nation can afford to overlook.

Let me lead you step by step from elementary code work right up to the firing squad. In the first place, you must understand that there is more than one kind of secret agent. There is, first, the General Spy, whose activities are unlimited. Then there is the man who specializes in bargain-counter and lunch-counter cases, and he is, of course, the Counter-Spy. Finally there is the Northern Spy, which hasn't anything to do with the subject except that it's good eating if you like apples.

But I am getting away from my theme. I always say an article is like a lady's stocking—it's important to keep the theme straight. I knew we'd get around to women sooner or later. Aren't you glad?

Easy for Redheads

On becoming a spy, you will have to learn to deal with feminine wiles. The temptation of a beautiful woman can be your downfall—if you're lucky. Of course, Marx, the Master Spy, is proof against blandishments of the sveltest brunettes and the most ravishing blondes on earth. On the other hand, a redhead can get anything out of me in two minutes flat.

Let me tell you about my first *femme fatale*, that suave, bejeweled agent of Hungroslavia. Her name was Mandolin, and I shall always remember that evening in her scented boudoir on the Rue de la Strapontin-Cassee. My mission was to wrest from her the blueprints of the fearsome Gatling gun. . . .

But I am getting ahead of my story. Let me tell you how the mission first started. Our spy outfit was stationed on a secret island off the French coast. We had all been through a terrifying period. We had run out of paper clips, and we could no longer file reports in sextuplicate. We had to have clips! One panic-stricken soul among us suggested we try a clip joint, but that would have been

Reprinted from *This Week* magazine, *New York Herald Tribune*, February 16, 1946, pp. 6, 20.

tantamount to dealing in the black market. I was running feverishly all over the island. I was ready to drop in my tracks, except that I don't run on tracks.

Wrest in Peace

Then the General approached me. "Marx," he said, "You must go to the mainland in a small, unseaworthy craft and then proceed to Paris on a small, ungroundworthy motorcycle. Once there you must wrest the blueprints of the fearsome Gatling gun from the beauteous Mandolin. May you wrest in peace."

I set out at midnight in a dory. The waves were so high that they broke over the gunwales (pronounced gunnels). All I could find to bail with was a funwale (pronounced funnel). *To make matters worse, the night was black as a tunwale (pronounced tunnel). This kind of humor is known as beating a dead horse, so let's drop it.*

Suffice to say, I eventually reached Paris and burst in upon the beauteous Mandolin. "Dear lady," I said as I took her in my arms, "I am not hemmed to fit the touch of your skirt!" (This is the way spies always talk to each other—code language.)

"Mandolin," I continued, "I have come to curry favor." I ran my fingers through her hair. "Sorry I forgot my currycomb." Then I prostrated myself before her. "Mandolin," I slavered, "I swear that your beauty has crazed me. Your eyes, how they shine! They shine like the pants of a blue serge suit!"

Blueprint Gourmet

At that moment the plans of the Gatling gun dropped from her bodice—I snatched them.

"Monster!" she shrieked. "For this night's work you shall reap dismay!"

"You've got it all wrong," I said. "I shall plow dismay—I won't be reaping till dis-august."

At that point Mandolin's lover, the Count de la Défense d'Afficher rushed into the room. I had to swallow the blueprints quick, and I must say they were the worst I've ever tasted.

"*Cochon!*" cried the Count. "What are you doing in my fiancée's apartment?"

"Well, right now I'm trying to find a bicarbonate of soda."

He advanced and slapped me across the cheek with his gloves. I could not let this challenge go unheeded. I produced my cardcase. "Take one, Monsieur," I snapped.

He did.

"What is it?" I said.

"Queen of spades."

"Pay me—I drew the ace."

This did not satisfy him, however, so I stalked away to my motorcycle and drove off in low dudgeon—I couldn't make high on the gasoline we were getting in those days.

This whole episode goes to prove an important point: A good spy must be able to take insults and hardships in his stride. He must keep constantly gruntled—the moment a spy becomes disgruntled he is of no use to anyone. For instance, let me tell you of another important case of mine. This one happened right in New Jersey.

As I sat one night swatting mosquitoes, I received three mysterious telephone calls. The first two were wrong numbers, the third was an acquaintance of mine, J. J. Fusty, who runs a large penwiper factory in Hoboken. "Come to me quick, Inspector," he pleaded.

I rushed right over. A butler ushered me into the drawing room where Mr. and Mrs. Fusty were waiting to greet me.

"Thank heaven you are here, Inspector," said Fusty. "Sit down anywhere."

I sat down in Mrs. Fusty's lap.

"Inspector," continued Fusty, "my business is going to rack and ruin. Labor is scarce. Supply is turning my hair gray. Price is dangling a sword over my head."

"Why don't you dangle a sword over Price's head and see how *he* likes it?"

"You don't understand, Inspector. There is worse trouble—a suspicious character is writing me letters, threatening to highjack my trucks."

Plunge to Work

"That's right down my alley," I said. "Do you have an inkling as to the fellow's identity?"

"None at all, except that he poses as an Army officer."

"Hah," I said, "anyone with half an eye could clear up this case. *Unfortunately, I don't happen to know anybody with half an eye, so I'll have to do the job myself.*"

Without further words I plunged out into the night. As luck would have it, I ran across a suspect that very evening. He was dressed in Army khaki, but my sharp eye noted that the insigne was not that of any Army outfit. I trailed him for three days, and his actions were most suspicious. Every day he would sneak out into the woods around town and meet up with a band of midgets. Then they would all go about setting fires.

I determined to bring my quarry to bay. So one evening as he trudged along the road with his midget band, I sprang from the bushes and confronted him. "I am Marx, the Master Spy," I snarled.

"Glad to meet you, Mr. Marx," he said. "I am Clarence Snood, Scoutmaster of the Beaver Troop."

Of course it was a bitter pill for me to swallow, but in a way I did not regret it—we all toasted marshmallows and became fast friends.

Get Rid of 'Ent

Incidentally, J. J. Fusty's business did go to rack and ruin. It is now known as Rack & Ruin, Inc., and I understand the new owners are making a go of it.

What, you may ask, is the practical use of spy work? Can it be applied to everyday life: Yes, I say. Persons with sound espionage training can overcome many social problems that would stagger ordinary householders.

Suppose, for instance, that boring Mr. and Mrs. Pratt down the street are about to call on you. If you and your wife have had spy training, you will immediately turn off all lights in the house.

While your wife prepares an eerie fire of bleached bones on the living-room hearth, you will disguise yourself as a mad butler. After quickly shaving your hair off, you will insert a dagger in your chest so that a conspicuous bloodstain will spread all over your shirt front. Then, when you welcome the Pratts at the front door, Mr. Pratt will probably laugh nervously and mumble something about not being able to stay long.

If the Pratts are difficult cases, I suggest hiding a dead Balkan minister in the coat closet (you should be able to pick one up cheap). When the Pratts are hanging up their wraps, the body will fall out at their feet. *There is no need to make introductions, even though they may express some curiosity as to who he is.*

The next step is to usher the Pratts into the living room where the bleached bones are crackling dismally. Your wife will have set out phials of poison on the coffee table (these should be clearly marked with skull and crossbones or you'll get into trouble with the Food and Drug Administration).

If you can get hold of a baby sitter to come over and clank some chains in the cellar, so much the better. But baby sitters are hard to get nowadays.

Drop a Line

By all the laws of averages, the Pratts should make their adieux within 20 minutes by the clock. But if they persist in sticking around, it is considered justifiable to take them out to the garden wall and shoot them down with rifles. Fastidious hosts will, of course, remember to supply eye bandages and a last cigarette.

Well, I think that just about covers the subject of spy work. If any of you have further questions, merely drop me a letter stating your age, weight, height and sex.

I'm particularly anxious to hear from a few blondes under 30 who enjoy canoeing.

4.

A MARX BROTHERS BIBLIOGRAPHICAL ESSAY

To write an autobiography of Groucho Marx would be as asinine as to read an autobiography of Groucho Marx.[1]
—Groucho Marx, just after completing his second autobiographical work

This bibliographical essay furnishes, in a logical manner, those key reference materials that are most helpful in studying the lives and careers of the Marx Brothers. All works are divided first by length and then by subject. The pivotal works discussed will also be found in the bibliographical checklist in Chapter 5.

The first section is devoted to book-length sources written about or by the comedians. The materials are then subdivided into four categories: Marx Brothers viewed by insiders, Marx on Marx, Marx critical studies, and Marx references. Though these books frequently have a focus Marx Brother, generally Groucho, they never entirely divorce themselves from the team, because the team was also family. This is best exemplified by Hector Arce's *Groucho*, which, despite the title, is easily the best Marx *Brothers* biography. Thus, each volume is treated as a group biography here.

The second section is comprised of shorter works and includes articles, interviews, book chapters, and monographs. It is subdivided into two parts: Marx Brothers critical and/or biographical pieces (categories often combined by authors writing on the Marxes), and Marx on Marx (including interviews).

There is also a brief account of existing Marx Brothers archives and film sources.

BOOKS

Marx Brothers Viewed by Insiders

There are two positive contradictions about Arce's *Groucho* (1979). First, it boasts a title that disguises its status as the best group biography of the team. Also, it is an insider volume (Arce was both a longtime Groucho friend and co-author with the comedian of *The Secret Word Is GROUCHO*), which avoids the general flaws of such works—it is generally *unbiased* and there is a wealth of *accurate* Marx Brothers information. (The volume runs 540 pages.) Though the absence of footnotes is disappointing, the author often cites references within the text. Marx Brothers aficionado Paul G. Wesolowski is cited as the book's chief researcher, but Arce was aided by the close cooperation of Groucho (the book is Groucho's authorized biography, though the comedian died before its completion) and interviews with, among others, Chico's first wife Betty, their daughter Maxine, and Norman Krasna, Groucho's close friend and co-writer on the film *The King and the Chorus Girl* (1937) and the Broadway play *Time for Elizabeth* (1948).

Unfortunately, while there is a four-page bibliography, it notes only materials that have appeared in book form—ironically neglecting most of the sources that have been referred to within the text. Since a text citation by nature is never complete, this is frustrating. The interested reader who wants to pursue further information from an article or evaluate it himself is forced to first play secretary (recording the partial reference) and then detective finding it. One might liken it to the hoary treasure-hunt tale, where only half a map is available. Moreover, even the bibliography has glaring omissions. For example, no mention is made of Groucho's many books, including the comedian's and Arce's joint project *The Secret Word Is GROUCHO*. This is especially surprising, since Arce did the introduction for *The Groucho Phile*, a volume that, as the title comically suggests, draws generously from Groucho's other works.

The best adjustment to such frustrations is to remind oneself that most insider books (be they on the Marx Brothers or the subject of your choice) provide little or no reference sources. Additional comfort comes from the factual detail that is there. This is the strength of the text. The sizable store of Marx information is also frequently showcased in an equally detailed look at the period settings in which the Marx Brothers drama occurred. For example, the book opens with an interesting examination of the late nineteenth-century New York into which the boys were born. Period frameworks such as these often provide an insightful sociologically critical perspective regarding the evolution of the Marx Brothers. Thus, with regard to the immigrant city of their youth, one senses the outsider nature of these later iconoclasts from day one. Moreover, comic use of language seems natural when your playground has a United Nations-style mixture of peoples. This is not the first time such analogies have been drawn, but they are nowhere else so effectively presented.

Arce also provides more commentary upon career than is typical of insider volumes, which often just focus upon the personal. However, his overview per-spectives upon movements and trends within the entertainment industry are neither as frequently drawn as his general historical perspectives, nor are they as insightful. Thus, one sometimes wishes for more critical analysis of the Marxes's work. For instance, Arce consciously avoids entering the controversy over the effect on their comedy of Thalberg's changes in their films.

Such expectations again illustrate the general excellence of the book, because more critical analysis is hardly a normal request of an insider volume. This author's only complaint with the traditional (personal) content of Arce's book is that in his frequent cross-cutting between mounds of information (a narrative technique no doubt employed to enliven the reading), some of the volume's little mini-dramas are never fully resolved. This is best exemplified by the plight of Groucho's oldest daughter, Miriam. Though much is revealed about her, it is by a bits-and-pieces method that cries out for both more information and the kind of overview with which Arce is frequently so effective. In this instance, such high expectations seem valid after Arce's moving sketch of the ties between Miriam and the pivotal character of the same name she inspired in Norman Krasna's play *Dear Ruth* (see Chapter 1 of this volume). Arce heightens the fascination by giving the reader Miriam's own frightening answer to her chemical dependency as an adult: "I do everything to fulfill my father's feelings about women. He hates them, and I prove him right."[2] This analysis demands that more be said about the daughter who also received affection and whose cynical sense of humor was so much like her father's.

Again, one's desire for more of Arce actually compliments the detail he has provided and the insatiable reader appetite it has provoked. Moreover, the very inclusion of an observation like Miriam's underlines the critical honesty Arce brings to an affectionately honest look at Groucho and his Brothers. It also makes a joke of one *Groucho* reviewer's complaint that the book is not funny.[3] A valu-able and ongoing message of the book—which *is* periodically buttressed with comedy examples—is that the Marx Brothers (particularly Groucho) could con-tinue to play effectively at being funny while their personal lives were often any-thing but amusing. Indeed, Arce's book at times even provides the black comedy of life, such as King "Leer" Groucho being afflicted with sexual dysfunction.

Though in no way an unobtainable book, Arce's *Groucho* has never been as readily available as it might have been. Correspondence with researcher Wesolow-ski revealed that a large number of the volumes were water damaged in storage. And, insurance policies being what they are, it was more profitable for the pub-lisher to destroy the damaged books without replacing them. How ironically fitting that the best volume on the absurd Marxes should itself fall victim to absurdity! Groucho no doubt would have especially enjoyed the comic paradox and just as possibly might have observed, "It's the *high-water mark* of Marx literature."

Next in importance as a Marx Brothers insider author is a writer Groucho called "Hemingway."[4] Of course, he used the name sarcastically, and only during the early days of an apprentice writer he was actually supporting—his son Arthur. Arthur's second-place finish is a result both of insight and productivity, because he has done two books of special Marx Brothers interest: *Life with Groucho* (1954) and *Son of Groucho* (1972). While the author of this book means for the second-place standing to be taken highly, Arthur would probably be more likely to call it his fate in life. He nicely capsulized the phenomenon in his second title. *Son of Groucho* was also how the headlines frequently ran in his very successful amateur tennis days as a contemporary of the young Bobby Riggs. Though it might seem cruel, it is also relevant to add he was a perennial runner-up in tennis, too.

As the child of a famous parent, Arthur hardly has a corner on the also-ran status. But then he has also drawn attention to the fact. As *Los Angeles Times* book reviewer Burt Prelutsky comically observed of a writing career which has been dominated by the subject of the Marxes (Arthur also co-authored the Broadway play *Minnie's Boys*, 1970): "One sometimes gets the feeling that had the Marx Brothers not been born, Arthur . . . would have had to invent them."[5] But then as the gung-ho soldier said to the critic of a controversial, escalating military action, "Don't knock it; it's the only war we've got." Similarly, the student of the Marxes is tempted just to be equally appreciative that the Arthur works exist. Except for Maxine Marx's much too short *Growing Up with Chico* (1980), none of the numerous other Marx Brothers children have graced the scene with a book at this printing. This temptation is not, however, an option for the author surveying the works, especially since both works are flawed in what they say and in how they say it.

Let this author address the latter point first, because it implies that Arthur is a poor writer. This is not the case, especially with regard to the warmly written and received *Life with Groucho*, a book whose original dust jacket carries the comically asterisked subtitle: *A Son's-Eye View*. The point is, *Son of Groucho* reveals that the first story had been considerably softened. This might best be documented by *Life with Groucho*'s most endearing characteristic—the frequent comic footnotes by Groucho. For example, Chapter 8 begins: "FATHER NEVER WANTED to play Hamlet." Groucho added: "I don't even want to see it."[6] Earlier, Arthur had called his father the "most literate" of his Brothers, to which Groucho dryly footnoted: "Faint praise."[7]

What a lovely addition for a biography to have! The Groucho footnotes are funny. They are insightful. In this case, they subliminally reinforce the image being drawn—the caring father helpfully reading and comically enriching his child's work. Oh, that all biographies had this autobiographical reinforcement! But as the comically criticized Hamlet might have added here, had he done consulting work—"ay, there's the rub!" *Arthur* wrote these footnotes, *not Groucho*. One could defend Arthur by saying that the statements are true to his father both in comic spirit and in content. In fact, there is frequent evidence elsewhere that documents that Groucho was of the opinion to have said such things. For instance, after Arthur observes how difficult it is to get a gift for someone who has "every earthly belonging a man could want," "Groucho" adds—"Except

Marilyn Monroe."[8] Monroe, who in her early career had made a brief but hardly unnoticed appearance with Groucho at the close of the Marxes's *Love Happy* (1949), was someone Groucho thought unusually attractive. Thus, to verify this, one might either consult the comedian's initial autobiography, *Groucho and Me* (1959) or his *The Marx Bros. Scrapbook* (1973, co-authored with Richard J. Anobile), which is obscenely graphic about Groucho's sexual thoughts concerning Monroe during the production of the film.[9] One could even further defend Arthur by noting that Groucho would use a similar footnote effect in his later *Memoirs of a Mangy Lover* (1963).

Despite such defenses, Arthur's addition of "Groucho" quotes seems an opportunist act—a further prettifying (cosmetic comedy) of a figure not quite so warm and fatherly. In fact, *Son of Groucho* reveals that besides not authoring the comically reinforcing footnotes to his son's *Life with Groucho*, Groucho's response to the book in manuscript form was just the opposite—a threat to sue. These are called bombshells. Thus, the best thing about the second book is what it reveals about the first. One should hasten to add that Groucho does not suddenly become a "Daddy Dearest" figure, but considerably more wrinkles are exposed.

A "creative" act such as the "Groucho" footnotes does reveal, however, much about the son and, indirectly, the father as well. Arthur is a survivor, and that seems to have been a key lesson of a childhood with Groucho. Just as the first wives of Chico and Groucho (see Chapter 1) sometimes had to fend for themselves on the road (while touring with their husbands), Groucho's children were frequently put in that position. This is especially true as the youngsters reached adulthood, because as both books thoroughly document, Groucho was often wonderful to be around when they were children. But it was as if growing up was a betrayal to the efforts Groucho had taken to celebrate their childhoods. One further *Son of Groucho* bombshell nicely exemplifies Arthur's survivor nature.

Arthur had not shown the *Life with Groucho* manuscript to his father until after it had been accepted by a publisher and the serial rights had been sold to *The Saturday Evening Post*. This was not done out of deceitfulness, or he would not have shared the manuscript with Groucho in the first place. But from past experiences with his domineering father, Arthur knew the importance of working from a point of success. Otherwise, even as a son, Arthur would—as the anti-heroic anthem of comedian Rodney Dangerfield goes—"get no respect."

In this situation, however, Arthur still ended up Dangerfield. Groucho did not like the book in manuscript form. Among other things, he was especially bothered by two items—one general, one specific. In the former case, he felt he had been made to look like a tightwad; in the latter, Groucho was upset by a sentence from a quoted letter he had written his son concerning Groucho's divorce from Arthur's mother.

Arthur was correct in not agreeing with these complaints. His descriptions of his father's spending habits were hardly negative. Rather, they made Groucho out to be a delightful eccentric (see Chapter 1). And the offensive quote—"If you're even in the neighborhood again, drop in"—was really a classic example of pathos when the tender content of the complete letter is taken into effect.[10] It revealed a sensitivity Groucho often seemed unwilling to share. But how does one resolve such a father-son dilemma? For Arthur the survivor, the eventual answer proved quite simple. He merely requested two copies of his book's galleys (a final printed copy of a work to be proofed before publication), and gave one to his father, telling him to make whatever changes he thought necessary. However, the only galley proof Arthur returned to the publisher was his own. Groucho's extensively revised version was simply discarded.

Arthur's actions soon received a double endorsement. The book was a great critical and commercial success, and Groucho created no further problems concerning it. Arthur hypothesized that his father's initial opposition might have been caused by Groucho's need to remain number one in the family, a possibility Arce also examines. However, an example Arthur provides in support of this stance can also be interpreted quite differently. Nearly paralleling the publication of *Life with Groucho*, the scandal sheet *Confidential Magazine* made a number of disparaging comments about both Groucho's television show and his interest in young women. But in this case, where the threat of suing was certainly justified, Groucho merely penned a one-sentence letter of delightful comic surprise: "If you persist in publishing libelous articles about me, I will have to cancel my subscription."[11]

Arthur posits that Groucho felt unthreatened by the *Confidential* author but that the home-grown variety (Arthur) was something else. While a certain jealousy might have been at work, Groucho's scandal sheet letter to the editor also represents the many contradictions about the man and offers additional reinforcement, in part, of Groucho's comedy persona—a dirty old man who never felt any compulsion to hide the fact. Besides, it was publicity, and as the real story behind the *A Night in Casablanca* letters revealed (see Chapter 1), publicizing "letters" made great newspaper copy.

One final *Son of Groucho* bombshell must be noted. It concerns a lesson Arthur learned about handling his father from baseball legend Leo Durocher. And again, it represents the son writing something as "Groucho," though this time with the comedian's approval—a 1953 *Colliers* article-length letter to New York Giants manager Durocher on "What's Wrong with the Giants."[12] Father and son visited the Giants during spring training to get some photographs of a uniformed Groucho interacting with the team. But at the last moment Groucho decided he did not want to wear the uniform, which, of course, would kill most of the pictures' article-accompanying comic effect. At this point Durocher unconsciously provided Arthur with his lesson. Durocher, a friend of Groucho's, told the comedian, "Don't be a fucking prima donna."[13] And he gave Groucho five minutes to put the thing on or he would do it himself. Groucho then tried at least to avoid wearing the baseball shoes, but Durocher's forcefulness totally carried the day. Pictures of Groucho in *full uniform* accompanied the article, Arthur's lesson was: "He's [Groucho] a bully, and if you don't bully him right back, he'll trample all over you."[14] This is a provocative statement considering that Arthur would later be in a custody fight over Groucho where his side would accuse the opposition (Groucho companion Erin Fleming) of, among other things, verbal abuse.

Regardless of how one judges this, or any other, pronouncements by Arthur, his books offer invaluable insights into the world of the Marxes, particularly one Groucho Marx. One needs, however, to think of the two Arthur books focused on here as one volume, in order to obtain a full picture of his subject. With regard to *Son of Groucho*, this can be a problem because for some, such as *Los Angeles Times* reviewer Burt Prelutsky, one learns more about Arthur Marx than is absolutely necessary for a fruitful life. But then, *Son of Groucho* is an autobiography of sorts, and to examine the child is to receive another view of the parent. Personally, this author was more bothered by sloppy research, from repeated stories (generally not told as effectively in *Son of Groucho*) to the wrong year and general scenario being given for the Marx Brothers's Christmas 1930 trip to Europe, something Arthur had managed to record correctly in *Life with Groucho*.[15] Still, problems aside, Arthur's books are required reading for students of the Marxes.

The next insider volume of note is from another Marx Brothers child—Chico's Maxine. Her *Growing Up with Chico* (1980) is especially important because, of the three main performing Marx Brothers, her father was the only one not to write his memoirs. Moreover, Chico's contributions to the act have not generated the ongoing interest normally accorded to Groucho and Harpo. Thus, there is not as much written about him. Not only does Maxine's book change this, but she is "most persuasive," as theatre and film critic/historian Walter Kerr has observed, in establishing "her father's indispensability" to the team.[16] This "indispensability" was true both on stage and camera and behind the scenes (see Chapter 1). While not brusquely casting earth mother Minnie aside, Maxine both performs some necessary redistribution of significance (from Minnie to Chico), and examines Minnie with a realism that is refreshingly rare in Marx Brothers literature.

Besides providing new insights, Maxine underlines what should be obvious but is frequently lost in the laughter: both Groucho and Harpo (whose comedy personae often precluded their having scenes together) needed someone off whom to play, and Chico was generally that someone. Moreover, Chico was the interpreter between his Brothers—the link that made them a team. And he did all this while still maintaining a comedy persona of his own.

Like her cousin Arthur's *Son of Groucho*, Maxine's volume is, in part, an autobiography. But unlike Arthur's second Marx book, rare would be the complaint that there is too much on the author in *Growing Up with Chico*. In fact, the only real disappointment about Maxine's work (besides the occasional citing of wrong dates) is its brevity. *Growing Up with Chico* runs only 180 pages, merely *one-half* the length of Arthur's *second* Marx book. Part of this briefness is no doubt due to the fact that Chico was not as available to his child as Groucho was to Arthur. This was a result both of Chico not being the homebody Groucho was and Harpo would become, and Maxine's placement in a boarding school.

While tastefully documenting Chico's womanizing and gambling nature, Maxine still manages to portray her father in a warm light. Such ongoing affection nicely compliments the friendly charm and loyalty for which this man is celebrated. Moreover, while he was not around as much as some fathers, he brought a certain Peter Pan magic when he did appear, from the day he took a young Maxine out of school for some parent-approved hooky to the elegant 1930s life-style Chico provided for a while in the real fantasyland called Hollywood. He was not hard to love. Thus, one might best compliment the book by saying it is "essential reading for students of the Marxes," meaning "its got [*sic*] something of Chico in it."[17]

The next insider book to be examined is actually the first volume ever devoted to the team—Kyle Crichton's *The Marx Brothers* (1950). The book was quite possibly an after effect of a 1947 plan for a "film biography tentatively titled *The Life of the Marx Brothers* [which would star the] ... Marxes and incorporate their best routines from vaudeville days. . . ."[18] Such a plan was quite possibly precipitated by the phenomenal success of *The Jolson Story* (1946, which also spawned the 1949 sequel *Jolson Sings Again*). Regardless, while the Marx Brothers biography film was never made, the book had direct ties to the Brothers. "Essentially they had hired Crichton to write the book based on stories they told him."[19] Crichton does not seem to have limited himself to this, but the Brothers certainly must have approved of the text. First of all, the copyright is owned by the five Brothers, who are also prominently caricatured on both the cover and the title page. Second, the Brothers helped promote the book. For example, as reported by *Newsweek*, Groucho was comically pitching the Crichton book even before it was published. Thus, Groucho claimed the volume was "dirt cheap at $3. Here's a book about five men. Broken down (and believe me there is no one more broken down than these five men) it comes to a measly 60 cents for each brother."[20]

Crichton's book is largely a detailed look at the prefilm Marxes. Of the volume's twenty-three chapters, the team does not arrive in Hollywood until number twenty-two! Even then the chapter mistakenly implies *Animal Crackers* was shot in Hollywood. Such an error nicely capsulizes the kind of attention given their films. But the book remains rich in early detail. The opening comically pictures the Marx Brothers flat just as this side of chaos, and thoroughly describes an incident of a dropped paper bag filled with water which made young Chico a "neighborhood hero."[21]

The latter example is especially important, because besides showcasing the detailed anecdotal method the book will follow, it underlines the significance of Chico from page one. Again and again he is credited with having made the difference in the Marxes's climb to the top, especially with his off-stage wheeling and dealing. But in the passing years this was largely obscured by both the ongoing myth of Minnie (ironically, the Crichton book was originally titled *Mother of the Two-a-Day*) and the many Groucho-focused Marx Brothers books which followed (thus the impact of Maxine's book thirty years later). Crichton's work, therefore, offers a strong, though unacknowledged, foundation for *Growing Up with Chico*'s managerial celebration of Chico. The stage/screen importance of Chico to the team, while not absent from Crichton's book, is more fully examined in Maxine's writing.

For those concerned about biography by anecdote, seldom a recommended style among writing instructors, it can be justified in *The Marx Brothers* for three reasons. First, Crichton was dealing directly with the Brothers themselves, though unfortunately, the exact degree of this involvement is unknown. Second, at that time (1950), few film subjects were being given much scholarly detail anyway. This is reiterated both by the amount of time it took for *any* Marx Brothers book to appear and the fact that the team's films are given such short shrift in Crichton's work. Second, like Robert Lewis Taylor's classic but then just-published biography of a Marx Brothers contemporary—*W. C. Fields: His Follies and Fortunes*—it is sometimes possible for a work to capture the spirit of its subject through retelling stories about it. Such is the case with Crichton's book.

The final volume of the insider category is Charlotte Chandler's *Hello, I Must Be Going: Groucho & His Friends* (1978). As if designed to follow Crichton's focus on the early years in *The Marx Brothers*, Chandler's hefty volume (568 pages) is a chronicle of Groucho in his eighties. But Chandler should have added *& His Marx Brothers Memories* to her *Groucho & His Friends* subtitle, because the Marx Brothers years are frequently the subject of discussion. And discussion is an apt phrase, because the book is generally done in an interview/conversation format, both between Groucho and the author, as well as between the comedian and a number of his friends.

Fittingly, this largely oral history grew out of a 1974 Groucho interview Chandler did for *Playboy* magazine.[22] Groucho was so impressed with the interview (his letter to *Playboy* praising Chandler's job is included in the book[23]), that Chandler was often made part of his 1970s entourage. A sometimes long-term Groucho houseguest, Chandler was given a rare behind-the-scenes invitation to the later world of Groucho. Moreover, Groucho further assisted Chandler by providing her with tape recorder access to his friends, frequently with the comedian's participation.

Unfortunately, the book tends to meander. The best thing about it is the title, from the Groucho song, but a more apt musical title would have been the Nat "King" Cole standard "Ramblin' Rose." Moreover, much of the material has appeared elsewhere and been better showcased. One of the people interviewed had observed that the old Groucho was still funny, but his delivery was not what it had been. This critique could also be applied to the book itself, especially since Groucho does a lot of the talking. Thus, while much of the material is still amusing, despite Groucho's abbreviated telling, it is also sad because of one's memory of what actually had been.

The same sadness permeates this portrait of Groucho in old age—the memory of what he had been. He is still quite lucid and sometimes amusing, but his long-time trait of always "being on" now often seems forced. Forced also describes many of the book's recorded conversations between Groucho and his younger celebrity friends. People like Woody Allen and Bill Cosby appear to be verbally scrambling just to maintain the most basic of conversations.

The book is best when it avoids Groucho's famous younger friends and focuses on the comedian's cronies and colleagues from the past, such as the segment with Groucho friend and writing partner Norman Krasna. Among other things, Krasna reveals that in his Groucho family-inspired play *Dear Ruth*, "A lot of the jokes were little family jokes that were real. A lot of it just echoes of the dinner table talk at Groucho's house."[24] Other contributing friends from the early days include such Marx Brother screenwriters as Morrie Ryskind, George Seaton, Nat Perrin, and Robert Pirosh (a list which accents the high esteem Groucho had for writers). In addition, the comedian was more insightful when old friends were there to trigger memories. Though the segments with veteran friends are more valuable, there are again recycled material and a repetition of subjects.

Also of special interest is an altogether too short segment with Zeppo and Gummo. Most interesting are Zeppo's comments, which while not all new, provide a more detailed look at Zeppo than one normally encounters. Moreover, Zeppo is directed (something Chandler does too little of in the book) to discuss life after the Marx Brothers. Besides addressing the irony that the denigrated straight man was probably the funniest Brother in real life, it also suggests he was the most versatile, with success in everything from the agency business to the machinist trade. He even invented a wristwatch that could warn a potential victim of an approaching heart attack!

What one comes away from the book wanting is more personal analysis of what has been recorded. The sheer bulk of Chandler's recordings does, however, anticipate the central theme of her next book, *The Ultimate Seduction* (1984, co-dedicated to Groucho). As suggested by Pablo Picasso, one of the subjects in a volume on diverse artists, "Always you [the artist] put more of yourself into your work [regardless of your original motives], until one day . . . you *are* your work. . . . That is the ultimate seduction."[25] Thus, Groucho in old age often seems to be pressing as he unloads the expected insults. But how could anyone compete on a day-to-day basis with the unaging comic cynicism of *Duck Soup*? Groucho's ultimate seduction has finally proved to be too demanding.

Marx on Marx

As in the previous category of insider volumes, where Groucho is the focus Brother in all but one volume, such is the case here. But before examining the mini-library of Groucho-authored or co-authored books, the exception must be noted—*Harpo Speaks!* (1961, Harpo with Rowland Barber). It seems only appropriate that when the silent one finally spoke, his should be the most important of the books authored by the Brothers.

This author has already indirectly underlined this by the frequency with which he quoted from *Harpo Speaks!* in Chapter 1. The richness of the volume is, in part, a result of the decision not to soften everything by describing it comically, which is typical of Groucho's biographical writing. Moreover, Harpo attempts a full chronicle in his nearly 500-page autobiography, a more ambitious task than Groucho attempted in any one of his books. Of course, Harpo is not always good about specifics, like dates. And one is reminded of a 1937 Marx Brothers interviewer (Harry Long) who was bothered by Harpo always calling him Mr. Benson. The explanation: "Don't mind him," soothed Groucho. "He just can't remember names. He's crazy. He calls everybody Mr. Benson."[26] While Groucho even manages to close this comic information with a topper of a joke, Harpo did sometimes simplify personal contacts in this manner. But despite occasional problems with specifics, Harpo provides a more well-rounded look at the Brothers—especially concerning the difficult early years, both at home and as very young performers. Like Crichton's *The Marx Brothers*, which the comedian mentions, *Harpo Speaks!* is best at capturing the spirit of the Marxes. And though again dealing with anecdotes, one is a generation closer to the source, as the teller was also part of the group.

The 1985 reprinting of the volume, which for years had been one of the most sought-after books among students of film comedy, offers two additional bonuses. There is an afterword by one of Harpo's sons (Bill; see also Chapter 1 of this book) and a poem, "Ode to the Silent Harp," by his widow Susan. (The delightful caricatures in both the original volume and the reprint are also by Susan.) Thus, a measure of Harpo's happy marriage and family life (see Chapter 1) is reinforced further by these special additions, years after his death. Harpo's book, like his image in other Marx Brothers literature, is hard to top.

If *Harpo Speaks!* had not appeared, this category would have been titled "Groucho on Groucho." The mustached Marx, who grew his own after retiring the greasepaint variety, authored or co-authored the following volumes: *Beds* (1930), *Many Happy Returns: An Unofficial Guide to Your Income-Tax Problems* (1942), *Groucho and Me* (1959), *Memoirs of a Mangy Lover* (1963), *The Groucho Letters: Letters from and to Groucho Marx* (1967), *The Marx Bros. Scrapbook* (1973, co-authored with Richard J. Anobile), *The Groucho Phile* (1976), and *The Secret Word Is GROUCHO* (1976, with Hector Arce). Thus, books by Groucho appeared in five successive decades. In addition, there were the 1937 screenplay *The King and the Chorus Girl* and the 1948 Broadway play *Time for Elizabeth* (both co-authored with Norman Krasna). Such a list is a tribute to the most literary of the Marxes, especially since his formal education was minimal (the punster in Groucho might have labeled himself a "bookMarx").

One must add a qualifier, however, in at least two instances. Official Groucho biographer Hector Arce (close friend of and co-author with Groucho of *The Secret Word Is GROUCHO*) convincingly states that both *Beds* and *Many Happy Returns* were done in uncredited collaboration with Groucho friend and writer Arthur Sheekman.[27] That sort of arrangement was typical for the time. It would be a number of years before the credit "with such-and-such" became an accept-able admission. One is bothered more here only because Groucho took great pride in being an author, and in *Groucho and Me*, he devotes a page to denigrating autobiographies that lean on another author who receives only miniscule billing.[28] In Groucho's defense, the relative contributions of each man are not known. Moreover, their comedy writing styles are similar, something indirectly borne out through their close friendship, their work together on comedy sketches, and the fact that Groucho had substituted for Sheekman in writing the latter's Chicago newspaper column. Perhaps most telling, however, is a co-authored let-ter by Groucho and Sheekman to the comedian's longtime friend Dr. Samuel Salinger.[29] Though primarily by Groucho, the Sheekman interjections are so close to the Groucho persona that one is sometimes confused over just who is writing. Interestingly enough, the letter begins with Sheekman at the typewriter and Groucho up and talking—a working style that Groucho and Krasna used in their collaborations.

The Groucho books can be broken into two broad categories. While they are all graced with comedy, three of them are essentially humor books: *Beds*, *Many Happy Returns*, and *Memoirs of a Mangy Lover*. All the rest, especially the late examples, deal more specifically with Groucho's life and career (often as a Marx Brother), though there are pure comedy detours on all of them. *The Groucho Letters*, of course, represents a cross section of the public and private man.

The humor books are frequently antiheroic in nature (see Chapters 1, 2, and 3), with the publication dates of the first two (1930 and 1942) nearly represent-ing decade markers around what might be called the antiheroic heyday—the 1930s. This is only logical, since the Marx Brothers could claim both involve-ment in the evolution of the comic antihero in American humor as well as fre-quent contact with many of its greatest practitioners.

One might also posit that the comic antihero is also an easier figure by which to lure sympathetic *readers*, as opposed to stories featuring a more aggressive narrator. Groucho friend and contemporary W. C. Fields, whose screen character fluctuated between con man and antihero, clearly opted for the latter path when he authored his *Fields for President* (1940). Despite the title and Fields's book-opening combination of politician and con man (possibly a redundancy of terms), the work is more a comic celebration of the nonpolitical antihero. In fact, one of Fields's chapters, "How to Beat the Federal Income Tax—and What to See and Do at Alcatraz," might have influenced if not inspired Groucho's comedy in-come tax guide, *Many Happy Returns*, which appeared just two years later. Interestingly, the delightful comedy caricatures that compliment both works were drawn by the same artist, Otto Soglow.

Many Happy Returns is Groucho's most sustained single-topic humor volume, maintaining its comedy income tax focus for nearly one hundred pages. *Beds* runs twenty-five pages fewer while comically addressing everything one can do in bed ... except for IT—to borrow a period euphemism for sex. Drawings and photos entertainingly pad both volumes, with the 1976 reissue of *Beds* tastefully but still comically showcasing Groucho in bed with a number of celebrities, from Burt Reynolds to Phyllis Diller (truely an antiheroic situation).

Memoirs of a Mangy Lover is longer than the combined lengths of *Beds* and *Many Happy Returns*, but it is more a comedy anthology of Groucho essays *sometimes* focusing on love, or to be more antiheroically precise—the frustrations of love. For the student of the Marx Brothers, Groucho's last humor volume is the most interesting, because there are also several stories about the early years and his Brothers. When coupled with this and the lateness of its appearance (four years after his autobiography, *Groucho and Me*), an argument could be made for including it in the more reminiscence-focused volumes of Groucho's last years. After all, it does include *Memoirs* in the title. But besides emphasizing funny over family or films, the book is most significant when seen as a barometer or Groucho's comic literary tendencies. Being last, longest, and most varied, it is a comedy summation. And the total is truly antiheroic.

One is especially reminded of Robert Benchley, who was not only pivotal to the comic antiheroic movement but also a Groucho friend and a writer greatly admired by the comedian. Indeed, *Groucho and Me*'s antiheroic dedication had been to Benchley and five other frequently antiheroic writers (George S. Kaufman, Ring Lardner, S. J. Perelman, James Thurber, and E. B. White), "Without Whose Wise and Witty Words My Life Would Have Been Even Duller. . . ." Thus, Groucho's essay, "When Pigeons Fly In, Love Flies Out," has parallels with Benchley's delightful piece "Down with Pigeons."[30] And Groucho's "The Pariah of Hollywood Am I," about the comedian's inability to break into the film community's fast-lane set, is reminiscent of Benchley's lengthy essay "My Untold Story," where the writer not only has trouble being involved in New York and Hollywood party scenes—he cannot even find them![31]

All this is not to suggest that Groucho is merely derivative. After all, he, too, had been in on the ground-floor evolution of the antihero (see Chapter 2). However, if one remains concerned about Benchley's possible influence on Groucho, it should also be remembered that Benchley's writing has had a phenomenal influence on a host of ohter pivotal antiheroic writers, from James Thurber to Woody Allen, not to mention the general public. In fact, Thurber nicely summarized both the debt and the admiration of other writers and himself in a comic 1956 observation: "one of the greatest fears of the humorous writer is that he has spent three weeks writing something done faster and better by Benchley in 1919."[32]

The second category, Groucho-authored volumes, those generally geared toward reminiscences of his life and career, appropriately begins with his autobiography, *Groucho and Me*, the first and most important of these works. Consistent for both a writer of humor books and an individual who was always "on," *Groucho and Me* is a very funny autobiography. However, it generally laughs itself around the type of poignant realism that makes *Harpo Speaks!* such an insightful book. For example, Harpo described the towns the young team would play during their Grade Z vaudeville days with a detail befitting the era's muckraking journalists. Conversely, given a similar siutation, Groucho played it comically—"We played towns I would refuse to be buried in today, even if the funeral were free and they tossed in a tombstone for lagniappe."[33]

Though seemingly a comic dead end, such a tendency indirectly reiterates a commonly noted trait of Groucho—his inability to open up with people, whether close friends or his book-reading public. In a sense, this difference between Groucho and Harpo is also true of their performing personae. For instance, Groucho (unless victimized by his Brothers) can use his fast patter to direct attention elsewhere from his persona. Moreover, his frequent comic teacher-like roles, whether as an actual teacher in *Fun in Hi Skule* or his old professor-like stance on *You Bet Your Life*, allow Groucho to be asking (not answering) the questions. In contrast, Harpo's silence frequently invites discourse, while his serious harp solos seem to *reveal* his character's added depth, as well as vulnerability. Consistent with this is the fact that while Harpo was seemingly Groucho's favorite brother, he was not particularly fond of Harpo's silent yet more open comedy character. The consistency continued while in comedy character, for Groucho was fond of undercutting, through direct address to the viewer, forthcoming harp solos.

In the early, rambling pages of *Groucho and Me*, the comedian characterizes all men as islands unto themselves.[34] While this is quickly followed by some jokes, the ongoing point of these pages is to minimize just how much of the real person is revealed in any autobiography. This is not your typical autobiographical opening, though there is a certain absurd appropriateness for it in a Marx Brother autobiography. As quoted at the beginning of this chapter, Groucho later would be even more bald about his feelings on writing an autobiography. Though this, too, is followed by a joke, a mock-heroic comparison of Groucho and Lawrence of Arabia, it again reveals the internalized nature of the man, and his tendency to use humor as a mask.

Appropriately, chapter 22 of *Groucho and Me* even opens with Groucho's editor still waiting for more intimate details about the comedian's life. Son Arthur's later response to the volume might also be described as still waiting— Arthur notes there is very little in the book about his sister Miriam, their mother, and himself.[35] A capsulized example of this autobiographical neglect is Arthur's additional comment that while there are no pictures of Miriam and himself in the book, there are five that include Groucho's youngest, still-at-home daughter, Melinda. Besides accenting Groucho's preference for children over adults—even when those adults are also his children—this demonstrates the comedian's ability to compartmentalize unpleasant things, be it the marriage to Arthur's and Miriam's mother that would end in divorce, or the fact that Miriam's drinking and general instability had led to her being institutionalized for a time in the 1950s, the decade in which *Groucho and Me* appeared.

Autobiographical blind spots such as these are hardly unusual. For instance, Charlie Chaplin's *My Autobiography* devotes all of a single paragraph to one of his unpleasant marriages. Ironically, it is precisely this ability to scissor out the unpleasant that helped make Chaplin and Groucho such great artists—nothing got in the way of their comedy. For the very same reason, it was often less than pleasant to live with Chaplin and Groucho. Arthur himself had chronicled a perfect example of this single-mindedness in *Son of Groucho.* During a dinner argument Groucho had sent his wife from the table because "I can't be upset when I have to be funny in front of an audience in an hour."[36]

Despite this occasional necessity for the reader to interpret between the lines, *Groucho and Me* is still a generally informative work that follows the artist's career more closely than many autobiographies. Moreover, in his own way Groucho can be very informative. For example, his extended discussion of comedy as a "trial-and-error" phenomenon is seemingly sincere and very modest, considering his celebrated wit.[37] Fittingly, however, even here he includes a famous example of a clown suppressing inner torment. Groucho briefly recounts the story of the suicidal patient whose doctor prescribes a visit to Grock, the greatest of clowns, only to discover later that his patient is Grock. Thus, *Groucho and Me* is well worth reading, paling only when compared to an autobiography as unique as *Harpo Speaks!*

The second most recommended book of Groucho's nonhumor volumes is *The Groucho Phile.* As the title suggests, the book draws material from all his works except the controversial *The Marx Bros. Scrapbook.* (There is also an excellent introduction by Hector Arce.) But it goes well beyond being a collection of previously published material. Indeed, at first glance, it appears to be simply a picture book. And even if that were the extent of its contents, it would well be worth acquiring, because there is a wealth of private photographs, publicity stills, and reproductions of posters, as well as letters, obscure articles, and related Marx Brothers materials. This includes a number of lovely color duplications, generally of Marx Brothers posters. But there are also color photos of the author and his last home, as well as a full-page shot of Groucho as Ko-Ko, the Lord High Executioner, from a 1960 television production of Gilbert and Sullivan's *The Mikado.* Gilbert and Sullivan had been a longtime passion of the comedian's, and being able to star in such a production "fulfilled a lifelong ambition."[38] Though not previously noted in this volume, Groucho's passion for spending evenings listening to Gilbert and Sullivan records sometimes sent family and associates to a point of distraction, from first wife Ruth to the writers for his television show *You Bet Your Life.*

The Groucho Phile goes beyond being a pictorial history of the Marxes, however. There is a lengthy running commentary (including those excerpts from earlier books by Groucho) and captions that are frequently both detailed and amusing. One such caption, from a series of Groucho photos documenting a World War II bond tour, reminded him of a Minneapolis censorship he had suffered on the trip. His microphone cord was pulled simply for telling the crowd this story: "I knew a girl in Minneapolis once. She used to come over to see me in St. Paul. She was known as the tail of two cities."[39] Groucho's local color was sometimes off-color to others.

The next recommended Groucho volume is *The Marx Bros. Scrapbook* (with Richard J. Anobile). As the title suggests, it showcases reproductions of the type offered in *The Groucho Phile*, although neither so many nor any in color. But the real emphasis is on the interviews with surviving Marx Brothers, Harpo's Widow Susan, professional associates who were often close friends, and two 1930s reporters who covered the first stop (Salt Lake City) of the *Night at the Opera* road tour.

There are nine chapters, each beginning with an excerpt from a lengthy career overview interview with Groucho. Except for the last chapter, which is all Groucho, the other chapters include at least one additional interview. They are, in order of appearance: Gummo, Jack Benny (who toured with the Brothers in vaudeville), frequent Marx Brothers writer Morrie Ryskind, *The Cocoanuts* director Robert Florey, Marxes film writers Harry Ruby and Arthur Sheekman (who sometimes collaborated with Groucho), Zeppo, Susan Marx, reporters Harry and Morrie Guss, and Marxes movie writers George Seaton and Nat Perrin.

Anobile's interviews are sometimes insightful, with generally well-directed questions (the lack of such direction, when there were questions, being a problem of Chandler's interviews in *Hello, I Must Be Going*). But what was most *revealing* about the volume was the often bawdy stories of friends, family, and associates, which Groucho related in equally bawdy terms. Groucho himself was later shocked, having assumed his taped interviews were to be laundered first. Thus, he brought a $15 million lawsuit against the publisher, distributor, and Penthouse Publications Ltd., which was running excerpts of the book. He also attempted to stop distribution of the book. But, since Groucho had signed the contracts, Anobile prevailed.

The public response was divided. While garnering some excellent reviews, many were shocked, including some positive reviewers. In fact, that seemed part of the attraction—that one of the shocking Marxes could still do it in the early 1970s. And this acceptance was not hurt by the fact that the 1960s renewal of interest in the Marxes had not abated.

Along more somber lines, there were those who felt the book's publication represented a Groucho who had now become a victim of age. While Groucho friend and biographer Hector Arce was noncommital about the question of age-impaired judgment, he later termed the Anobile interview a "shabby exercise."[40] He also undercut Anobile's preparation for the work by noting incorrect phonetic spellings of some names from the transcribed interviews.

As in all controversies, important things become misplaced. Regardless of how one feels about a totally uncensored Groucho, the book would be worth reading simply for the other interviews and related Marx Brothers materials, such as its inclusion of some Harpo and Alexander Woollcott letters. (The candid interview with Harpo's widow is also one of the book's plusses, although Anobile himself is not as well prepared here.)

The Groucho Letters comes next on this ordered list of Groucho books. It, too, was published on a wave of publicity but of an earlier and more positive nature than *The Marx Bros. Scrapbook*. The upbeat catalyst for the volume was the Library of Congress's earlier request for Groucho's correspondence. When a delightfully amusing book by a certifiable American legend has been further ennobled by a stamp from on high (*Newsweek*'s review stated the Groucho correspondence was already "enshrined in the Library of Congress"[41]), the man and his work are not so much reviewed as celebrated. Such was the case with *The Groucho Letters*.

The book, with an introduction by Arthur Sheekman, is divided into ten letter categories: "Movie Business," "Private Life," "Touching on Television," "Groucho and Other Men of Letters," "Grouchy," "Broadway and Hollywood," "For Publication," "Friends Abroad," "The Faintly Political Scene," and "Short Shrift."

Though it is still a most valuable volume, this author has become somewhat jaded by having gone through both the complete collection of Groucho letters at the Library of Congress as well as the long-term correspondence with Dr. Samuel Salinger (now housed at the State Historical Society of Wisconsin in Madison). This broader spectrum, though not always as amusing, nor with such celebrated correspondents (the book features exchanges with literary greats such as T. S. Eliot, James Thurber, and E. B. White), is in many ways the more revealing. This is especially true of the Salinger letters, which begin much earlier (the late 1920s versus the book's largely 1940s and 1950s focus, though a few late 1930s letters are included).

As already demonstrated by excerpts in Chapter 1 of this volume, the Salinger letters, written with less of an eye on history and to a noncelebrity friend, often have an honesty and earthiness not to be found in *The Groucho Letters*. In fact, a reader familiar with these letters is little shocked by the contents of *The Marx Bros. Scrapbook*. Interestingly enough, however, as early as 1931 Salinger must have queried Groucho about a book of their correspondence, because the comedian wrote:

> Its [*sic*] too bad that these letters aren't better literature than they are, because then someday in the distant future when one of us became famous [Groucho is being modest], they could be published in two volumes in a cardboard box and called, The Doctor looks at the actor, or footlights and tonsils, and no one would buy the books [the sales of Groucho's *Beds*, from the previous year, had not been large, a probable reaction to the onset of the depression], except your friends and my friends, which makes a total of three sales in all [like Groucho's, Salinger's sense of humor could be very biting]. At any rate its [*sic*] a fine idea and one that should be given very little thought.[42]

The wittiness of this reply notwithstanding, *The Groucho Letters* often seems much more self-consciously polished, coming as it did from a man who was now possibly more willing to admit being famous. Indeed, *The Reporter*'s rave review of the volume used it as a platform to bemoan the decline of such sophisticated communication.[43] That the entertainingly slick took precedent might best be capsulized by noting that the book opens with Groucho's now celebrated letters to Warner Brothers comically belittling the studio's alleged complaint about the Marxes using the title *A Night in Casablanca.* Yet, a Groucho letter to Salinger reveals that this began as a manufactured publicity stunt (see Chapter 1).

The final Groucho-authored book in this ranked overview, *The Secret Word Is GROUCHO*, was also the last one to appear (1976). Though obviously focused on Groucho's *You Bet Your Life* television show, right down to a title which plays upon the program's most comically prized gimmick—saying the "secret word" and making the duck come down—the book still manages to donate space to pertinent material from both the Marx Brothers years and Groucho's transition period between the team's breakup and the radio beginnings of *You Bet Your Life.*

The book fluctuates between the observations of Groucho and those of a number of the program's key participants, from producer John Guedel to Groucho's second banana George Fenneman. While this supporting cast provides numerous insights to both the program and the period (such as the communist witch hunting), even here Marx Brothers material slips in, such as the revelation that for a time Groucho, Harpo, and Chico acted as an audience warmup before the show would begin! One also receives a more detailed look at Gummo the agent as he represented Brother Groucho.

The scope of the book's participants, including former writers, underlines the fact that this was often a scripted "ad-lib" show (see Chapter 1). While there is understandably occasional fudging on the issue, depending upon who is speaking, one leaves the book thinking Groucho never just winged it, despite his skills along these lines.

Marx Critical Studies

There are surprisingly few book-length critical studies of the Marxes. The purist probably would admit to none, though there are at least three candidates: Allen Eyles's *The Marx Brothers: Their World of Comedy* (1969), Paul D. Zimmerman and Burt Goldblatt's *The Marx Brothers at the Movies* (1968), and Joe Adamson's *Groucho, Harpo, Chico and Sometimes Zeppo* (1973). Additional comments will also be directed at William Wolf's *The Marx Brothers* (1975) and at Martin A. Gardner's unpublished New York University doctoral dissertation, "The Marx Brothers: An Investigation of Their Films as Satirical Social Criticism" (1970).

Adamson's book is both the most ambitious and the most unorthodox in its presentation. Running 464 pages in length, it attempts to emulate the Marxes comically at the same time that it is being informative. And as even its title suggests, it is often a funny book. In fact, one seriously hopes that the previously mentioned critic (see note 3) who did not find *Groucho* funny enough to suit its subject has not missed Adamson's work. Indeed, since this work predates *Groucho*, maybe that reviewer's humor standard comes from Adamson.

Regardless, Adamson feels self-conscious about getting too deep dish on the Marxes, so he disguises his insights with yucks. But it is still criticism. (Or, as Adamson the stand-up critic might have said, "You can take the Marxes out of the comedy but you can't take the comedy out of the Boys.")

Adamson focuses his attention on the team's thirteen films, as well as examining their sometimes neglected stage career, especially prior to Broadway. Besides his comedy criticism, Adamson sketches the background of each film production in detail. He has researched extensively, drawing from an impressive collection of publications and from extensive interviews with pivotal people involved in the productions. (While the book is not footnoted, there are ambitious chapter notes and an excellent bibliography.) In addition, Adamson sweetens his make-'em-laugh critical stance by periodically including generous dialogue excerpts from the films. It is obviously a volume to be recommended strongly, though its laugh-first golden rule sometimes gets in the way of the scholarship.

British film historian Eyles's *The Marx Brothers* should be one's next critical step. Though not as detailed in the background of each film (it is less than half the length of Adamson's work), its critical commentary is the equal of that in *Groucho, Harpo, Chico and Sometimes Zeppo.* Eyles supplements his book's Marx Brothers film focus with brief but perceptive chapters on the team's "Background," the "Fifties," and the Marxes's influence with regard to entertainment "Trends and Traditions." The footnoted work also includes an annotated Marx Brothers filmography, a short Margaret Dumont appendix/filmography, a post-vaudeville nonfilm timeline of Marx Brothers professional activities (helpful but incomplete), and an annotated bibliography. Moreover, Eyles's writing is knowingly peppered with a broad spectrum of pertinent cultural and historical detail, which can make the reading most rewarding. (Though not as frequent, such bonus additions also occur in Adamson's work.)

The Zimmerman/Goldblatt book most resembles the Eyles work, although it is neither as broad in scholarly scope nor as devoted to a critical commentary. While plot synopses appear in both books (with Adamson more apt to recycle blocks of dialogue), the Zimmerman/Goldblatt text is much more dependent upon them. In fact, former *Newsweek* film reviewer Zimmerman's goal in *The Marx Brothers at the Movies* (he wrote the text and graphic artist Goldblatt provided an extensive collection of stills) was to "come as close as I could to the experience of the films in print. So that if somebody wanted to 'see' *Duck Soup*, they could do it by spending twenty minutes with the book."[44] (This was, after all, the pre-videotape age.) The quote, from a 1984 revisionist article on the work entitled "A Rather Mistreated Book" documents that even in the 1960s it did not receive all the attention it deserved. Still, the volume does go beyond the plot synopsis. When Zimmerman offers commentary, beyond a straight rehashing of plot, it is generally of merit. Moreover, the volume is exceptionally rich in pictorial content. This is only fitting, since the catalyst for the book's publication contract was to showcase Goldblatt's extensive collection of Marx Brothers film stills. (A filmography is interspersed throughout the study by way of each chapter opening with the credits for the film on which it focuses.)

Film critic Wolf's *The Marx Brothers* is part of the underrated series "Pyramid Illustrated History of the Movies." Though some might label Wolf's volume a survey biography, the emphasis is clearly on ongoing critical assessment of the Marxes's films, with a brief but worthwhile concluding chapter on their influence. The work also includes a bibliography and a two-part filmography—one section devoted to their team films, a second chronicling solo appearances of the Brothers. As with all the volumes in this Pyramid series, the book is a pointedly concise look at pivotal artists on the American scene. And the mixing of critical commentary with an abbreviated biography allows the reader to use the book as a convenient point of reference when going through weightier Marx Brothers tomes.

Gardner's "The Marx Brothers" dissertation is an amazingly detailed examination of the Marxes's satirization of society. Extensively researched, both on the Marxes and period literature during their filmmaking days, Gardner's work minutely places their satirical topics in historical perspective. The breadth of his documentation is best demonstrated by merely noting the three categories into which he groups Marx Brothers satire: history, politics, and the economy; manners and customs; and literature and popular entertainment.

The extreme detail Gardner brings to the correlation between reality and Marx Brothers satire is best exemplified when he examines *Duck Soup* as a comic undercutting of paranoia in international diplomacy. While his filmic example is Groucho's extreme vacillation of moods toward the ambassador of Sylvania (Louis Calhern), Gardner's historical illustration is the paranoid one-time belief that World War I was a conspiracy between munitions manufacturers to gain profits.[45] The analogy is valid, the insight excellent. But what is not revealed is that Gardner's line of thinking actually parallels an earlier *Duck Soup* script, which casts Groucho as a munitions salesman! This script, from a period when the property was still known as *Cracked Ice*, even includes the following Groucho sales pitch:

> Gentlemen, do you realize that ammunition was never cheaper? Right now you can get two sixteen-inch shells for the price of one and shoot twice as far for half the money. With every five thousand dollar purchase we throw in a Big Bertha [a huge German cannon]. If you don't like her you can throw her right out again.[46]

Thus, while Gardner was not aware of this early script (now housed in the special collection of the Academy of Motion Picture Arts and Sciences Library), it is a nice compliment to his ability to correlate Marx Brothers satire to the real world.

Gardner's dissertation also boasts an introductory chapter on satire, an overview chapter on the Marxes's film career, and a very impressive bibliography—though this also includes a great deal of material related to the subjects satirized, rather than the Marxes.

One only wishes that Gardner had spent additional time addressing the significance of his correlations. Obviously there is some of this, but too often there is a tendency simply to move on to the next example. However, with all the positives Gardner's work has to offer, it is a complaint upon which this author will not dwell.

Marx Brothers References

The key reference texts on the Marxes are: three film script collections, *A Night at the Opera* (1972), *A Day at the Races* (1972, both from "The MGM Library of Film Scripts" series), *Monkey Business/Duck Soup* (1972, "Classic Film Scripts" series), and editor Richard J. Anobile's two picture-book (frame-by-frame) examinations of the team's work, *Why A Duck?: Visual and Verbal Gems from the Marx Brothers Movies* (1971) and *Hooray for Captain Spaulding!: Verbal & Visual Gems from "Animal Crackers"* (1974).

The two volumes from "The MGM Library of Film Scripts" series are especially interesting. Unlike many published "scripts," which simply turn out to be dialogue continuity from the finished film (plus character action), these two volumes contain both the original script for the picture in question and the dialogue and action that eventually graced the final film. In each instance, the variations are significant. For example, in the original script for *A Night at the Opera*, the Marxes's anarchy is nicely culminated with the opera house burning down[47] as opposed to the actual staging of the performance. (This is reminiscent of the originally scripted idea to burn down the college in Paramount's *Horse Feathers*; in the final version the three-ring marriage completes the film.)

One should not, however, forget Adamson's *Groucho, Harpo, Chico and Sometimes Zeppo* qualifier about these MGM Marx script collections: they do not note all the changes that took place before the "original" script was finished. In fact, the title of an earlier Adamson essay says it much more directly: "The Seventeen Preliminary Scripts of *A Day at the Races*." (This will be examined later in the chapter.)

The double volume *Monkey Business/Duck Soup* collection, from the "Classic Film Scripts" series, unfortunately follows the dialogue continuity (with character action) approach. It is, however, convenient to have what are argumentatively their two best films, both from Paramount, in one volume. (*A Night at the Opera* and *A Day at the Races* are easily the best of their MGM films, with some still championing *Opera* as their greatest movie.)

Continuity by another name might be spelled Anobile. As the subtitles of both these volumes suggest, they are composed of selected dialogue and frame enlargements. Anobile, who was also responsible for the controversial *The Marx Bros. Scrapbook* (done with Groucho), has become a one-man industry in this type of reference work, having completed nearly a dozen of these volumes, ranging from *A Fine Mess!: Verbal and Visual Gems from the Crazy World of Laurel and Hardy* (1975) to Woody Allen's *Play It Again Sam* (1977). In fact, the models for both these extremes—the multiple-film focus Laurel & Hardy book and the single-film Allen volume—were Anobile's Marx Brothers works. Thus, while *Hooray for Captain Spaulding!* concentrates on *Animal Crackers*, *Why a Duck?* includes scenes from *The Cocoanuts, Monkey Business, Horse Feathers, Duck Soup, A Night at the Opera, A Day at the Races, At the Circus, Go West*, and *The Big Store*. For the record, legal problems kept Anobile from including scenes from *Animal Crackers* and *Room Service*, while he credited mediocre material as the reason for excluding *A Night in Casablanca* and *Love Happy*.

Why a Duck? appeared before the *Scrapbook* dispute and even featured an introduction by Groucho. (There is also a preface by *New York Times* cultural news editor Richard F. Shephard.) *Hooray for Captain Spaulding!* following the *Scrapbook*, with an introduction by Anobile, where he briefly refers to the controversy.

The books are both entertaining (their original purpose) and convenient for making a quick check of a scene, provided Anobile has showcased the material in question. In terms of frame enlargement quality, frequently atrocious in even the best of publications, these books are excellent. Of course, the videotape revolution has made this kind of book somewhat antiquated. But as critic Otis Ferguson said in a 1935 review of *A Night at the Opera*, Groucho "would be funny in still photographs."[48] Thus, you might save a little space on your bookshelf, or the coffee table, for these two books.

SHORTER WORKS

Marx Brothers Critical and/or Biographical Essays

Any number of essay-length critical and/or biographical pieces (categories often combined by authors writing on the Marxes) might have been chosen. This section, proceeding chronologically, examines some of the most important. When an author is responsible for more than one pivotal essay, all his work is grouped together. The same principle is applied to journals that have been unusually rich in their examination of Marx Brothers material.

It is most fitting that a section devoted to shorter pieces on the Marxes should begin with the writing of Alexander Woollcott (see also Chapter 1). In fact, there is a triple justification involved. First, as possibly New York's most influential critic during the 1920s, his rave *New York World* review of the Marxes's 1924 *I'll Say She Is!* established the team on Broadway. Second, in the succeeding years he wrote, for various publications, several additional influential pieces on the family. Third, though the later essays might at first seem best categorized as biographical sketches, there is such an insightfully epic portrayal of Harpo and/or his mother as to qualify the writing as mythological criticism.

The Harpo slant was, of course, there from the beginning, with that first Woollcott essay even entitled "Harpo Marx and Some Brothers." But in such

Harpo-focused essays as the 1928 *New Yorker* "Portrait of a Man With Red Hair" (red being the color of Harpo's wig) and the 1934 *Cosmopolitan* (having combined with Hearst's *International*) "A Strong Silent Man" Woollcott celebrated the man behind the persona while affectionately describing an entertaining family background not inconsistent with the Marxes's public image. And though Woollcott might deny a critical stance, as he does at the beginning of "Portrait," he seldom neglects observations along these lines (often comparing Harpo to Chaplin). For instance, the same "Portrait" states: "this clown's [Harpo's] art, like ... Mr. Chaplin's, does know no frontier [national boundaries] , and in a deeper sense he will never be in a strange land at all."[49]

Mother Minnie receives an even more sustained buildup in the lengthy "A Mother of the Two-a-Day," which traces Minnie's and the team's long vaudeville apprenticeship (anthologized in Woollcott's 1928 *Going to Pieces*). This was later followed by a similar, though briefer and more elegant, homage to Minnie's status as founder and one-time leader of the Marxes. Unfortunately, the catalyst was Minnie's death and Woollcott's September 28, 1929, *New Yorker* column, "Shouts and Murmurs," became a special "Obituary."

As is normal for the student of comedy, which Woollcott was, his works are often full of humor. And while such is the case with the aforementioned essays, two additional Woollcott pieces showcase it even more. As if emulating an on-going theme of the Marxes, that things are not what they seem, a "Marxian" Woollcott wrote an article entitled "My Friend Harpo" (see the 1934 Woollcott essay collection, *While Rome Burns*), which really is about the critic's dog, though the wording is ambiguous enough to keep one in the dark throughout much of the reading. And in the piece "I Might Just as Well Have Played Hooky," Woollcott comically ponders the importance of education, since minimally educated friends like Harpo are doing so nicely. (This is anthologized in Woollcott's 1943 *Long, Long Ago*.)

All in all, Woollcott's writing helped both to celebrate the Marxes (their talent *and* their long climb to the top) and to focus special attention upon two family members—Minnie and Harpo. Woollcott's added bonus to the reader was that these two special people seemed well worth knowing in real life—something that is never a given in the world of entertainment.

Robert Benchley, who like Woollcott later became a friend of the team, authored two especially entertaining reviews of the Broadway Marxes. Writing for *Life* (the humor magazine, not the later pictorial), his accounts of *I'll Say She Is!* (entitled "The Marx Brothers") and *Animal Crackers* (entitled "Harpo, Groucho, Chico, Zeppo and Karl") are first and foremost important because he recognizes the true importance of the team. In fact, at one point in "The Marx Brothers" his enthusiasm has become so great that he comically undercuts himself—"We hate to be like this...."[50] The same review refreshingly notes the significance of vaudeville as the supplier of comedy talent for Broadway. (W.C. Fields had followed a similar route the previous year, 1923, when he made it big on Broadway after years in vaudeville.)

"Harpo, Groucho, Chico, Zeppo and Karl" (besides having a title that was then a more original comic play upon "Marxism"), is most important as a period gauge of the reluctance many felt about overanalyzing comedy. That is, much of the review is a comic attack on becoming too cerebral in one's examination of the admittedly great Marxes.

Normally, this sort of anticritical comedy stance (which often includes the patentedly foolish comment: the artist in question never intended such-and-such an interpretation) turns this author's face into a grimace not unlike a Harpo Gookie, forcing him to voice an avalanche of protesting wordage which might best be reduced to a now classic bit of critical defense: "Trust the tale not the teller." That is, regardless of the author's point or lack of a point, if a work so moves an audience member to a certain critical stance, then that analysis is perfectly valid. This is important to note here for two reasons. First, this is a position still present in more contemporary Marx criticism, as already noted of Joe Adamson's *Groucho, Harpo, Chico and Sometimes Zeppo*. Second, the Marx Brothers, like many performers past and present, were basically of the same position. (See Groucho's modest views on his comedy in this chapter's earlier examination of *Groucho and Me*.)

Pioneer popular culture critic Gilbert Seldes, best known for his still insightful book *The 7 Lively Arts*, was someone more inclined to critical analysis. In fact, one excellent later essay on the Marxes, Clifton Fadiman's *Stage* review of *A Night at the Opera*, even opens with a comic promise about not being too deep à la Seldes: "Just to remove that frightened, I-think-I-hear-Gilbert-Seldes look from your face."[51] Regardless of this image, two interesting *New Republic* Seldes pieces are brief reviews of both the Marxes's last Broadway production, *Animal Crackers*, and their first film adaptation, *The Cocoanuts*. In the former, 1928, critique he insightfully aspires to a variety of subjects, such as: the Marxes are really anything but a team, being "four separate comedians who occasionally work together."[52] Moreover, he posits an early justification of the "why" of Groucho's nonstop speech: that is consistent with the comedian's own views on the subject—the sheer numbers of saturation comedy should provide for some success. Seldes's 1929 film review is best seen as a perceptive critic's first look at the big-screen Marxes, after having closely followed their stage career. Moreover, he indirectly reminds one how *The Cocoanuts*'s director, Robert Florey, might have seemed like a good choice at the time. That is, Florey had earlier directed the shoestring-budgeted film *The Death of a Hollywood Extra*. Though Seldes says little more about this abstracted short subject (an attack on the callousness of the Hollywood system), a screening of the film showcases a mindset seemingly not out of line with the anti-establishment Marxes. Unfortunately, the actual Florey/Marxes relationship did not prove so harmonious (see Chapter 1).

An excellent companion for Seldes's piece on *Animal Crackers* (the play) is the *New York Times*'s lengthy review of the same production. Especially interesting is the unofficial rise in comedy recognition being accorded Chico, compared to their Broadway beginnings when the praise was focused upon Harpo and Groucho. The essay is also stimulating when either discussing the nihilist nature of the team or when drawing parallels between *Animal Crackers* and *I'll Say She Is!*, which the reviewer still preferred.

Before moving on from Seldes, his 1937 book *The Movies Come from America* should be noted because he frequently addresses the importance of the Marx Brothers to early sound comedy (particularly in Chapter 5). Seldes credits W. C. Fields, Disney, and the Marxes with literally saving screen comedy after the sound era threatened to destroy it. Moreover, he perceptively provides reasons both for and against defining the team as surrealists, in that matter.

Four additional 1920s pieces nicely represent a cross section of what one can encounter when surveying Marx Brothers literature. First, John B. Kennedy's 1926 *Colliers* essay, "Slapstick Stuff," provided both a biographical overview of the family (among other details, Zeppo was not yet a decision-making member of the team), and an analysis of their comedy as dependent upon being "clean and crude—for there's money in the old slapstick."[53] The key example given is Harpo's classic routine of the tidal wave of stolen silverware which is known to drop from the "innocent's" sleeve.

Second, B. F. Wilson's 1928 *Motion Picture Classic* article "The Mad Marxes Make for the Movies" merits inclusion for a number of *wrong* reasons. While celebrity pieces invariably showcase discrepancies through the years as "facts" are retold, especially with the Marxes (where a whole family is involved in the telling and retelling), this Wilson essay sets a new high in low standards. From mislabeled pictures to a text that is still confused about just which Brother is which, the piece graphically demonstrates there were still worlds left for the Marxes to conquer as they prepared to enter the movies. Ironically, when the article turned to criticism, it followed generally insightful though already somewhat standard avenues by beginning with a section on Harpo and then likening him to Chaplin.

Third, a 1928 Heywood Broun column, "It Seems to Me" (in the *New York Telegraph*) touches upon a wide gamut of Marx Brothers topics. They range from Broun's view that the Marxes have not been affected by the intellectual attention that had flawed Chaplin's work to a fascinating description of backstage activity during an actual Marx Brothers Broadway production. In fact, with regard to the latter, Broun observed that he watched the Marxes so frequently from backstage that his epitaph might well read, "Here lies Heywood Broun (Who?), killed by getting in the way of the scene shifters at a Marx Brothers show."[54] An interesting sidelight to the piece is that Groucho was evidently pleased with it, because he included the column in correspondence with longtime Chicago friend Dr. Samuel Salinger. (See Chapter 1 for more on Groucho's friendship with Salinger, as well as his relationship with Broun.)

One should also note at this point another, later Marx Brothers-focused "It Seems to Me" Broun column from an early 1939 *New York Journal American*. Besides being an entertaining overview of Groucho's radio speech of support when Broun ran for Congress years before (see Chapter 1), the column interestingly notes the international political flack the group was then receiving from the right. For example, Mussolini had recently told his citizens not to laugh at the Marxes. (Of course, *Duck Soup* had been banned earlier in Italy.)

Fourth, Howard W. Fensterstock's 1929 *Parade* magazine article pretty much says it all in the title: "A Journalistic Scream: An Imaginary Interview with the Marx Brothers." Like the propensity of Marx criticism to include comic biography elements, there is also a tendency, though not as frequent, for authors to emulate the team. Besides being more comically successful than Adamson's book-length attempt, Fensterstock's tongue-in-cheek introduction indirectly suggests the reason for this imaginary interview—the popular wish that one's favorite performers are exactly the same off-stage. In Fensterstock's case, he should have been signed to write a Marx picture, because he has so comically captured the Marxes as to improve upon many a future movie scene, including the bestowal of some comedy to Zeppo!

In the early 1930s the great British documentary producer, theorist, and critic John Grierson reviewed *Animal Crackers* (in a 1930 issue of *The Clarion*) and *Monkey Business* (a 1931 edition of *Everyman*). Later anthologized as "The Logic of Comedy" in *Grierson on Documentary*, this seemingly unlikely source produces one of the most compelling examinations of the Marxes still to be done. In fact, coming early in their film career, the piece even gives a sense of impending tragedy as Grierson twice anticipates the Hollywood destruction of these uniquely anarchistic clowns. Besides foreseeing this industry tinkering (Thalberg's homogenizing of their characters), he also farsightedly recognizes black comedy aspects of their comedy. This is especially true of his provocative interpretation of the *Animal Crackers* close, with Harpo's spray-gun knockout of the whole cast, including the comedian, being translated by Grierson as comically insane murder by the Marxes's resident madman, Harpo. (A more traditional "reading" of the scene would be to assume Harpo's spray is something less than lethal, such as ether.)

His writing is so rich that even the asides are significant. For instance, he sees parallels between Groucho and the comedy of Robert Benchley and Donald Ogden Stewart, even mentioning the latter's book *Crazy Fool* (all of which will be examined later as applicable to the complete Marx Brothers team). And as one might assume, his analysis of their comedy personae is equally knowledgeable, especially Harpo, whom Grierson favors. Thus, his comparison of the sudden comic energy of Harpo's destruction of the passport setting (papers and documents being broadcast all over) with Chaplin's broken pillow scene in *The Gold Rush* (where feathers fly everywhere) immediately provides one with a better appreciation of both comedians.

Variety's reviews are invariably thorough, but during the early 1930s they were particularly rich for students of the Marx Brothers. Principal among them are film reviews of *Animal Crackers* and *Duck Soup*, and a radio review of Groucho and Chico's short-lived 1932-1933 radio series *Beagle, Shyster and Beagle*. The *Animal Crackers* and *Beagle pieces* are provocative because of their examination of early 1930s audiences for stage, screen, and radio (see Chapter 1, where both essays are discussed).

Variety's review of *Duck Soup* is unique because of its farsightedness. At a time when many critics were panning what is now often considered the team's greatest work (*The New York Sun* reviewer called it a "nose dive"[55]), *Variety* gives it a contemporary-sounding review. And, as always, there is informative detail, from a possible origin for the film's now celebrated mirror sequence (a Schwartz Brothers routine), to well-deserved recognition for Edgar Kennedy's supporting role. The significance of Zeppo is even noted, yet by needing to consult the film's press kit for examples, Zeppo still comes off a bit tarnished. (Though rare here and in its other early 1930s Marx Brothers reviews, *Variety*'s later chronicles of the team's lesser MGM films are sometimes flawed by a pressing need, as with this reference to Zeppo, to say the positive thing.)

Variety's notation of the *Duck Soup* jettisoning of the musical solos of Harpo and Chico also brings to mind the meticulousness of the publication's last Marx Brothers film review. Surveying *Horse Feathers* the previous year, it stated:

> On the matter of formula, the harp and piano numbers were repeated against the Marxes's personal wishes but by exhibitor demands to the studio. The piano is oke, but the harp reprise . . . substantiated the boys' negative opinion that that tended to slow up the comedy.[56]

This is a valuable insight in suggesting that the Marxes were especially amenable to *Duck Soup* director Leo McCarey's pure comedy focus.

Variety's *Duck Soup* review also comically states that the "Story is a mythological kingdom burlesque that could easily have been written by a six-year-old with dust in his eyes."[57] Not only is this a good example of a review that is frequently entertaining as well as enlightening (Margaret Dumont is described as "high, wide and handsome"), but the mythical kingdom comment also focuses attention upon something frequently neglected in more recent commentary on the film's serious political satire. Though such contemporary "readings" are very important, it should be remembered that *Duck Soup*, like so many post-*Animal Crackers* Marx Brothers films, also works as a film parody vehicle. In this case the target is the propensity of Hollywood to set many early 1930s films in some cute little mythical Balkan country.

In 1932 a great deal of quality Marx Brothers literature appeared. The first was Antonin Artaud's "Les Frères marx au Cinema du Panthéon" in the January 1, 1932, *Nouvelle Revue Française*. Examining *Animal Crackers* and *Monkey Business* he likens them to comedy poems of a surrealistic nature. He sees *Monkey Business* as the best of the two, describing its close as a song of revolt. Besides his then unique linking of the Marxes and surrealism, his comments are probably most important for two things he says about Americans. First, in almost an aside, he credits this sort of film as being uniquely American. But then he offers what might be called an ongoing prophesy on American neglect of the insights provided by their humor. Essentially saying it is their loss if they do not go beyond the laughter (as if responding to the anti-interpretation remarks of some American critics highlighted earlier in the chapter), Artaud closes with further hosannas to the Marxes.

Most, however, of this bumper crop of 1932 Marx Brothers criticism was clustered in the second half of the year (their 1932 film release, *Horse Feathers*, having opened in August), the most visible and prestigious attention was their August 15, 1932, cover article in *Time* magazine (see the Chapter 1 examination).

Photoplay writer Sara Hamilton, author of several highlighted articles in the bibliographical chapter of this author's *W. C. Fields: A Bio-Bibliography* (1984), also had 1932 insights to offer upon the Marxes. The most pointed observation in her July article, "The Nuttiest Quartette in the World" was a comparison between the team and Lewis Carroll:

> Like the tea party in "Alice" when the March Hare, sadly dipping his broken watch up and down in the tea, remarked to the Mad Hatter he didn't think he should have put the butter in the watch as the Hatter suggested, as now it wouldn't go at all. Whereupon the Mad Hatter shrugged and answered, "Well, it was the best butter." . . . So it is with the Marxes.[58]

The Lewis Carroll-Marx comparison represents an important, early recognition of the literary significance with which one might judge the team. It is only through an elevation of this nature that a true appreciation of the unique Marx Brothers characters is possible. Film theorist André Bazin would later articulate just this point while writing about Chaplin—drawing an important analogy between a gifted performer of the twentieth century and "mythic" literary heroes of the past.[59] Critic and historian Gerald Weales notes the meaningfulness of Hamilton's literary observation in his generally insightful essay *"Duck Soup"* (to be examined later in this chapter), but he then generally pooh-poohs the remainder of Hamilton's piece as typical fan magazine stuff. But Hamilton's essay should not be so lightly dismissed, because it is another Marx Brothers article that richly combines the biographical with the critical. Moreover, even its comical throwaway lines, such as "Chico (Leo) who performs on a piano as no self-respecting piano was ever performed on before. . ." can provide perceptive understanding. That is, Hamilton reminds one that Chico's anti-establishment persona (and those of his Brothers) is further reinforced by his comically unorthodox playing, including "shooting the keys"—hardly the standard technique taught by most piano instructors.

An anti-traditional playing style is also, of course, true of Harpo's musical solos. Indeed, one of the hoariest of Marx tales relates how after the team first achieved some success the musically gifted and self-taught Harpo decided to treat himself to harp lessons. But his playing was so unorthodox that during the first lesson Harpo did all the teaching as his "instructor" asked question after question. Harpo decided to take no more lessons.

Alexander Bakshy's August 1932 review of *Horse Feathers* offers both praise and an interesting suggestion: Marx madness could have been further maximized had the Brothers more fully integrated their comedy to its college campus setting. Bakshy then has some fun coining academic titles for team members. For example, Chico would become "the head of the college speakeasy and professor of bootlegging" (areas in which he was involved during the movie).[60] But Bakshy's suggestion has comedy merit. Certainly Groucho's biology lecture, or his attempt at a lecture since he must contend with his Brothers as students, is both a comedy delight and an effective comedy use of setting which has no real classroom followup in the film. Though, to the Marxes's defense, the college locale was so rich that the team found lots of pertinent comedy outside the classroom, such as the football climax.

Of special added interest is the fact that the Bakshy piece is one of the few reviews in which a team member's response is known. Groucho scornfully observes in a letter:

This weeks [*sic*] *Nation* [August 31, 1932] . . . carries a review of the picture [*Horse Feathers*], in which the critic [Bakshy] shows the world how he would have written the picture. These boys [critics] are all authors, and the proof of it, is the fact that they get sixty five dollars a week, and the author who actually writes the picture gets nine hundred.[61]

Of course, Groucho was no doubt feeling justifiably untouchable as an artist just then, after the team's recent gracing of the cover of *Time*, which is also noted in the letter (see Chapter 1).

Consistent with such *Time* cover significance, *Horse Feathers* also generated two especially provocative reviews from Europe. The comments of British critic Francis Birrell, in his *New Statesman and Nation* essay "The Marx Brothers" (October 1, 1932) are most engrossing when he, like Hamilton, comments upon Marx Brothers ties with the world of Lewis Carroll. Though Birrell would no doubt have a fit of superiority at such linkage to a fan magazine author (his review, at times, takes elitism to new heights of arrogance), his writing works best as an expanded look at Carroll and the Marxes.

That Birrell should also briefly conjure up the term surrealism in his review makes for a fitting transition to the other European piece—Philippe Soupault's praise of *Horse Feathers* in *L'Europe Nouvelle*, also in October (the eighth) of 1932. It is appropriate because Soupault was a pioneer figure in the surrealistic movement, though he does not specifically apply the term in his discussion of the Marxes.

Soupault's views on *Horse Feathers*, and on the Marxes in general, are much more upbeat than Birrell's (who, among other things, is bothered by the ongoing stage mannerisms of the team, though he finds this film to be their most cinematic to date). Soupault is much more democratic in his analysis of the Marxes. Thus, while Birrell can praise the team and still suggest its derivative, British nature from Carroll and Edward Lear, Soupault sets the Marxes and several other film comedians aside as representative of the truly unique American film comedy, which easily tops all other national cinemas in its rich array of comedians. He is also fully fleshing out what Artaud only suggested in an aside.

Soupault is at his most stimulating, however, when he uses the Marxes as a metaphor for a deforming comic mirror in which one sees exaggerations of himself and the world around him. He goes on to suggest what was a much more arresting observation in 1932—that the team represents how individuals might behave if social laws were not restrictive.

As if underlining the importance of both the Birrell and Soupault pieces, as well as constituting an appropriate close to a year especially fascinating in Marx Brothers literature, the December 1932 *Living Age* reprinted excerpts (though with little added commentary) from both essays under the title "As Others See Us." Such early recognition of the pieces is commendable, though it is unfortunate that the Artaud essay was not included.

Early 1933 continues this foreign focus one article further with Louis Chavance's often perceptive "The Four Marx Brothers: As Seen by a Frenchman" in *The Canadian Forum*. Chavance covers a wide spectrum of topics and is most interesting when discussing the cartoon nature of the Brothers. He reminds the reader that *Monkey Business* (the most recent Marx film discussed) has a story composed by caricaturists—S. J. Perelman and Will B. Johnstone. Though he neglects to mention Arthur Sheekman (credited with additional dialogue) and the often almost comedic ensemble construction of a Marx script, his point is well taken. As he notes, Perelman was a regular contributor to the humor magazine *Judge* (where he did cartoons and essays), and Johnstone did a daily cartoon in the *New York World-Telegraph*.

While Gerald Weales's essay, discussed previously, does not mention Chavance's article, a key Weales point could be applied here—that the richest ground for exploring the roots of zany Marx comedy would be American popular culture rather than esoteric European isms. Though Weales sometimes seems overly dogmatic about this, it seems a position well taken. In fact, the Soupault piece indirectly suggests the same thing when it touches upon America's unique school of film comedy.

Chavance's essay is also insightful when it traces the progressively more cinematic nature of the Marx Brothers films, feeling they have fully arrived as *movie* comedians with *Monkey Business*. (For additional period commentary on this, see especially John Mosher's *New Yorker* review of *Monkey Business*.)

Because Chavance's essay is so multifaceted, however, he is not beyond stumbling once or twice. Most problematic is his look at early Marx family history, such as recycling their mother's publicity-motivated appropriation of Minnie Palmer's identity (see Chapter 1). The interweaving of biography and criticism is common in Marx literature. And Chavance's overall message—that early hardship encouraged comedy inventiveness—is essentially true, though his biographical "facts" often land wide of the mark.

The November 1933 release of *Duck Soup* did not produce the same catalyst for the rich analysis of the team which had occurred the previous year. Ironically, one could claim just the opposite happened. That is, this great film was panned by many 1930s critics. Thus, significant comments are often found in reviews which state the film is seriously flawed. For example, *The Nation*'s William Troy had numerous problems with *Duck Soup* (such as Harpo "is becoming definitely tiresome"[62]), yet Troy's review is important because it includes an early claim (Weales calls it the first,[63] but it is predated by Grierson) linking the team with the "crazy-fool" comedy of the post–World War I era.

Along the same lines—a damning review that still manages to be thought-provoking—is Meyer Levin's *Esquire* piece on *Duck Soup*. After unbelievably calling it their weakest film, Levin celebrates the significance of Harpo (quite unlike Troy), while perceptively analyzing his persona. (The examination includes a short but thoughtful comparison of Harpo and Chaplin.) Levin's overall plea is for more of a Harpo focus in future Marx Brothers films, something that began and ended with the much later *Love Happy*.

Somewhat similar to the *Esquire* piece is *Time* magazine's review, which also manages to criticize the film yet elevate Harpo. But the Harpo commentary in *Time* takes two additional twists. First, it acknowledges his important comic meanness, which would later be controversially softened by MGM (see Chapter 1). Second, with a qualifier like "Admirers of Harpo should be particularly pleased with his horrid actions in *Duck Soup*,"[64] the piece also includes a tone of condescension under which many depression era personality comedians had to work. Though this elitist stance occurred in many period publications, a more specific example would be a later *Time* review of the Marxes's *Go West*: "Like W. C. Fields, Groucho, Harpo and Chico Marx are seemingly funny to their admirers, idiotic to others."[65]

As the earlier *Variety* review of *Duck Soup* demonstrated, however, the film was not without supporters. Especially interesting is Rob Wagner's positive appraisal of the film in the November 18, 1933, *Rob Wagner's Script*. It merits extra points because he gives *Duck Soup* director Leo McCarey part of the credit, besides reminding readers that the director both teamed and molded the slower comedy pace of Laurel & Hardy. This appreciation of McCarey's guidance of *Duck Soup*, though not accepted fact, was not quite the critical norm of 1933.

An interesting conclusion to the period material on *Duck Soup* is Edwin Schallert's short essay in the January 1, 1934, *Los Angeles Times*—"Marx Brothers Due for Vacation from Movies." As the title suggests, this was hardly a piece as upbeat as the rave reviews from *Variety* and *Rob Wagner's Script*. Yet, while Schallert was aware of the less-than-ideal reception that the film had received, he was equally cognizant (unlike many contemporary Marx doomsayers) that movies had hardly heard the last of the Marxes—"*Duck Soup* was scarcely a fadeout or anything like that. . . ."[66]

The next major catalyst for Marx Brothers literature was the great comeback success accorded the November 1935 release of *A Night at the Opera*. But just prior to this two radically different essays of interest appeared. The first was Clara Beranger's *Liberty Magazine* article, "The Woman Who Taught Her Children to Be Fools." This was the baldest deification of Mother Minnie yet. She is credited with everything from giving her boys their nicknames to being a writer on the production that sealed Harpo's silence (*Home Again*, actually authored by Uncle Al Shean). Yet when not building a monument to Minnie, Beranger's article is an interesting combination of biography and criticism that defines their comedy through their unorthodox childhood.

Unlike the Beranger piece, with its Woollcottish mythic overtones carried to an extreme, the secone essay was directly tied to the forthcoming release of *A Night at the Opera*. It was a Hollywood news column in the *New York Times* that on October 20, 1935, had focused on the apparent success of the Marxes's road-tour test of material for their first MGM film. It was in part subtitled "The Marxes as Guinea Pigs for a Stage-Screen Experiment," and author Douglas W. Churchill had assembled a mini-overview of recent Marx history and criticism, from their commercial decline at Paramount to Thalberg's softening of their characters as MGM Marxes. Churchill correctly predicted "a renaissance of the Marxes impends."[67]

The renaissance began November 15, 1935, the United States release date of *A Night at the Opera*. *Newsweek* called it "the best film the brothers—or any other comedians—have made."[68] *New York Times* critic Andre Sennwald was a bit closer to the mark when he observed, "If *A Night at the Opera* is a trifle below their best, it is also considerably above the standard of laughter that has been our portion since they quit the screen."[69] Regardless, there is a Noah's ark of hosanna reviews from which to choose. Three of the most interesting are by Sennwald, Otis Ferguson, and Clifton Fadiman. While each is an excellent critic, Ferguson and Sennwald occupy a special status for this author because of their fascinating period pieces on W. C. Fields, which this writer explored earlier in *W. C. Fields: A Bio-Bibliography*. Moreover, a case could be made for calling Ferguson the best American film critic of the 1930s. (And Sennwald would most certainly have been in contention for that honor had he not died tragically of gas poisoning in early 1936—at the age of only twenty-eight.)

Ferguson and Sennwald have the talent to be both critically perceptive and comic at the same time. For example, their commentary upon recycled material in *A Night at the Opera* has Sennwald observing: "Even when their gags sound as if they were carved out of Wheeler and Woolsey with an ax, the boys continue to be rapturously mad."[70] And Ferguson piles on even greater comic overstatement (a stance consistent with the Marxes's overstatement) when he notes the film "drives off with whole wagonloads of the Keystone lot without so much as putting the fence back up; it has more familiar faces in the way of gags and situations than a college reunion."[71]

While both critics generally praise the film, their ability to be entertainingly cognizant of its less-than-perfect nature (whether it is old material or the romantic subplot they both also found problematic) in the face of a Marx Brothers "renaissance," speaks highly of their skills to rise above contemporary hoopla. (See also Ferguson's later reviews of *A Day at the Races* and *Go West*. Though not as sagacious as his *A Night at the Opera* commentary, Ferguson always merits attention. Sennwald, of course, did not live to critique another Marx Brothers film.)

The third focus review of *A Night at the Opera*, Fadiman's *Stage* magazine critique, initially seems to be of the pure praise "renaissance" school. The author opens with his comic anti-analysis Gilbert Seldes slap, and then calls the film not only the Marxes's "funniest" but "a distinct step forward in American film comedy."[72] But what then follows is the single most perceptive period review of a Marx film. First there is a lengthy, provocative examination of the Marxes's work along comic overstatement lines (plus a comedy theory comparison to W. C. Fields). Second, ties between the film and the antiheroic world of James Thurber are made (a position examined in Chapters 1 and 2 of this volume). Third, as much as Fadiman likes the film, he is bothered by extremes of vulnerability under which Groucho and Harpo labor in two scenes (the softening of their screen characters). Fourth, his critical comments are constantly bolstered by a detailed knowledge of the Marx Brothers scene. Thus, his remarks are enriched with added background, unusual for the standard review. For example, he considers an earlier script plan to burn the opera; he closes with some projections for future Marx Brothers films . . . two of which end up being made! Fifth, like Sennwald, he found the comic artistry of Harpo to have reached a new high. (Ferguson was especially enamored of Groucho.) Sixth, as a final catch-all, Fadiman also touches upon everything from censorship concerns to an informal plea celebrating the inherent significance of this outrageous fun.

Appropriately, one can follow Fadiman's most stimulating of period reviews with an article of ambitious proportions—Alva Johnston's "The Marx Brothers: The Scientific Side of Lunacy." The previous year (1935) Johnston had done an insightful three-part series on W. C. Fields for *The New Yorker*, a subject to which he would later return with a 1938 *Saturday Evening Post* essay "Who Knows What Is Funny?"

As the subtitle of Johnston's Marx article indicates, the main thrust of his piece was an exploration of the methodical way in which the team honed its *A Night at the Opera* material via the MGM road-tour test. Or, as Johnston comically overstated, "The only possible advance in efficiency would be to load the public on belt conveyors and make it laugh with mechanical ticklers."[73] One might best underline the tour's attention to detail, as well as credit the improvising collaborator nature of the Brothers, by noting that during the last week on the road, court reporters were hired to record every line so that neither the latest script doctoring nor the latest ad-libbing would be lost.

Johnston's piece also devotes considerable space to family background. And while Minnie is again given honored status—"The greatest of all the Marxes"—the material does not slide into the biographical fantasy that flawed Beranger's earlier "The Woman Who Taught Her Children to Be Fools."[74] In fact, it even reports on a talent of the father, which is often neglected. Frenchie was a "born recruiting sergeant" at packing his sons' early theatres "with horny-handed enthusiasts thundering applause."[75]

Johnston's straight biographical observations can also serve a sociological critical stance, such as his chronicle of their career-long needs for improvisation. And while his Marx essay is not quite so rich as his Fields material—which had the added perception of also being about a friend—it is well worth examining. In fact, even the Johnston aside about public conveyor belts can have special merit. Thus, early in the article he insightfully links the Brothers with what now might best be called twentieth-century literature of the antihero and with such writers as Robert Benchley.

Fittingly, Johnston's article, with its gag-testing focus, has an excellent companion piece in Teet Carle's 1937 "Laugh Stock: Common and Preferred," which examines both *A Night at the Opera* and *A Day at the Races*. However, because Carle is an insider (a studio publicist), his essay is a more detailed look at this most conscientious of comedy approaches. For example, he relates a gag from the tour and the not-yet-released film, where, in preparation for conducting a physical examination, Groucho (or, should one say, Dr. Hugo Z. Hackenbush) removes his wristwatch to wash. But when he discovers Dr. Leopold X. Steinberg (Siegfried Rumann playing another of his delightfully pompous characters) checking out his watch, Groucho deliberately throws it into his basin of water and cracks, "I'd rather have it rusty than missing." That seemingly effortless bit of comedy was the product of much testing. Three different words were used at the close of the punch line: missing, disappear, and gone. On the Marxes's tour "*Gone* and *disappear* were each used forty-four times; *missing* got fifty voicings. Every time, the latter word brought the biggest laugh."[76]

Besides such a fascinatingly detailed look at comedy testing, Carle's essay has two other points recommending it. First, it contains both a Marx Brothers mini-article and illustrations by no less a figure than James Thurber. Thurber's parody review, its very title undercutting intellectual pretentiousness—"*Der Tag aux Courses*" (*A Day at the Races*), is a comic analysis that showcases a keen awareness of past Marx Brothers films and an affectionate affinity with them. It is a further underlining of the aforementioned ties between the comic antiheroic literary movement and the Marxes.

Second, Carle's essay also examines the Marxes in terms of both comedy theory and some of their basic rules on the subject, for instance: avoid jokes about national heroes. Thus, Chico's original aviation speech in *A Night at the Opera* claimed that "Lindbergh just tried a second trans-Atlantic flight but ran out of gas half-way across and had to turn back."[77] But road tour audiences did not laugh until Chico substituted himself for Lindbergh in the story. This personalized touch is also true of Carle's comedy theory approach, which investigates the notion that there is a Marx Brother deep inside everyone.

There were other Carle pieces over the years (see the "Marx on Marx" shorter works section for a highlighted Carle interview with Harpo). One might best note both Carle's continuing interest and the time span this entailed by briefly examining his 1978 *Los Angeles* magazine article "'Fun' Working with the Marx Brothers? Horsefeathers!" Though the title might suggest some sort of muckraking revelations, the article simply states they were hardly a publicist's dream and occasionally touches upon the subject as it moves on to their Paramount commercial decline, Margaret Dumont, and the MGM road testing of material. Carle's material is good, especially his Marx Brothers "straight woman"-entitled contrasting of Dumont and Thelma Todd.[78] Though there is a minor flaw or two, such as Carle having forgotten less ballyhooed Marx road-testing tours after *A Day at the Races*, he was a publicist who thankfully never learned the word retire.

It is pertinent at this point to note both that Dumont won the 1937 Screen Actors Guild Best Supporting Actress award for *A Day at the Races* and remind readers that women were hardly the heart of the Marx Brothers audience. Thus, besides being an excellent article, it is most appropriate that female reviewer Cecelia Ager's Dumont-focused review of *A Day at the Races* should now be examined. Ager's brief but comically insightful celebration of Dumont likens her to "the stuff of which our pioneer women were made . . . a lady who asks but little and gets it."[79] Fittingly, in light of Dumont's later award, Ager asks in comic overstatement for appropriate recognition for the actress, like maybe a statue or a national holiday. Dumont's devotion to Groucho knows no reason, despite her constant Marx Brothers victimization. Thus, she is "on display again in *A Day at the Races*, where once again her fortitude is nothing human. It's godlike."[80]

Among the other *A Day at the Races* reviews worth noting, one might best begin with the *New York Times*. In the second half of the 1930s the newspaper would seem to replace *Variety* as the major organ of publication that most judicially critiques Marx Brothers work while also adding information of related interest. Unfortunately, this often meant covering a team in decline. But from today's perspective, these *Times* pieces are more realistically to the point, something not always true of other Marx Brothers reviews during the same period.

Of particular interest at this point are four recommended *A Day at the Races* reviews from the chronologically listed "Notes" section of Joe Adamson's Marx Brothers book. Adamson's style is generally to cite but not single out reviews. Thus, there is an added curiosity to examining the selections. Besides the aforementioned *New York Times* piece, he suggests reviews in *Literary Digest*, *Commonweal*, and *The Nation*. However, in the first two cases, the selections do not live up to their advanced billing. This is especially true of the brief *Commonweal* coverage, which is more Marx Brothers enthusiasm than insight.

Mark Van Doren's review from *The Nation*, though, is interesting. Entitled "Harpo & Co.," it is a celebration of what might best be called the new Harpo. While Van Doren does not juxtapose the aggressive Paramount Harpo with the more homogenized MGM variety, his description of the clown (in terms of innocence and childlike nature) is consistent with the change. Though this author cannot embrace Van Doren's revision, it is an interesting period look at a critic who could. (Unfortunately, today's more socially conscious reader might also be bothered by Van Doren's lengthy examination of Harpo's veritable Pied Pipering of a black community during one scene of the film.)

Briefly moving from 1937 film to 1937 radio, Aaron Stein's review of Groucho and Chico, "Mad Marxes Guest Star on Radio," is both perceptive and easily applied to the complete team's work on stage and screen. (See Chapter 1 for a more extensive examination of this article.)

One might close the discussion of 1930s literature on the Marxes with comments on any number of pieces, but this author has limited observations to three essays—Frank S. Nugent's 1938 "Speaking of Comedy," Marie Seton's 1939 "S. Dali + 3 Marxes =   ," and James Feibleman's 1939 "The Comedy of Everyday Life: The Marx Brothers." The Nugent article, though it focuses on *Room Service*, is not to be confused with his earlier *New York Times* review of the film. In "Speaking of Comedy" Nugent methodically yet effectively repeats the refrain "Comedy is a matter of taste" as he proceeds to examine the subject.[81] Consequently, his discussion of the Marxes, in general as well as in *Room Service*, also touches upon other 1930s comedy contemporaries—Chaplin, Fields, and Harold Lloyd. Eventually he observes that comedy is also "a matter of restraint. Since the Marxes are unrestrainable, they should not have been turned loose upon [the structured] *Room Service*, which is not good Marx and not nearly so effective as the play."[82] Though that critical stance (that *Room Service* was not good Marx) seems pedestrian today, period examinations of the film were often more positive. Even Nugent's earlier *Room Service* review flirted with this particular position: "the Marxes haven't made it [*Room Service*] any funnier; but neither has their presence interfered to any large extent with the disorderly progress of an antic piece."[83] (See Chapter 1 for the team's reservations about *Room Service*.)

The Seton article, besides noting the team's dislike of the film, is a survey of surrealist artist Salvador Dali's fascination with the Marxes, particularly Harpo— the most surreal of the family. Moreover, the essay is accompanied by five Marx Brothers-inspired Dali drawings. They represent part of a series of Dali drawings that were done as an abstract storyboard of sorts for an equally abstract and unrealized team-inspired Dali script. (Luis Buñuel and Dali were responsible for the still provocative classic *Un Chien andalou*, 1928, generally considered the beginning of surrealist cinema.) The point of Seton's article, which also touches upon Lewis Carroll, is that the Brothers are actual surrealist performers. Indirectly, the essay and its drawings (generally focused upon Harpo; the originals are hung in the comedian's living room) additionally chronicles Harpo's ongoing love affair with the intelligentsia.

Strangely enough, or should one say surrealistically enough, the Seton article makes no mention of Dali's provocative 1937 essay "Surrealism in Hollywood." Though not limited to the Marxes, or more precisely to Harpo, the pantomimist still manages to be the heart of the article. Thus, after praising the dreamlike state of *Animal Crackers*, Dali calls Harpo "the most fascinating and the most surrealistic character in Hollywood."[84] However, from this point on the Dali article itself becomes a bit surreal:

> I met Harpo for the first time in his garden. He was naked, crowned with roses, and in the center of a veritable forest of harps (he was surrounded by at least five hundred harps). He was caressing, like a new Leda, a dazzling white swan, and feeding it a statue of the Venus of Milo made of cheese, which he grated against the strings of the nearest harp.[85]

This is called an interesting first impression. And while one assumes this is a flight of fancy by Dali, he does occasionally return to planet Earth. For example, he states Harpo "adores" such things as his "beautiful wife" and "'soft' watches."[86] Harpo was, of course, just then in the early phases of his very happy marriage to lovely film actress Susan Fleming. Soft watches is obviously a reference to Dali's frequent tendency to feature melted timepieces in his paintings. (It also reminds one of Harpo's surrealistic safeguarding of a childhood watch—from the pawning hands of Chico—by removing its hands. See Chapter 1.) Moreover, in Dali's favor, even his most outlandish statements do not seem that far removed from the world of the Marxes. For instance, Harpo was known for sometimes playing his harp in the nude, with guests occasionally being introduced into the most revealing of first impressions. And the Marxes were famous for pranks, some of which involved nudity. For example, one classic story (there are numerous variations) has them becoming so disgusted at the long waits to which they were subjected by their very busy MGM producer Irving Thalberg that he eventually found them nude in the waiting room—roasting potatoes in the fireplace. Thus, while Dali has obviously been up to his old shocking self in this article, it is a surrealistic credit to his key subjects that the exaggeration often seems not that extreme. Regardless, the essay should be required reading for students of the Marxes and/ or surrealism, and is a natural companion piece to Seton's article. (A Dali drawing of Harpo that accompanies the artist's essay is, in addition, one of the five later reproduced for Seton's "S. Dali + 3 Marxes =   .") One should, in addition, review the pertinent 1932 comments of Artaud, Birrell, and Soupault, as well as both those from Seldes's 1937 volume *The Movies Come from America* and *The New Statesman and Nation* December 16, 1939, review of *At the Circus*. The latter case provides the provocative observation:

> The circus ring is where by tradition the Marxes belong . . . to see them . . . [*At the Circus*] running with clowns, and firing Margaret Dumont from a cannon, reminds us of the real origins of their humor, which is by no means specifically modern as the surrealist interpreters of it would like to suggest.[87]

The final 1930s essay to be discussed, Feibleman's "The Comedy of Everyday Life: The Marx Brothers," is drawn from chapter 5 of his watershed book, *In Praise of Comedy: A Study in Its Theory and Practice.* As the title of the Marx Brothers segment suggests, Feibleman sees the team's work as a comic attack upon contemporary American life, from the world of real estate to horse racing.

In particular, he focuses upon such favorite Marx targets as business, medicine, entertainment, romance, and sex. Because Feibleman sees Groucho as both an embodiment of the team's humor and the greatest of its members, most examples are drawn from the mustached one's comic pox upon the language. Despite the still-valuable insights Feibleman's writing has given the study of comedy and the Marxes, in the 1930s he felt a justification was in order for his work. His defense is as rich as his analysis and bears quoting, because of that richness and as a supplement to both this author's earlier comments on the subject and Groucho's sometimes dismissal of deeper meanings to his comedy:

> To know how far he [Groucho] is able to analyze his own humor would throw some light upon his individual intelligence but little or none upon the meaning of comedy. . . . Comedy addressed to the public is public comedy, and hence absolutely available for analysis to meanings which are themselves objective meanings. It should by now be a recognized truth that the artist is not always the best aesthetician; and similarly the comedian is not always the best expositor of his comedy.[88]

Pivotal Marx Brothers literature from the 1940s is not nearly so plentiful as in the decade just examined, for four reasons. First, and most apparent, the team broke up in 1941 following the release of *The Big Store*. While they reteamed for *A Night in Casablanca* in 1946 and *Love Happy* (1949, though not generally released until 1950, and with Groucho largely absent), there was not the steady, almost one-film-a-year average of 1929-1941. Consequently, there is no large store of film reviews and articles which a new product is forever generating (as was the case in the 1930s). This is underlined by the fact that the best of the 1940s Marx literature is clustered around the 1946 release date of *A Night in Casablanca*. Second, although there continued to be a Marx Brothers following, the later films prior to *Casablanca* had shown a definite decline. As the *New York Times*'s sympathetic review of *The Big Store* observed: "one would have to admit that the picture has many a dull stretch, that the tricks have been overworked, that the boys are slowing down, etc., etc."[89] Ironically, this is probably best summed up by the earlier title for *The Big Store—Bargain Basement*. Third, at least during the war years, the Marx brand of anti-establishment film comedy would hardly have been in the patriotic norm. For instance, Abbott and Costello were phenomenally popular at the time in a series of films that highlighted different branches of the military services, starting with *Buck Privates* (1941). Fourth, because the solo activities of the Marxes often involved a return to America's hinterland (such as war bond rallies, or the touring of the band for which Chico fronted), some of the better Marx period articles have been lost or forgotten by having appeared in less-than-mainstream publications (for example, the September 10, 1943, *Dallas Morning News* interview "Arthur (Harpo) Marx, Surrealist Comedian").

An interesting starting point for this 1940s literature is Edward Buzzell's *New York Times* article, "Mocked and Marred by the Marxes." Besides having directed the Marxes in *At the Circus* and *Go West*, Buzzell was an old performing friend from vaudeville and Broadway. Though the article includes the standard team comments, such as "no one can 'handle' a Marx brother," there are also intriguing observations.[90] For instance, he reveals why he "was the guy without a sense of humor."[91] Laughing at the Marxes, as with most comedians, merely encourages them to run more comically amuck. Thus, Buzzell neither laughed at their ad-libs nor attempted to match repartee with the Brothers (despite being a former comedian). This revelation is especially interesting because although numerous Marx Brothers directors were accused of being "without a sense of humor," there was probably more than a little of this Buzzell principle (maintaining a comedy distance) present in their behavior. Discussing this subject also allowed Buzzell to include some Marx Brothers ad-lib material. For example, he once told Harpo he was not stalking the villain slowly enough, and the comedian replied, "But I'm a silent actor—not a stalking one."[92] Buzzell went on to defend them:

> It isn't that they don't know any better or are obstinate. But theirs is a non-conformist sort of comedy and the spontaneity which makes them great laugh stars often gets out of the boundaries of the camera's range finder.[93]

The piece makes one wish that all the Marx directors had been given a similar opportunity. Of course, the frequent tensions between the Marxes and directors might also have produced some X-rated observations, not unlike Groucho's comments in the controversial later *Marx Brothers Scrapbook*.

With *The Big Store* as the Marxes's announced retirement piece, Britain's *Spectator* produced an important 1941 review that was more a moving tribute to their body of work. Critic Edgar Anstey stated:

> Among the players who have contributed to cinema history only Chaplin ranks higher than these three clowns . . . no pretentiousness ever survived the friendly investigations of Harpo and Chico, and that no social, political or economic skullduggery ever found Groucho at a loss for a nimble oration.[94]

Truly the Brothers's stock in Britain had come a long way since the penny-throwing incident of the 1920s (see Chapter 1).

On April 1 *Life* magazine brought out a Marx Brothers pictorial spread entitled "How to Be a Spy," which should not be confused with the Groucho-authored essay reprinted in Chapter 3. *Life*'s tongue-in-cheek April Fool's gift to the nation was a mock-heroic guide to espionage through comic pictures (usually featuring Groucho) with comic titles. Credit for this patriotic service was given to Groucho.

The March 16 issue of *Colliers* carried Jim Marshall's "warning" article about "The Marx Menace." Though heralding the arrival of their forthcoming (early May) *A Night in Casablanca*, it combines the now familiar Marx essay pattern of colorful family history (starting with Minnie) and some critical commentary. However, in this instance the history is justified as a reminder, since the team has been absent from the screen since 1941. It opens with a winsome anecdote about an implied Groucho ad-lib from the team's New York stage days. This was still the time of old-fashioned iceboxes, and Groucho observed during Harpo's musical solo, "I wonder if I remembered to empty the pan under the icebox."[95] It brought the house down and would continue to do so for months. The point was, according to Groucho, "Humor is like that—you can't tell, most of the time, what an audience is going to laugh at."[96] Yet, Marshall later applies an excellent post-World War II comedy overview to their antics: "The Marxes's best friend probably is the regimentation of modern life and their refusal to accept it."[97]

These radically different items—the little, everyday anxiety of remembering to empty the icebox pan versus rebellion from societal regimentation—also nicely demonstrate the broadness of the team's work and their ongoing ties with the evolution of the comic antihero.

In May 1946 *Movieland* magazine published "The Royal Family of Riot," a tribute at its best when it is revealing Harpo as the Brother to appeal to when a team decision is necessary. There is, of course, more family history, a review of the Casablanca title dispute with Warner Brothers (this was later revealed to be a publicity stunt and was also dealt with in the Marshall piece), an overview of the making of *A Night in Casablanca*, comments on why film production is getting old for the team, the comic life of their business secretary, and a brief look at the Marx children—the most publicly visible one at this time being Chico's Maxine, "who appears on the 'Sherlock Holmes' broadcasts, and other radio programs."[98] The article ends on a breezy note as it discusses "the merry, mad Marx Brothers" and their activities since the completion of the film.[99] However, one cannot help but feel a little sad when it is revealed that Chico (whose perennial money problems are not mentioned) is off to Rio de Janeiro to fill a nightclub date. It undercuts the article's ongoing theme that the Marxes, unlike the classic image of comedians as being sad, are a merry bunch. Not surprisingly, the only Chico quote included in the article concerned his desire (financial need?), unlike his Brothers, to make another film—"But what can I do if these other guys are too lazy to make one?"[100]

The critical reception of *A Night in Casablanca* is best summed up, as noted in Chapter 1, by James Agee's May 25 review in *The Nation*, where he ranks flawed Marx Brothers above most everything else.[101] The focus of his critique is the satirical greatness of Groucho, which he introduces by confessing, "Only a mash-note, or the work of several weeks, could contain my regard for Groucho."[102]

If companion review material is desired, one might best turn to D. Mosdell's later critique (September) of the film in *The Canadian Forum*. It is insightful, recognizing "Chico's real function . . . as interpreter between Harpo and Groucho, and to make it possible . . . for them to act in the same picture." (Maxine's later description of Chico's role was comic "catalyst"—see both Chapter 1 and the book section of this chapter). But of more interest here is Mosdell discussing Agee on Groucho. Among other things, Agee had claimed that the satirical Groucho had always been burdened by an audience incapable of following all his verbal slapstick. Mosdell counters by observing that Groucho's use of "slapstick pantomime [no doubt meaning his pulsating eyebrows, ready leer, and the crouching walk] makes some of the oldest and worst lines in the world sound funny."[103] Both authors are, in fact, correct; Groucho's comedy often fluctuated from one type to another. Regardless of one's position, the two reviews work nicely together.

Prior to Mosdell's piece, *New York Times* film critic Bosley Crowther had written an affectionate celebration of the Marxes. Entitled "Those Marx Men," it more than made up for the *Times*'s earlier soft panning review of *A Night in Casablanca*. Crowther's article was especially engaging because it spoke with a great deal of entertainment common sense. Interestingly, he recalls Groucho's 1941 team retirement explanation (about their anticipating the public's dislike; see Chapter 1). Then he gently takes Groucho to task, saying, "Those were hard words from a comic who had been (and still was, to our mind) one of the most delightful people that had ever socked and buskined on the screen."[104] Crowther then offers critical forgiveness for the earlier decline of their last films—"no matter how 'stale' the pattern seemed, there was [*sic*] always a few priceless moments that made up for any other lack."[105] His examples range from the comic dismantling of the wooden boxcars for fuel during the finale of *Go West* to Groucho's *At the Circus* observation, after an important wallet has been tucked into an alluring bosom—"There must be some way I can get that without getting into trouble with [movie censor] Will Hays."[106] Crowther goes on to say, "They are in a class with Charlie Chaplin and the best that the Keystone age produced."[107] Thus, like Agee and Mosdell, Crowther is thankful just to have the team back.

The following year (April 1947) Columbia College professor Richard Rowland authored what is still one of the most critically absorbing Marx Brothers essays. Aptly titled "American Classic," it both offered insight and heralded the arrival of the team as cinema greats who had withstood the test of time. Post-World War II America was nostalgic for its comedy cinema past. Rowland's piece anticipates Agee's 1949 influential essay "Comedy's Greatest Era," which celebrated the silent era but still managed to cite the Marxes as rare examples of great comedians in the largely arid sound era. MGM re-released some of the team's work in the late 1940s, and in 1950 the Crichton biography of the Brothers appeared. But the Marxes did not represent wistfulness for a simpler comedy past. Their comedy lessons about the complex modern world seemed even timelier. Rowland recognizes this and even slides into an unacknowledged commentary about what would now be described as black comedy:

perhaps the anarchy of their comedy—"Look! No hands!" Chico explains joyfully as their air liner tears down the [*A Night in Casablanca*] runway with only an inexperienced Harpo in the pilot's seat—is hard for us to bear. But that is our fault and not theirs. We [the modern world] are driving with no hands; perhaps that is no longer a joke. Perhaps that is why they [the Marxes] are less funny [in *A Night in Casablanca*] to us today.[108]

Rowland's essay is must reading.

Current Biography 1948 (1949) has an excellent bibliographical, critical over- view of the team under the group heading of "Chico Marx, Groucho Marx, Harpo Marx." It touches upon everything from surrealism to Groucho's ownership of a minor league baseball team. Its chronological commentary also notes significant Marx literature, as well as closing with a bibliography. Ironically, sources cited in the text are usually not included in the bibliography. Still, it is a valuable survey, both for the apprentice follower of the team as well as the longtime supporter who wishes to review Marx Brothers basics.

As one moves to significant 1950s Marx Brothers literature, there is a real danger of drowning in the paper deluge of articles focusing on Groucho and his very popular radio/television program *You Bet Your Life*. This author has ad- dressed the challenge in two ways. First, the majority of these pieces are so fasci- nated by Groucho's comic observations (and no doubt the ease with which it helps the reporter fill a writing assignment) that the comedian should rate co- author status. Thus, the best of these are examined later in the article-length "Marx on Marx" category of this chapter. Second, the more prestigious and critically minded 1950s Groucho articles, such as the *Time* and *Newsweek* cover pieces, qualified legitimately as Marx *Brothers* literature because the former team was also a natural topic of the week. Even here, however, space is invariably reserved for Groucho sayings.

A third category that could be applied to Groucho pieces heavily laden with the comedian's quips might have merited consideration by dint of being un- acknowledged recycling (as ad-libs) of material from the team days. The best example of this is writer Leo Rosten's 1950 *Look* magazine piece "Groucho . . . The Man From Marx." Rosten, also the author of a story upon which one of Groucho's later solo movies would be based—*Double Dynamite* (1951)—has done an entertaining but misleading article. For an examination of some of the Marx Brothers roots that Rosten has inadvertently omitted to credit, see come- dian/author Steve Allen's excellent "Groucho Marx" chapter in his 1956 *The Funny Men*. Fittingly, when Rosten's 1958 "The Lunar World of Groucho Marx" appeared in *Harper's* magazine (with ties of its own in the *Look* essay), it was more conscious of the earlier Marx Brothers's world. He again recycles, without acknowledgment, some of this material in his later essay "Groucho," from the 1970 Rosten book *People I Have Loved, Known or Admired*. This final variation includes some interesting remarks on both the con man fan Groucho played in *Double Dynamite*, Emil Keck, and how author Rosten was pleased with the comedian's performance.

A better 1950s starting point is the *New York Times* piece "Groucho in Mufti," from April 23, 1950. As the title suggests, the focus of the article is on the noncostumed Groucho. But it still finds time for some background on the early years and the team. Moreover, it is a good look at both the early *You Bet Your Life* and Groucho's initial apprehension about the show being a "comedown."[109] In addition, as noted in Chapter 1, the article also shows a Groucho who is still sensitive that his new audience not be offended.

Both Groucho cover pieces for *Newsweek* (May 15, 1950) and *Time* (December 13, 1951) devote space to the other family comedy team members. In tone the articles seemingly take their cues from the type of picture showcased on their covers: *Newsweek* has an amusing photograph of Groucho smiling; *Time* features a pensive drawing of the comedian. Thus, *Newsweek*'s article is longer, lighter, and more comically entertaining (including dialogue between Groucho and quiz guests), while *Time* is more analytical about Groucho's humor career, including an overview of his memorable film roles. (See also Chapter 1 for more on these articles.)

In 1954 British author John Montgomery's *Comedy Films: 1894-1954* was published. The book's "Chapter Sixteen: The Eccentrics," was primarily devoted to the Marxes and W. C. Fields. Unfortunately, the Marx material is an eclectic jumble of anecdotes and team background that does anything but flow together. In fact, even the anecdotes are frequently flawed in the telling. Other than Montgomery's recognition of the superiority of the Marxes's early films, this segment can only be recommended for some perceptive but uncredited quotes from the team. For instance, Chico explains the team's popular success:

> The reason why people like to see us doing any tomfool thing that comes into our heads is quite simple. It's because that's how every normal person would like to act, once in a while . . . when Harpo makes a run at one of his blondes he goes at it like a three-quarter back [*sic*, undoubtedly meant halfback or quarterback] . . . . We can't afford to have inhibitions. . . . If Harpo had any hesitation about jumping at every woman he sees, he would offend people and probably never get past the censor. But he goes at it so hard that it's just plumb crazy, and can't be in bad taste.[110]

In a decade (the 1950s) when critiques of the Marx Brothers films are at a premium, André Martin's lengthy examination of the team rather stands out. Entitled "Les Marx Brothers ont-ils une âme?", it appeared in the February, March, May, and June 1955 issues of the celebrated film journal *Cahiers du Cinéma*. While not all Marx films are dealt with, it is still a detailed study that also includes some script excepts.

Through the 1950s and early 1960s Groucho would be a favorite subject of *TV Guide*. And in 1954 one of the more interesting articles appeared—"The Truth About Groucho's Ad Libs." As examined in Chapter 1, what was both a given about Groucho's career since vaudeville days and a foundation of *You Bet Your Life* was drawing closer attention.

Steve Allen's essay on Groucho, *The Funny Men*, devotes a considerable amount of space to the same ad-lib issue. But Allen also makes some valuable observations on the general nature of Groucho's humor, as well as references to related materials like the original Rosten essay, or Arthur Marx's *Life with Groucho*. Allen's later Groucho essay, from his 1981 book *Funny People*, spends more time on the team and is more provocative (both because he did not find them that funny and because he could not accept them as screen comedians— being forever *stage* comedians to him).

The following year (1957) William Cahn's *The Laugh-Makers—A Pictorial History of American Comedians* appeared, with a portion of chapter 10, "For Laughing Out Loud," devoted to the Marxes. Despite the title, the volume generally offered considerable commentary (a later revision of the book was retitled *The Great American Comedy Scene*). But unfortunately, the Marx segment mistakenly opens by suggesting the team once included all five brothers and soon largely limits itself to quoting Marx material.

That same year (1957) the Marxes were much better served in film historian Arthur Knight's *The Liveliest Art: A Panoramic History of the Movies*. In a segment of his chapter "The Movies Learn to Talk," he credits the Marxes and W. C. Fields with being "the real flowering of comedy in the sound film."[111] Again teamed with the equally anti-establishment film contemporary W. C. Fields, Knight calls them "an almost perfect balance of sight and sound, marred only by the occasional *scènes obligatoires* of Harpo playing the harp and Chico the piano."[112]

Holiday magazine published Harry Kurnitz's "Return of the Marx Brothers" in January 1957. Kurnitz, a Groucho friend from MGM days, begins by remembering a scene from his favorite film: Groucho's not-quite-late-enough horse-drawn carriage arrival in *A Night at the Opera*, when he nearly has to see part of the dreaded festivities.

The point of the article, as suggested in the title, is that Marx Brothers MGM classics like *A Night at the Opera* would now be available for view on the small screen (television). But Kurnitz covers a wide range of topics with wit and understanding. For instance, with Groucho as his obvious focus, he explores the myth that a great comedian has to be sympathetic. He also gently kids Arthur Marx's *Life with Groucho*, vaguely claiming that he does not quite recognize the "sentimentalist" portrayed therein.[113] This assessment became obvious to most people only after the publication of Arthur's second Groucho book. And while not addressing it directly, Kurnitz's homage to past Marx glories also reflects the then contemporary view that comedy was in severe decline. (This will be examined further in the article-length "Marx on Marx" section). There is, however, time for comments on Groucho's passion for the plight of the local baseball team (the minor league Hollywood Stars), where the comedian thoughtfully gave advice to players: "You don't hit hard enough to be a wife-beater" ("advice" Rosten also remembered Groucho sharing). Though the line is more likely to make today's reader wince than laugh, this is, after all, the long-ago off hours of an often misogynist comedian. Kurnitz nicely but sentimentally (one should never cast stones) ties all this together at the close with "those who are too young to know what they're missing are again referred to television and the revival houses. As for me, I have my memories."[114]

An unusual but fitting close to 1950s literature on the Marxes would be "beat generation" crown prince Jack Kerouac's July 1959 *Playboy* poem "To Harpo Marx." While the decade's significant writing on the Brothers was meager, this poem might be seen as a harbinger of the attention the Marx Brothers would soon receive in the anti-establishment 1960s. It also reminds one of Kerouac's frequent earlier references to Groucho in his classic novel and beat-generation Bible, *On the Road*. While the 1950s were generally a politically conservative time, with things like communist witch hunting blunting the field of pointed satire, Marx-Brothers style, it is appropriate that a legitimate period outsider like Kerouac should embrace the team. As William Wolf said of the team's ongoing popularity:

> In a period of repression or tension, a Marx Brothers film offers relief. In a period of free thought and political renaissance, the antics of the Marxes underscore, illustrate, and reinforce the prevailing mood.[115]

Kerouac's poem was a lament to the past greatness of Harpo—the films he and his Brothers no longer made. Thus, several stanzas begin with the question, "When did you [Harpo]" perform such and such a routine?[116] And the poet is familiar with Harpo's material, from dropping silverware to his bicycle chasing of a blonde (complete with the essential baited fish pole protruding over the handlebars). In addition, Kerouac inquires as to whether Harpo (who had then just made a nightclub appearance in New Orleans) was now old. Consequently, the poet has moved from questions about old films to old age itself, which cannot help but make the reader ponder the incongruity of Harpo's Pan-like persona growing old. But more than this, the poem might best be read as Kerouac's own statement on the then topical issue of the 1950s decline of comedy.

One might best look at 1960s literature on the Marxes by starting with S. J. Perelman's comical "The Winsome Foursome," in the November 1961 issue of *Show*. (The article, plus a short addition, later surfaced in both the posthumous Perelman book *The Last Laugh* and the September 1961 *Esquire*.) There are other Perelman-Marx Brothers essay/interviews of interest (some of which will be examined shortly), but "The Winsome Foursome" is the one most frequently noted. It is a comic chronicle of how Perelman and *I'll Say She Is!* author Will B. Johnstone were hired to write a Marx Brothers picture and the response they later received from the Marxes and their entourage to an early version of what would eventually become *Monkey Business*. The seldom quoted subtitle of the essay provides a Perelman capsulization of the experience—"How to go batty with the Marx Brothers when writing a film called 'Monkey Business'" (see also Chapter 1).

Perelman had earlier written "Week End with Groucho Marx" for *Holiday*'s April 1952 issue (later anthologized as 'I'll Always Call You Schnorrer, My African Explorer"). Though the main focus of the essay is a short comic visit with

12. Groucho and his youngest daughter Melinda on the set of *A Girl in Every Port* (1952). (Photograph courtesy of the Wisconsin Center for Film and Theater Research.)

Groucho during the production of the comedian's film *A Girl in Every Port*, it includes an intriguing opening. Perelman does everything but call himself a twelve-year-old Marx Brothers groupie as he comically describes his haste to get to a 1916 performance of *Home Again* and the joy the performance gave him. Besides being amusing in Perelman's own verbal slapstick manner (at one point he quotes himself as an agitated youngster saying, "The holley had a trot-box! I mean, the trolley had a hotbox."[117]), the opening is important for three reasons. First, while Perelman most definitely had a later impact upon the Marxes, it is fascinating to find him so enamored of (and maybe a little influenced by) the team at a young age. (See Chapter 1 for more on Perelman and the Marxes.) Second, Perelman's opening also finds him describing the New York Cunard dock scene from *Home Again*. Interestingly enough, the basic scenario idea that initially got the Marxes to sign Perelman and Johnstone was simply the team as stowaways on an ocean liner. Thus, the youngster who loved the Marxes in a program featuring an ocean liner disembarkation would later present them with an ocean liner movie premise. Third, Perelman's childhood joy in this opening for everything Marxian contrasts sharply with his later, seemingly vindictive, views about the Marxes, possibly because his brief, early association with them sometimes eclipsed a lifetime of writing. Eric Lister's 1985 book on the author was even entitled *—Don't Mention—The Marx Brothers: Reminiscences of S. J. Perelman*. Regardless, there seems little question that working with them was very difficult:

> I did two films with them, which in its way is perhaps my greatest distinction in life, because anybody who ever worked on any picture for the Marx Brothers said he would rather be chained to a galley oar and lashed at ten-minute intervals than ever work for these sons of bitches again.[118]

While Groucho himself found Perelman the essayist very funny, he felt Perelman's impact on the team's screen comedy was minimal. See also Perelman interviews in the *New York Times Magazine*, "That Perelman of Great Price Is 65" (January 26, 1969) and *Sight and Sound*'s "Perelman in Cloudsville" (Autumn 1978). Needless to say, there was a falling out with Groucho (see especially *The Marx Bros. Scrapbook*), though there was a reconciliation of sorts before the comedian's death. For an interesting joint interview with Groucho and Perelman while they were still on friendly terms, see Kenneth Tynan's "Groucho, Perelman and Tynan Talk About Funny Men" in *The Observer* (London, June 14, 1964), which appeared as the "Funny World of Groucho and Perelman" in the *Los Angeles Times* (June 28, 1964).

Before leaving this Perelman subdivision it is imperative to note a mistake that frequently crops up in the highlighted pieces: that the Marxes were bombing in London just prior to starting production on the film *Monkey Business*. This failure, and the penny-throwing incident that accompanied it, actually occurred on the team's previous British visit (see Chapter 1).

The deaths of Chico (1961) and Harpo (1964) produced numerous career-in-review tributes. The best of these was probably Bosley Crowther's *New York Times* salute to Harpo. It wins this honor because it demonstrates again Crowther's proven sensitivity to the whole team (he describes Chico as "tossing off humorous non sequiturs in tortured Italian dialect"[119]) and the added insight he brought to Harpo. Most especially, this meant Crowther's observation that the harp solos were pivotal to giving the added depth of pathos to the Chaplin-like mischief maker's persona. He added, "There was no common sense in the character. It was a whimsey, a hare-brained caricature. But it sweetly suggested life's derangements and something of its haunting mystery."[120]

Two foreign journals made 1965 a big year for both the Marxes and American film comedy in general. In February the British *Films and Filming* published Allen Eyles's "Great Films of the Century: *A Night at the Opera.*" Eyles's essay is a mini-version overview of the Marxes by way of *A Night at the Opera.* Especially interesting is his section on the British critical reaction to the film. (See also this author's earlier assessment of Eyles's book *The Marx Brothers: Their World of Comedy.*) Between July 1965 and January 1966 *Films and Filming* also serialized a lengthy philosophy-of-comedy thesis by Raymond Durgnat which would later surface in expanded book form as *The Crazy Mirror: Hollywood Comedy and the American Image.*

Durgnat's chapter on the Marxes, "Four Against Alienation," is nothing short of brillant. Whereas the rest of the book is always stimulatingly provocative, the material is often rather eclectic, as Durgnat attempts to touch bases with a large number of comedians. Possibly the Marx Brothers essay works so nicely because they are also eclectic. Regardless, Durgnat is most fascinating when examining the persona of each Brother and how all three personae then become a "three-pronged attack on society."[121] The essay closes with an interesting examination of what would best be called the black comedy of *Duck Soup.*

Due to Durgnat's often scatter-gun approach—he is rather a stream-of-consciousness comedy critic—the passing references to the Marxes elsewhere in the book (so often not worth your time in other volumes) are frequently fascinating. Especially good in his comedy breakdown of the basic Groucho-Margaret Dumont encounter as an example of the axiom that "all the best jokes are a collection of little jokes."[122]

February 1965 also saw the *Cahiers du Cinéma*'s publication of an extensive interview with celebrated comedy filmmaker Leo McCarey, the director of *Duck Soup.* The time devoted to this film, however, is not lengthy. And despite McCarey's clear impact, the director expressed frustration at the difficulty of bringing change to Groucho's verbal persona. Ironically, McCarey had done just that in the famous "mirror" sequence, where Groucho and Harpo (dressed as Groucho) do one of screen comedy's great *silent* routines. The interview is sometimes very similar to author/director Peter Bogdanovich's later "Oral History" interview with McCarey for the American Film Institute, which can only be examined at their Los Angeles library. (See both Chapter 1 and this author's earlier book, *Leo McCarey and the Comic Anti-Hero in American Film*, though the latter focus is not on McCarey's personality clown films. Also, archivist/author Charles Silver's 1973 *Film Comment* piece "Leo McCarey: From Marx to McCarthy" provides an excellent examination of some of the comedy gifts the director brought to *Duck Soup*.)

In 1966 George Oppenheimer, who wrote for the Groucho-Chico radio show *Flywheel, Shyster and Flywheel* and later helped script *A Day at the Races*, wrote his autobiography—*The View from the Sixties*. While references to the Marxes are hardly voluminous, there is interesting background material to both these productions and related subjects—generally in Oppenheimer's chapter 4, "The Sound State." For instance, though Oppenheimer does not express the grief of a Perelman with regard to writing for the team, he does explain how it could become a problem: "If producers are uncertain and insecure, your average comic is almost psychotically so. A joke that seemed to him hilariously funny the night before becomes a stale gag the following morning."[123]

In 1968 film critic/author Andrew Sarris published his auteur Bible—*The American Cinema: Directors and Directions, 1929-1968*. However, he reserved one chapter, "Make Way for the Clowns!" for comedians who did not direct themselves (excepting his inclusion of Jerry Lewis). His Marx Brothers segment is frequently perceptive—"Groucho's confrontations with Miss Dumont seem much more the heart of the Marxian matter today than the rather loose rapport among the Marx Brothers themselves."[124] But predictably for an auteurist, the team loses artistic points for Sarris for not having been in charge of direction. Still, it is a stimulating overview that is indirectly strengthened further (like all well-written surveys) by the easy availability of comments on other pivotal film comedians.

The following year (1969) British film critic and author David Robinson published his *The Great Funnies: A History of Film Comedy*. Though interesting, the scope of the volume, including numerous stills, severely limits what can be said about any one comedian. His brief remarks on the Marxes are largely limited to an examination of their "crazy . . . or surrealist style in comedy."[125] Of more significance that year was the publication of Raymond Durgnat's *The Crazy Mirror* and Joe Adamson's *Cinema Journal* (Spring 1969) article "The Seventeen Preliminary Scripts of *A Day at the Races*." This was later incorporated into Adamson's *Groucho, Harpo, Chico and Sometimes Zeppo*, examined earlier in the chapter. Two other Adamson articles that also found their way into his book are "Film Favorite: Joe Adamson on *Monkey Business*" (*Film Comment*, Fall 1971) and "Duck Soup the Rest of Your Life" (*Take One*, December 8, 1971).

Attention on the Marx Brothers escalates further in the 1970s. In 1970 prolific film author and critic Leonard Maltin published *Movie Comedy Teams* (updated in 1985) with a chapter devoted to the Marxes. Though the book is somewhat uneven, it is the best available on teams. And its Marx Brothers chapter is a good career survey, though this author often found himself scribbling counter-

points in the book's margins. For instance, Maltin found unobtrusive the romantic, musical subplot of *A Night at the Opera.*

Maltin also did a chapter on the Marxes for his later excellent *The Great
Movie Comedians: From Charlie Chaplin to Woody Allen* (1978). Maltin prepared the book while serving as guest director of the "Museum of Modern Art's
Bicentennial Salute to American Film Comedy." This second Maltin essay on the
Marxes is shorter, but his analysis of the team's personae is both more pointed
and more entertaining. For instance, Maltin credits the success of Chico's humor
to his

> utter sincerity in his outlandish character and dialogue. Chico's Italian
> heritage is about as authentic as a three-dollar bill, but he never lets down
> his guard (although his wife was known to reprimand him during screen-
> ings of his films, "Chico, your accent is slipping").[126]

Maltin also insightfully uses Grierson's earlier-cited essays. Each Marx chapter in
both Maltin books includes a team filmography, with the earlier essay adding the
Brothers's solo film appearances.

This was also the year (1970) *Minnie's Boys* played on Broadway. The play
was not the commercial and critical success for which authors pray. But the always insightful critic and author Walter Kerr has written a review which is both
a fun tribute to the spirit of the Marxes and a sympathetic look at the challenges
of staging the lives of such a phenomenon. Thus, his April 1970 *New York Times*
review joins the recommended reading list. As a side note it might be added that
Groucho was a fan of Kerr's, including this highlighted review (see *The Groucho
Phile*). There are, however, two other Kerr pieces of note.

Kerr's 1976 comments on the "Museum of Modern Art's Bicentennial Salute"
produced an article whose focus is reflected in the title: "The Marx Brothers and
How They Grew." Obviously aware that he could not go into detail on the
whole subject of film comedy, he chose a favored element (the Marxes) and
wove his commentary on the team throughout the essay. The result is a provocative piece that asks a lot of questions, just as this retrospective of American film
comedies was supposed to do, and come to think of it, questions (from language
to leadership) are what the Marxes are all about . . . after the laughter.

The third Kerr piece is his 1981 review of Maxine Marx's *Growing Up with
Chico*. As with his other featured critiques, Kerr uses an event as a showcase
both for an artist's work and Kerr's own artistry in the field of analysis. Thus,
while Maxine has given the student of the Marxes a unique book-length look at
the most obscure of the featured team members, Kerr gives one the best essay-
length study of Chico. (See Chapter 1 comments on the book and the review,
especially in terms of Chico as the all-important comedy "catalyst" for the team.)
For more of Kerr on the Marxes, one might also examine his 1967 volume
Tragedy and Comedy. Though his comments on the team are brief, they are provocative; for instance, he does not see Groucho as a figure of anarchy.

In 1971 Gerald Mast's *A Short History of the Movies* (now in its third edition) appeared. While hardly lengthy in its examination of the Marxes, Mast provides an excellent big picture view. For instance, "The Marx Brothers combined the great traditions of American physical comedy with a verbal humor that perfectly suited their physical types."[127] Besides being knowledgeable about the Marxes's significance at the start of the sound era, such a statement encourages one to examine the team in the broader context of American humor. And though the Marxes have been receiving hosannas for decades, Mast is thought-provoking when he ranks several Marx routines (such as the stateroom sequence in *A Night at the Opera* or the less well-known real "midget" room scene in *At the Circus*) as being equal to the best of the long-celebrated silent comedies.

Film critic Stanley Kauffmann's 1972 anthology (with Bruce Henstell) *American Film Criticism: From the Beginnings to Citizen Kane* offers convenient access to significant period reviews of five Marx Brothers films. Each of the highlighted critics has been examined earlier in this chapter: Gilbert Seldes on *The Cocoanuts*, John Mosher on *Monkey Business*, Alexander Bakshy on *Horse Feathers*, Meyer Levin on *Duck Soup*, and Clifton Fadiman on *A Night at the Opera.*

In 1973 Mast wrote the best historical overview of film comedy yet available—*The Comic Mind: Comedy and the Movies* (now in its second edition). His observations upon the Marxes also merit high praise, such as his analysis of each Brother's persona, with relationship to sound. His conclusion here results in more evidence for labeling Groucho, within the team, a comic antihero: "The irony that a bumbling foreign speaker [Chico] renders a mute clown's [Harpo] honks, beeps, and whistles into English so it can be understood by the supreme verbal gymnast [Groucho] plays a role in every Marx Brothers film."[128]

As in his Marx comments from the earlier text, Mast is good at putting the team into historical perspective. Thus, *The Comic Mind* enriches the reader's sense of American film comedy continuity in the Marxes's work, as Mast draws parallels with such early film anarchists as John Bunny and Mack Sennett. Mast is also convincing in his preference for the team's Paramount films as opposed to their work at MGM. Related to this juxtapositioning of studios are some interesting thoughts on the earthy sexuality of the team's destructive comedy. In fact, Mast's closing comments on the subject would seem to be an open invitation to explore the frequently black comedy nature of the team: "The interrelation of sexuality and iconoclasm in the Marx Brothers' Paramount films is a constant— and constantly unspoken—source of all the effects that follow."[129] Mast on the Marxes represents more highly recommended reading.

The year 1971 also saw *Cinema*'s (London) publication of Geoffrey Brown's "The Marx Brothers," an essay that anticipates Mast's claim for parity with silent comedy's great moments. That is, Brown has authored a fascinating comparison of Buster Keaton's world with that of the Marxes. For example: "Exposed to the elements in the natural world the brothers seem out of place. Unlike Keaton they flourish within an enclosed area where they can effectively rampage about."[130] Thus, for the Marxes, it is best to undercut the pomposity of modern man in those manmade settings that have come to symbolize the rigidity, be it the academic hall of *Horse Feathers* or the president's cabinet room in *Duck Soup*. In addition, this ongoing examination of Keaton's comic orderliness and Marx Brothers chaos takes one into other significant issues, such as the effect of the censorship code upon the team, or the essential card-playing nature of their comedy—at the expense of everything else, including any satirical message.

William Donnelly undertook the most ambitious of projects in his Winter 1971-1972 *Velvet Light Trap* essay—"a theory of the comedy of THE MARX BROTHERS." Donnelly's theory or "gestalt of Marxian comedy" is interesting, as it literally charts character variations from two extremes—the spontaneous craziness of Harpo to the "totally conventional" Margaret Dumont (who receives team status).[131] But the real significance of the piece comes in his evaluations of three major Marx Brothers critical evaluators—Antonin Artaud, Allen Eyles, and Andrew Sarris, with Walter Kerr also being considered but not granted a unique Marxian critic status. (All four are dealt with earlier in this chapter.) Not surprisingly, since Donnelly is assuming a revisionist stance, he has reservations about the Marx views of each of the cited critics. What he says will not always win converts, but it is intellectually stimulating and challenges the reader to reevaluate where he/she stands on the Marxes (no pun intended).

In 1971 Andrew Bergman's *We're in the Money: Depression America and Its Films* was published. Originally a doctoral dissertation at the University of Wisconsin, it is a sociological look at American films of the 1930s. While not without controversy, such as his chapter on screwball comedy, it remains a pivotal work on the films of depression America.[132]

Bergman's chapter 3, "Some Anarcho-Nihilist Laff Riots," focuses on the Marx Brothers and W. C. Fields, with the Marxes receiving the lion's share of the attention. But descriptions of the Marxes's comedy are often equally true of Fields's art: "The Depression did not create their comedy; that craft had been mastered by years on the road, playing vaudeville stages and Broadway. But the Depression endorsed it and made it a national pastime."[133]

With regard to the Marxes, Bergman focuses on their Paramount years, particularly *Duck Soup*. He makes interesting use of period critics, particularly Antonin Artaud. But the big mystery under discussion is why *Duck Soup* proved such an initial critical and commercial failure (though Bergman somewhat overplays its failure nature). The answer lies in timing—the release of a wild attack on all things political coinciding with the tenuous, early days of a new American government during the depression (see Chapter 1). In *Duck Soup* the Marxes used black comedy ahead of its time, just as Fields did in *The Fatal Glass of Beer*—another acclaimed film that was initially not well received. Sociologically for Bergman, this meant that "the most desperate years of our national experience produced our most desperate comedy."[134]

In 1973 comedy film historian Donald W. McCaffrey's book *The Golden Age of Sound Comedy: Comic Films and Comedians of the Thirties* appeared. Chapter 4, "Zanies in a Stage-Movieland," is a Marx Brothers career overview that focuses upon what McCaffrey calls their "golden period"—1931-1937.[135] This involves the following films: *Monkey Business, Horse Feathers, Duck Soup, A Night at the Opera*, and *A Day at the Races*. Other issues discussed are the stage-oriented nature of much of the team's work, the now-boring romantic and/or musical subplots involving other characters, a brief look at some other period comedy teams, and comic Marx Brothers dialogue excerpts. It is an above average survey enriched by its inclusion in a volume completely addressed to 1930s film comedy.

Colin L. Westerbeck, Jr.'s 1974 *Commonweal* article, "Marxism," discusses the ongoing Marx Brothers revival and keys upon *Animal Crackers*, which had just been re-released following a lengthy court battle over ownership. But from this platform he also insightfully compares the team to W. C. Fields, who, with the Marxes, are his essential 1930s screen comedians. Westerbeck also debates Andrew Sarris's claim that the hokey world created for the team was not appropriate for their off-the-wall comedy:

> Anarchy isn't comical in a real world, so their films have to pose and sustain a noticeably artificial one, a world peopled with theatrical conventions like Margaret Dumont's stuffy dowager rather than real human beings who might win our sympathy for the abuse they suffer from the film's stars.[136]

One might debate Westerbeck's view that "Anarchy isn't comical in a real world" when discussing a more recent black comedy such as *Dr. Strangelove* (1964), where Stanley Kubrick's attention to detail often has a documentary-like nature. However, it is most applicable to the Marxes. In fact, there would seem to be proof of Westerbeck's view in the *Duck Soup* war scenes at the film's close. Periodically, real or seemingly real war footage is intercut with the patently false and comic *interior* headquarters of the Marxes. On those occasions the comedy is derailed. This is best exemplified when Harpo appears to be recruiting on a real battlefield with the sign "Join the Army and see the Navy." Regardless of one's view here, Westerbeck's essay is stimulating and documents well the state of the Marx Brothers revival in 1974.

In 1975 Thomas H. Jordan's *The Anatomy of Cinematic Humor* was published, with a central part of the book being his monograph-length essay on the Marxes. Jordan is especially good at character delineation, be it the team members themselves or their comedy villains.

Edward Edelson's 1976 film comedy survey *Funny Men of the Movies* devotes chapter 7 to "The Marx Revolution." It is the most modest of surveys, even mistakenly stating that all five Marx Brothers were, for a time, concurrently in the team.

In 1977 the Stuart Byron and Elisabeth Weis-edited book *The National Society of Film Critics on Movie Comedy* appeared. The anthology contains contemporary essays, often in film revival format, of a wide spectrum of comedy subjects, from Mack Sennett to Luis Buñuel.

Movie Comedy contains two Marx Brothers essays—the already examined Andrew Sarris piece and Richard Schickel's "The Marx Brothers." The Schickel essay is a brief but very well-concentrated look at their comedy characters. For instance, after Schickel examines both Groucho's confidence scheme nature and his need to insult, the critic observes that the comedian's "hatred for the conventional was so immense that he could not forbear his insults even if they placed his economic goals in jeopardy."[137] He also grants the team unique bridge status between the silent and sound comedians. Word for word, this is probably the richest of the shorter Marx Brothers essays.

Roger Rosenblatt's May 21, 1977, *New Republic* essay "At the Circus Go West" is a darkly comic and finally very moving look at the Groucho conservator flight between his secretary/companion Erin Fleming and son Arthur Marx. Rosenblatt manages to weave a contemporary commentary on the court battle out of scenes from old Marx Brothers films. Such an outrageous juxtapositioning (which seems especially fitting for a Marx Brother) works because of Rosenblatt's wit and his audacity to express it—both also cornerstones of Groucho's dark comedy.

Groucho's death in August 1977 produced countless tributes and/or career overviews. Three are of special significance. First, there is the *Newsweek* piece "Comedy's King Leer." Author Charles Michener has skillfully written the slickest of conventional homages. It masterfully juggles the life and comic times of the most prominent Marx (save Karl), from poverty days with Saint Minnie to the wealthy celebrant who delighted in addressing his correspondence with T. S. Eliot to "Dear Tom." Michener even closes his essay with a fashionable touch of the dark side when he repeats Groucho's sneer to a fan who was happy to make his acquaintance: "I've known him for years, and I can tell you it's no pleasure."

In contrast to Michener's excellent traditional homage, film author David Thomson's *Take One* (November 1977), "Groucho Marx: A Retrospective" is that rare iconoclastic tribute to an iconoclast. His very analysis reads like the black comedy poetry of which Groucho seemed to be a pioneer—"Groucho could have played nearly any protagonist from Buñuel—pirapic thrust turning to rubber, mordant longing that hovers between rape and flowers, and booby traps dogging every act of assertion."[138] Thomson's searing style is equally and provocatively insightful about the team:

> the Marx Brothers are the single most emphatic evidence we have of the macabre ridiculousness of family attachments . . . unable to escape being brothers, but thoroughly alien to one another. Except that Chico could interpret for Harpo, leaving Groucho in more entrenched, poignant solitude, a talker to himself who buttonholes stupid listeners deaf to his slippery poetry.[139]

Thomson's "tribute" tends to linger longer than most.

One might best close these obituaries of note by briefly examining that by a close Groucho friend—Goodman Ace. In his *Saturday Review* "Top of My Head" column (February 18, 1978) entitled "Personal," he writes a letter to the departed Groucho explaining he is busy putting together a "handsome scrapbook of all the reviews your life got from the obit writers. . . ."[140] After Ace fails to resist contemplating a possible Groucho ad-lib to the eccentric act of writing to a dead man (imagining the comedian saying he will pick it up at the "dead letter" office), Ace critiques the general nature of the obituaries. His pronouncement is that they focused too much on Groucho as a misanthrope. According to Ace, Groucho's stinging wit "intended no insults—that you [Groucho] were having fun with people and hoped they would fend and parry and join in. . . ."[141] One can think of exceptions, such as his reply to condescending Marx director Sam Wood's statement that you can't make actors out of clay. Groucho's lovely comeback: "Nor directors out of Wood." Still, Ace's defense of the Groucho insult has much merit, especially in reference to the comedian's later years. Besides, it is a gesture befitting a close friend, something that proves in and of itself that Groucho was more than just insult. (For additional Groucho-focused "Top of My Head" columns by Ace, see the April 1, 1972, and November 2, 1974, issues of the *Saturday Review*. (See also Ace's Groucho-related "The People Won't Understand It," from the April 1975 *Yale Alumni Magazine*.)

Groucho's death was also the catalyst for an interesting 1977 *New York Times* essay on black comedy entitled "Cruelty vs. Compassion Among the Comics." Actor Richard Whelan contrasted the comedy *and* compassion of *You Bet Your Life* to the darker humor of *Saturday Night Live*, with the latter coming up wanting. One should also see Chevy Chase's (formerly of *Saturday Night Live*) later published 1977 *New York Times* convincing reply, "Chevy Chase: I'm Not Mr. Cruel."

In 1978 *New York* magazine produced two Marx articles that merit notation. In August Charlotte Chandler adapted material from her book *Hello, I Must Be Going* in order to write the Margaret Dumont piece "What Are They Laughing At, Julie [Groucho]?" In August John Alan Friedman did "A Memory of Groucho" based upon one of the Erin Fleming-orchestrated parties of the comedian's last years. Its primary interest is in the child-parent relationship that surfaces when Groucho and Erin interact. The article is done not vindictively, but rather with a matter-of-fact honesty that is refreshing after all the hell or halo extremes since used to describe Fleming. Truth most often resides in middle grounds.

In writing this volume, countless reviews from the many media in which the Marxes excelled have been consulted, with numerous ones being recommended in this chapter. But near the top is Dick Cavett's 1979 *New Republic* critique of Hector Arce's *Groucho*. This author, never a big fan of Cavett the television personality, sees in this essay a sensitivity for which most authors under review would kill. However, the reviewer's sensitivity can prove distracting from the focus book. For example, when Cavett comments on the gifts and goblins with which Groucho forever had to cope, an analogy is drawn from Diana Trilling's one-time speculation, in a Marilyn Monroe essay, on a law of negative compensation, where "the greatly gifted must suffer agonies proportionate to their talents. . . ."[142] Poignant additions such as this are the norm here. Moreover, Cavett both knowledgeably highlights key Arce points while often enriching them with observations of his own. While this does occasionally allow Cavett to indulge himself in that personality game of being Mr. Name Dropper (Cavett knew Groucho), the general effect is most positive. (See chapter 7 of Cavett's and Christopher Porterfield's *Cavett*. Besides showcasing some perceptive insider observations on Groucho, the chapter reproduces several letters Cavett received from the comedian.)

In recent years books on film comedy and the Marxes continue to appear with increasing alacrity, such as James Robert Parish and William T. Leonard's detailed guide *The Funster* (1979) or Jeffrey Robinson's *Teamwork: The Cinema's Greatest Comedy Teams* (1981). But the most deserving of special attention is Gerald Weales's *Canned Goods as Caviar: American Film Comedy of the 1930s* (1985). Each chapter in the book focuses on a single comedy classic, with the Marxes's feature appropriately *Duck Soup*. Weales, a professor of English at the University of Pennsylvania, gives the film its most scholarly detailed look yet, while also making it a microcosm of the Marx world. As noted earlier in this chapter, Weales is especially taken with removing the surreal definitions of American "Marxism" in order to reveal its roots in this country's "crazy-fool" or comic antihero movement. Also especially rich is his discussion of pivotal 1930s critics and his notation of a wealth of source material. Unlike so many film comedy texts, which are often simply overgrown picture books, Weales puts the intellectual excitement of several good books in each chapter.

In 1980 the first series of reference books appeared in *Magill's Survey of Cinema: English Language Films*. Each volume is composed of contemporary critiques of significant English language films. The essays, written specifically for the project, are approximately three pages in length, contain principal cast and credits, and are arranged alphabetically.

The Marx Brothers films reviewed in the first series are *Animal Crackers*, *Monkey Business*, and *A Night at the Opera*. In 1981 a second series of volumes was published in *Magill's Survey of Cinema*. Three additional Marx films are reviewed: *A Day at the Races*, *Duck Soup*, and *Horse Feathers*.

Besides listing cast and credits, the volumes include story synopses, comments on the central players' careers at the time of the film's release, and critical analysis drawing upon both the film's initial response and its reputation today. Thus, for a generally capsulized look at a specific Marx Brothers film, or that of another favorite, the Magill series is a good starting point.

Obviously, pertinent material upon the Marxes continues to appear. But for the last several years the key source has been the little magazine edited by Paul G. Wesolowski aptly titled *The Freedonia Gazette*, or as each cover page "modestly" states—"*The* Magazine Devoted to the Marx Brothers." Though Drexel Hill, Pennsylvania (the home of *The Freedonia Gazette*), might not have been one's first guess as the location of a Marx Brothers journal, issue after issue produces material of interest. Though without footnotes, articles frequently have a scholarly attention to detail and address issues of academic interest. The following essays are particularly interesting. Kipp Wessel's "Comrade Harpo" (November 1980) chronicles Harpo's celebrated trip to the Soviet Union. Peter Dixon's "Groucho in Britain" (Summer 1981) examines Groucho's attempt at a United Kingdom version of *You Bet Your Life*. Dixon, who would later be the British editor of *The Freedonia Gazette*, also authored a thorough look at the Marxes's 1922 "First Appearance in Europe" (Winter 1981). Wesolowski's "The Marx Brothers' Paramount Contract" (Winter 1981) scrutinizes the document over which the team took the studio to court in 1933. And in a two-part follow-up article (Summer and Winter 1982) Wesolowski inspects "The Contract That Almost Was," a proposed agreement between the Brothers and United Artists for the distribution of an independent, team-produced film, had the Marxes been able to break with Paramount. "Erin Fleming, Who Made His Life Worth Living" (Summer 1983) is an issue-length, diary-like look at the 1977 Bank of America vs. Erin Fleming trial. The following summer (1984) the journal included an article on Groucho's third wife "Eden Marx." Previous to that Wesolowski did a piece on the alleged Marx-Warners title controversy "Brother Against Brother" (Winter 1983), and Dennis P. deLoof wrote an issue-length essay, "A Constructive Analysis of Three Early Marx Brothers Films" (Spring 1984). And Robert Bader later compiled "Needle Marx" (Summer 1986), a "complete" Marx Brothers discography.

Marx on Marx

As with the "Marx on Marx" book section of this chapter, this category is again dominated by Groucho. It examines chronologically both important essays by the Brothers and interviews with them, though in the latter case, the original titles of some articles often obscure their interview nature.

Between Broadway commitments the 1920s Marxes sometimes returned briefly and lucratively to vaudeville. During a 1925 return Groucho agreed to contribute to *The New Yorker* (also founded in 1925) a series of comedy pieces entitled "Vaudeville Talk." The June 20, 1925, contribution included the following dialogue:

VA: . . . Where would you be today if it wasn't for your wife?
VI: I'm not sure. I've got three or four good telephone numbers.
VA: Ah, it's a wonderful feeling to go home at night and have the little woman waiting for you.
VI: You bet it is, if it's a little woman, but if it's a big woman, it's dangerous.

—Julius [Groucho] H. Marx.[143]

One gets a better idea of Groucho's early writing style by reading his 1928 *New York Times* piece "Up from Pantages" or the 1929 *New Yorker* essay "Press

Agents I have known." Both deal with the frustrations of show business. The former chronicles the early days ("Pantages" being a bargain basement vaudeville circuit). Much of the material would later be recycled in Groucho books. For example, his tale of the Texas landlady who served chili for every meal was expanded upon when it was included in the 1963 *Memoirs of a Mangy Lover.* Besides being fleshed out (the primary difference was that the second version added, or revealed, a sexual subplot), the material is quite similar. "Press Agents I Have Known" shows a now successful star still suckered by the press agent pitch and promise. Though not as antiheroic as his early 1940s pieces, both essays showcase a figure of frustration—perfectly in keeping with the antiheroic nature of the pivotal *New Yorker.* Of course, this was only fitting, since Groucho was occasionally writing for *The New Yorker.*

The 1929 *Theatre Magazine*'s "Confessions of the Marx Brothers" is interesting for two reasons. First, it displays comically just how disinterested the team could become with an interview. Groucho and Chico spend most of their time providing interviewer Sylvia B. Golden with the right answers . . . to the *wrong* questions. For example, when asked his age, Chico replies, "Golf and bridge."[144] As if this were not comically clear enough, Groucho closes his segment with a straight answer to the question of any pet aversion: "interviews." While Harpo's section is naturally (and literally) blank, it is only with Gummo (even then long out of the group) that a degree of rationality appears—but only a degree: "Why 'Gummo'? Because I said I'd never stick to the stage."[145] Second, as if to differentiate further straight man Zeppo from the comic trio, the youngest Marx is poignantly direct about his less-than-central position in the team (see Chapter 1). The only humor here is purely ironic, such as his interview-closing answer to why "Zeppo": "No reason for it, just the same as my being in *Animal Crackers.*"[146]

While the scrambled nature of most of this interview obviously reinforces the desired zany image that was to the team's benefit, the Marxes genuinely did not like giving interviews. Through the years there would be more of these Loony Tune "information" sessions.

As if underlining his enjoyment at dismantling interviews, Groucho even incorporates some interviewer baiting into the beginning of his 1931 *Saturday Evening Post* article "Bad Days Are Good Memories." For instance, "Did I plan to play Hamlet? [a popular question then being asked of Chaplin] No, we couldn't think of playing any town under 100,000."[147] More to the point, however, he uses a onetime interviewer's question on his happiest memory to write an article befitting a *groucho.* That is, as the title says, "Bad Days [if past] Are Good Memories." He then proceeds to discuss several sorrowful yet comically rendered stories from his entertainment past. His happiest memory, and therefore his most pitiful experience, was being stranded on the road in Colorado as a boy, which then necessitated his driving a grocery wagon to earn train fare home. The most accessible later rendering of this anecdote appears in *Groucho and Me.* And as noted of this book earlier in the chapter, Groucho specialized in drawing humor from unhappiness. Perversely, though not a focus of this piece, Groucho also enjoyed interjecting shock into happy times. Thus, there is even kind of a contrary appropriateness to a cold reading of the Groucho title "Bad Days Are Good Memories."

Through the years Marx Brothers comments (generally Groucho's) have been used as entertaining filler in countless eclectic-minded articles. This kind of story has been avoided herein because of the propensity of articles entirely devoted to the team. However, an exception has been made concerning the Groucho observations included in a 1931 article on prominent passengers disembarking in New York from the North German Lloyd liner *Europa*. Groucho and family are returning from the Marxes's very successful London engagement, only to have the comedian subject his loved ones to a lengthy, embarrassing delay due to his joke to customs officials about being a smuggler (see Chapter 1). Though the incident is not noted in the piece, Groucho calls into question the varying policies of government institutions like immigration and customs—"How about the pilgrims, were they bothered with all this landing card and visa business? Did a guard stand on Plymouth Rock waiting for them?"[149]

Drawing attention to this is important for three reasons, besides the simple fact it is funny. First, it provides timely period evidence that Groucho's "joke" did occur. Second, it demonstrates an almost immediate transition by Groucho of the painful to comedy. (Though, of course, in time it will undoubtedly be a "Good Memory.") Third, it emphasizes all the more how appropriate it would be, in retrospect, that the team's next film was *Monkey Business*, where they would attack the stuffiness associated with ocean liner travel, including humorless customs officials.

The July 1932 *Silver Screen* featured an interview with Harpo entitled "Roses, Love and Shotguns From Harpo Marx." It attempts to get at the real Harpo and whether girl-chasing is as important off-screen as on. Like a Groucho comedic essay, this question allows Harpo to relate stories from his vaudeville past. As if to match the heady Charlie Chaplin-Harpo comparisons that open the piece, Harpo eventually relates a tale of a lost love which could be ranked with Chaplin's lifelong lament over an un-acted-upon love. Such is the stuff of clowns growing serious.

A January 1933 *Cinema Digest* article, "Censorship for Interview: Hollywood's Wild Idea," briefly examines a studio protection idea where all interviews would have to pass a review before publication. However, the brunt of the article is devoted to revealing the interview tendencies of several major stars. Not surprisingly, they are described as usually staying in character. The explanation is that they are always testing comedy ideas. And if Groucho is doing a magazine piece, one is advised that there is even less chance of a successful interview, because the comedian will be saving it for his own piece. Moreover, it adds that since the Marxes have gone "literary," they are just generally not good interview subjects. Fittingly, a degree of affection seems apparent in the following two Harpo pieces.

"Harpo Marx Talks" appeared in the November 12, 1933, edition of the *New York Times*. The focus was on his forthcoming trip to the Soviet Union, as well as his "regular pilgrimage to the little fishing village of Etretat [France] . . . to hear 'the greatest harp player in the world,'"[149] an eccentric recluse who must be visited in her attic. Both subjects are later addressed in Harpo's autobiography, the title of which, *Harpo Speaks!*, is reminiscent of this article's heading.

If there was a suggestion of slight affectation in the *Silver Screen* piece, à la the missed love, it is much more pervasive here, as Harpo receives the interviewer in a dressing gown of the "yellowest, blackest and zigzaggiest decorations . . . and he wore it aggressively. The monogram that struggled to assert itself through the zigzags was H. M. And a very large golden harp sat . . . in the middle of the room."[150] Other than going on to describe Harpo's first answer as being given while "puffing complacently on his cigarette," this less than positive tone about Harpo gradually fades from the interviewer's comments.[151] It seldom surfaces elsewhere in the Harpo literature, with the exception of Oscar Levant's 1940 anthologized essay, "Memoirs of a Mute," which is much more bald about comically suggesting Harpo was into a somewhat affected life-style, from placing an important but unread book in a prominent place in his home to captivation with the intelligentsia and other prominent notables. One also, of course, might interpret Woollcott's earlier noted essay on "My Friend Harpo" the dog as more darkly ironic than originally suggested. That is, Woollcott could have been comically suggesting that Harpo's loyal but often silent presence among the elite could be likened to the faithful family pooch. Regardless, despite Harpo's propensity for hobnobbing with the famous, he was rarely described in an affected manner.

"Harpo Marx Talks" also briefly addresses an eclectic assortment of topics, from the comedian's comments on the eccentric fan mail the team receives to the revelation that an earlier story about a $500,000 insurance policy on his fingers had been a publicity stunt.

Harpo's return from the Soviet Union on January 9, 1934, prompted a New York City news conference while he was still on board ship. For a sampling of the extensive newspaper coverage the following day, see "Harpo Marx Back, A Caviar Convert" in the *New York Times* (examined in Chapter 1). The very similar coverage in the *New York Herald Tribune* article, "Visit to Russia Looses [sic] Tongue of Harpo Marx," did add the Harpo comment, "I ignore my brothers when I get away from them."[152]

In a *New York Times* piece from the following year (November 17, 1935), "Plucking A Few Notes From Harpo," the comedian discusses very positively the action of road testing material for the movies. The proof of his convictions is, of course, the just-released (November 15, 1935) *A Night at the Opera*. Interestingly enough, Harpo claimed the team's next film would be released the following November with the title *Merry Christmas*. However, such was not the case, as the renamed film, *A Day at the Races*, did not surface until June 1937.

The May 1936 *Motion Picture* carried the Grace Simpson article "GROUCHO looks at CHARLIE," which might best be characterized by the essay's subtitle—

"The maddest Marx recalls the day when he 'discovered' the genius in Chaplin." The publication date coincided with America's latest state of Chaplinitis, *Modern Times* having been released earlier in the year. According to Groucho, the two comedians had gotten to know each other in their prefilm vaudeville days: "I said then he was the greatest fellow on the stage. I know now there will never be anyone like him. He's in a class all by himself, just as he has always been."[153]

Though not included in the article, Chaplin was a great admirer of Groucho's comedy. It is interesting that two such diverse great comedians should form a mutual admiration society. Even more remarkable, however, was Groucho's description of a then-recent (1936) dinner date these two acclaimed performers had had: "There we were, two comedians talking, completely terrified about life and our careers!"[154] Thus, it seems they were as much attracted by their on-going, uncalled-for anxieties (this being only a year after the great Marx Brothers comeback of *A Night at the Opera*), as by their respect for each other's comedy.

This is a unique admission/realization by Groucho, especially considering his normal blind spot to the ridiculousness of his fears (see Chapter 1 for his son Arthur's comments). Not surprisingly, though, Groucho seems immediately oblivious to his personal insight, because he goes on to exclude himself in some further comments on Chaplin which were equally true of himself:

> You would think, that by this time Chaplin would be more or less convinced that he had remarkable talent. But *no*! He was just as frightened as he had been when he first came to me and asked my advice [about initially entering the motion picture industry].[155]

For a time, however, this article revealed a Groucho whose discoveries were not limited to "the genius of Chaplin."

The following June (1937) a number of provocative interview pieces surfaced, coinciding with the release of *A Day at the Races*. On June 13 the *Los Angeles Times* ran the article "Three Marx Brothers Interviewed." But it was only marginally more informative than the earlier examined "Confessions of the Marx Brothers." Harpo was limited to "Peep, peep!" answers and his Brothers usually attempted to turn interviewer Philip K. Scheuer into a straight man. For instance, Groucho's reply to whether he had read Max Eastman's *Enjoyment of Laughter*, prompted the reply—"I enjoyed that from the minute I picked it up until I laid it down. Sometime I intend to read it."[156] This is recycled Groucho, because it is a close variation of a blurb the comedian had done for Perelman's first book, *Dawn Ginsbergh's Revenge*. This anticipates a later time, such as the aforementioned Leo Rosten article, where the ad-lib Groucho was really more a Marx with a memory.

The lack of information such group interviews generally produced no doubt sent many reporters to contemplating Howard W. Fensterstock's recourse—the previously noted *imaginary* interview. In this case, Scheuer seems to try the next best thing; he asks the Brothers about the one subject by which all Marxes were fascinated—women. His question was the tried-and-true: "What ten women would you take with you to a desert island?" Chico's answer proves the most interesting. And though he turns it into a joke, it is still revealing—"I'd just take any ten dames. On second thought, I'd let my wife pick them out and then we'd be sure they'd scare away the savages."[157]

Much more insightful was a Teet Carle interview with Harpo published the same day as the *Los Angeles Times* piece. Entitled "The Silent Member of the Marx Trio," it appeared in the *Brooklyn Daily Eagle*, though other papers undoubtedly ran the article. Carle reveals that despite Harpo's image of silence, he is a "veritable chatterbox . . . [off-screen, and the] easiest of the three [Marxes] to drag into conversation."[158] Carle also calls Harpo the most glib Marx in interviews, but this would seem true only of his "Peep, peep!" type answers. When isolated in a solo interview, Harpo is often very informative. This is proved again in Carle's own article, as Harpo talks at length about why his character does not speak:

> We Marxes . . . feel that the pantomime I do is definitely needed in our style. All of the talking and wise-cracking necessary is done by Groucho. Chico handles the dialogue [dialect?] well. Together, we take care of almost every other form of popular comedy. The only thing missing is pantomime. That is what makes clowns popular and I am needed in this field. It has been neglected so long in entertainment that I have always been proud to make a success of it.[159]

For Harpo, his "novelty" was based on silence. If he spoke, he felt his character would be lost. And Harpo remained true to that principle—he would later turn down a $55,000 offer to speak in *A Night in Casablanca*.

Harry Lang's *Motion Picture* article "A Day with the Mad Marxes" also appeared in June 1937. But as the title begins to suggest, interviewing the Brothers is next to impossible. Thus, Lang stops trying and turns the piece into a general article about the team, with an occasional, brief Marx comment.

This is also the approach taken by *Photoplay*'s Kirtley Baskette the following month (July 1937) in her "Hoodlums at Home." And though the comment that the Groucho and Chico marriages are completely happy is a farce, the article is straightforward about some issues, such as Chico's gambling. There is also the sense that the Brothers essentially ditched this interview-turned-straight article by turning the reporter loose on their families.

On September 18, 1938, Chico wrote "Time Marches on for the Marxes" for the *New York Times*. As was common in Groucho essays, Chico does a comic memory piece on the team's tough times in vaudeville. In fact, he credits himself instead of Groucho for the now-celebrated response to a displeased penny-throwing London audience (in effect, that they had come a long way and the audience could at least throw shillings). But exchanging anecdotes was not limited to Chico.

The next month (October, *Room Service* having been released on September 30) saw their favorite films listed in a special ongoing *New York Sun* column—

"My Ten Favorite Pictures." Initially, they merely listed their own films, including the Marxes's privately made silent film, but still falling short of ten, they added, "Hell, we haven't made that many pictures yet."[160] Their more serious list was: (1) *Cavalcade*; (2) *Stage Door*; (3) *The Informer*; (4) *Mr. Deeds Goes to Town*; (5) *Mutiny on the Bounty*; (6) *The Story of Louis Pasteur*; (7) *Alexander's Ragtime Band*; (8) *The 39 Steps*; (9) *Snow White and the Seven Dwarfs*; (10) *Three Smart Girls*.[161]

Chico again reminisces about the past in the November 14, 1939, *New York Sun* column "Picture Plays and Players." Subtitled "Chico, the Piano-playing Marx, Talks of the 'Marx Bros. at the Circus,'" (which had been released the previous month) columnist Eileen Creelman has a Marx who wants to talk only of William Saroyan's play *The Time of Your Life*. Because the production reminded Chico of his own cabaret piano-playing days, however, his memories initially focus on his early preteam days. With regard to films, the column is at its best when Chico is discussing why *Room Service* (their last film) was not an appropriate Marx Brothers vehicle (see Chapter 1).

For students of the Marxes, the big news of the 1940s was their on again-off again retirement from films. Two of the best interview pieces related to their 1941 split are the *Los Angeles Herald*'s "Marx Brothers, Sick of Movies, to Quit" (see Chapter 1) and the *New York Herald Tribune*'s "Groucho Plans to Write After Quitting Films." The latter showcases a decidedly somber Groucho, especially in terms of past interviews. Appropriately for his character (he was in the midst of what was to be their last group film), Groucho was reading Ambrose Bierce's *The Devil's Dictionary*. Besides discussing writing plans, Harpo's possible stage projects with Alexander Woollcott and Noel Coward are also considered. Late the previous year (November 27, 1940) Chico's postteam plans were chronicled in a *New York World Telegram* piece which is basically summarized in its lengthy, comic title: "Chico Is Not Sure What His Band Will Do But He Knows He'll Play Piano With An Orange."

In terms of Marx on Marx, the best article on their 1946 return in *A Night in Casablanca* is Mary Morris's "News: Girl Chases Marx Brothers," from the January 27 issue of *PM*. The piece is essentially divided into two parts, with a solo Harpo first discussing the old days and Woollcott (who had died earlier in the 1940s), followed by a separate session with Groucho, where topics were kept current. The later segment is the freshest, with Groucho discussing everything from motion pictures being too homogeneous an industry (as opposed to theatre and literature) to his fascinating desire for a stage production with political comment, à la "the Marx Brothers in Washington."[162] Groucho does not, however, become so serious as to forget just who he is. He closes the article by advising Ms. Morris that she would receive a longer interview next time if she wore a sweater.

Between the 1941 split and the 1946 re-teaming there was hardly an avalanche of interview-related articles, but there were some. In fact, Harpo even provided a new type . . . sort of. The real star of Francis Hayes's 1942 *Colliers* essay "Just a Gesture" is the miming Marx. The brief two pages of text are dwarfed by fifteen accompanying stills of Harpo in various grimaces and garbs, which provide the visual explanation. Also in 1942 Groucho proves most provocative in a Frederick C. Othman *New York World Telegraph* article "Comics Only ½-There, Holds Groucho Marx." With the team now broken up, Groucho is pitching for dramatic parts by claiming they are a piece of cake compared to comedy. Of course, this is not the best way to win new dramatic friends, but then this is Groucho, too. Regardless, he observes:

> Take the Robinsons and the Cagneys and the Rafts and all those other guys. They don't have to get up at 6 and start being funny at 8.... It's no trick to put your arms around Lana Turner and Priscilla Lane and say, "I love you," at 8 a.m. or 6, or 4, or 2.
>
> As far as I can figure it out, the straight actor keeps the wrinkles out of his clothes and the dandruff out of his hair and the rest of it just sort of falls into his arms. That's for me.[163]

So much for creating a groundswell of support from the dramatic field. But what about the title of the article? Well, Groucho did get around to comedians, too, as if he had to alienate everyone—"Comics have rattle-trap brains. They're on the fringe of idiocy. They're half out of this world. Sometimes I wish I was all the way out."[164] The dark close no doubt shows how frustrated the now solo Groucho was feeling, especially when compared to any of the earlier cited interviews. But the biting nature is still in Groucho character, just as the loner against the world stance is typical. Groucho has just revealed more to the public than was normal for him to do, at least at that time.

As noted earlier in the text, Groucho was especially prolific as an essayist during the 1940s (see the reprint of his 1946 "How to Be a Spy" in Chapter 3, as well as both his 1930 essay "My Poor Wife!" and an Edward R. Sammis interview with Groucho, "Those Mad Marx Hares...."). During the 1940s Groucho wrote a number of essays for the *New York Herald Tribune* Sunday magazine supplement *This Week*. They include an election year 1940 piece entitled "What This Country Needs"; a 1941 comic attack upon guests who have overstayed their welcome, "Do You Know Enough to Go Home?"; war-related homefront essays like "Groucho Marx Turns Himself in For Scrap" (1942), "How to Crank a Horse" (1943), and "How to Build a Secret Weapon" (1943); postwar issues like the housing shortage focus of "Standing Room Only" (1946) and the cold war backdrop of "How to Be a Spy" (1946); and the more general "Why Harpo Doesn't Talk" (1948).

Regardless of subject, the essays generally place Groucho in a comically antiheroic advising and/or complaining situation. Even the political stance of "What This Country Needs" (politics not generally being a topic of antiheroic humor) is made palatable in two ways. First, Groucho immediately denies that he is a candidate for vice president, which would also probably qualify as the most antiheroic of political positions. And second, Groucho quickly moves his comedy "Needs" into an eclectic very nonpolitical area, such as a "good ham sandwich."[165]

The antiheroic W. C. Fields, also an occasional contributor to *This Week*, might have acted as an unofficial inspiration for some of Groucho's topics during this time. For instance, in 1940 Fields authored the book *W. C. Fields for President*, the same year as Groucho's comic vice presidential candidacy. Fields's book had a chapter on income tax, a variation of which saw light as an article in *This Week*'s March 10, 1940, issue. Groucho would author a 1942 comic book-length look at income tax entitled *Many Happy Returns* (see also Groucho's January 24, 1942, *The Saturday Review* essay "Many Happy Returns!"). In 1938 Fields did a *This Week* essay entitled "My Rules of Etiquette," while Groucho wrote a 1940 *Liberty* magazine article "How I Beat the Social Game," which was a comic look at etiquette, Groucho-style. Such topic parallels with Fields are not noted to distract from Groucho's writing, just as the stylistic parallels he shared with the antiheroic Benchley (see Chapter 3) were not meant as a negation. Instead, they more clearly link him both to the period in which he was writing and to a comedy movement (of the comic antihero) with which he is not always associated.

Other 1940s Groucho pieces range from the Warner Brothers letters (for instance, see the December 22, 1945, *Saturday Review*) to the *Saturday Evening Post* issue of March 8, 1948, where he described "The Role I Liked Best . . ."— Dr. Hugo Z. Hackenbush of *A Day at the Races*. Late in the decade another Groucho variation began to surface. Due to the success of his *You Bet Your Life* program, articles began to appear featuring the comic banter of Groucho and his contestants. This is best exemplified by a 1949 *Life* article, "Groucho's Garland of Gags: They come in many colors, including off," which is entirely devoted to such gags. *You Bet Your Life* material would frequently highlight articles on Groucho for the next decade.

A four-week engagement at the great London Palladium, site of the Marxes's infamous penny victimization, prompted Harpo's 1950 *Esquire* article "Plenty of Guts." The title is a paraphrasing of a comment by Harpo's close friend George Burns, upon hearing that mediocre clarinetist Harpo would be playing that instrument in London. Naturally, of course, the engagement is a smash, including the clarinet, though Harpo comically fudges the issue by playing "I'm Forever Blowing Bubbles" while real bubbles come out of the instrument.

In earlier years Harpo had often seemed to be the Marx in highest ascendancy, whether as the 1920s protégé of Woollcott or as a 1930 representative (with Chaplin) of the bygone but revered silent comedy era. By the time of the team's initial 1941 breakup there was more of a parity situation; possibly Groucho was even the slight favorite. But it was still close. All that changed with the mega-hit status of *You Bet Your Life*. And nothing demonstrated that transition more fully than the 1951 article authored by Harpo, the former Marx crown prince— "My Brother GROUCHO." It is an often warmly comic essay, for instance tracing Groucho's cynicism to the fact that he was named after an uncle (Julius) thought to be possibly rich but who in reality was just the opposite, leaving no hoped-for inheritance. Harpo might have comically added that Groucho's tight

purse strings might therefore also be dated from the circumstances of his chris-
tening. But he does not, instead turning serious and polishing Groucho's penny-
pinching ways as an outgrowth of a poor childhood. Thus, the article flip-flops
between comic insights and more serious explanations of contrary Groucho characteristics. What it says is often entertaining, but the unwritten transition for
Harpo—from comic heights to his brother's chronicler—still leaves one somewhat
sad.

From the 1950s on, Groucho was the most watched and quoted of the Marx
Brothers, and one has only to choose from a flood of Groucho material. But
sometimes there are additional challenges. For instance, Groucho's son Arthur
now takes credit for writing the Groucho Marx-credited 1953 *Colliers* article,
"What's Wrong with the Giants." Regardless of which Marx was author, it is a
funny extended letter of advice to the Giant's then-manager Leo Durocher. In
tone and style (right down to its letter format), the article is pure Groucho. In
fact, Arthur might have out-Grouchoed Groucho. Perhaps this was even a warmup for the "Groucho" asides Arthur did for his 1954 *Life with Groucho.*

There are also Groucho asides in a 1955 *American Weekly* article written by
third wife Eden Marx (with Liza Wilson) entitled "My Life with Groucho." These
additions occur frequently enough that the comedian should have been given co-
author status. Regardless, it is an interesting look at the 1950s Groucho. Other
pieces of interest during this time range from a 1952 *Los Angeles Times* inter-
view/career overview entitled "King Leer Groucho Still Rules with Raised Brow,
Barbed Wit," to a 1954 *Variety* reprint of Groucho's monologue as master of
ceremonies at that year's Screen Writers Guild Awards.

For Groucho on Groucho, however, the meatiest year of the decade would
seem to have been 1957. The articles/interviews included a January *Los Angeles
Times* page one piece entitled "Why Groucho Sends Viewers," an April *TV
Guide* cover article called "Everyone's a Critic," celebrated personality author/
interviewer Pete Martin's *Saturday Evening Post*'s "I Call on Groucho" (May), a
July *Look* on "The Secret of Groucho," and a September *Newsweek* article
"The Stupider the Better." The last piece was the most provocative, though it
was not the first time he had attacked television:

> I don't watch TV in between TV appearances. Intellectually, it's a joke.
> But, unfortunately, it reflects the taste of the U.S. public. How many
> copies of the *Atlantic Monthly* are sold each month? How many *Confiden-
> tials*? People want what doesn't tax them.[166]

Even balder was his comment about contestants, which also found its way into
the title: "We don't have to have brains on our show. The stupider [the guests]
the better, just as long as they can talk. Anyway, the encyclopedic mind gets
pretty dull."[167] Interestingly enough, Groucho's comments did not seem to hurt
his standings with television viewers, inasmuch as the Nielsen ratings for 1957-
1958 (the season just starting after the *Newsweek* article appeared) included

You Bet Your Life in the top ten.[168] In fact, it was an improvement, insofar as the show had inadvertently not made the top ten the previous season, after five straight earlier appearances.

Besides the attractiveness to the print medium of a person obviously unafraid to speak his mind, Groucho was also an appropriate late 1950s spokesman (because of his enduring popularity) for a profession (comedy) diagnosed as being in decline. In fact, in another *Newsweek* piece from the following year (1958), "The Marx Brothers Now," each of the three team members were polled on the subject. Harpo felt not enough time was being devoted to developing comedy material; Chico blamed television's huge audience for literally eating up comedy routines. Groucho focused on satire:

> There are no more Marx brothers movies because we did satire, and satire is verboten today. The restrictions—political, religious, and every other kind— have killed satire. If Will Rogers were to come back today, he couldn't make a living. They'd throw him in the clink for being subversive. [169]

A *Los Angeles Mirror-News* column entitled "Groucho Diagnoses Our Ailing Comedy" (and appearing the same date as the just noted 1958 *Newsweek*— March 17) expanded further on Groucho's thoughts on comedy's decline. The comedian insightfully focused the blame on the communist witch hunting of Senator Joseph McCarthy: "Everybody became afraid to say what they were thinking. This affected comedy and comedians. There used to be a lot of comedians telling political jokes. Bob Hope is the only one left."[170] The comedian later added, "Many people don't seem to realize that the first thing which disappears when men are turning a country into a totalitarian state is comedy and comics."[171]

An absorbing companion piece to these comedy diagnoses is a more fundamental look at the genre in Chico's brief 1937 piece "Getting Laughs the Hard Way." Chico divides comedians into two camps—the "personally funny" and those "who know how to do funny things."[172] W. C. Fields is his example of a great personality comedian. The Marx Brothers represent the other variety, using "calculated gags, even test them in the theatre. We create funny material . . . rather than rely on naturally funny personalities. It's a hard way of getting laughs, but it's really the surest."[173] This "hard way" key brings one back full circle to Harpo's 1958 comment about the need for more time. (See also both the 1958 *New York Herald Tribune* piece "Candid Quipster," where Groucho focuses his thoughts on comedy to *You Bet Your Life*, and the 1961 *Los Angeles Mirror* letter/article "Groucho Enlightens [Al] Capp on the Marx Brand of Humor," with the comedian crediting the move to softer film characters as being a result of declining box office.)

Groucho's 1960 appearance in a television production of Gilbert and Sullivan's *The Mikado* also produced, strangely enough, additional comments on comedy from the comedian. *Newsweek*'s coverage (May 2) offered further Groucho thoughts on the decline of satire. And *TV Guide*'s article (April 23) found Groucho more introspectively revealing, though with a dose of the tongue-in-cheek: "Gilbert hated middle age, elderly women and Sullivan. I like Gilbert because he hated *everybody*. Not enough hatred in this world. That's why I admire [Jack] Paar. He slashes back."[174] Though Groucho is exaggerating, these are hardly inappropriate remarks from a comedian known for both outrageous misogynous and misanthropic observations.

The 1961 publication of Harpo's autobiography resulted in a great deal of increased visibility for the comedian, especially with a heavy round of author-related PR appearances (including a stop on *You Bet Your Life*). Obviously, this visibility was also reflected in print. For example, the *New York Herald Tribune*'s *This Week* magazine carried the article "Harpo's hilarious history of the greatest practical jokes of our time." (The following year *This Week* offered "Groucho's Who's Who of Great Ha-Ha's.") Harpo also did a 1961 comic essay for the *New York Post* entitled "Harpo Turns Over a New Leaf, Finds Sin in Filmland Phone Book." Yet, as with Harpo's pictorial support of the 1942 *Colliers* article, "Just a Jesture," the more appropriate (and memorable) 1961 print "appearances" were picture "essays." (See the *Life* pictorial entitled "Harpo Leers, Frowns . . . and Speaks," or the *New York Times*'s "Harpo in Toyland," which plugged his television special *The Wonderful World of Toys*.)

With the early 1960s deaths of Chico and Harpo, Marx on Marx articles (dominated by Groucho since the 1950s) obviously became his exclusive domain, except for the rare Zeppo or Gummo piece. During that decade, 1967 was especially rich in Groucho commentary. That year the New York Gallery of Modern Art saluted the Marxes with a film retrospective, as well as publishing a booklet called "a tribute to THE MARX BROS." Edited by gallery curator and program director Raymond Rohauer, it featured interviews with Groucho and Chico's daughter Maxine.

This was also the year *The Groucho Letters* was published (commented upon extensively in the Rohauer interview). Because the catalyst for the publication was the Library of Congress (see this chapter's book section), Groucho received increased attention. A brief but interesting Groucho commentary that touches on both the book and the retrospective can be found in Vincent Canby's *New York Times* article "Captain Spaulding Is Now a Lion" (which also includes a few words from Groucho-accompanying Zeppo). But countless pieces surfaced. In fact, Groucho gave what is probably his funniest letter-related interview the year before (1966) in the *New York Post*'s "A Few Remarx from Groucho."

As one moves into the 1970s Groucho on Groucho (and the Marxes in general) observations were surfacing all over. Four of the most ambitious interviews were *Take One*'s 1970 "Groucho Marx: Portrait of the Artist As an Old Man"; film critic Roger Ebert's 1972 *Esquire* piece "A Living Legend, Rated R" (see also Ebert's 1970 "Groucho Remembers Mama," in the *New York Times*); Richard J. Anobile's 1973 "Penthouse Interview: GROUCHO"; and Charlotte Chandler's 1974 "Playboy Interview: GROUCHO MARX"—see comments earlier in this chapter on Chandler's subsequent Groucho biography). It was hardly mere coincidence that Groucho's observations were appearing in adult magazines such as *Playboy* and *Penthouse*, inasmuch as the comedian's thoughts were equally salty. In fact, Anobile's interview is drawn from his controversial 1973 collaboration with Groucho, *The Marx Bros. Scrapbook*, over which the comedian unsuccessfully sued (see the book section of this chapter).

The *Penthouse* interview appeared at the end of 1973, and without directly acknowledging the controversy, the magazine quoted an Anobile-supplied quote from Groucho at the beginning of their working relationship: "I'm going to be eighty-three years old. At this age I don't give a damn what I say about anybody or what they say about me."[175]

Strangely enough, the *Take One* piece probably contained the most controversial comment of the lot and had nothing to do with sexuality. In an interview that originally took place in 1969, Groucho had been asked his views on the establishment, and he opined, "I think it's hopeless. This whole gang in Washington, at least half of them, are thieves. . . ."[176] But the zinger came later, when he was asked, years before Watergate, "Do you think there's any hope for [President] Nixon?" The comedian's response was, "No, I think the only hope the country has is Nixon's assassination."[177]

Variations of the interview had appeared earlier in some underground publications. One sensationalized version, with which the original interviewers had no connection, came to the attention of the office of the United States attorney general. For a brief time there was a chance Groucho might be prosecuted for what was construed as a threat to the president. As the interviewers noted, Groucho then "introduced his own brand of anarchy into the proceedings. He denied everything," to a reporter.[178] Eventually, the government decided not to prosecute.

If later controversial Groucho statements would have some whispering senility, this otherwise perfectly lucid interview demonstrates an earlier precedent for legal rhubarbs any time the outspoken Groucho voiced an opinion. However, Groucho was guilty of not recognizing (or not being able to recognize) changes in journalism, where everything could and would be printed. For example, in 1950s interviews with the comedian it was not unusual for the reporter to observe that some of Groucho's more interesting comments could not appear because this was a family publication. Moreover, as his long-term correspondence with Dr. Samuel Salinger demonstrates (see Chapter 1), Groucho's conversation frequently had an earthiness to it.

Other shorter, late-life interviews of note include a 1972 *Vogue* piece with Erin Fleming asking the questions, "Groucho Marx, The Comic's Comic"; the New York *Daily News*'s 1974 "Even at 83, Groucho's Not at Wit's End"; and the *Christian Science Monitor*'s 1975 "Groucho Marx: Lunch with a master at roasting the audience."

Surprisingly enough, a 1979 BBC-Television salute to Groucho, from its *The Hollywood Greats* series, produced an insightful but also provocative interview from Zeppo, including his crediting of show business involvement with possibly saving him from a life of crime (see Chapter 1). A special thank you is due *The Freedonia Gazette*, however, for bringing the interview to the public. As might be expected, only a fraction of Zeppo's comments made the Groucho salute. Thus, through a special arrangement with the BBC and "Hollywood Greats" producer Barry Norman, a transcript of the interview was acquired by *The Freedonia Gazette*. The magazine then ran it as a two-part series (Winter 1981, Summer 1982) under the title "Zeppo's Last Interview," since the youngest Marx Brother had died a few months after the BBC program had aired.

MARX BROTHERS ARCHIVES AND FILM SOURCES

There is no one library with an exclusive collection of writing by and about the Marx Brothers. Those that come the closest are the Library of Congress (Washington, D.C.); Margaret Herrick Library at the Academy of Motion Picture Arts and Sciences (Los Angeles); New York Public Library at Lincoln Center, which houses the Billy Rose Theatre Collection; and State Historical Society of Wisconsin (Madison, Wisconsin).

The Library of Congress is home for a great deal of Groucho's correspondence, much of which is reproduced in *The Groucho Letters*. These letters are housed in the Library's Manuscript Division (Madison Building) as the "Groucho Marx Papers."

The Library Reading Room (Jefferson Building) offers access to all major texts on the team. The Reading Room also provides availability of a wide cross section of periodicals, from which the obscure Marx Brothers article frequently can be found. The Library's Motion Picture, Broadcasting, and Recorded Sound Division (Madison Building) contains both some of their films, though only a few are yet available for reference screening and various material preserved on long-playing records (see this volume's Discography). The United States Copyright Office (Madison Building) contains a number of the team's copyrighted scripts.

The Academy Library contains several all-important clipping files on the Brothers, besides numerous other files on people of special interest to the student of the team. In addition, the academy's script collection was of great assistance to this study.

The Billy Rose Theatre Collection also contains several invaluable Marx Brothers clipping files, complemented as at the Academy by other pertinent files. Furthermore, there is an excellent collection of recorded material. The New York Public Library system has, appropriately, an outstanding collection of former New York City newspapers on microfilm; these were very helpful in tracing a number of nearly forgotten Marx Brothers articles. (While the files in the Billy Rose Theatre collection are invaluable, many articles have only partial reference citations and/or are in a deteriorating or incomplete state. Thus, the microfilm collection is pivotal, as one needs to play detective more often than even the traditional researcher.)

The State Historical Society of Wisconsin has Groucho's priceless correspondence with Salinger and an extensive collection of Marx Brothers film scripts, plus both the play script to *Animal Crackers* and film scripts for two Groucho solo efforts—*Copacabana* (1947) and *Double Dynamite* (1951). All these items fall under the heading "Groucho Marx Papers." In the State Historical Society's United Artists' legal files are the aforementioned *almost* 1933 contract between the Brothers and U.A., and the Paramount contract the team was then trying to circumvent. And as the number of so many of this text's still credits bears testimony, the State Historical Society's photo archives (in its Center for Film and Theatre Research) is excellent. Photo archives were also used at the academy and the Museum of Modern Art (New York).

Three other libraries proved helpful in this study. The University of Iowa's (Iowa City) main library, with its outstanding periodical collection, provided a large number of the Marx Brothers articles herein examined. The American Film Institute's (Los Angeles) Leo McCarey Oral History was very useful. And UCLA's Theatre Arts Library, within the University Research Library, allowed this author to examine several more Marx Brothers clipping files.

The majority of the Marx Brothers films have long been available for 16-mm film rental. All their films have appeared and continue to appear on American television, where the author originally viewed all of them. They are also becoming available on low-cost video tape and disc—a development that has already begun to revolutionize the study of the Marxes, as well as film itself.

NOTES

1. Groucho Marx, *Memoirs of a Mangy Lover* (New York: Bernard Geis Associates, 1963), p. 213.

2. Hector Arce, *Groucho* (New York: G. P. Putnam's Sons, 1979), p. 348.

3. Elizabeth Wheeler, "This Groucho biography misses the Marx" (*Groucho* review), *Los Angeles Times*, January 21, 1979, n.p.

4. Arthur Marx, *Son of Groucho* (New York: David McKay Company, 1972), p. 184.

5. Burt Prelutsky, "Facets of Groucho That Only a Son Could Know" (*Son of Groucho* review), *Los Angeles Times*, December 10, 1972, p. 15.

6. Arthur Marx, *Life with Groucho* (New York: Simon and Schuster, 1954), p. 61.

7. Ibid., p. 22.

8. Ibid., p. 145.

9. Groucho Marx, *Groucho and Me* (1959; rpt. New York: Manor Books, Inc., 1974), p. 9; Groucho Marx and Richard J. Anobile, *The Marx Bros. Scrapbook* (New York: Grosset & Dunlap, 1974), p. 251.

10. Arthur Marx, *Son of Groucho*, p. 282. For the whole letter, see Arthur Marx, *Life with Groucho*, pp. 245-246.

11. Arthur Marx, *Son of Groucho*, p. 291.

12. Groucho Marx (written by an uncredited Arthur Marx), "What's Wrong with the Giants," *Colliers*, July 18, 1953, pp. 13-15.

13. Arthur Marx, *Son of Groucho*, p. 266.

14. Ibid.

15. Ibid., p. 82; Arthur Marx, *Life with Groucho*, p. 138.

16. Walter Kerr, "Chico, the utterly indispensable Marx," *Los Angeles Herald-Examiner*, February 24, 1981, p. 81.

17. Ibid., p. B6.

18. "Movie Lines," *Newsweek*, September 15, 1947, p. 14. See also Paul G. Wesolowski's "The Life of the Marx Brothers," *The Freedonia Gazette*, Winter 1984, pp. 12–16.

19. Wesolowski, "The Life of the Marx Brothers," pp. 14–15.

20. "The Personal Pitch," *Newsweek*, June 12, 1950, p. 45.

21. Kyle Crichton, *The Marx Brothers* (Garden City, N.Y.: Doubleday & Company, 1950), p. 1.

22. Charlotte Chandler (uncredited interviewer), "Playboy Interview: GROUCHO MARX," *Playboy*, March 1974, pp. 59–60, 62, 66, 69, 72, 74, 184–185.

23. Charlotte Chandler, *Hello, I Must Be Going: Groucho & His Friends* (Garden City, N.Y.: Doubleday & Company, 1978), pp. 546–547.

24. Ibid., p. 418.

25. Charlotte Chandler, *The Ultimate Seduction* (Garden City, New York: Doubleday & Company, 1984), p. 3.

26. Harry Lang, "A Day with the Mad Marxes," *Motion Picture*, June 1937, p. 90.

27. Hector Arce, *Groucho*, pp. 169, 272.

28. Groucho Marx, *Groucho and Me*, pp. 11–12.

29. The Groucho letter later dated "1931 May?" in "The Groucho Marx Papers," Box 1, Folder 1 (Correspondence with Dr. Samuel Salinger, 1928–1938), State Historical Society of Wisconsin, Madison, Wisconsin.

30. Robert Benchley, "Down with Pigeons," in *From Bed to Worse: or Comforting Thoughts About the Bison* (New York: Harper & Brothers, 1934), pp. 175–182.

31. Robert Benchley, "My Untold Story," in *My Ten Years in a Quandry and How They Grew* (1940; rpt. Garden City, New York: Blue Ribbon Books, 1936), pp. 347–361.

32. Burton Bernstein, *Thurber: A Biography* (1975; rpt. New York: Ballantine Books, 1976), p. 227.

33. Groucho Marx, *Groucho and Me*, p. 117.

34. Ibid., p. 13.

35. Arthur Marx, *Son of Groucho*, p. 257.

36. Ibid., p. 68.

37. Groucho Marx, *Groucho and Me*, pp. 87–89.

38. Groucho Marx, *The Groucho Phile* (1976; rpt. New York: Pocket Books, 1977), caption for Groucho as Ko-Ko picture, n.p.

39. Ibid., p. 198.

40. Arce, *Groucho*, p. 447.

41. Paul D. Zimmerman, "Epistles of Groucho" (a review of *The Groucho Letters*), *Newsweek*, April 3, 1967, p. 94.

42. The Groucho letter later dated "1931" in "The Groucho Marx Papers," Box 1, Folder 1.

43. Martin Nolan, "Marxisms" (a review of *The* Groucho Letters), *The Reporter*, July 13, 1967, pp. 61–62.

44. Paul G. Wesolowski, "A Rather Mistreated Book," *The Freedonia Gazette*, Summer 1984, p. 14.

45. Martin A. Gardner, "The Marx Brothers: An Investigation of Their Films as Satirical Social Criticism," Ph.D. dissertation, New York University, 1970, p. 94.

46. "Cracked Ice" (*Duck Soup*), Temporary Script (January 6, 1932–should be 1933), p. 86, in Special Collections, Margaret Herrick Library, Academy of Motion Picture Arts and Sciences, Beverly Hills, California.

47. *A Night at the Opera* (New York: The Viking Press, 1972), pp. 83–95.

48. Otis Ferguson, "The Marxian Epileptic" (*A Night at the Opera* review), *New Republic*, December 11, 1935, p. 130.

49. Alexander Woollcott, "Portrait of a Man with Red Hair," *The New Yorker*, December 1, 1928, p. 36.

50. Robert Benchley, "The Marx Brothers" (*I'll Say She Is!* review, from *Life*, June 5, 1924), in *Benchley at the Theatre*, ed. Charles Getchell (Ipswich, Mass.: Ipswich Press, 1985), p. 35.

51. Clifton Fadiman, "A New High in Low Comedy" (*A Night at the Opera* review, from *Stage*, January 1936), in *American Film Criticism*, ed. Stanley Kauffman, with Bruce Henstell (1972; rpt. Westport, Conn.: Greenwood Press, 1979), p. 322.

52. Gilbert Seldes, *Animal Crackers* review, *New Republic*, November 14, 1928, p. 352.

53. John B. Kennedy, "Slapstick Stuff," *Colliers*, July 10, 1926, p. 28.

54. Heywood Broun, "It Seems to Me," *New York Telegraph*, 1928 citation incomplete, in "The Groucho Marx Papers," Box 1, Folder 1.

55. John S. Cohen, Jr., *Duck Soup* review, *New York Sun*, November 24, 1933, in "Marx Brothers Files," Billy Rose Theatre Collection, New York Public Library at Lincoln Center.

56. *Horse Feathers* review, *Variety*, August 16, 1932, p. 15.

57. *Duck Soup* review, *Variety*, November 28, 1933, p. 20.

58. Sara Hamilton, "The Nuttiest Quartette in the World," *Photoplay*, July 1932, p. 27.

59. André Bazin, "Charlie Chaplin," in *What Is Cinema?*, vol. 1, selected and trans. by Hugh Gray (1958; rpt. Los Angeles: University of California Press, 1967), p. 144.

60. Alexander Bakshy, "Madness from Hollywood" (*Horse Feathers* review), *The Nation*, August 31, 1932, p. 199.

61. The Groucho letter later dated "1932?" in "The Groucho Marx Papers," Box 1, Folder 1.

62. William Troy, *Duck Soup* review, *The Nation*, December 13, 1933, p. 688.

63. Gerald Weales, "*Duck Soup*," in *Canned Goods as Caviar: American Film Comedy of the 1930s* (Chicago: University of Chicago Press, 1985), p. 57.

64. *Duck Soup* review, *Time*, November 20, 1933, p. 39.

65. *Go West* review, *Time*, December 23, 1940, p. 46.

66. Edwin Schallert, "Marx Brothers Due for Vacation from Movies," *Los Angeles Times*, January 1, 1934, Part II, p. 13.

67. Douglas W. Churchill, "News and Gossip from Hollywood: The Marxes as Guinea Pigs for a Stage-Screen Experiment...," *New York Times*, October 20, 1935, Section 10, p. 5.

68. "Screen: *A Night at the Opera* Will Win Converts to Marxism" (review), *Newsweek*, November 23, 1935, p. 29.

69. Andre Sennwald, *A Night at the Opera* review, *New York Times*, December 7, 1935, p. 22.

70. Ibid.

71. Otis Ferguson, "The Marxian Epileptic," (*A Night at the Opera* review), *The New Republic*, December 11, 1935, p. 130.

72. Clifton Fadiman, "A New High in Low Comedy" (*A Night at the Opera* review), p. 323.

73. Alva Johnston, "The Marx Brothers: The Scientific Side of Lunacy," *Woman's Home Companion*, September 1936, p. 12. (A condensed version of this article also appeared later in *Readers Digest* as "Those Mad Marx Brothers," October 1936, pp. 49–52.)

74. Ibid., p. 13.

75. Ibid.

76. Teet Carle, "Laughing Stock: Common and Preferred," *Stage*, March 1937, p. 48.

77. Ibid., p. 50.

78. Teet Carle, "'Fun' Working with the Marx Brothers? Horsefeathers!" *Los Angeles* magazine, October 1978, p. 145.

79. Cecelia Ager, *A Day at the Races* review, in *Garbo and the Night Watchman: A Selection from the Writings of British and American Film Critics*, ed. Alistair Cooke (London: Jonathan Cape, 1937), p. 310.

80. Ibid., p. 311.

81. Frank S. Nugent, "Speaking of Comedy," *New York Times*, September 25, 1938, Section 9, p. 5.

82. Ibid.

83. Frank S. Nugent, *Room Service* review, *New York Times*, September 22, 1938, p. 27.

84. Salvador Dali, trans. for *Harper's Bazaar* by George Davis, "Surrealism in Hollywood," *Harper's Bazaar*, June 1937, p. 68.

85. Ibid.

86. Ibid., p. 132.

87. *At the Circus* review, *The New Statesman and Nation*, December 16, 1939, p. 893.

88. James Feibleman, chapter 5, "Illustrations from Modern Comedians," in *Praise of Comedy: A Study in Its Theory and Practice* (New York: Russell & Russell, 1939), p. 225.

89. *The Big Store* review, *New York Times*, June 27, 1941, p. 14.

90. Edward Buzzell, "Mocked and Marred by the Marxes," *New York Times*, December 15, 1940, p. 6.

91. Ibid.

92. Ibid.

93. Ibid.

94. Edgar Anstey, *The Big Store* review, *The Spectator* (Britain), October 3, 1941, p. 331.

95. Jim Marshall, "The Marx Menace," *Collier's*, March 16, 1946, p. 24.

96. Ibid.

97. Ibid., p. 71.

98. Gertrude Shanklin, "The Royal Family of Riot," *Movieland*, May 1946, p. 65.

99. Ibid.

100. Ibid., p. 64.

101. James Agee, *A Night in Casablanca* review, *The Nation*, May 25, 1946, p. 636.

102. Ibid.

103. D. Mosdell, *A Night in Casablanca* review, *The Canadian Forum*, September 1946, p. 139.

104. Bosley Crowther, "Those Marx Men," *New York Times*, August 18, 1946, Section 2, p. 1.

105. Ibid.

106. Ibid.

107. Ibid.

108. Richard Rowland, "American Classic," *Hollywood Quarterly* (now *Film Quarterly*), April 1947, p. 268.

109. Val Adams, "Groucho in Mufti," *New York Times*, April 23, 1950, Section 2, p. 9.

110. John Montgomery, "Chapter Sixteen: The Eccentrics," in *Comedy Films: 1894-1954* (1954; rpt. London: George Allen & Unwin, Ltd., 1968), p. 227.

111. Arthur Knight, "The Movies Learn to Talk," in *The Liveliest Art: A Panoramic History of the Movies* (New York: The Macmillian Company, 1957), pp. 173-174.

112. Ibid., pp. 174-175.

113. Harry Kurnitz, "Return of the Marx Brothers," *Holiday*, January 1957, p. 98.

114. Ibid.

115. William Wolf, *The Marx Brothers* (New York: Pyramid Publications, 1957), pp. 133, 136. (The quote is uncut but photographs on two pages make the page citation appear as though it were edited.)

116. Jack Kerouac, "To Harpo Marx" (poem), *Playboy*, July 1959, p. 44.

117. S. J. Perelman, "Week End with Groucho Marx," *Holiday*, April 1952, p. 59.

118. Joe Adamson, *Groucho, Harpo, Chico and Sometimes Zeppo* (New York: Simon and Schuster, 1973), p. 170.

119. Bosley Crowther, "The Silent Articulator," *New York Times*, September 30, 1964, p. 43.

120. Ibid.

121. Raymond Durgnat, chapter 25, "Four Against Alienation," in *The Crazy Mirror: Hollywood Comedy and the American Image* (1969; rpt. New York: Dell, 1972), p. 154.

122. Durgnat, chapter 7, "How Many Laughs Can Dance on the Point of a Gag," in *The Crazy Mirror*, p. 50.

123. George Oppenheimer, chapter 4, "The Sound Stage," in *The View from the Sixties* (New York: David McKay Company, 1966), p. 100.

124. Andrew Sarris, chapter 10, "Make Way for the Clowns!" in *The American Cinema: Directors and Directions, 1929-1968* (New York: E. P. Dutton & Co., 1968), p. 247.

125. David Robinson, "The 'Thirties," in *The Great Funnies: A History of Film Comedy* (New York: E. P. Dutton and Co., 1969), p. 108.

126. Leonard Maltin, chapter 13, "The Marx Brothers," in *The Great Movie Comedians: From Charlie Chaplin to Woody Allen* (New York: Crown Publishers, 1978), p. 134.

127. Gerald Mast, chapter 11, "The American Studio Years: 1930-1945," in *A Short History of the Movies*, 3d ed. (1971; rpt. Indianapolis: Bobbs-Merrill Educational Publishing Co., 1981), p. 233.

128. Gerald Mast, chapter 17, "The Clown Tradition," in *The Comic Mind: Comedy and the Movies*, 2d ed. (1973; rpt. Chicago: University of Chicago Press, 1979), p. 283.

129. Ibid., p. 287.

130. Geoffrey Brown, "The Marx Brothers," *Cinema* (London), No. 8, 1971, p. 29.

131. William Donnelly, "A theory of the comedy of The Marx Brothers," *The Velvet Light Trap*, Winter 1971/1972, p. 15.

132. Screwball comedy and Bergman are discussed more fully in Wes D. Gehring, *Screwball Comedy: A Genre of Madcap Romance* (Westport, Conn.: Greenwood Press, 1986).

133. Andrew Bergman, chapter 3, "Some Anarcho-Nihilist Laff Riots," in *We're in the Money: Depression America and Its Films* (New York: New York University, 1971; rpt. New York: Harper and Row, 1972), p. 31.

134. Ibid., p. 41.

135. Donald W. McCaffrey, chapter 4, "Zanies in a Stage-Movieland," in *The Golden Age of Sound Comedy: Comic Films and Comedians of the Thirties* (New York: A. S. Barnes and Company, 1973), p. 81.

136. Colin L. Westerbeck, Jr., "Marxism," *Commonweal*, June 14, 1974, p. 333.

137. Richard Schickel, "The Marx Brothers," in *The National Society of Film Critics on Movie Comedy*, ed. Stuart Byron and Elisabeth Weis (New York: Penguin Books, 1977), p. 47.

138. David Thomson, "Groucho Marx: A Retrospective," *Take One*, November 1977, p. 42.

139. Ibid., p. 41.

140. Goodman Ace, "Top of My Head: Personal," *Saturday Review*, February 18, 1978, p. 48.

141. Ibid., p. 49.

142. Dick Cavett, "*Groucho* by Hector Arce" review, *The New Republic*, June 30, 1979, p. 30.

143. Julius [Groucho] H. Marx, "Vaudeville Talk," *The New Yorker*, June 20, 1925, p. 14.

144. Sylvia B. Golden, "Confessions of the Marx Brothers," *Theatre Magazine*, January 1929, p. 48.

145. Ibid.

146. Ibid.

147. Groucho Marx, "Bad Days Are Good Memories," *The Saturday Evening Post*, August 29, 1931, p. 12.

148. "Europa Has a Rough Trip," *New York Times*, February 15, 1931, p. 18.

149. "Harpo Marx Talks," *New York Times*, November 12, 1933, Section 9, p. 5.

150. Ibid.

151. Ibid.

152. "Visit to Russia Looses [*sic*] Tongue of Harpo Marx," *New York Herald Tribune*, January 10, 1934, in the "Marx Brothers Files," Billy Rose Theatre Collection.

153. Grace Simpson, "GROUCHO looks at CHARLIE: The maddest Marx recalls the day when he 'discovered' the genius in Chaplin," *Motion Picture*, May 1936, p. 39.

154. Ibid., p. 83.

155. Ibid.

156. Philip K. Scheuer, "Three Marx Brothers Interviewed," *Los Angeles Times*, June 13, 1937, Section III, pp. 1, 3.

157. Ibid., p. 3.

158. Teet Carle, "The Silent Member of the Marx Trio," *Brooklyn Daily Eagle*, June 13, 1937, p. C3.

159. Ibid.

160. "My Ten Favorite Pictures: No. 18—The Marx Brothers," *New York Sun*, October 8, 1938, in "Marx Brothers Files," Billy Rose Theatre Collection.

161. Ibid.

162. Mary Morris, "News: Girl Chases Marx Brothers," *PM*, January 27, 1946, p. 8.

163. Frederick C. Othman, "Comics Only ½-There, Holds Groucho Marx," *New York World Telegraph*, March 30, 1942, p. 8.

164. Ibid.

165. Groucho Marx, "What This Country Needs," *This Week, New York Herald Tribune* Sunday magazine supplement, June 16, 1940, p. 9.

166. "The Stupider the Better," *Newsweek*, September 2, 1957, p. 52.

167. Ibid.

168. Tim Brooks and Earle Marsh, *The Complete Directory to Prime Time Network TV Shows: 1946-Present* (New York: Ballantine Books, 1979), p. 804.

169. "The Marx Brothers Now," *Newsweek*, March 17, 1958, p. 104.

170. Hal Humphrey, "Groucho Diagnoses Our Ailing Comedy," *Los Angeles Mirror-News*, March 17, 1958, "Marx Brothers Files," Margaret Herrick Library, Academy of Motion Picture Arts and Sciences.

171. Ibid.

172. "Getting Laughs the Hard Way," in the "Marx Brothers Files," Billy Rose Theatre Collection.

173. Ibid.

174. "Groucho Tackles 'The Mikado,'" *TV Guide*, April 23, 1960, p. 14.

175. Richard J. Anobile, "Penthouse Interview: GROUCHO," *Penthouse*, December 1973, p. 106.

176. Robert Altman, Jon Carroll, and Michael Goodwin, "Groucho Marx: Portrait of the Artist As an Old Man," *Take One*, September/October 1970, p. 12.

177. Ibid.

178. Ibid., p. 10.

5.

BIBLIOGRAPHICAL CHECKLIST OF KEY MARX BROTHERS SOURCES

BOOKS ABOUT AND/OR BY THE MARX BROTHERS

Adamson, Joe. *Groucho, Harpo, Chico and Sometimes Zeppo.* New York: Simon and Schuster, 1973.

Anobile, Richard J., ed. *Hooray for Captain Spaulding!: Verbal and Visual Gems from "Animal Crackers."* New York: Darien House, 1974.

————. *Why a Duck?: Visual and Verbal Gems from the Marx Brothers.* New York: Darien House, 1971; rpt. New York: Avon Books, 1973.

Arce, Hector. *Groucho.* New York: G. P. Putnam's Sons, 1979.

Bogdanovich, Peter. "Leo McCarey Oral History." Los Angeles: American Film Institute, 1972. Available only there.

Chandler, Charlotte. *Hello, I Must Be Going: Groucho & His Friends.* Garden City, N.Y.: Doubleday & Company, 1978.

Crichton, Kyle. *The Marx Brothers.* Garden City, N.Y.: Doubleday & Company, 1950.

Day At the Races, A. 1972; rpt. New York: The Viking Press (The MGM Library of Film Scripts), 1974.

Eyles, Allen. *The Marx Brothers: Their World of Comedy.* New York: A. S. Barnes & Co., 1969; rpt. New York: Paperback Library, 1971.

Martin, André, "Les Marx Brothers ont-ils une âme?" In *Cahiers du Cinéma,* February 1955 (pp. 2–16), March (pp. 24–32), May (pp. 17–60), and June (23–35).

Marx, Arthur. *Life with Groucho.* New York: Simon and Schuster, 1954.

————. *Son of Groucho.* New York: David McKay Company, 1972.

Marx, Groucho (with uncredited assistance possibly coming from Arthur Sheekman). *Beds.* 1930; rpt. Indianapolis: Bobbs-Merrill Company, 1976.

Marx, Groucho. *Groucho and Me.* New York: Bernard Geis Associates, 1959; rpt. New York: Manor Books, 1974.

———— . *The Groucho Letters: Letters from and to Groucho Marx.* New York: Simon and Schuster, 1967.

———— . *The Groucho Phile.* Indianapolis: Bobbs-Merrill Company, 1976; rpt. New York: Pocket Books, 1977.

———— . *Many Happy Returns: An Unofficial Guide to Your Income Tax Problems.* New York: Simon and Schuster, 1942.

———— . *Memoirs of a Mangy Lover.* New York: Bernard Geis Associates, 1963.

———— , and Richard J. Anobile. *The Marx Bros. Scrapbook.* New York: Grosset & Dunlap, 1974.

Marx, Groucho (with Hector Arce). *The Secret Word Is GROUCHO.* New York: G. P. Putnam's Sons, 1976; rpt. New York: Berkley Publishing Corporation, 1977.

Marx, Harpo (with Rowland Barber). *Harpo Speaks!* 1961; rpt. New York: Freeway Press, 1974; rpt. New York: Limelight Editions, 1985. (Latest edition also contains poem by Harpo's widow, Susan, and an essay by son Bill.)

Marx, Maxine. *Growing Up with Chico.* Englewood Cliffs, N.J.: Prentice-Hall, 1980.

Night at the Opera, A. New York: The Viking Press (The MGM Library of Scripts), 1972.

Sinclair, Andrew, ed. *Monkey Business and Duck Soup.* 1972; rpt. Letchworth, England: Lorrimer Publishing (Classic Film Scripts Series), 1981.

Wolf, William. *The Marx Brothers.* New York: Pyramid Publications, 1975.

Zimmerman, Paul D., and Burt Goldblatt. *The Marx Brothers at the Movies.* New York: G. P. Putnam's Sons, 1968; rpt. New York: Berkley Publishing Corporation, 1975.

SHORTER WORKS ABOUT AND/OR BY THE MARX BROTHERS

Ace, Goodman. "Age" ("Top of My Head" column), *Saturday Review*, November 2, 1974, p. 51.

———— . "'The Peoples Won't Understand It,'" *Yale Alumni Magazine*, April 1975, pp. 30–32.

———— . "Personal" ("Top of My Head" column), *Saturday Review*, February 18, 1978, pp. 48–49.

———— . "Report on Groucho" ("Top of My Head" column), *Saturday Review*, April 1, 1972, p. 4.

Adams, Val. "Groucho in Mufti," *New York Times*, April 23, 1950, Section 2, p. 9.

Adamson Joe. "Duck Soup the Rest of Your Life," *Take One*, December 8, 1971.

———— . "Film Favorite: Joe Adamson on *Monkey Business*," *Film Comment*, Fall 1971, pp. 55–57.

Adamson, Joseph. "The Seventeen Preliminary Scripts of *A Day at the Races*" (cover story), *Cinema Journal*, Spring 1969, pp. 1–9.

Agee, James. *A Night in Casablanca* review, *The Nation*, May 25, 1946, p. 636.

Ager, Cecelia. *A Day at the Races* review. In *Garbo and the Night Watchmen.* Edited by Alistair Cooke. London: Jonathan Cape, 1937, pp. 310–311.

Allen, Steve. "Groucho Marx." In *The Funny Men.* New York: Simon and Schuster, 1956, pp. 237–251.

——— . "Groucho Marx." In *Funny People.* New York: Stein and Day Publishers, 1981, pp. 193–215.

Altman, Robert, Jon Carroll, and Michael Goodwin. "Groucho Marx: Portrait of the Artist As an Old Man," *Take One,* September/October 1970, pp. 10–16.

Animal Crackers review (the play), *New York Times,* October 24, 1928, p. 26.

Animal Crackers review, *Variety,* September 3, 1930, p. 19.

Anobile, Richard J. "Penthouse Interview: GROUCHO," *Penthouse,* December 1973, pp. 106, 108, 112, 132, 189–190.

Anstey, Edgar. *The Big Store* review, *The Spectator,* October 3, 1941, p. 331.

Artaud, Antonin. "Les Frères Marx au Cinéma du Panthéon," *Nouvelle Revue Française,* January 1, 1932, pp. 156–158.

"As Others See Us" (contains excerpts of reviews by Francis Birrell and Philippe Soupault—see also entries under those names), *Living Age,* December 1932, pp. 371–372.

At the Circus review, *The New Statesman and Nation,* December 16, 1939, pp. 892–893.

Bader, Robert. "Needlemarx," *The Freedonia Gazette,* Summer 1986, pp. 8–13.

Bakshy, Alexander. "Madness from Hollywood" (*Horse Feathers* review), *The Nation,* August 31, 1932, pp. 198–199.

Baskette, Kirtley, "Hoodlums at Home," *Photoplay,* July 1937, pp. 38–39, 113–114.

Benchley, Robert. "The Marx Brothers" (*I'll Say She Is!* review, 1924) and "Harpo, Groucho, Chico, Zeppo and Karl" (*Animal Crackers* play review, 1928). In *Benchley at the Theatre: Dramatic Criticism, 1920–1940.* Edited by Charles Getchell. Ipswich, Mass.: Ipswich Press, 1985, pp. 35–36, 86–87.

Beranger, Clara. "The Woman Who Taught Her Children to Be Fools," *Liberty Magazine,* June 3, 1935, pp. 22–25. (Reprinted Winter 1972 and Summer 1976.)

Bergman, Andrew. Chapter 3, "Some Anarcho-Nihilistic Laff Riots." In *We're in the Money: Depression America and Its Films.* New York: New York University Press, 1971; rpt. New York: Harper and Row, 1972.

Big Store, The, review, *New York Times,* June 27, 1941, p. 14.

Birrell, Francis. "The Marx Brothers" (*Horse Feathers* review), *New Statesman and Nation,* October 1, 1932, pp. 374–375.

Broun, Heywood. "It Seems to Me" column, *New York Journal American,* 1939 (citation incomplete). In "Marx Brothers Files," Billy Rose Theatre Collection, New York Public Library at Lincoln Center.

——— . "It Seems to Me" column, *New York Telegraph,* 1928 (citation incomplete). In "The Groucho Marx Papers," Box 1, Folder 1 (Included in correspondence with Dr. Samuel Salinger, 1928–1938), State Historical Society of Wisconsin Archives, Madison, Wisconsin.

Brown, Geoffrey, "The Marx Brothers," *Cinema,* No. 8, 1971, pp. 29–31.

Buzzell, Edward. "Mocked and Marred by the Marxes," *New York Times,* December 15, 1940, p. 6.

Cahn, William. Chaper 10, "For Laughing Out Loud." In *The Laugh Makers: A Pictorial History of American Comedians*. New York: G. P. Putnam's Sons, 1957, pp. 136–140, 142. (Later revision entitled *The Great American Comedy Scene*.)

Calman, Mel. "Perelman in Cloudsville," *Sight and Sound*, Autumn 1978, pp. 248–249.

Canby, Vincent. "Captain Spaulding Is Now a Lion," *New York Times*, April 13, 1967, p. 45.

Carle, Teet. "'Fun' Working with the Marx Brothers? Horsefeathers!" *Los Angeles* magazine, October 1978, pp. 142, 145–146, 148, 150.

——— . "Laughing Stock: Common and Preferred," *Stage*, March 1937, pp. 48–50.

——— . "The Silent Member of the Marx Trio," *Brooklyn Daily Eagle*, June 13, 1937, p. C3.

Carroll, Kathleen. "Even at 83, Groucho's Not at Wit's End," New York *Daily News*, June 30, 1974, p. 7.

Cavett, Dick. *Groucho* review, *The New Republic*, June 30, 1979, pp. 30–32.

Cavett, Dick, and Christopher Porterfield. "Chapter 7." In *Cavett*. New York: Harcourt Brace Jovanovich, 1974; rpt. New York: Bantam Books, 1975, pp. 201–215.

Chandler, Charlotte. "Playboy Interview: GROUCHO MARX," *Playboy*, March 1974, pp. 59–60, 62, 66, 69, 72, 74, 185–186.

——— . "What Are They Laughing at, Julie?" *New York*, February 20, 1978, pp. 60–63.

Chase, Chevy. "Chevy Chase: I'm Not Mr. Cruel," *New York Times*, October 2, 1977, Section 2, p. D35.

Chavance, Louis. "The Four Marx Brothers As Seen by a Frenchman," *The Canadian Forum*, February 1933, pp. 175–76.

"Chico Is Not Sure What His Band Will Do But He Knows He'll Play Piano with an Orange," *New York World Telegraph*, November 27, 1940 (n.p. cited). In "Marx Brothers Files," Billy Rose Theatre Collection, New York Public Library at Lincoln Center.

Churchill, Douglas W. "News and Gossip from Hollywood: The Marxes as Guinea Pigs for a Stage-Screen Experiment," *New York Times*, October 20, 1935, Section 10, p. 5.

Creelman, Eileen. "Picture Plays and Players: Chico, the Piano-playing Marx, Talks of Marx Bros. at the Circus," *New York Sun*, November 14, 1939, p. 16.

Crowther, Bosley. "The Silent Articulator," *New York Times*, September 30, 1964, p. 43.

——— . "Those Marx Men," *New York Times*, August 18, 1946, Section 2, p. 1.

Cunningham, James P. *A Day at the Races* review, *Commonweal*, July 2, 1937, p. 267.

Dali, Salvador. "Surrealism in Hollywood," *Harper's Bazaar*, June 1937, pp. 68–69, 132.

Daney, Serge, and Jean-Louis Noames, "Leo et les aléas" (McCarey interview), *Cahiers du Cinéma*, February 1965, pp. 11–20.

Day at the Races, A, review, *New York Times*, June 18, 1937, p. 25.

Delehanty, Thorton. "Groucho Plans to Write After Quitting Films," *New York Herald Tribune*, April 20, 1941 (n.p. noted). In "Marx Brothers Files," Billy Rose Theatre Collection, New York Public Library at Lincoln Center.

deLoof, Dennis P. "A Constructive Analysis of Three Early Marx Brothers Films," *The Freedonia Gazette*, Spring 1984, pp. 3–23.

Dixon, Peter. "First Appearance in Europe!" *The Freedonia Gazette*, Winter 1981, pp. 9–12.

——— . "Groucho in Britain," *The Freedonia Gazette*, Summer 1981, pp. 9–12.

Donnelly, William. "A theory of the comedy of THE MARX BROTHERS," *The Velvet Light Trap*, Winter 1971/1972, pp. 8–15.

Duck Soup review, *Newsweek*, December 2, 1933, p. 33.

Duck Soup review, *Time*, November 20, 1933, pp. 38–39.

Duck Soup review, *Variety*, November 28, 1933, p. 20.

Durgnat, Raymond. Chapter 25, "Four Against Alienation." In *The Crazy Mirror: Hollywood Comedy and the American Image*. Plymouth, England: Latimer Trend & Co., 1969; rpt. New York: Dell, 1972, pp. 150–158. (For insightful Durgnat comments on the Marxes outside this chapter see pages 50 and 82.)

Ebert, Roger. "Groucho Remembers Mama," *New York Times*, March 1, 1970, pp. 1, 11.

——— . "A Living Legend Rated R," *Esquire*, July 1972, pp. 140–143, 172, 174.

Edelson, Edward. Chapter 7, "The Marx Revolution." In *Funny Men of the Movies*. New York: Doubleday & Company, 1976; rpt. New York: Pocket Books, 1980, pp. 59–72.

"Eden Marx," *The Freedonia Gazette*, Summer 1984, pp. 9–11.

Eells, George. "The Secret of Groucho," *Look*, July 9, 1957, pp. 30–34.

Elderkin, Phil. "Groucho Marx: Lunch with a Master at Roasting the Audience," *Christian Science Monitor*, October 28, 1975, p. 17.

"Erin Fleming, Who Made His Life Worth Living," *The Freedonia Gazette*, Summer 1983, pp. 4–17.

"Europa Has a Rough Trip," *New York Times*, February 15, 1931, p. 18.

Eyles, Allen. "Great Films of the Century: A Night at the Opera," *Films and Filming*, February 1965, pp. 16–20.

Fadiman, Clifton. "A New High in Low Comedy" (*A Night at the Opera* review), from *Stage*, January 1936. In *American Film Criticism: From the Beginning to Citizen Kane*. Edited by Stanley Kauffman, with Bruce Henstell. New York: Liveright, 1972; rpt. Westport, Conn: Greenwood Press, 1979, pp. 322–328.

Feibleman, James. Chapter 5, "Illustrations from Modern Comedians." In *In Praise of Comedy: A Study in Its Theory and Practice*. New York: Russell & Russell, 1939, pp. 223–230.

Fensterstock, Howard. "A Journalistic Scream: An Imaginary Interview with the Marx Brothers," *Parade*, August 1929, pp. 11, 27–28.

Ferguson, Otis. *A Day at the Races* review, *The New Republic*, June 30, 1937, p. 222.

——— . "The Marxian Epileptic" (*A Night at the Opera* review), *The New Republic*, December 11, 1935, p. 130.

——— . "Methods of Madness" (*Go West* review), *The New Republic*, January 27, 1941, p. 117.

"Few Remarx from Groucho, A," *New York Post*, June 4, 1966 (n.p. noted). In "Marx Brothers Files," Billy Rose Theatre Collection, New York Public Library at Lincoln Center.

Fleming, Erin. "Groucho Marx, The Comic's Comic, Has the Last Word About Women, Maybe," *Vogue*, July 1972, pp. 88–89, 111.

Friedman, Josh Alan. "A Memory of Groucho," *New York*, August 28, 1978, pp. 98, 100, 102.

Gardner, Martin A. "The Marx Brothers: An Investigation of Their Films as Satirical Social Criticism." Ph.D. dissertation, New York University, 1970.

"Getting Laughs the Hard Way,"1937 (citation incomplete). In "Marx Brothers Files," Billy Rose Theatre Collection, New York Public Library at Lincoln Center.

Golden, Sylvia B. "Confessions of the Marx Brothers," *Theatre Magazine*, January 1929, p. 48.

Grierson, John. "The Logic of Comedy." In *Grierson on Documentary*. Edited by Forsyth Hardy. London: Faber and Faber, 1947; rpt. Los Angeles: University of California Press, 1966, pp. 52–57. (Marx Brothers segments originally appeared as an *Animal Crackers* review in *The Clarion* of December 1930 and a *Monkey Business* review in the *Everyman* of October 15, 1931.)

"Groucho Enlightens [Al] Capp on the Marx Brand of Humor," *Los Angeles Mirror*, February 15, 1961 (n.p. noted). In "Marx Brothers Files," Special Collections, Margaret Herrick Library, Academy of Motion Picture Arts and Sciences, Beverly Hills, California.

"Groucho Marx" (cover story), *Time*, December 31, 1951, p. 29.

"Groucho Rides Again" (cover story), *Newsweek*, May 15, 1950, pp. 56–59.

"Groucho's Garland of Gags: They Come in Many Colors, Including Off," *Life*, November 2, 1949, pp. 139–140.

"Groucho's SWG [Screen Writers Guide] Monologue," *Variety*, March 1, 1954, pp. 6, 18.

"Groucho Tackles 'The Mikado,'" *TV Guide*, April 23, 1960, pp. 10–11, 14.

Hamilton, Sara. "The Nuttiest Quartette in the World," *Photoplay*, July 1932, pp. 27, 90–91.

"Harpo in Toyland," *New York Times Magazine*, November 5, 1961, p. 82.

"Harpo Leers, Frowns . . . and SPEAKS," *Life*, May 19, 1961, pp. 65–66.

"Harpo Marx Back, a Caviar Convert," *New York Times*, January 10, 1934, p. 24.

"Harpo Marx Talks," *New York Times*, November 12, 1933, Section 9, p. 5.

Hayes, Francis. "Just a Gesture," *Colliers*, January 31, 1942, pp. 14–15.

Horse Feathers cover story, *Time*, August 15, 1932, pp. 24–25.

Horse Feathers review, *Variety*, August 16, 1932, p. 15.

Humphrey, Hal. "Groucho Diagnoses Our Ailing Comedy," *Los Angeles Mirror-News*, March 17, 1958. In "Marx Brothers Files," Special Collections, Margaret Herrick Library, Academy of Motion Picture Arts and Sciences, Beverly Hills, California.

Jenkins, Dan. "Everyone's a Critic" (Groucho cover story), *TV Guide*, April 27, 1957, pp. 21–23.

Johnston, Alva. "The Scientific Side of Lunacy," *Woman's Home Companion*, September 1936, pp. 12–13, 73–74.

Jordan, Thomas H. "The Marx Brothers." In *The Anatomy of Cinematic Humor*. New York: Revisionist Press, 1975, pp. 89–157.

Kauffman, Stanley, ed., with Bruce Henstell. *American Film Criticism: From the Beginning to Citizen Kane*. New York: Liveright, 1972; rpt. Westport, Conn.: Greenwood Press, 1979. Marx Brothers contents: *The Cocoanuts* (Gilbert Seldes); *Monkey Business* (John Mosher); *Horse Feathers* (Alexander Bakshy); *Duck Soup* (Meyer Levin); and *A Night at the Opera* (Clifton Fadiman).

Kennedy, John B. "Slapstick Stuff," *Colliers*, July 10, 1926, p. 28.

Kerouac, Jack. "To Harpo Marx" (poem), *Playboy*, July 1959, p. 44.

Kerr, Walter. "Chico, the Utterly Indispensable Marx," *Los Angeles Herald-Examiner*, February 24, 1981, p. 86.

———. Chapter 12, "The Clown Gives Scandal." In *Tragedy and Comedy*. New York: Simon and Schuster, 1967, pp. 245–247.

———. "The Marx Brothers and How They Grew," *New York Times*, June 7, 1976, p. 37.

———. "Those Four Boys Onstage Honored The Marx Bros." (*Minnie's Boys* review), *New York Times*, April 5, 1970, Section 2, p. 3.

Knight, Arthur. Chapter 4, "The Movies Learn to Talk." In *The Liveliest Art: A Panoramic History of the Movies*, New York: The Macmillan Publishing Co., 1957.

Krasna, Norman. *Dear Ruth*. New York: Dramatists Play Service, 1944.

Krasna, Norman, and Groucho Marx. *Time for Elizabeth*. New York: Dramatists Play Service, 1949.

Kurnitz, Harry. "Return of the Marxes," *Holiday*, January 1957, pp. 95, 98.

Lang, Harry. "A Day with the Mad Marxes," *Motion Picture*, June 1937, pp. 38–39, 90–92.

Levant, Oscar. "Memoirs of a Mute." In *A Smattering of Ignorance*. Garden City, N.Y.: Garden City Publishing Co., 1942.

Levin, Meyer. *Duck Soup* review, *Esquire*, February 1934, p. 131.

Lister, Eric. Chapters 1 and 2. In *–Don't Mention–The Marx Brothers: Reminiscences of S. J. Perelman*. Topsfield, Massachusetts: Merrimack, 1985, pp. 2, 5, 11–12.

"Lord High Groucho," *Newsweek*, May 2, 1960, p. 80.

McCaffrey, Donald W. Chapter 4, "Zanies in a Stage-Movieland." In *The Golden Age of Sound Comedy: Comic Films and Comedians of the Thirties*. New York: A. S. Barnes and Company, 1973, pp. 74–88.

Magill, Frank, ed. *Magill's Survey of Cinema: English Language Films* (first series), 4 vols. Englewood Cliffs, N.J.: Salem Press, 1980. Marx Brothers contents: *Animal Crackers* (Howard J. Prouty, vol. 1); *Monkey Business* (Ronald Bowers, vol. 3); and *A Night at the Opera* (Howard H. Prouty, vol. 3).

———. *Magill's Survey of Cinema: English Language Films* (second series), 4 vols. Englewood Cliffs, N.J.: Salem Press, 1981. Max Brothers contents:

A Day at the Races (Juliette Friedgen, vol. 2); *Duck Soup* (Rob Edelman, vol. 2); and *Horse Feathers* (Ralph Angel, vol. 3).

Maltin, Leonard. Chapter 13, "The Marx Brothers." In *The Great Movie Comedians: From Charlie Chaplin to Woody Allen*. New York: Crown Publishers, 1978, pp. 132–141.

——. "The Marx Brothers." In *Movie Comedy Teams*. 1970; rpt. New York: Signet, 1974 (Revised 1985).

Marshall, Jim. "The Marx Menace," *Colliers*, March 16, 1946, pp. 24, 71.

Martin, Pete. "I Call on Groucho," *Saturday Evening Post*, May 25, 1957, pp. 31, 85–86, 89.

"Marx Brothers Now, The," *Newsweek*, March 17, 1958, pp. 104, 106.

"Marx, Chico, Groucho, Harpo." In *Current Biography 1948*. Edited by Anna Rothe. New York: The H. W. Wilson Company, 1949, pp. 425–430.

Marx, Chico. "Time Marches on for the Marxes," *New York Times*, September 8, 1938, Section 10, p. 4.

"Marx Cinemania," *A Night at the Opera* review, *Literary Digest*, June 26, 1937, pp. 22–23.

Marx, Eden Hartford (as told to Liza Wilson, plus frequent Groucho asides), "My Life with Groucho," *American Weekly*, September 4, 1955, p. 12.

Marx, Groucho. "Bad Days Are Good Memories," *Saturday Evening Post*, August 29, 1931, pp. 12, 82–83.

——. "The Customers Always Write," ("Trade Winds" column), *Saturday Review*, December 22, 1945, p. 20.

——. "Do You Know Enough to Go Home?" *This Week, New York Herald Tribune* Sunday magazine supplement, March 23, 1941, pp. 6, 29.

——. "Groucho Marx Turns Himself in for Scrap," *This Week, New York Herald Tribune* Sunday magazine supplement, November 8, 1942, p. 6.

——. "How I Beat the Social Game," *Liberty Magazine*, October 19, 1940, pp. 32–33.

——. "How to Be a Spy," *This Week, New York Herald Tribune* Sunday magazine supplement, February 16, 1946, pp. 6, 20. (See reprint in Chapter 3 of this volume.)

——. "How to Be a Spy" (pictorial), *Life*, April 1, 1946, pp. 65–66, 68, 70.

——. "How to Build a Secret Weapon," *This Week, New York Herald Tribune* Sunday Magazine supplement, November 7, 1943, p. 11.

——. "How to Crank a Horse," *This Week, New York Herald Tribune* Sunday magazine supplement, April 4, 1943, p. 8.

——. "Many Happy Returns!" *Saturday Review*, January 24, 1942, p. 14.

——. "My Poor Wife!" *Colliers*, December 20, 1930, pp. 15, 59. (See reprint in Chapter 3 of this volume.)

——. "Press Agents I Have Known," *The New Yorker*, March 9, 1929, pp. 52, 54–55.

——. "The Role I Liked Best...," *Saturday Evening Post*, March 8, 1948, p. 115.

——. "Standing Room Only," *This Week, New York Herald Tribune* Sunday magazine supplement, November 17, 1946, pp. 18, 28.

——. "Up from Pantages," *New York Times*, June 10, 1928, Section 8, p. 2.

——. "Vaudeville Talk," *The New Yorker*, June 20, 1925, p. 14.

——— . "What This Country Needs," *This Week, New York Herald Tribune* Sunday magazine supplement, June 16, 1940, pp. 9, 30.

——— . (authorship now claimed by son Arthur). "What's Wrong with the Giants," *Colliers*, July 18, 1953, pp. 13–15.

——— . "Why Harpo Doesn't Talk," *This Week, New York Herald Tribune* Sunday magazine supplement, December 12, 1948, pp. 22, 48.

——— . (with Leslie Lieber). "Groucho's Who's Who of Great Ha-Ha's," *This Week, New York Herald Tribune* Sunday magazine supplement, March 11, 1962, pp. 15, 20.

Marx, Harpo. "Harpo's Hilarious History of the Greatest Practical Jokes of Our Time," *This Week, New York Herald Tribune* Sunday magazine supplement, July 16, 1961, pp. 4–5, 12.

——— . "Harpo Turns Over a New Leaf, Finds Sin in Filmland Phone Book," *New York Post*, Apirl 18, 1950, p. 4.

——— . "My Brother GROUCHO," *Coronet*, February 1951, pp. 131–135.

——— . "Plenty of Guts," *Esquire*, November 1950, pp. 84–85, 128, 130.

Mast, Gerald. Chapter 11, "The American Studio Years: 1930–1945." In *A Short History of the Movies*, 3d edition. 1971; rpt. Indianapolis: Bobbs-Merrill Educational Publishing, 1981, pp. 233–235.

——— . Chapter 17, "The Clown Tradition." In *The Comic Mind: Comedy and the Movies*, 2d edition. 1973; rpt. Chicago: University of Chicago Press, 1979, pp. 281–288.

Michener, Charles. "Comedy's King Leer," *Newsweek*, August 29, 1977, pp. 78–79.

Moffitt, John C. "Censorship for Interviews Hollywood's Wild Idea," *Cinema Digest*, January 9, 1933, pp. 9–12.

Montgomery, John. Chapter 16, "The Eccentrics." In *Comedy Films: 1894–1954*, 2d edition. 1954; rpt. London: George Allen & Unwin, 1968, pp. 225–230.

Morris, Mary. "News: Girl Chases Marx Brothers," *PM*, January 27, 1946, pp. 6–8.

Mosdell, D. *A Night in Casablanca* review, *The Canadian Forum*, September 1946, pp. 138–139.

"My Ten Favorite Pictures," *New York Sun*, October 8, 1938 (n.p. noted). In "Marx Brothers Files," Billy Rose Theatre Collection, New York Public Library at Lincoln Center.

Night at the Opera, A, review, *Newsweek*, November 23, 1935, pp. 29–30.

Norman, Barry. "Zeppo's Last Interview" (two parts), *The Freedonia Gazette*, November 1981 (pp. 5–7) and Summer 1982 (pp. 6–9).

Nugent, Frank S. "Speaking of Comedy," *New York Times*, September 25, 1938, Section 9, p. 5.

Oppenheimer, George. Chapter 4, "The Sound Stage." In *The View from the Sixties: Memories of a Spent Life*. New York: David McKay Company, 1966, pp. 99–101, 123–127.

Othman, Frederick. "Comics Only ½-There, Holds Groucho Marx," *New York World Telegraph*, March 30, 1942, p. 8.

——— . "Marx Brothers, Sick of Movies, to Quit," *Los Angeles Herald*, April 10, 1941, pp. 2, 13.

Parish, James Robert, and William T. Leonard (with Gregory W. Mank and Charles Hoyt). "The Marx Brothers." In *The Funsters.* New Rochelle, N.Y.: Arlington House Publishers, 1979, pp. 463-475.

Perelman, S. J. "Going Hollywood with the Marx Brothers," *Esquire,* September 1981, pp. 60-64, 66.

———. "Week End with Groucho Marx," *Holiday,* April 1952, pp. 59, 126-133. Retitled "I'll Always Call You Schnorrer, My African Explorer," in *The Most of S. J. Perelman.* New York: Simon and Schuster, 1958, pp. 624-631.

———. "The Winsome Foursome: How to go batty with the Marx Brothers when writing a film called 'Monkey Business,'" *Show,* November 1961, pp. 35-38.

"Personal Pitch, The," *Newsweek,* June 12, 1950, p. 45.

"Plucking a Few Notes from Harpo," *New York Times,* November 17, 1935, Section 9, p. 4.

Prelutsky, Burt. "Facets of Groucho That Only a Son Could Know" (*Son of Groucho* review), *Los Angeles Times,* December 10, 1972, pp. 1, 15.

"Refineries' Five-Star Theatre for Every Type of Radio Listener" (Includes a review of *Beagle, Shyster and Beagle*), *Variety,* December 6, 1932, p. 34.

Robinson, David. "The 'Thirties." In *The Great Funnies: A History of Film Comedy.* New York: E. P. Dutton and Co., 1969, pp. 104-105, 108-109, 111.

Robinson, Jeffrey. "The Marx Brothers." In *Teamwork: The Cinema's Greatest Comedy Teams.* New York: Proteus, 1982, pp. 41-55.

Rohauer, Raymond. "Tribute to the Marx Bros.," Gallery of Modern Art 6-page program, 1967. Largely comprised of Rohauer's "An Interview with Groucho Marx," pp. 2-5.

Room Service review, *Modern Screen,* December 1938, p. 18.

Rosenblatt, Roger. "At the Circus Go West," *New Republic,* May 21, 1977, pp. 60-62.

Rosenfield, John. "Arthur (Harpo) Marx, 'Surrealist Comedian,'" *Dallas Morning News,* September 10, 1943, p. 8.

"Roses, Love and Shotguns from Harpo Marx," *Silver Screen,* July 1932, pp. 24-25, 58-59.

Rosten, Leo. "Groucho." In *People I Have Loved, Known, or Admired.* New York: McGraw-Hill Book Company, 1970, pp. 59-75.

———. "Groucho . . . The Man from Marx," *Look,* March 28, 1950, pp. 76-78, 81-84.

———. "The Lunar World of Groucho Marx" (cover story), *Harper's,* June 1958, pp. 31-35.

Rowland, Richard. "American Classic," *Hollywood Quarterly* (now *Film Quarterly*), April 1947, pp. 264-269.

Salmaggi, Bob. "Candid Quipster," entertainment supplement, *New York Herald Tribune,* July 27, 1958, pp. 5-6.

Sammis, Edward R. "Those Mad Marx Hares: As Revealed by the Fifth Marx Brother to Edward R. Sammis," *Photoplay,* February 1936, pp. 26-27. (See reprint in Chapter 3 of this volume.)

Sarris, Andrew. "Make Way for the Clowns." In *The American Cinema: Directors and Directions, 1929-1968.* New York: E. P. Dutton and Co., 1968, pp. 246–248.

Schallert, Edwin. "Marx Brothers Due for Vacation from Movies," *Los Angeles Times,* January 1, 1934, Part II, p. 13.

Scheuer, Philip K. "Three Marx Brothers Interviewed," *Los Angeles Times,* June 13, 1937, Section III, pp. 1, 3.

Schickel, Richard. "The Marx Brothers" (1962). In *The National Society of Film Critics on Movie Comedy.* Edited by Stuart Byron and Elisabeth Weis. New York: Penguin Books, 1977, pp. 47–48.

Scott, John L. "King Leer Groucho Still Rules with Raised Brow, Barbed Wit," *Los Angeles Times,* February 10, 1952, Part IV, pp. 1, 10.

Seldes, Gilbert. *Animal Crackers* (stage) review, *The New Republic,* November 14, 1928, pp. 351–352.

———— . Chapter 5. In *The Movies Come from America.* New York: Charles Scribner's Sons, 1937.

Sennwald, Andre. *A Night at the Opera* review, *New York Times,* December 7, 1935, p. 22.

Seton, Marie. "S. Dali + 3 Marxes =   ," *Theatre Arts,* October 1939, pp. 734–740.

Shanklin, Gertrude, "The Royal Family of Riot," *Movieland,* May 1946, pp. 58–59, 64–65.

Silver, Charles. "Leo McCarey: From Marx to McCarthy," *Film Comment,* September 1973, pp. 8–11.

Simpson, Grace. "GROUCHO looks at CHARLIE," *Motion Picture,* May 1936, pp. 39, 82–83.

Smith, Cecil. "Why Groucho Sends Viewers," *Los Angeles Times,* January 27, 1957, pp. 1, 5.

Soupault, Philippe. *Horse Feathers* review, *L'Europe Nouvelle,* October 8, 1932, p. 1202.

Stein, Aaron. "Mad Marxes Guest Star on Radio," *New York Post,* September 15, 1937 (n.p. noted). In "Marx Brothers Files," Billy Rose Theatre Collection, New York Public Library at Lincoln Center.

"'Stupider the Better, The,'" *Newsweek,* September 2, 1957, p. 52.

Thomson, David. "Groucho Marx: A Retrospective," *Take One,* November 1977, pp. 41–42.

Thurber, James. "James Thurber presents *Der Tag Aux Courses,*" *Stage,* March 1937, p. 49.

Troy, William. *Duck Soup* review, *The Nation,* December 13, 1933, p. 688.

"Truth about Groucho's Ad Libs, The," *TV Guide,* March 19, 1954, pp. 5–7.

Tynan, Kenneth. "Funny World of Groucho and Perelman," *Los Angeles Times,* June 28, 1964, pp. 1, 35.

Van Doren, Mark. "Harpo & Co." (*A Night at the Opera* review), *The Nation,* July 10, 1937, p. 53.

"Visit to Russia Looses [*sic*] Tongue of Harpo Marx," *New York Herald Tribune,* January 10, 1934 (n.p. noted). In "Marx Brothers Files," Billy Rose Theatre Collection, New York Public Library at Lincoln Center.

Wagner, Rob. *Duck Soup* review. In *Selected Film Criticism 1931–1940.* Edited by Anthony Slide. Metuchen, New Jersey: The Scarecrow Press, 1982, pp. 70–71. (Originally appeared in *Rob Wagner's Script*, November 18, 1933, p. 8.)

Ward, J. A. "The Hollywood Metaphor: The Marx Brothers, S. J. Perelman, and Nathanael West," *The Southern Review*, Summer 1976, pp. 659–672.

Weales, Gerald. Chapter 3, *"Duck Soup."* In *Canned Goods as Caviar: American Film Comedy of the 1930s.* Chicago: University of Chicago Press, 1985, pp. 54–83.

Wesolowski, Paul G. "Brother Against Brother," *The Freedonia Gazette*, Winter 1983, pp. 3–5.

——— . "The Contract That Almost Was" (two parts), *The Freedonia Gazette*, Summer 1982 (pp. 16–18) and Winter 1982 (pp. 16–17).

——— . "The Marx Brothers' Paramount Contract," *The Freedonia Gazette*, Winter 1981, pp. 13–14.

Wessel, Kipp. "Comrade Harpo." *The Freedonia Gazette*, November 1980, pp. 7–8, 18.

Westerbeck, Colin L., Jr. "Marxism," *Commonweal*, June 14, 1974, pp. 332–333.

Whelan, Richard. "Cruelty vs. Compassion Among the Comics," *New York Times*, October 2, 1977, p. D-29.

Wilson, B. F. "The Mad Marxes Make for the Movies," *Motion Picture Classic*, February 1928, pp. 48, 78.

Woollcott, Alexander. "Harpo Marx and Some Brothers" (*I'll Say She Is!* review), *New York World*, May 19, 1924 (n.p. noted). In *The Marx Bros. Scrapbook* by Groucho Marx and Richard J. Anobile. New York: Grosset & Dunlap, 1974, p. 61.

——— . "I Might Just as Well Have Played Hooky." In *Long, Long Ago.* New York: World Book Company, 1943, pp. 176–182.

——— . "A Mother of the Two-a-Day" (from *Saturday Evening Post*, June 20, 1925). In *Going to Pieces.* New York: G. P. Putnam's Sons, 1928, pp. 35–66.

——— . "My Friend Harpo." In *While Rome Burns.* New York: Grosset & Dunlap, 1934, pp. 37–41.

——— . "Obituary [of Minnie Marx]," *The New Yorker*, September 28, 1929, p. 54. See also Woollcott's *While Rome Burns.*

——— . "Portrait of a Man with Red Hair," *The New Yorker*, December 1, 1928, pp. 33–36.

——— . "A Strong, Silent Man," *Cosmopolitan* (Hearst's *International* combined with *Cosmopolitan*), January 1934, pp. 56–57, 108.

Zinsser, William. "That Perelman of Great Price Is 65," *New York Times Magazine*, January 26, 1969, pp. 24–27, 72, 74, 76.

APPENDIXES

CHRONOLOGICAL BIOGRAPHY

Constructing a chronological biography necessitates using all one's sources. Earlier time lines exist in Allen Eyles's *The Marx Brothers: Their World of Comedy* (1969; the line is limited to some professional activities), Charlotte Chandler's *Hello, I Must be Going: Groucho and His Friends* (1978, a Groucho time line), and André Martin's "Les Marx Brothers ont-ils une âme?" in *Cahiers du Cinéma* (a four-part 1955 series, with the February installment a time line-length article).

Aug. 1887   Leonard "Chico" Marx born to Simon "Frenchie" and Minnie Marx in New York. Frenchie is Manhattan's worst tailor and Minnie a housewife and future entertainment manager. (Chico's daughter Maxine provides this birth date for her father—see *Growing Up with Chico*—but March 22 is the most frequently cited. Could the pun-loving Chico have encouraged this in order to be the Marx of March?

Nov. 23, 1888   Adolph, later Arthur, "Harpo" Marx born.

circa 1889   Margaret Dumont born.

Oct. 2, 1890   Julius "Groucho" Marx born.

circa 1890s   Minnie's brother Al Shean (changed from Schoenberg) organizes and stars in the influential vaudeville comedy and musical act the Manhattan Comedy Four. He is later half of the famous comedy team Gallagher and Shean.

1893   Milton "Gummo" Marx born. Most obscure of the Brothers, since he did not appear in any films. (An 1897 birth date is sometimes also cited.)

Feb. 25, 1901   Herbert "Zeppo" Marx born.

1905   Groucho begins entertainment career as part of the Leroy Trio.

1906   Groucho plays the office boy in a production of *The Man of Her Choice*.

1907   Chico becomes song-plugger for a Pittsburgh music house. The same year "The Three Nightingales" first surface—comprised of Groucho, Gummo and Mabel O'Donnell.

1908   With the addition of Harpo, "The Three Nightingales" become a foursome. Earlier in the year O'Donnell had been replaced by Lou Levy.

1910   Minnie moves the family from New York to Chicago. In Chicago the Nightingales briefly become The Six Mascots. Also in this year the Brothers organize and begin touring in *Fun in Hi Skule*.

1912   Chico joins the act—the first professional union of the three pivotal Marxes—Groucho, Harpo, and Chico.

1913   Their act has evolved into *Mr. Green's Reception*.

1914   Uncle Al Shean writes *Home Again* for his nephews. It gives their careers a boost. This is also the year they would receive their famous nicknames.

1915   The team plays the Palace.

1916   The family's home base becomes a farm just outside of Chicago. Chico marries Betty Karp. They have one child, Maxine, and later divorce.

1917   Gummo drafted into the army; Zeppo is drafted into the team.

1918   The Marxes mount a musical comedy entitled *The Street Cinderella*.

circa 1919   New York again becomes the Marx family home.

Feb. 1920   Groucho marries Ruth Johnson, a dancer featured with Zeppo in the Home Again troupe.

1920   The Marx Brothers privately finance their movie debut in a silent short subject, *Humorisk*.

Feb. 1921   Benny Leonard, lightweight boxing champion, finances them in *On the Mezzanine Floor.*

July 1921   Arthur Marx is born to Ruth and Groucho.

1922   The Marxes's act has evolved to a variation of the *Mezzanine— On the Balcony.*

Summer 1922   Unsuccessful British tour.

Summer 1923   *I'll Say She Is!* opens in Philadelphia.

May 19, 1924 *I'll Say She Is!* opens on Broadway.

1925   Harpo has a small supporting role in the romantic comedy feature film *Too Many Kisses.*

Dec. 9, 1925 *The Cocoanuts* opens on Broadway.

Apr. 1927   Zeppo marries Marion Benda. They have one child, Tim, and later divorce.

May 1927   Miriam Marx born to Ruth and Groucho.

Summer 1928   Harpo accompanies Alexander Woollcott to Europe.

Oct. 23, 1928 *Animal Crackers* opens on Broadway.

Mar. 1929   Gummo marries Helen con Tilzer, the widow of composer Russell con Tilzer. They have two children, Robert and Kay.

May 1929   The filmed version of *The Cocoanuts* is released.

1929   *College Humor* magazine serializes Groucho's book *Beds.*

Sept. 13, 1929 Minnie Marx dies in New York.

Oct. 1929   Groucho and Harpo eventually lose fortunes in the stock market crash.

1930   *Beds* appears in book form.

Sept. 1930   The filmed version of *Animal Crackers* is released.

Jan. 5, 1931 The Marxes have a smash opening and subsequent run at the London Palace.

1931   The Marxes move to California.

Sept. 1931   *Monkey Business* is released.

Apr. 9, 1932   Chico is injured in an automobile accident; the production of *Horse Feathers* is delayed.

Aug. 1932   *Horse Feathers* is released.

Aug. 15, 1932   Groucho, Harpo, Chico, and Zeppo make the cover of *Time*, in a scene from *Horse Feathers*.

Nov. 28, 1932   Groucho and Chico have a short-lived radio program—*Flywheel, Shyster and Flywheel.* (Groucho, as Flywheel, gets double billing.)

Mar. 9, 1933   The team temporarily breaks with Paramount.

Apr. 1933   The team incorporates. They hope to produce; there are talks with United Artists about distributing.

May 1933   Differences settled with Paramount.

May 11, 1933   Frenchie Marx dies in California.

July 1933   Gummo moves to California. His New York clothing business has gone bankrupt. He would help manage the team.

Nov. 1933   *Duck Soup* is released. What is now considered the team's greatest film, with their only auteur director, Leo McCarey, goes largely unappreciated upon its release. Harpo leaves for Soviet Union tour.

Jan. 9, 1934   Harpo's New York press conference upon return from a very successful Soviet Union tour. He is the first American to entertain in Moscow after the U.S. officially recognizes the Soviet Union.

Mar. 1934   Groucho and Chico have another short-lived radio program—the *Marx of Time.*

Mar. 30, 1934   Groucho makes public Zeppo's letter of resignation from the team.

Aug. 1934   Groucho takes off the mustache and appears in a summer theatre production of *Twentieth Century*.

Sept. 1934   The team signs with MGM.

Summer 1935   Road tour of *A Night at the Opera* material.

Nov. 1935	*A Night at the Opera.* released. Major critical and commercial success.
Summer 1936	Road tour of *A Day at the Races* material.
Sept. 14, 1936	Irving Thalberg dies.
Sept. 28, 1936	Harpo marries actress Susan Fleming. They will eventually adopt four children (Billy, Alex, Jimmy, and Minnie).
Mar. 29, 1937	Groucho co-scripts with friend Norman Krasna the Warner Brothers film *The King and the Chorus Girl.*
June 1937	*A Day at the Races* released.
Nov. 1, 1937	Groucho and Chico are convicted of copyright infringement involving radio material. They appeal.
1937	Margaret Dumont wins the 1937 Screen Actors Guild "Best Supporting Actress" Award for her role as Mrs. Emily Upjohn in *A Day at the Races.* Team agent Zeppo signs the group to a lucrative RKO contract to star in the film adaptation of the hit Broadway play *Room Service.*
Apr. 1938	The appeal is upheld.
Sept. 1938	The filmed version of *Room Service* is released. It proves to be a disappointment.
1939	During the first half of the year Groucho and Chico are regulars on the radio program *The Circle* (also known as *The Kellogg Show*).
Sept. 25, 1939	*The Man Who Came to Dinner* opens on Broadway. The character Banjo is based upon Harpo.
Oct. 1939	*At the Circus* is released, with the team again under the MGM banner, as they will be on their next two films.
Late 1930s	Arthur Marx has become a prominent tennis player.
Dec. 1940	*Go West* is released.
Apr. 1941	Marxes announce the breakup of the team.
Dec. 1941	*The Big Store* is released.
1941–1942	Groucho is a regular on the *Rudy Vallee-Joan Davis Sealtest Show.* Harpo appears in a stage production of *The Man Who*

Came to Dinner, playing the part which was based on his own character.

Jan. 1942   Chico begins to tour successfully with a band for which he fronts.

July 1942   Groucho and Ruth are divorced.

1942   Groucho's book *Many Happy Returns* is published.

1943   *Stage Door Canteen* is released. Harpo joins many guest stars. During the war years he is active entertaining the troops, as well as appearing in stage revivals of *The Yellow Jacket* as well as *The Man Who Came to Dinner*.

1943–1944   Groucho has his own radio program—*The Pabst Show*. Groucho manages to continue his wartime entertainment of troops by doing some programs from camp locations.

Dec. 13, 1944   Norman Krasna's *Dear Ruth* opens on Broadway. The central family is loosely based upon Groucho's household.

1944   Chico appears in the revue *Take a Bow*.

July 1945   Groucho marries Kay Marie Gorcey, former wife of actor Leo Gorcey.

May 1946   *A Night in Casablanca* is released. The team is briefly reunited.

Aug. 1946   Melinda Marx is born to Kay and Groucho.

1947   Chico suffers a heart attack in Las Vegas, where he has been performing. He temporarily retires.

July 1947   *Copacabana* is released. Groucho co-stars with Carmen Miranda.

Oct. 27, 1947   Groucho's *You Bet Your Life* is first broadcast on radio.

Sept. 27, 1948   The Groucho and Krasna-authored *Time for Elizabeth* opens on Broadway for a very short run.

Apr. 1949   Through *You Bet Your Life* Groucho wins a Peabody Award (radio's highest honor) as best entertainer.

June 1949   Harpo and Chico's successful British tour is topped off with a London Palladium engagement.

Mar. 1950   *Love Happy* is released. The final reteaming of the Marx Brothers, though largely a Harpo-Chico vehicle. Sometimes is listed as a 1949 release.

May 12, 1950   Groucho and Kay divorce.

May 15, 1950   Groucho makes the cover of *Newsweek*.

July 1950   Groucho signs a very lucrative contract to jump networks with *You Bet Your Life*, from CBS to NBC (the program debuted on ABC). Gummo is Groucho's agent.

Oct. 2, 1950   Chico's television show *The College Bowl* first telecast. A half-hour musical comedy on ABC, it lasts a season.

Oct. 5, 1950   Groucho's *You Bet Your Life* first telecast, though it continues for a time on radio.

1950   The Kyle Crichton-authored biography *The Marx Brothers* appears. The Brothers own the copyright. Groucho makes a guest appearance in the feature film *Mr. Music*.

Jan. 23, 1951   Groucho receives an Emmy Award as "Most Outstanding Personality" of 1950.

Dec. 1951   *Double Dynamite* is released. Groucho co-stars with Frank Sinatra and Jane Russell.

Dec. 31, 1951   Groucho makes the cover of *Time*.

1952   *A Girl in Every Port* is released. Groucho co-stars with Marie Wilson and William Bendix.

Summer 1954   Groucho combines business with pleasure on a trip to Europe, where he films commercials for De Soto (his television sponsor). Daughter Melinda and soon-to-be third wife Eden Hartford accompany him. They visit Groucho and Melinda's ancestral home.

July 16, 1954   Groucho and Eden marry.

1954   Arthur Marx's *Life with Groucho* published.

May 9, 1955   Harpo guests on *I Love Lucy*, and they re-enact the mirror scene from *Duck Soup*.

1957   Groucho makes an unbilled guest appearance in the feature film *Will Success Spoil Rock Hunter?* Groucho, Harpo and Chico appear in the feature *The Story of Mankind*, but never together.

1957–1960   Groucho and Eden do *Time for Elizabeth* in summer stock.

1958   Chico plays a dramatic role on television in *Next to No Time* (*Playhouse 90*). Chico marries Mary DeVithas.

Mar. 8, 1959   Chico and Harpo star in the *G. E. Theater* television production of *The Incredible Jewel Robbery*. Groucho makes an unbilled appearance at the close.

Apr. 1959   The Marxes begin work on a television pilot, *Deputy Seraph*, which is permanently shelved when Chico's poor health makes him uninsurable.

Sept. 1959   Zeppo marries Barbara Blakely.

1959   Groucho's autobiography *Groucho and Me* is published. Chico tours in *The Fifth Season*, without his Italian character.

Apr. 29, 1960   Groucho stars in a television production of *The Mikado* (*Bell Telephone Hour*).

Dec. 22, 1960   Harpo plays his first dramatic role on television in *Silent Panic* (*June Allyson Show*).

1961   Harpo's autobiography, *Harpo Speaks!* (with Rowland Barber) is published. Harpo makes several silent television appearances in April and May to promote the book. The programs include *The Ed Sullivan Show*, *I've Got a Secret*, *Candid Camera*, and *The Groucho Show* (the final season title of *You Bet Your Life*).

Sept. 21, 1961   Last regular telecast of NBC's *You Bet Your Life*, which was called *The Groucho Show* the final season.

Oct. 11, 1961   Chico dies.

Jan. 11, 1962   *Tell It to Groucho* is first telecast. This CBS variation of *You Bet Your Life* fails—last telecast May 31, 1962.

1963   Groucho's *Memoirs of a Mangy Lover* published.

Sept. 28, 1964   Harpo dies.

June 1965   *Groucho* first telecast. This BBC variation of *You Bet Your Life* fails.

1965   *Hollywood Palace* television appearance of Groucho and Margaret Dumont. Dumont dies later that year.

1967   *The Groucho Letters* published.

1968   Groucho appears briefly in the feature film *Skidoo*.

Feb. 1969   Zeppo and Albert D. Herman patent their heart wristwatch invention; it monitors the heart and sounds an alarm if there is a problem.

Dec. 1969   Groucho and Eden divorce.

Mar. 26, 1970   *Minnie's Boys* (co-authored by Arthur Marx) has a brief Broadway run.

1971   Groucho meets Erin Fleming. She will become his companion/manager.

May 6, 1972   Groucho performs a one-man show at Carnegie Hall.

May 1972   The French government makes Groucho a *Commander dans l'Orde des Arts et des Lettres.* The award ceremony takes place at Cannes, where Groucho is guest of honor during the city's internationally known film festival.

Dec. 1972   Zeppo and Barbara divorce. She will later marry Frank Sinatra.

1972   Arthur Marx's *Son of Groucho* is published.

Apr. 2, 1974   Groucho receives a special Oscar from the Academy of Motion Picture Arts and Sciences for the "brilliant creativity and unequaled achievement of the Marx Brothers in the art of motion picture comedy."

May 23, 1974   New premiere (Los Angeles) of the 1930 *Animal Crackers*, which, because of legal questions concerning copyright, had not been commercially shown for years. Groucho is present.

June 23, 1974   The New York premiere of *Animal Crackers* produces Marx Brothers fan pandemonium as Groucho is nearly crushed just trying to get into the theatre.

1974   The controversial *Marx Bros. Scrapbook* is published.

1974   *You Bet Your Life* becomes a hit in syndication.

Oct. 2, 1975   Los Angeles mayor Tom Bradley declares it "Groucho Marx Day." It is the comedian's eighty-fifth birthday.

1975   Groucho is awarded special Emmy.

1976   Groucho's *The Groucho Phile: An Illustrated Life* published, as is his *The Secret Word Is GROUCHO* (with Hector Arce).

Jan. 1977   Hollywood Hall of Fame inducts Groucho, Harpo, Chico, and Zeppo.

Mar. 1977   Groucho enters hospital for hip operation; Erin Fleming becomes his temporary conservator (through the authority of legal Groucho documents signed several years before).

Apr. 1977   Arthur Marx attempts to become conservator. Neither he nor Fleming ends up with the position.

Apr. 21, 1977   Gummo dies.

Aug. 19, 1977   Groucho dies.

Oct. 1977   Bank of America (executors of Groucho's estate) sues Fleming for almost one and a half million dollars. A 1983 decision against Fleming (but for considerably less money) is currently under appeal.

Nov. 1979   Zeppo dies.

1980   Maxine Marx's *Growing Up with Chico* is published.

1985   *Harpo Speaks!* reissued with special additions "afterwords"—a Harpo poem by his widow Susan, and a son's view by Bill Marx.

FILMOGRAPHY:
THE MAJOR WORKS

The following filmography was constructed from such key listings as Paul D. Zimmerman and Burt Goldblatt's *The Marx Brothers at the Movies* (1968), Allen Eyles's *The Marx Brothers: Their World of Comedy* (1969), Simon and Schuster's classic film scripts of *Monkey Business and Duck Soup* (1972), Viking Press's MGM Library of Film Scripts for *A Night at the Opera* (1972) and *A Day at the Races* (1973), William Wolf's *The Marx Brothers*, period film reviews, and—of course—the original film credits themselves, when available. (Film scholar Anthony Slide helpfully pointed out the rarely noted *The House That Shadows Built*.) Writing credits frequently do not fully showcase the contributing talent, since a large pool was usually drawn upon, from gag men to the Marxes themselves. Moreover, the team's key work was made during the "studio era" (1930-1945), when it was tantamount to heresy to cross craft lines. Thus, performers performed, writers wrote. . . .

PARAMOUNT

1929   *The Cocoanuts* (96 minutes).
        Producer: Walter Wanger. Directors: Robert Florey and Joseph Santley. Screenplay Adaptation: Morrie Ryskind. Based on stage production *The Cocoanuts*: George S. Kaufman and Morrie Ryskind; music and lyrics: Irving Berlin. Cast: Groucho (Mr. Hammer), Harpo (Himself), Chico (Himself), Zeppo (Jamison), Mary Eaton (Polly Potter), Oscar Shaw (Bob Adams), Katherine Francis (Penelope), Margaret Dumont (Mrs. Potter), Cyril Ring (Harvey Yates), Basil Ruysdael (Hennessey), Sylvan Lee (Bell Captain), Gamby-Hale Girls and Allan K. Foster Girls (Dancers).

1930   *Animal Crackers* (98 minutes).
Director: Victor Heerman. Screenplay: Morrie Ryskind. Continuity: Pierre Collings. Based on stage production *Animal Crackers*: George S. Kaufman and Morrie Ryskind; music and lyrics: Bert Kalmar and Harry Ruby (including "Hooray for Captain Spaulding"). Cast: Groucho (Captain Jeffrey T. Spaulding), Harpo (The Professor), Chico (Signor Emanuel Ravelli), Zeppo (Horatio Jamison), Lillian Roth (Arabella Rittenhouse), Margaret Dumont (Mrs. Rittenhouse), Louis Sorin (Roscoe W. Chandler), Hal Thompson (John Parker), Margaret Irving (Mrs. Whitehead), Kathryn Reece (Grace Carpenter), Robert Greig (Hives, the butler), Edward Metcalf (Inspector Hennessey), The Music Masters (Six Footmen).

1931   *Monkey Business* (77 minutes).
(Herman Mankiewicz produces.) Director: Norman McLeod. Screenplay: S. J. Perelman and Will B. Johnstone. Additional Dialogue: Arthur Sheekman. Cast: Groucho, Harpo, Chico, Zeppo (Playing Themselves as Stowaways), Thelma Todd (Lucille), Tom Kennedy (Gibson), Ruth Hall (Mary Helton), Rockcliffe Fellowes (Joe Helton), Ben Taggart (Captain Corcoran), Otto Fries (Second Mate), Evelyn Pierce (Manicurist), Maxine Castle (Opera Singer), Harry Woods ("Alky" Briggs), "Frenchie" Marx (Extra on Ship and at Dock).

1932   *Horse Feathers* (68 minutes).
Director: Norman McLeod. Screenplay: Bert Kalmar, Harry Ruby, S. J. Perelman, and Will B. Johnstone. Music: Bert Kalmar, and Harry Ruby (including "I'm Against It"). Cast: Groucho (Professor Quincey Adams Wagstaff), Harpo (Pinky), Chico (Barovelli), Zeppo (Frank Wagstaff), Thelma Todd (Connie Bailey), David Landau (Jennings), Florine McKinney (Peggy Carrington), James Pierce (Mullens), Nat Pendleton (McCarthy), Reginald Barlow (Retiring President of Huxley College), Robert Greig (Professor Hornsvogel), E. J. LeSaint and E. H. Calvert (Professors in Wagstaff's Study), Edgar Dearing (Bartender), Sid Saylor (Slot Machine Player).

1933   *Duck Soup* (70 minutes).
(Herman Mankiewicz produces.) Director: Leo McCarey (Responsible for much of the visual comedy, including the classic mirror sequence). Screenplay: Bert Kalmar and Harry Ruby. Additional Dialogue: Arthur Sheekman and Nat Perrin. Music and Lyrics: Bert Kalmar and Harry Ruby (including "This Country's Going to War"). Cast: Groucho (Rufus T. Firefly), Chico (Chicolini), Harpo (Pinkie), Zeppo (Bob Rolland), Raquel Torres (Vera Marcal), Louis Calhern (Ambassador Trentino), Margaret Dumont (Mrs. Teasdale), Verna Hillie (Secretary), Leonid Kinsky (Agitator), Edmund Breece (Zander), Edwin Maxwell (Secretary of War), Edgar Kennedy (Lemonade Peddler), William Worthington (First Minister of Finance), George MacQuarrie (First Judge), Fred Sullivan (Second Judge), Davison Clark (Second Minister of Finance), Charles B. Middleton (Prosecutor), Eric Mayne (Third Judge).

METRO-GOLDWYN-MAYER

1935   *A Night at the Opera* (92 minutes).
(Irving Thalberg producing.) Director: Sam Wood. Screenplay: George S. Kaufman and Morrie Ryskind. Additional Material: Al Boasberg. Story: James Kevin McGuinness. Cast: Groucho (Otis B. Driftwood), Chico (Fiorella), Harpo (Tomasso), Kitty Carlisle (Rosa), Alan Jones (Ricardo), Walter King (Lassparri), Siegfried Rumann (Herman Gottlieg), Margaret Dumont (Mrs. Claypool), Edward Keane (The Captain), Robert Emmet O'Connor (Detective Henderson), Billy Gilbert (Engineer's Assistant), Leo White, Jay Eaton, and Rolf Sedan (Aviators).

1937   *A Day at the Races* (109 minutes).
(Irving Thalberg production; he died after the road tour.) Director: Sam Wood. Cast: Groucho (Dr. Hugh Z. Hackenbush), Chico (Tony), Harpo (Stuffy), Allan Jones (Gil), Maureen O'Sullivan (Judy Standish), Margaret Dumont (Mrs. Emily Upjohn), Leonard Ceeley (Whitmore), Douglas Dumbrille (Morgan), Esther Muir (Miss Nora—"Flo"), Siegfried Rumann (Dr. Leopold X. Steinberg), Robert Middlemass (The Sheriff), Vivien Fay (Solo Dancer), Ivie Anderson and the Crinoline Choir (Singers), Charles Trowbridge (Dr. Wilmerding), Pat Flaherty (Detective), Frank Dawson and Max Lucke (Doctors).

RKO-RADIO

1938   *Room Service* (78 minutes).
Producer: Pandro S. Berman. Director: William A. Seiter. Screenplay: Morrie Ryskind. Based upon stage production *Room Service*: John Murray and Allen Boratz. Cast: Groucho (Gordon Miller), Chico (Harry Binelli), Harpo (Faker Englund), Lucille Ball (Christine), Ann Miller (Hilda), Frank Albertson (Leo Davis), Donald MacBride (Gregory Wagner), Cliff Dunstan (Joseph Gribble), Philip Loeb (Timothy Hogarth), Philip Wood (Simon Jenkins), Alexander Asro (Sasha), Charles Halton (Dr. Glass).

METRO-GOLDWYN-MAYER

1939   *At the Circus* (87 minutes).
Producer: Mervyn LeRoy. Director: Edward Buzzell. Screenplay: Irving Brecher. Music: Harold Arlen. Lyrics: E. Y. Harburg (including "Lydia, the Tattooed Lady"). Cast: Groucho (Attorney J. Cheever Loophole), Chico (Antonio), Harpo (Punchy), Kenny Baker (Jeff Wilson), Florence Rice (Julie Randall), Eve Arden (Peerless Pauline), Margaret Dumont (Mrs. Dukesburg), Nat Pendleton (Goliath), Fritz Feld (Jardinet), James Burke (John Carter), Jerry Marenghi (Little Professor Atom), Barnett Parker (Whitcomb), Frank Orth (Lunchroom Attendant).

1940   *Go West* (80 minutes).
         Producer: Jack Cummings. Director: Edward Buzzell. Screenplay: Irving
         Brecher. Music and Lyrics: Gus Kahn and Roger Edens, Bronislau
         Kaper, Charles Wakefield Cadman. Cast: Groucho (S. Quentin Quale),
         Chico (Joe Panello), Harpo ("Rusty" Panello), John Carroll (Terry
         Turner), Diana Lewis (Eve Wilson), Walter Wolf King (Beecher), Robert
         Barrat ("Red" Baxter), June MacCloy (Lulubella), George Lessey (Rail-
         road President), Mitchell Lewis (Halfbreed), Tully Marshall (Dan Wilson),
         Harry Tyler (Telegraph Clerk).

1941   *The Big Store* (83 minutes).
         Producer: Louis K. Sidney. Director: Charles Reisner. Screenplay: Sid
         Kuller, Hal Fimberg, and Ray Golden. Story: Nat Perrin. Music: Hal
         Borne. Lyrics: Sid Kuller and Hal Fimberg. Cast: Groucho (Wolf J. Fly-
         wheel), Chico (Ravelli), Harpo (Wacky), Tony Martin (Tommy Rogers),
         Virginia Grey (Joan Sutton), Margaret Dumont (Martha Phelps), Douglas
         Dumbrille (Mr. Grover), William Tannen (Fred Sutton), Marion Martin
         (Peggy Arden), Virginia O'Brien (Kitty), Henry Armetta (Guiseppi),
         Anna Demetrio (Maria), Paul Stanton (George Hastings), Russel Hicks
         (Arthur Hastings), Bradley Page (Duke), and Charles Holland.

UNITED ARTISTS (distributor; independently produced)

1946   *A Night in Casablanca* (85 minutes).
         Producer: David L. Loew. Director: Archie L. Mayo. Screenplay:
         Joseph Fields and Roland Kibbee. Additional Material: Frank Tashlin.
         Music: Werner Janssen. Music and Lyrics: Ted Synder, Bert Kalmar and
         Harry Ruby (the song "Who's Sorry Now"). Cast: Groucho (Ronald
         Kornblow), Harpo (Rusty), Chico (Corbaccio), Lisette Verea (Beatrice
         Rheiner), Charles Drake (Lt. Pierre Delmar), Lois Collier (Annette),
         Dan Seymour (Captain Brizzard), Lewis Russell (Galoux), Harro Hellor
         (Emile), Frederick Gierman (Kurt), Siegfried Rumann (Count Pfeffer-
         man, alias Heinrich Stubel).

1949/   *Love Happy* (85 minutes).
1950   Producer: Lester Cowas (Presented by Mary Pickford). Director: David
         Miller. Screenplay: Frank Tashlin and Mac Benoff. Story: Harpo.
         Special Effects: Howard A. Anderson. Cast: Groucho (Detective Sam
         Grunion), Harpo (Himself), Chico (Faustino the Great), Ilona Massey
         (Madame Egilichi), Verra-Ellen (Maggie Phillips), Marion Hutton
         (Bunny Dolan), Raymond Burr (Alphonse Zoto), Bruce Gordon (Hanni-
         bal Zoto), Melville Cooper (Throckmorton), Leon Belasco (Mr. Lyons),
         Paul Valentine (Mike Johnson), Eric Blore (Mackinaw), Marilyn Monroe
         (Grunion's Client).

FILMOGRAPHY: OTHER SCREEN WORK

1920   *Humorisk.*
        A lost, silent, short subject privately funded by and starring the Marx Brothers. Not released.

1925   *Too Many Kisses* (Paramount).
        Harpo has a small supporting role in a feature film.

1931   *The House That Shadows Built* (Paramount).
        The Marxes do a sketch from *I'll Say She Is!* in this feature tribute to Paramount.

1932   *Hollywood on Parade* (Paramount).
        A short subject with brief off-screen footage of Groucho, Harpo, and Chico and their families.

1933   *Hollywood on Parade* (Paramount).
        A short subject with Chico, W. C. Fields, Buster Crabbe, and the Earl Carroll Girls.

1935   *La Fiesta de Santa Barbara* (MGM).
        A *color* short subject whose cast includes Harpo, Buster Keaton, Judy Garland (Francess Gumm), Gary Cooper. (Harpo is seen in his red wig.)

1937   *The King and the Chorus Girl* (Warner Brothers).
        Norman Krasna and Groucho did the screenplay.

1943   *Screen Snapshots No. 2* (Columbia).
        A short subject with Groucho doing a radio broadcast.

Screen Snapshots No. 8 (Columbia).
Groucho, Harpo, and Chico in a short subject whose other stars include the Ritz Brothers, Gene Autry, and Tyrone Power.

Stage Door Canteen (A Sol Lesser Production, released by United Artists).
Harpo appears in a feature-length all-star production whose cast includes Katharine Hepburn, Tallulah Bankhead, Helen Hayes, and Ethel Merman.

1945   *All Star Band Rally* (Twentieth Century-Fox).
A short subject whose cast includes Harpo, Bob Hope, Bing Crosby, Frank Sinatra, Betty Grable, and Carmen Miranda.

1947   *Copacabana* (A Sam Coslow Production, a United Artists release).
A feature starring Groucho and Carmen Miranda. Groucho is Lionel Q. Devereaux, and his Kalmer and Ruby number "Go West Young Man" features both the costume and spirit of the old Groucho.

1950   *Mr. Music* (Paramount).
Groucho makes a guest appearance in this feature and does a comic song "Life Is So Peculiar."

1951   *Double Dynamite* (RKO).
A feature starring Frank Sinatra, Jane Russell, and Groucho.

1952   *A Girl in Every Port* (RKO).
A feature starring William Bendix, Marie Wilson, and Groucho.

1957   *Will Success Spoil Rock Hunter?* (Twentieth Century-Fox).
A Frank Tashlin-directed feature, with Groucho making an unbilled cameo at the close.

The Story of Mankind (Warner Brothers).
An all-star feature with the Brothers appearing in separate segments. Groucho (Peter Minuit), Harpo (Isaac Newton), Chico (A Monk), Eden Mark (Laughing Water), Melinda Marx (Early Christian Child).

1958   *Showdown at Ulcer Gulch* (Shamus-Culhane Productions).
Commercial short for *The Saturday Evening Post*. Groucho and Chico appear with a cast which includes Ernie Kovacs, Bob Hope, and Bing Crosby.

1968   *Skidoo* (Paramount).
Groucho appears briefly in this Otto Preminger-directed feature.

SELECTED
DISCOGRAPHY

"You know you haven't stopped talking since I came here? You must have been vaccinated with a phonograph needle."
— Rufus T. Firefly (Groucho) to Mrs. Teasdale (Margaret Dumont) in *Duck Soup* (1933)

The following selected discography is limited to those long-playing (LP) commercial albums devoted entirely to one or more of the Marx Brothers. (Material that appears to have been bootlegged, something involving several Marx Brothers albums, has also been eliminated.)

As with this author's previous books on Charlie Chaplin and W. C. Fields, the starting point for this section was the collections of several major libraries. This was expanded with titles from the author's collection, as well as those of friends and colleagues. But the greatest single checklist was Robert Bader's definitive Marx discography, "Needle Marx," from the Summer 1986 issue of *The Freedonia Gazette*. In fact, the Bader list is so extensive it even contains discs where the Marxes merely surface in the album cover art.

Because Marx material has been, and continues to be, released in a number of packaging arrangements, even a selected discography with the aforementioned restrictions does not purport to be complete and final. However, the following chronological listing is both an effective illustration of the ongoing interest in the Marxes (as is the bootleg phenomenon) and more than a good foundation for the student of their many skills.

1952   *Hooray for Captain Spaulding and Other Songs by Harry Ruby and Bert Kalmar Sung by Groucho Marx* (Decca DL-5405).

Harp by Harpo (RCA Victor LPM-27).

1957   *Harpo* (Mercury MG-20232 and Wing MGW-12164; A dozen songs by Harpo, with an orchestra accompaniment that includes his son Bill).

1958   *Harpo at Work* (SR-60016, stereo; A dozen more Harpo numbers, again with son Bill in the accompaniment).

1960   *The Mikado Starring Groucho Marx* (Columbia Masterworks OS-2022, stereo; Television soundtrack to the 1960 television production—see the Chronological Biography).

1968   *The Marx Brothers—Original Voicetracks from Their Greatest Movies* (Decca DL-79168; Material from their Paramount films).

1972   *An Evening with Groucho* (A&M SP-3515, two-record set; Groucho's 1972 Carnegie Hall performance, as well as the Iowa State University warmup—in Ames—and a later San Francisco show).

1974   *Three Hours Fifty-Nine Minutes Fifty-One Seconds with The Marx Bros.* (Murray Hill Records 931680, four record set; An extensive collection of radio broadcasts, primarily from the 1940s. But the time span ranges from 1937 promotional program for *A Day at the Races*, to a 1972 KFI 50th Anniversary show greeting from Groucho. While the Groucho material easily dominates, there is an interesting range of items, from two mock interviews with Harpo to music from Chico Marx and his orchestra—including Mel Torme, who sang for a time with the group; Other Marx albums which have been drawn entirely from this four-record set are: *The Very Best of the Marxes*—in two 1977 volumes, each being a two-album collection; the 1977 *Groucho on Radio*).

1974   *Groucho Marx: When Radio Was King!* (Memorabilia Records MLP 733; A 1950 *You Bet Your Life* and material from the Groucho-Chico 1938 radio routine *Hollywood Agents*—see also *Three Hours Fifty-Nine* . . .).

1978   *Groucho Marx!* (Mark 56 758; A Contrast of *You Bet Your Life* radio material from nearly a decade apart).

   Groucho (Nostalgia Lane NLR-1021; More *You Bet Your Life* on radio—two 1958 programs, one with Ernie Kovacs, another with Groucho's youngest daughter Melinda and Candice Bergen).

   Groucho Marx—You Bet Your Life (Golden Age GA-5021; Broadcasts from 1957 and 1958).

1979   *Marx Movie Madness* (Radiola No. MR-1097; Radio broadcasts promoting *Duck Soup*, *At the Circus*, *Go West*, and *A Day at the Races*).

INDEX